The Problem of Negligent Omissions

Investigating Medieval Philosophy

VOLUME 1

The Problem of Negligent Omissions

Medieval Action Theories to the Rescue

By

Michael Barnwell

BRILL

LEIDEN • BOSTON
2010

This book is printed on acid-free paper.

Library of Congress Cataloging-in-Publication Data

Barnwell, Michael.
The problem of negligent omissions : medieval action theories to the rescue / by Michael Barnwell.
p. cm. -- (Investigating medieval philosophy ; v. 1)
Includes bibliographical references and index.
ISBN 978-90-04-18135-9 (hardback : alk. paper) 1. Action theory. 2. Negligence. 3. Philosophy, Medieval. I. Title. II. Series.

BF619.5.B37 2010
170'.42--dc22

2010020324

ISSN 1879-9787
ISBN 978 90 04 18135 9

This book is dedicated to
Marilyn McCord Adams
Teacher, Mentor, Scholar and Friend

CONTENTS

SERIES EDITOR'S NOTE

Michael Barnwell's study is the first in a new series, *Investigating Medieval Philosophy*, which will feature books that take an analytical approach to philosophy of the Middle Ages. 'Analytical' is meant here in a broad sense, to designate the style of philosophy predominant in Anglophone philosophy departments. There are many ways to approach medieval philosophy within this broadly analytical frame. At the more exegetical extreme, a writer might stick to explaining medieval texts, keeping close to the medieval authors' own questions and priorities, while presenting the material in terms readily comprehensible to contemporary philosophers. At the other, more speculative extreme, the discussion might be aiming to solve a problem in philosophy today, using medieval ideas and arguments. There are many intermediate approaches, and many variations that are not captured by this continuum. *Investigating Medieval Philosophy* is open to all of them.

Barnwell is, as he explains in his beautifully clear and explicit introduction, at the speculative end of the continuum. He wishes, as a philosopher, to examine the problem of Negligent Omissions. Suppose I have promised to write you a reference and to send it in before the deadline, but I negligently omit to do so. I am clearly blameworthy, and yet it is difficult to explain the sense in which my failure to write it in time was voluntary in the way that moral responsibility seems to require. There was no moment at which I chose not to write it by the deadline. Had I remembered about it when there was just time, I would have stopped everything and rushed to write it. This is, very roughly speaking, the problem Barnwell wants to tackle, and he has turned to medieval philosophers because he believes their analyses and arguments provide him with the tools he needs to solve the problem. He is not interested in medieval authors for their own sake, but he sees them as a rich and neglected repository of ideas for the contemporary philosopher. Yet even readers whose interests are historical will find Barnwell's engaged analyses of thinkers such as Aristotle, Anselm, Aquinas, Scotus and Suárez valuable. Just as medieval philosophy is a resource for the philosopher today, so the skills and questionings of working philosophers are a resource for understanding medieval philosophy.

John Marenbon, March, 2010

PREFACE

This book is the result of work spanning the past decade concerning what I take to be one of the most common occurrences in day-to-day life and, at the same time, one of the most vexing problems in philosophy – the occurrence of culpable negligent omissions. Oddly, the problem of negligent omissions has been almost entirely neglected (no pun intended) in philosophical discourse. Indeed, it is often not recognized as a problem at all until the puzzling aspects of negligent omissions are pointed out. This book (which, so far as I know, is the only one addressing this topic) intends to do exactly that. It will point out why this problem is indeed a problem and will then proceed to offer a solution.

In formulating this solution, I draw upon one of my other loves – medieval philosophy. Given the richness of medieval philosophical thought, it only stands to reason that some of those resources could be mined and applied to contemporary philosophical problems such as that of negligent omissions. It is this that I endeavor to do in the present monograph. The book is thus a sort of hybrid between being a 'constructive' and an 'historical' (specifically, 'medieval') philosophical project. As such, it will diverge in some ways from both classical constructive and historical philosophical approaches. Obviously, I regard these divergences as positive and as providing additional, valuable ways in which philosophy can be done. It is thus my hope that this book fosters the production and acceptance of similar methodological approaches. Since I say much more about my methodology in the Introduction, I will say no more here regarding this topic. Finally, I want to mention my desire that this book begins a serious philosophical discussion of negligent omissions. Given the prevalence of the concept in our day-to-day lives (not to mention the legal profession!) it seems that our profession has failed to live up to its duty by not having seriously investigated this phenomenon.

In some ways, I dread beginning to thank the many people responsible for this book for fear that I will 'negligently omit' some. I offer my apologies in advance to those whom I will have inevitably forgotten. I must start by thanking the person to whom this book is dedicated: Marilyn McCord Adams. Without her, not only would I not have ever been able to get this book published, but I would never have become a philosopher at all! I am still amazed at the energy and attention she has dedicated toward me while, at the same time, continuing to perform her own research and teaching. I could not have asked for a better mentor, and I consider myself among the most fortunate of philosophers to have had the chance to spend several years studying under her guidance. To her and her husband, Robert Adams, I owe a debt that I cannot repay for the innumerable ways in which they have assisted me throughout the years. Thank you!

In addition to Marilyn and Robert, I wish to thank all the professors at Yale who taught me how to think. Michael Della Rocca, Tad Brennan, David Kelsey and Todd Ganson all played special roles in much of this manuscript coming to fruition. My student colleagues while at Yale also provided invaluable assistance, both while I was at Yale and afterwards. Particular mention goes to Edward Waggoner, Maurice Lee, Mary Beth Willard, Jennifer Shea, and Frederick Simmons. I also want to thank Yale University for its resources in general and for a Leylan Writing Fellowship in particular, all of which allowed me to write much of this manuscript.

John Marenbon merits special recognition for believing in my work and giving me the opportunity to share it in this series. His constant and speedy assistance throughout this process has been invaluable. I also want to thank Marcella Mulder at Brill who has guided me along the process of submitting this manuscript. Tobias Hoffmann deserves special mention for having provided very complete, extensive, and helpful comments on a prior version of this manuscript. He has in addition continued to offer helpful advice during the revision process. If future readers pay even half the attention to this manuscript that Hoffmann has, I will consider myself lucky. I have also benefited from various conversations with Thomas Williams, Scott MacDonald, Jorge Gracia and Colleen McCluskey. Kevin Boddecker, moreover, graciously provided very essential editing assistance. I am not sure that I could have turned this manuscript in on time if it had not been for Kevin's magnanimousness and perseverance.

To my colleagues in the philosophy department at Niagara University, I offer a sincere 'thank you' for the various ways in which they have supported this project. I consider them all among my best friends and could not envision being any happier in a philosophy department. Working at Niagara University in general, moreover, is a pleasure. I thank the administration for its continued support for my research. In particular, a Summer Research Stipend granted by Niagara University helped me solve one particularly problematic portion of this manuscript. In addition, I want to thank the department's support staff, including the student aides who provided important support in the days immediately running up to the manuscript's completion. Jaclyn Eckel deserves special mention for her exceptional helpfulness and attention to detail.

Finally, I want to thank my family. My parents, Roy and Sandra Barnwell, have always supported me in almost any endeavor I have been interested in. Their goal since I was small was that I be able to devote as much time to my studies as possible. I hope that they see in this book some of the fruits of all they have done for me. My wife, Joyce, deserves an immense amount of credit for doing all that was possible so as to lessen my stress in the writing of this book. The patience and love she has demonstrated over the past four years is in many ways unimaginable and indicative of just what a wonderful person she is. Finally, I must thank my sons, Greydan and Devan, for being the lights of my life. As I am writing this, Devan is due to be born at any moment. Indeed, it is his impending birth that motivated me to finish this manuscript. Greydan has been a constant source of joy and encouragement and has helped me keep the different aspects of my life in perspective. To these, and a host of innumerable others I have no doubt negligently omitted, I offer sincerest thanks.

Michael Barnwell
Department of Philosophy
Niagara University, NY 14109–2043
October 29, 2009

LIST OF ABBREVIATIONS

AI - Affectio Iustitiae.

AC - Affectio Commodi.

B1 - An agent can be metaphysically free (i.e. possess superabundant sufficiency) without possessing dual affections.

C1 - In sins of negligent omission, culpability seems to lie somehow in the failure to have the foresight or knowledge of the subsequent omission. It seems not to lie in willing against one's better knowledge.

C2 - Negligent ignorance requires that there must be some time when the agent actually, actively knew that she should attempt to know those things of which she is now negligently ignorant.

Complac - A unit of 'psychic power' resulting from the performance of *complacere*.

ContinualComp - The continual performance of *complacere* on an intellection.

FSKR - That an intellection be of some imperfect/indistinct status is adequate such that the will can culpably perform, or fail to perform, some act of complacere related to that intellection.

ITV - Intellectual Tunnel Vision.

LII - Lingering Indistinct Intellection.

MOI - Mere Obligation Intellection.

NO - Negligent Omission.

P1 - It being the case that one perfect and distinct intellection exists in the intellect, many indistinct and imperfect intellections are able to inhere [in the intellect].

P2 - It being the case that one intellection is inhering in the intellect but is not being cognized as an object, the will is able to will and take pleasure (*complacere sibi*) in the object of that intellection, and in that intellection, and it is able not to take pleasure.

P3 - It being the case that the will is taking pleasure in an intellection, the intellection is made stronger and intensified; it being the case that the will is not taking pleasure in or nilling [an intellection], the intellection is weakened in intensity and set aside (*remittitur*).

PA3 - How can there be inconsideration (either voluntary or involuntary) in a case in which something has been offered to the intellect and has caused a certain disposition in it, given that this created disposition implies some form of consideration?

PNR - Point of No Return. The latest point at which an obligation could be fulfilled.

RB1 - An agent cannot be metaphysically free (i.e. possess superabundant sufficiency) without possessing dual affections.

SKR - Every volition necessarily requires an intellection naturally prior, although simultaneous in duration.

TEF - Time of Expected Fulfillment.

V1 - The perfectly voluntary consists of an act in which there is (a) 'full' knowledge of the end by a rational agent along with (b) an inner principle of action by which it moves itself towards that end.

V2 - The perfectly voluntary consists of that which is 'from the will' (*a voluntate*).

VT1 - The virtual phenomenon must be preceded by an 'actual' phenomenon.

VT2 - The virtual phenomenon must not have been revoked since the relevant original actual phenomenon.

VT3 - The actual phenomenon has left behind an aliquid that somehow influences (*influit*) that which is virtual.

VT4 - This *aliquid* probably consists of some sort of appetitive/ phantasmatic movement.

WMI - Will Moving the Intellect.

INTRODUCTION

WHAT'S THE PROBLEM?

I. Sins of Negligent Omission: What They Are and Why They Are Puzzling

The task of this book is to discover how negligent omissions can consistently be considered blameworthy and, in a theological context, sinful by appealing to medieval and scholastic theories of action.[1] In order to explain why this task merits a book-length discussion, I need first state in general terms what a fault, or sin, of negligent omission is as understood in this work: it is a case of blameworthiness in which an agent omits to perform some action which she is under obligation to, and morally-speaking should, do.[2] Furthermore, the omission must come about not as a result of the agent intentionally omitting the action. Rather, the omission is unintended. If she had remembered her obligation, she would have fulfilled it. We can even assume that she would have wanted to fulfill it *if only* she had remembered it. The problem is that she happened not to think about it. Moreover, an agent who commits a negligent omission did not intend, nor try to bring it about, that she not think about her obligation. Nevertheless, the conventional

---

[1] I will occasionally refer to negligent omissions as 'sins.' My use of the term should not be construed as implying that what I say regarding negligent omissions can be applied only within a theological system. To the contrary, I use the term simply to pick out blameworthy occurrences or non-occurrences, whether that blameworthiness can be construed as theological or not. The advantages of using this term is that many of the writers in this study couched their discussion of blameworthiness in terms of 'sin,' and it helps make explicit that there is theological application for the conclusions produced by this book if so desired.

[2] I am intentionally leaving vague the notion of what 'being obligated' amounts to other than the fact that the agent must be aware that she is under an obligation. I have no intention of developing an ethical/philosophical system of obligation and prefer instead to leave the notion vague at this point. I will say, however, that in general when I speak of an obligation, I am referring to an act which, if omitted by an agent, would cause the agent to be considered blameworthy. Of course, this statement only begs the question as to what 'blameworthiness' consists of. The answer to this will vary depending on the thinker. For the medieval Christian thinkers, it can be said that 'blameworthiness' will in general be coextensive with their notions of sin. I do not believe that I need to delve any deeper than this into the understanding of 'obligation' for the purposes of this book.

wisdom is that she is blameworthy because she should have 'seen to it' that she not omit the action.

Faults of negligent omission (hereafter, 'NO') merit consideration because it is not fully clear how they qualify as blameworthy or sinful in the first place. Although I will expand upon this problem in the first chapter, allow me briefly to explain here. It is often thought that the imputation of sin or blameworthiness is made on the basis of the intentions of the agent; if the agent did not intend the sinful result, the agent is not regarded as having sinned.[3] In other words, the mental, intentional state of the agent is the primary factor in determining whether an action is to be imputed to the agent as sinful or culpable.

The puzzling aspect of sins of NO is that in these 'sins,' a mental, intentional state regarding the omitted obligation is absent. In such cases, the agent is under some obligation to perform some action *x*, yet omits performing *x not* as a result of intentionally omitting to perform *x*, but rather as a result of seemingly *inadvertently* omitting to perform *x*. Based upon what was just said above, the absence of an intentional state with respect to some sinful action *x* would seem to absolve the agent from any blameworthiness; if the agent did not intend the sin, the agent is not held responsible for it (i.e. she did not sin). Philosophers and theologians from Aristotle to Suárez to the present time, however, have held that such omissions *are* blameworthy. Even though the agent omits to do that which she should as a result of her not thinking about her obligation to do it, the agent is nonetheless regarded as blameworthy for not performing that action.

The purpose of this book will be to specify the locus of voluntary, culpable blameworthiness in the causal history of a NO. In other words, where did the agent go wrong? Where could and where should she have done something differently? It is difficult to maintain that she 'went wrong' at the time she failed to fulfill her obligation. As we have already said, at that time she was unaware of her obligation; otherwise, she would have fulfilled it.

At the same time, it seems not possible to place the blame in some earlier attempt to try to forget the obligation. If an agent had done this, the resulting omission would not be negligent, as we understand it. The type of NO we are concerned with is that in which the agent apparently

[3] Incidentally, the same position is often held in regard to merit. That is, if an agent did not intend to do a good action, then even if the result of the action in and of itself is good, the agent thereby deserves no merit.

did not try to bring it about that she be ignorant of her obligation. If she had done so, the resulting omission would be somewhat more 'intentional' than negligent for our purposes; consequently, we cannot place the locus of voluntary culpable blameworthiness in an earlier attempt to cause the subsequent ignorance of the obligation.

II. A Lack of Scholarship, and Two Inadequate 'Gut Reaction' Solutions to the Problem

The topic of negligent omissions has itself been neglected in scholarly literature and discussions. Not only are books on negligent omissions absent, but there is also a nearly-complete lack of any secondary material on this topic: an initial review of *Philosopher's Index* yields only two articles on this topic! As the author of one of those two articles laments, the class of negligent omissions has been left "without any adequate framework of analysis because philosophical discussion has been focused in the opposite direction."[4] Given that this distinction is of such crucial importance to philosophical theories of action, this lacuna is surprising at best, and inexcusable at worst.

In the lack of existing scholarship, there seem to be two 'gut-reaction' answers to the problem of NO's. The first I call the 'think harder' solution. According to it, a person is liable for an omission because she *could* recall awareness of her obligation to mind. She 'knows' about her obligation insofar as knowledge of it is in the recesses of her mind, and if she would only 'think harder' before omitting to fulfill it, she could recall it from memory. Since she could think harder and thereby recall it from memory, she is blameworthy because she does not in fact do so.

This solution has always seemed exceedingly unsatisfactory to me. I will grant that theoretically an agent could recall some obligation that is in the recesses of her mind. But why should we expect that an agent, at the time she must fulfill her obligation, would know to 'think harder'

[4] Patricia G. Smith, "Contemplating Failure: The Importance of Unconscious Omissions," *Philosophical Studies* 59 (June, 1990): 159–176. The other article is: Jeffrey Hause, "Voluntariness and Causality: Some Problems for Aquinas' Theory of Responsibility," *Vivarium* 36, no. 1(March 1998): 55–66. There have been a mere handful of other articles that make reference to the problem, such as Scott MacDonald, "Primal Sin" in *The Augustinian Tradition*, ed. Gareth B. Matthews (London; Berkeley: Univ. of California Press, 1999), 110–139.

at that time? It will not do to say that she would know to 'think harder' at that time because that is the time at which she is to fulfill her obligation, for if she is currently unaware of her obligation, she has no way of knowing that she is at the time her obligation should be fulfilled. In other words, if the 'think harder' solution were to work, the agent would need to know at the appropriate time *that* she must 'think harder.'

For example, consider a situation in which a man named 'John' is morally obligated (on account of a promise) to pick up another man 'Des' from the airport at 7:00. At 7:00, John is watching TV and just happens to have no thought about picking up Des. Of course, John theoretically *could* think harder at 7:00 to see if he is forgetting anything. But what reason does he have to do that? He is not expected to think harder at all times. And since he is unaware of his obligation, 7:00 seems just like any other time. It is consequently difficult to blame John for not 'thinking harder' at 7:00 so as to fulfill his obligation. I thus find the 'think harder' solution, as it is, inadequate.

It has been suggested to me that my dissatisfaction with the 'think harder' solution is based upon my having constructed a straw man out of the proponent of it. When people say that the negligent omitter failed because she could have 'thought harder,' what they really have in mind is that the agent failed to exercise the virtue of prudence by either precipitously rushing into doing something other than her obligation or failing to exercise the proper amount of circumspection and caution in deciding what action to take. And if the 'think harder' solution is presented in this way (its proponents say), then my dissatisfaction with it will supposedly cease.

Thomas Aquinas may have this 'think harder' solution in mind when he writes that inconsideration (*inconsideratio*) is a special sin contained under prudence's vice, imprudence. In explaining this point, he even says (using language relevant to our discussion) that inconsideration occurs when an agent "neglects to attend to those things from which upright judgment proceeds."[5] 'Thinking harder' would thus consist in not neglecting to attend to those things needed to form a right judgment

---

[5] Respondeo dicendum quod consideratio importat actum intellectus veritatem rei intuentis. Sicut autem inquisitio pertinet ad rationem, ita iudicium pertinet ad intellectum, unde et in speculativis demonstrativa scientia dicitur iudicativa, inquantum per resolutionem in prima principia intelligibilia de veritate inquisitorum diiudicatur. Et ideo consideratio maxime pertinet ad iudicium. Unde et defectus recti iudicii ad vitium inconsiderationis pertinet, prout scilicet aliquis in recte iudicando deficit ex hoc quod contemnit vel negligit attendere ea ex quibus rectum iudicium procedit. Unde manifestum est quod inconsideratio est peccatum. (*Summa Theologica* IIa-IIae,

about what to do. John, therefore, supposedly did not 'think hard' enough because he neglected to pay attention to the things he should have paid attention to.

While it is possible to identify 'thinking harder' with thinking about the details needed to make a right judgment in any particular situation, doing so does not seem to explain our worry with regard to NO's like John's. If John's not picking up Des is a result of his not thinking about relevant details, and if thinking about relevant details is a form of 'thinking hard,' then indeed John's failure results from his not 'thinking hard' enough. But this tells us nothing about how John is responsible for his 'not thinking hard enough = not thinking about the relevant details he needed to think about.' Nor does it tell us how John could 'think harder = think about the relevant details' in this situation since he is *ex hypothesi* not even aware that he is not considering relevant details. Part of the reason NO's are so puzzling is that the agent is not supposedly aware that he is not thinking about something he should and yet is held accountable for not thinking about that. It is this puzzle that demands explanation, and simply saying the agent should 'think harder' appears not to address it at all.

It might be replied that what defenders of the 'think harder = think about the relevant details' approach really have in mind is that such failures to think harder are blameworthy because they arise from a lack of the virtue prudence. It is because someone lacks circumspection or caution, each an element of prudence, that a person fails to think about all he should think about.[6] A negligent omission is thus ultimately blameworthy because the agent lacks this virtue in some sense or other.

I am willing to grant that such a failure in virtue may be a cause of some NO's. Instances of negligent omission caused by such failures, however, are not puzzling at all – they simply result from a prior blameworthy failure to properly attain some virtue. It is thus not these instances of NO's (i.e. those resulting from a failure to obtain prudence) that I am interested in. I will thus avoid analyzing NO's in terms of

---

q.53, a.4). Unless otherwise noted, all Latin quotations of Aquinas are from the Leonine edition, located at: http://www.corpusthomisticum.org/iopera.html. All translations, unless otherwise noted, are mine.

[6] See, for example, Thomas Aquinas's *Summa Theologica* IIa-IIae, q.49, aa.7–8. Indeed, the prior reference to *ST* IIa-IIae, q.53, a.4 in which inconsideration is discussed (and from which we derived the 'think harder = think about relevant details' formulation) is couched in terms of a lack of the virtue prudence. Cf. also IIa-IIae, q.53, a.3.

virtue. Later in this "Introduction," I devote a section to the role virtue will play (or rather, not play) in my treatment. The following should suffice for now: I assume there are some NO's not ultimately explicable in terms of a lack of virtue which are nonetheless blameworthy. For example, it is plausible to assume that John is a virtuous person in general and that his omission to pick up Des does not arise from any lack of virtue. It is *these* NO's, NO's that can not be so clearly traced to some character flaw, that are puzzling and demand explication. And the 'think harder' solution, as presented, does not seem to provide the needed explication.

The other 'gut reaction' answer I call the 'tie a string around the finger' solution.[7] According to it, the agent made a mistake by not taking some special, extra precautions so as to ensure that she remember her obligation. For example, John could have set his alarm clock at 7:00 to remind him of his obligation, or he could have placed post-it notes (with his obligation written on them) all over his apartment such that he could not help but look at them and be reminded. According, then, to the 'string around the finger' solution, the locus of John's culpability lies at the point in which John could have taken some sort of extra precautions such as these but did not.

As I will point out, this solution is appropriate for certain cases of obligation. There are some instances in which the time until one can fulfill the obligation is so long, and/or the circumstances are such, that the agent would reasonably be expected to take extra precautions. For example, if John knows he is the type of person who forgets everything, then this circumstance may justify the expectation that he take special precautions. Similarly, consider a case in which Des is arriving to undergo an organ transplant later that evening. Given the serious consequence that Des's life would in that case be in danger if John failed to pick him up, extra precautions so as to remind John of his obligation may be called for.

Despite the occasional applicability of the 'tie a string around the finger' approach, it is inadequate. In the first place, not all cases of blameworthy omission are such in which extra precautions are reasonably expected. If the circumstances are not so serious, if there is not an extensive time span until the time at which the obligation should be

[7] The name is taken, of course, from the old idea that one ties a string around her finger to remind her of something.

fulfilled, and if the agent is not constituted so as to be frequently forgetful, no such precautions need necessarily be taken. Certainly, after all, there are cases of negligent omission in which we believe we rightfully blame an agent for an omission and yet would not have expected her to take special precautions. Secondly, even in those cases in which special precautions are reasonably expected, it is not at all times clear that the agent is aware that circumstances are such so as to justify special precautions. If we are to blame the agent on account of failing to take such precautions, we would need to have a way in which to understand her as knowing at that time she should take such special precautions. Otherwise, the failure to take such precautions would itself be a NO in need of explanation.

As a result, both the 'think harder' and 'tie a string around the finger' solutions are inadequate for solving our problem. Despite these inadequacies, it will ultimately be the case that the solution I propose will point out a kernel of truth in each of these solutions. In fact, my ultimate solution can in one sense be understood as demonstrating in what way the 'think harder' and 'tie a string around the finger' solutions are basically correct. As presented here, however, these solutions lack the sophisticated philosophical machinery to be adequate in and of themselves. We will have to wait until we have explored medieval and scholastic action theories before such machinery will become available to us.

III. Typology

I am going to treat what I regard as three different 'types' of NO. Each of these 'types' have certain features making them qualitatively different from each other, differences that will justify slightly separate treatments. Despite these differences, it will turn out that the problem of where the locus of culpability is in all of them can be solved in a similar way. In the concluding chapter, I will treat the three types separately and show how they are ultimately to be resolved based upon the model I will have proposed by that point. For the time being, I want to introduce the three types.

A. *Type-1 NO's*

Stated generally, Type-1 NO's are NO's in which the agent was reasonably expected to keep in mind continuously her obligation until the time for its fulfillment so as to ensure not forgetting about it. The following is an example.

> Sample 1: At 6:55 p.m., John promises, and is thus morally obligated in some sense, to pick up his friend Des at the airport, for which he will need to leave at 7:00. At 6:56, a mere one minute after promising Des, John begins watching television and subsequently forgets to leave at 7:00 to pick Des up. It is not until 9:00, when Des calls John to ask him where he is, that John realizes he has omitted to fulfill his obligation.

It seems not to be asking too much to expect John to keep in mind his obligation to pick up Des for a mere five minutes.[8] His omission, therefore, seems to be blameworthy on account of his failure to continue to keep in mind his obligation.

Before moving on, let me make one further note. Although the example is phrased in terms of the time span between the time at which John undertook the obligation and the time at which it is to be fulfilled, this time-span is not necessarily the relevant one for determining what type of NO a certain omission is. The relevant time span is that between the last time a person has awareness of her obligation and the 'time of its expected fulfillment' (referred to hereafter as 'TEF'). For example, it could be the case that John promised Des yesterday and merely recalls his promise at 6:55. In such a case, John was under no obligation yesterday to keep that promise continuously in mind until today. However, given that he does recall it a mere five minutes before TEF, he is *at that point* expected to keep that obligation continuously in mind. There is no excuse for him now to mentally set it aside. If John then proceeds to set it aside after recalling it at such a short time before TEF, the resulting NO is Type-1; in the time period running immediately to TEF since last recalling it he could have been reasonably expected to keep it in mind continuously.

For sake of simplicity, I will often refer to time spans as that between undertaking the obligation and TEF. This is because at the point of undertaking the obligation, the agent was at least at that point aware of her obligation; otherwise, she could not be obligated. Nonetheless, the reader should be cautioned that the relevant time span for determining which type of NO ultimately ensues is that between the last full awareness of one's obligation and TEF.

---

[8] If this does seem too long to some, let the time be shorter. The point is that there is some time span short enough such that an agent can be reasonably expected to keep in mind her obligation continuously until that obligation is to be fulfilled.

B. *Type-2 NO's*

Type-2 NO's are the most challenging and problematic to explain. They furthermore seem to be the most prevalent in our day-to-day lives. They are those NO's in which the time span between one's last full awareness of the relevant obligation and TEF is (i) too long for the agent reasonably to be expected to keep in mind continuously her obligation until TEF, and yet (ii) too short, nor are the circumstances serious enough, such that the agent should take extra precautions. The following is an example.

> Sample 2: John arrives at his apartment at 4:30 and, at that time, makes a promise, and is thus morally obligated in some sense, to pick up his friend Des at the airport tonight. He will need to leave at 7:00 in order to do this. Knowing that he has two and a half hours, he begins watching TV. As it turns out, he becomes so engrossed in the show he is watching that he forgets to pick up Des. It is not until 9:00, when Des calls John to ask him where he is, that John realizes he has omitted to fulfill his obligation.

I will discuss Type-2 NO's in depth in chapter 6. There it will become apparent that such NO's are best understood as splitting into two further variations that I will call Variation A and Variation B. Not much can be said about these variations before we have explored some of the details presented in that chapter. Let it suffice for now to say that Type-2/Variation A NO's would be those in which an agent, upon realizing she has omitted an obligation, has the immediate reaction "I knew I was forgetting something." By contrast, Variation B NO's are those in which the recognition that one forgot about an obligation kind of 'hits the agent out of the blue,' so to speak. In NO's of this latter variation, the agent had *completely* forgotten about the fact that she had to do anything.[9]

---

[9] It may seem that Type-2 NO's are incoherent. It appears as if for any obligation, either precautions must be taken (thus issuing in a Type-3 NO) or not in which case the obligation must be able to be kept continuously in mind. Indeed, this disjunction points out why Type-2 NO's are especially problematic and thus are the main topic of this book. The disjunction *seems* to be a true one, and yet if it is, there are no Type-2 NO's. Nonetheless, we typically recognize that there are Type-2 NO's. For example, if my wife calls me an hour before I leave work and asks me to pick up bread on my way home, I'm not necessarily expected to write post-it notes on my car to remember to pick up bread. Nor, it seems, can I continuously keep in mind my obligation to pick up bread. Nonetheless, if I fail to remember to pick it up, there is a very good chance that *ceteris paribus* (e.g., I didn't receive bad news from a relative or something like that that would justify my forgetting), I am blameworthy for forgetting to pick up the bread. The task of this book can thus be viewed as a way in which to reconcile the existence of blameworthy Type-2 NO's with the disjunction noted at the beginning of this note.

C. *Type-3 NO's*

I have basically already explained a Type-3 NO. It is the type of NO in which the time span between last awareness and TEF is long enough and/or the circumstances such so as to justify expecting the agent to take special precautions. In other words, it is the type of NO in which the 'tie a string around the finger' solution is applicable. Please note, however, that simply saying the 'tie a string around the finger' solution is applicable does not mean that Type-3 NO's pose no problem. We must still, as mentioned above, explain how an agent can be expected to know that she should 'tie a string around her finger,' for if she does not know this, failing to do so is itself a NO in need of explanation.

Note in addition that the last statement brings up a significant problem for our task. As stated, we must find a way to posit that the agent knows she must take such special precautions. However, if an agent explicitly knows she must do this and yet fails to do so, the resulting ignorance of her obligation would seem to be more intentional. This would further seem to imply that the ultimate omission is not so much negligent as somehow intended.

I point out this problem here for it will be one that plagues us throughout our task and will be present in regard to NO's of all types. To solve NO's, we will have to find some way to posit some sort of knowledge in the agent while, at the same time, avoiding the implication that that piece of knowledge entails the resulting omission is less negligent and more foreseen and intended. In other words, if we assume that the agent has some sort of knowledge, that knowledge must be had in a way that is somewhat active[10] and yet does not cause the category of negligent omissions to collapse into that of intentional ones. My ultimate solution, and its dependence upon a concept called 'virtual knowledge,' will aptly walk this fine line.

Finally, I want to mention that Type-3 scenarios will turn out to be the least problematic and easiest to solve. Furthermore, the solution to the problem of culpability for them will be evident from the solution given for Type-1 and Type-2 NO's. Consequently, I do not explicitly deal again with Type-3 NO's until the final chapter, at which time I show how my model adequately explains their culpability.

---

[10] More will be said shortly about the fact that knowledge must be somewhat active.

There is no precise algorithm for figuring out which type any one NO may be, and there need not be one for the purposes of this inquiry. Every situation will be specific and which type any specific NO is will depend upon the particular circumstances involved. Ultimately, the three types are differentiated based upon the reasonable expectations one could expect of any one agent. Of course, reasonable expectations will vary depending on who the agent is, the importance of the matter at hand, and the time factor involved. This explains the repeated references to the time factor and importance aspects throughout the rest of the book. The descriptions given should be sufficient to give a sense of the three different types, and I take it all persons are familiar with all three types in their own lives.

D. *Types of NO vs. Types of Scenario*

I will often refer to 'types' of scenarios in a way that corresponds to types of NO. For example, in Sample 1 John is in a Type-1 scenario since, if all things stay as they are and a NO occurs, it will be a Type-1 NO. Given, however, that NO's are ultimately determined by the time between *last awareness of one's obligation* and TEF and not necessarily by the time span between first undertaking an obligation and TEF, an agent could be in more than one 'scenario' during the causal genesis of a NO.

For example, imagine that John initially promised Des four days ago. In that case, John is reasonably expected to take special precautions to remind himself to pick up Des at 7:00 four days hence. If John does not take such precautions, happens not to think again about his obligation, and therefore omits to pick up Des, his NO will by of Type-3. Accordingly, John is in a Type-3 scenario upon initially undertaking the obligation.

It could be the case, however, that John was initially in a Type-3 scenario but ended up committing a Type-1 NO. Let it be the case, for example, that John had written a note to himself about his obligation four days ago. He saw it at 6:55 on the night he was to pick up Des. Having been thus reminded of his obligation, he felt safe in throwing the note away. He subsequently began watching TV and forgot his obligation. His NO in that case was a Type-1 NO. Even though at his first awareness of the obligation he was in a Type-3 scenario, he could reasonably be expected to keep his obligation in mind continuously until 7:00 once he was reminded of his obligation at 6:55. Accordingly, at 6:55 he entered a Type-1 scenario and his resulting NO was of Type-1.

As will become apparent, Type-2 scenarios often become Type-1 scenarios. This causes no problem for our explication and I mention the issue here only to avoid potential confusion. In chapter 6 I spend a section elaborating on this particular possibility and why such changes of scenario ought to be expected and pose no problem.

IV. Clarifications Regarding the Approach of this Book

A. *Methodology*

There are different ways to do medieval philosophy. One way (and what is perhaps most prevalent) is to focus on problems that medieval writers themselves focused upon, and to focus upon them in the same way that medieval thinkers did. According to this approach, the medieval philosopher's own conception of a problem or topic would define and delimit the range of inquiry. In such an approach, one would attempt to determine what so-and-so thinks about such-and-such a topic. Such an approach can be very beneficial in solving some current debates in medieval scholarship. For example, there are heated discussions about whether Aquinas himself was a voluntarist or an intellectualist when it came to the will.[11] To solve such a question, a contemporary scholar may perform an exegesis of various passages throughout an author's corpus so as to make an argument that the medieval philosopher either thought one way or another (or, perhaps, even changed one's mind during the course of his career).

Alternatively, a scholar of medieval philosophy may simply want to bring to light or clarify some point that has in general been overlooked in a medieval thinker's writing. In a related vein, a text on medieval philosophy may try to present the entirety of an author's thought on a particular point. One could, for example, be interested in presenting

[11] See, for example: Jeffrey Hause, "Thomas Aquinas and the Voluntarists," *Medieval Philosophy and Theology* 6 (1997): 167–182; Colleen McCluskey, "Intellective Appetite and the Freedom of Human Action," *The Thomist* 66 (2002): 421–456; Patrick Lee, "The Relation between Intellect and Will in Free Choice According to Aquinas and Scotus," *The Thomist* 49 (1985): 321–342; Eleonore Stump, "Aquinas's Account of Freedom: Intellect and Will," *The Monist* 80 (1997): 576–597; David M. Gallagher, "Free Choice and Free Judgment in Thomas Aquinas," *Archiv für Geschichte der Philosophie* 76 (1994): 247–277; Tobias Hoffmann, "Aquinas and Intellectual Determinism: The Test Case of Angelic Sin," *Archiv für Geschichte der Philosophie* 89 (2007): 122–156; Scott MacDonald, "Aquinas's Libertarian Account of Free Choice," *Revue Internationale de Philosophie*, 52 (1998): 309–328.

what so-and-so thought about ethics, or virtue, or action, or eschatology in general.[12] To do so would require reaching into all aspects of an author's corpus and presenting a wide, varied, and (hopefully) coherent system of an author's thought on a particular field of inquiry.

Let me be clear that from the outset that I am *not* following, nor am I trying to follow, these approaches in executing the argument of this book. While the techniques just mentioned are themselves valuable and yield important insights, this book will follow a very different course. This book is concerned with a particular contemporary problem – negligent omissions. Furthermore, it is concerned with understanding negligent omissions in a particular way – the way in which an agent omits to uphold a particular obligation she has. As such, I am imposing my own typology of negligent omissions throughout the book; it is this typology that is the subject matter of this book. Accordingly, I will not, nor will I attempt, to focus on the problems the medievals themselves focused upon. (Indeed, as I will discuss in a bit, the medievals really did not focus per se upon the problem in which I am interested in this book.) Rather, I will try to appropriate insights the medievals had so as to help solve the problem under discussion – the problem of NO's as we have defined here.

Because I am focused on imposing my own typology and am ultimately using medieval thinkers' thoughts so as to help advance my own purposes with regard to NO's, it has seemed to some that I am 'cherry-picking' from their writings, so to speak. I suppose that, in a way, I am. But that need not carry the negative connotation usually associated with that phrase. Indeed, I believe quite the opposite is the case. By doing so, I do not distort the meaning of those thoughts. Furthermore, I take it as a compliment to the medieval period of philosophy that their insights could be used to solve contemporary problems in philosophy. Indeed, one would hope that if the medievals are to be relevant to philosophy as conducted in the present day (a claim unfortunately denied by many in the philosophical profession), then some of their arguments could be lifted out of their medieval context and applied to contemporary questions. And if they are to be so used, then some so-called cherry-picking is necessary. If Scotus or Suárez said something

[12] Examples include: Katherin Rogers, *Anselm on Freedom* (Oxford, New York: Oxford University Press, 2008); Anthony Kenny, *Aquinas on Mind* (New York: Routledge, 1993); Eleonore Stump, *Aquinas* (New York: Routledge, 2003).

or made an argument that could be used to advance a solution to the problem of negligent omissions, then it would in my opinion be a disservice to their work not to so use that argument.

Solving the problem of NO's, as defined here, is my topic. Accordingly, I use the writings of medieval philosophers to the extent that they help me do so. Proceeding in this way entails that my treatment of the medievals will greatly differ from the approaches mentioned at the beginning of this section. While I will certainly do a significant amount of exegesis and will occasionally offer particular interpretations, I will not ultimately be concerned in this present work with ascertaining or explaining the entirety of an author's thought on any one particular subject. While doing so is a valuable enterprise in itself, it is a different kind of project from this one. (Indeed, I would not have space left over to solve the problem that is the focus of this book were I to proceed in the former way.) I therefore beg the reader who may be used to historical philosophy being done in some other style to accept this work in the way it is intended and not to expect that I will fully explain the overall views of the particular authors. Although I will, at many times, engage in various exegetical debates relevant to particular points, my doing so will always be with a view toward solving the problem of NO's.

Furthermore, I shall occasionally draw inferences based upon my exegesis of certain writers as to what they either would have to say based upon what they have said, or what they could say based upon what they have said. Some have asserted that doing such is not doing medieval philosophy per se. For example, I was once criticized for having supposedly ceased doing historical philosophy near the end of chapter 3 in which I draw out certain Anselmian inferences based upon his statements regarding the will. To be honest, I am puzzled by such a criticism since it is not clear how a person quits doing historical philosophy once he stops performing a strict exegesis of texts and tries to discuss where that exegesis would logically lead. Nonetheless, it is (so far as I am concerned) irrelevant whether drawing or suggesting such inferences is strictly considered historical philosophy. My real concern is whether I can successfully apply those inferences and suggestions (regardless whence they arose) to elucidating and ultimately solving the problem of NO's. And if I can, then I am definitely doing philosophy whether or not doing such fits any one particular definition of doing *historical* philosophy. And if I can do such philosophy by appealing to thoughts written down by medieval philosophers, then all the better for medieval philosophy. Doing so shows that not only is medieval philosophy interesting and valuable in its own right, but that it can be appropriated by philosophers today who often ignore this great period of thought.

I should also mention that since my main emphasis will be to solve the problem of NO's, there will be times at which what may count as an adequate solution in one context of doing medieval philosophy may not count in this context. For example, I discuss Aquinas's thought in relation to NO's in chapter 4 by trying to find a way in which the ignorance that precedes an omission can be voluntary despite not being directly willed. A colleague once pointed out to me that I had overlooked Aquinas's answer in *ST* Ia-IIae, q.6, a.8. In that passage, Aquinas states that ignorance can be voluntary when a person, on account of negligence, does not take the effort to learn what he should know.[13] This colleague thus claimed that Aquinas had resources to solve my problem which I had overlooked.

If one were doing medieval philosophy in such as way as to determine whether Aquinas himself thought NO's resulting from ignorance of what one could have known were voluntary and thus blameworthy, then indeed, this text would be decisive and important. But so far as my purposes are concerned, it is in large part irrelevant. For I am not primarily interested in trying to determine whether Aquinas thought such ignorance could be blameworthy. Instead, I am trying to determine *how* such ignorance can be blameworthy, and that is not necessarily explained in this passage. With regard to the problem of NO's caused by being ignorant of one's obligations, I am interested in what sense we voluntarily *can* know something that we should or ought to know if we don't occurrently think of the fact that we should know that (or alternatively, how we can know that we ought to gain some knowledge if we do not occurrently think of the fact that we should gain that knowledge). It is this question that ultimately has to be answered in order to solve NO's. And passages that do not bear on this question will thus sometimes be overlooked even when, viewed from a different context of doing medieval philosophy, they would be directly relevant.

[13] Hoc igitur modo dicitur ignorantia, sive cum aliquis actu non considerat quod considerare potest et debet, quae est ignorantia malae electionis, vel ex passione vel ex habitu proveniens, sive cum aliquis notitiam quam debet habere, non curat acquirere; et secundum hunc modum, ignorantia universalium iuris, quae quis scire tenetur, voluntaria dicitur, quasi per negligentiam proveniens (Ia-IIae, q.6, a.8).

Given that my primary goal is to solve the problem of NO's per se and not necessarily to explaining the entirety of different medieval thinkers' views on particular subjects, one may wonder why I have bothered appealing to the medievals at all. The answer, I hope, has already become obvious. The medieval period was a time at which philosophical reasoning arguably reached a, if not 'the,' high point. Given the immense talent and resources devoted to philosophical thinking during this period, it is only to be expected that some of their thoughts could be helpful to contemporary philosophers. I thus see no need to reinvent the wheel, so to speak. If something a medieval philosopher said can help solve a contemporary problem (or spurs a thought that subsequently solves a problem), then it should be used. And I am convinced that philosophers from the medieval period could help us solve many problems, if only they were not themselves so neglected by contemporary practitioners in the profession. To begin to remedy this particular instance of negligent omission is thus part of the purpose of this book.

B. *A Clarification of Terms: Knowledge and Ignorance*

I want to comment on my use of the terms 'ignorance' and 'knowledge' in reference to NO's. According to one common understanding of these terms, an agent is considered to have 'knowledge' of a fact *x* and is not necessarily ignorant of *x* if *x* is in the recesses of her mind such that the she has learned it and can recall it. In other words, a known fact need not be 'occurrent' to be knowledge. Regarded in another way, however, knowledge is coterminous with 'occurrent' knowledge, and ignorance can refer to something that one knows in the recesses of one's mind yet is not presently aware of or cognizing. It is in the latter sense that I use the terms knowledge and ignorance in this book.

When an agent fails to fulfill her obligation, she is *at that time* 'ignorant' of her obligation. This does not mean that she has no cognitive access to that information whatsoever; she could recall it given the right circumstances and prompting. Nonetheless, if she has no current awareness or cognition of her obligation at all, I will consider her not to 'know,' but to be 'ignorant' of her obligation.

After all, of what use is 'knowledge' that is in the recesses of one's mind at the time an obligation is to be fulfilled if that knowledge is not *before* the agent's mind in any way? If an agent is supposed to act based on knowledge, that knowledge had better be somewhat active, somewhat occurrent; otherwise, the agent's action is indistinguishable from what her action would have been if she had never learned the non-occurrent piece of information in the first place.[14] In other words, since I am concerned with actions and lacks thereof, the only type of knowledge that is relevant is knowledge of which one is aware or is cognizing in some way or other. So-called 'knowledge' of which one is not currently aware can have no influence upon one's action and is, for that reason, indistinguishable from ignorance for our purposes.[15]

For this reason, I will often use the terms 'ignorance,' 'not-thinking-about,' 'temporarily not-thinking-about,' 'inconsideration/not considering,' 'not being aware,' 'not cognizing' and others similar to these interchangeably and synonymously. And by 'knowledge' I do not mean something one has at one point learned. It must be somewhat active so as to influence action. I will accordingly use 'knowledge,' 'awareness,' 'consideration,' 'deliberation,' 'cognizing' and similar terms somewhat interchangeably. And again, by adopting this practice I am not denying that there is some utility in the typical usage in which something that has been learned before but of which one is not presently aware can be called knowledge. Nonetheless, such usage is irrelevant in the current context that deals with actions and lacks thereof.

This usage of 'ignorance' and 'knowledge' raises a couple of questions that I should quickly discuss before proceeding. First, it may be wondered whether the ignorance involved is, as the medievals referred to it, vincible or invincible (able and not able to be overcome, respectively). Since the type of NO discussed in this book is *ex hypothesi* blameworthy, and invincible ignorance completely excuses, any ignorance that would cause a NO must be vincible.[16]

Another worry is that this usage conflates true ignorance with 'habitual knowledge,' knowledge that is not actual but that the agent can

---

[14] Suárez is particularly insistent on this point. See chapter 8. In addition, cf. my "Voluntary Inconsideration, Virtual Cognition, and Francesco Suárez," *Southwest Philosophical Studies* 31 (Spring 2008).

[15] As the reader may guess from this statement, in Chapter 2 I will reject the common interpretation of Aristotle's akratic that he is to be regarded as blameworthy because he had knowledge that was merely possessed but not used. Non-used knowledge is, in my opinion, irrelevant for evaluations of action, and thus, as far as action is concerned, one might as well be ignorant of such knowledge.

[16] Cf., for example, chapter. 4, *DM* q.3, a.8 and *ST* Ia-IIae, q.76, a.3.

make actual.[17] But to call a certain piece of knowledge 'habitual' does not explain *how* an agent can be expected to actualize some knowledge that is, at present, not actualized. And as will be seen, to give such an explanation is essential to this book's project of solving NO's. Since ultimately a piece of knowledge is either actualized (in some sense) or not, relying upon the notion of habitual knowledge, without explaining *how* such non-actualized knowledge can be actualized, would be to dodge the issue so far as the present project is concerned. I will thus avoid appealing to 'habitual knowledge.' Nonetheless, it may turn out that the ultimate results of this inquiry could be used in order to illuminate exactly what those who refer to 'habitual knowledge' have in mind by the term.

C. *The Bracketing of Virtue*

Others have often suggested to me that an agent's character, or virtue, could explain the occurrence, and thus the imputability, of a NO. In one sense, this is no doubt true. If somebody has voluntarily formed a character such that she does not take her obligations seriously, then she will probably commit NO's and those NO's would be imputable to her insomuch as they resulted from that voluntarily-formed flawed character. But in those cases, the imputability of NO's is not puzzling or interesting at all. As a result, such NO's are *not* the focus of this book. Instead, this book is focused on how individual NO's can be voluntary and imputable abstracting from the character of the agent committing them. One might say this is an act-, as opposed to a character-, based investigation.

There are a couple of ways in which this act-based orientation can be motivated. First, let us suppose that many NO's do result from a flawed character. Such a flawed character, if it is to be imputable to the agent, must have been voluntarily formed by the agent. And such flawed formation could itself have been the result of individual voluntary NO's which did not themselves necessarily result from a previously-formed character (lest a regress begins). Therefore, even the virtue theorist should be willing to admit that there may be NO's not ultimately explicable by reference to character. And if so, then my act-based approach should be amenable even to the virtue theorist.

---

[17] Tobias Hoffmann, in "Aquinas and Intellectual Determinism," relies upon this notion in his explanation of Aquinas's view of the first angels' sin.

Moreover, I take it that the most virtuous people can sometimes commit voluntary, blameworthy NO's that are not the result of any flaw of character – even virtuous agents can sometimes makes mistakes.[18] Suppose, for example, that John is very virtuous and that his forgetting Des is in no way a result of any flaw in his character. Given this, I take it that it is still possible that John's NO can be voluntary and thus is to be imputed to him (certainly Des would agree). And if so, then I have a particular NO that is not ultimately traceable to character and which presents the philosophical puzzle with which this book began. Such NO's, those not traceable to character, are the kinds I will be dealing with.

On account of my bracketing issues related to character, some medieval texts that many readers might initially think are relevant to my problem will not be. Aquinas, for example, discusses the virtue of prudence and its relation to various acts in *ST* IIa-IIae, qq.47–56. How the virtue of prudence affects one's actions certainly seems relevant to the question of NO's. Indeed, q.54 is specifically about negligence. And indeed, if my aim were to discuss Aquinas's ethical theory in general, or how he would explain NO's resulting from character, such texts would be required. But that is not my aim. My aim is to explain NO's from the so-called 'act-based' perspective. Therefore, texts which appeal to virtue, character, or habit (such as the ones in *ST*) will not play a role in this particular study.

D. *The* Ex Hypothesi *Blameworthiness of NO's in this Book*

I should explicitly note that when I discuss NO's in this book, they are *ex hypothesi* blameworthy or sinful. This needs to be explicitly noted for a couple of reasons. When I mention to others that I work on the potential blameworthiness of negligent omissions and explain it to them by means of examples similar to those above, I often receive the following retort: "Yes, but wouldn't John's omission not be blameworthy if he forgot to pick up Des because he got a call that a relative had died in the meantime." Indeed, it probably would not be

[18] Of course, it is possible that certain virtue theorists may disagree with me here and assert that any blameworthy action is ultimately a result of that agent's not being *completely* virtuous and thus can still be traced to a character flaw in some sense. If one holds this position, then the reasoning presented in this paragraph will not be convincing. Indeed, unless the reasoning in the prior paragraph holds, the problem of NO's would not be interesting to such a virtue theorist in any case.

blameworthy; forgetting one's obligations because of some other crisis is no doubt often excusable. Put in terms we used above, there are cases in which one's ignorance of one's obligation is indeed invincible because of some overriding circumstance. But this is irrelevant to my project. I am proceeding under the assumption that, those cases notwithstanding, there are other cases of NO's which *are* voluntary and blameworthy. And I am simply trying to find a way in which such NO's can be voluntary, given that some voluntary NO's exist. Along these same lines, I am not interested in offering any sort of algorithm by which one could determine whether any particular case of omission is voluntary or not. Instead, I simply aim to explain how, given the *ex hypothesi* assumption that there are blameworthy NO's, they could be philosophically regarded as voluntary.

On a related note, it has been noted that even the medievals themselves did not think that agents could possibly keep in mind, or pay sufficient attention to, all of their obligations so as to avoid sinning.[19] This too may indeed be the case, but is likewise irrelevant to my project. A particular NO is either blameworthy or not – and if it is, then I simply want to explain how it may be that the agent could be considered to have fulfilled the conditions for voluntariness.

E. *Varieties of Negligence and the Repeated Use of Stock Illustrations*

It has been pointed out to me that the examples used in this book (especially the ones concerning John and Des) focus on promise-keeping and thus fail to take into account the entire range of NO's. While it may indeed be the case that many of the samples explain NO's by means of failure to keep some promise, the failure to keep promises is not what characterizes NO's so far as this book is concerned. NO's, as understood here, center on the failure to fulfill some obligation. I have simply found that using illustrations in which the obligation is to keep a promise is effective. Despite some of the illustrations relying on promise-keeping, the conclusions of this study should be easily applicable to any NO in which one fails to fulfill some obligation.

Some may nonetheless think that the focus on failure to fulfill obligations does not cover the entire range of NO's. It has, for example, been suggested to me that one can negligently omit to learn one's

---

[19] Cf. Aquinas's *De Veritate* 24.13; *ST* Ia-IIae q.74, a.3, *ad* 2; q.109, a.8–10; Scotus *Ordinatio* II, d.28.

obligations in the first place.[20] Note, however, that such a negligent omission accords with my emphasis on obligation, for a person is only blamed for not learning her obligations if she had a prior obligation to learn those subsequent obligations. I am thus not convinced that there are NO's not characterized by a failure to fulfill some sort of obligation. If, however, there are indeed such NO's, they are simply not relevant to this study. To explain how NO's, understood as failures to fulfill obligations, can be voluntary is a serious and difficult enough task in itself.

I am also not interested in discussing some cases that, in some respects, may resemble NO's. For example, there can be the case in which an agent plans to commit a blameworthy act and negligently omits to do so. While my ultimate diagnosis might be able to explain how he could be regarded as having voluntarily omitted to commit the diabolical act despite not having intended to omit it (and thus could provide his evil overlord a reason for holding him responsible for failing to carry out some evil assignment), I will have nothing to say on whether such an agent is ultimately blameworthy (because of his intention) or not (because of perhaps getting lucky). To describe necessary and sufficient conditions for blameworthiness and exoneration is not this book's concern.

As the preceding paragraph implies, I am also not interested in discussing how 'moral luck' is related to the blameworthiness of NO's, a phenomenon that nonetheless seems to plague the problem of NO's. For example, suppose that two persons in the same Type-3 scenario each fail to take the needed special precautions. Before TEF, one of them is just randomly, by pure chance, reminded of her obligation by something that is said on the radio while the other is not. The former thus remembers and fulfills her obligation while the latter does not. In other words, the former has no 'sin of NO' and the latter does, despite the fact that they both similarly failed to take the same steps. I simply want to state at the outset that I am not going to address such issues surrounding moral luck, blame, or the lack thereof in this book. The task of identifying a specific locus of culpability for NO's that do in fact occur is a challenging enough task for the present project.

Similarly, I am not necessarily interested in explaining how bosses and CEO's can be charged with negligence because of mistakes made by those working under them. (If, however, the boss or CEO had a

[20] For Aquinas's discussion of this issue, see *ST* Ia-IIae, q.19, a.6.

particular obligation to oversee certain processes and failed to perform those obligations, then my account could apply.) I am likewise not concerned with any legal, as opposed to moral, understandings of negligence or blameworthiness.

Finally, the reader should be prepared to encounter a stock set of examples throughout the book. While I do vary my illustrations at a couple of points, the reader will nonetheless encounter John and Des repeatedly throughout the text. And though I realize that the repeated use of the same basic scenario can be tedious, I believe it best to use the same set of examples so as to foster clarity of the points being made. I thus beg the reader's patience.

V. Structure of the Book and Authors Studied

I attempt to solve the problem of the locus of culpability in sins of negligent omission by drawing from the writings of Aristotle, Anselm, Aquinas, Scotus[21] and Suárez. It may be initially puzzling that I have chosen to focus on these authors in an attempt to solve my problem since only two of them (Aquinas and Suárez) commented on anything even close to the idea of NO's. Furthermore, there is almost no secondary literature written about their views on NO's. Nonetheless, I have chosen these authors because their writings either (i) contain important foundational views for approaching the topic, (ii) discuss other topics in ways in which certain implications relevant to the idea of sins of NO can be drawn, (iii) offer distinctive insights particular to the problem of NO's, (iv) draw distinctive insights specifically as a result of the writings of one or more of the other authors discussed, or (v) various combinations of these reasons.

In the end, I find that certain elements drawn from Scotus's and Suárez's thought can be combined to provide a powerful model for solving the problem of NO's. Furthermore, the details of that model largely agree with some of the insights made with regard to other writers in this study. I conclude by stating that the utility of the model provides reason to believe that the insights of medieval and scholastic thinkers can be applied to contemporary philosophical and theological problems.

---

[21] Some of the writings we will be discussing with regard to Scotus may not be Scotus's own writings. Indeed, many of them may ultimately be from the pen of his secretary, William of Alnwick. I discuss these issues in Chapter 5.

In the opening two chapters, I first problematize the question of how NO's can be blameworthy in terms of Aristotelian notions of voluntariness. I then examine Aristotle's akratic in an attempt to understand how robust one's knowledge must be such that an act or omission related to that knowledge can be considered voluntary.

In chapter 3, I explore Anselm's notion of the will as 'affection.' I make the point that, if Anselm is to be consistent, his understanding of the *affectiones* as characterized by something called the 'strong conditional' entails that the first rational creature's initial sin (who for him is the 'devil') would have to have been a sin of negligent omission. Sins of NO can thus be viewed as playing an important role in the history of theological thought, and a solution to problem of the culpability of NO's is thus shown to be vital to many theological discussions.

In chapter 4, I turn to Aquinas, one of the few authors who explicitly write about NO's. Through an exploration of several points in his action theory, I come to make the significant insight that in every sin of NO, the voluntariness, and thus the culpability, must lie (for Aquinas) in a separate non-negligent sin of omission.

In chapters 5 and 6, I begin my constructive proposal by offering a way in which to understand Scotus and the 'doctrine of indistinct intellections' as applicable to Type-1 and Type-2 NO's. At the end of these chapters, NO's of the two types will have largely been solved although in each case a few issues will remain.

In chapter 7, I discuss Scotus's unique adaptation of Anselm's *affectiones*. We there discover that he adapts them in such a way that they do not imply (contra Anselm) the devil's first sin would have to be a NO. In addition, we see how a Scotist understanding of the affections provides the answer to one of the issues left unresolved at the end of chapter 6.

In chapter 8, I explore Suárez's notions of the 'indirectly voluntary' and his understanding of how 'inconsideration' (not-thinking-about/ignorance) can be indirectly voluntary. We come to discover two important concepts, 'virtual' reflection/knowledge, and the idea of the will moving the intellect (WMI), concepts that will become crucial for solving the problem of NO's.

I conclude the study by showing how Scotist and Suárezian elements can be combined into a model that explains wherein lie the blameworthiness and voluntariness in the causal history of NO's. This model is then compared to the insights garnered from the other three thinkers.

CHAPTER 1

THE PROBLEM MAY LURK IN ARISTOTLE'S *ETHICS*

In this chapter, I will accomplish a few general tasks. First, I will discuss Aristotle's basic notion of voluntariness. In doing so, I will explore his claim that knowledge is required for voluntariness, and I will probe into some issues surrounding his understanding of ignorance and its relation to voluntariness. This discussion will moreover lead to the realization that the problem of negligent omissions may even lurk in one of Aristotle's most basic distinctions between types of ignorance: the distinction between 'ignorance of particular circumstances' and 'ignorance of universals.' The results of this chapter will thus partially point out the necessity of solving negligent omissions so as to ground Aristotle's own action theory. Perhaps more importantly, however, the work of this chapter will also enable us to problematize NO's in terms of Aristotelian (and thus medieval) understandings of voluntariness and ignorance. As will become apparent, the solution to the puzzle of NO's will depend largely on how we are to understand Aristotle's claim that knowledge is required for voluntariness and that ignorance, in some cases, removes voluntariness.

I. Aristotelian Agency

A. *The Basic Notion of Voluntariness*

Although Aristotle lacks the theological concept of 'sin,' he nonetheless believes there are certain actions one is obligated not to perform and blamed if one does.[1] For such an action to be culpably ascribed to an

[1] I do not believe a full exploration of exactly which actions one is required to perform is necessary. First, the class is very broad and varies with the individual (e.g. some persons are required to perform certain actions that others are not). More importantly, such an investigation into the details of this issue in regard to Aristotle's theory does not advance our investigation, given that the important issue is not what one is obligated to do, but rather (as indicated in the Introduction) *given* that one is obligated to do something, how can she be or not be held responsible for omitting to do it.

agent, however, that action must be 'voluntary' (*hekousion*).[2] Discerning under which conditions Aristotelian voluntariness obtains, however, is somewhat difficult.

In the first place, it will not be correct to say (as it is for some other authors in this study) that the voluntary is that which issues from the faculty of the will. Aristotle, as is widely recognized, has no concept of the will as faculty.[3] Second, Aristotle's development of the notion of *hekousion* is at times problematic. Not only does he explicate it in different ways in various texts,[4] he also (seemingly unwittingly) attributes two distinct senses to it.[5] In addition to meaning what we now commonly call 'voluntary,' i.e. a description of an action that is intended and inherently linked to praise or blame, *hekousion* can also mean 'willing' (in the sense of wanting to, and as opposed to 'unwilling').[6] These are two logically distinct meanings, either of which may be appropriate depending upon the situation.[7]

Despite this problem, it is possible to state Aristotle's conditions for *hekousion* in the sense we are interested in. An act is voluntary in this sense if "the moving principle is in the agent himself, he being aware of

[2] "Since virtue is concerned with passions and actions, and on voluntary passions and actions praise and blame are bestowed, on those that are involuntary pardon, and sometimes also pity, to distinguish the voluntary and the involuntary is presumably necessary for those who are studying the nature of virtue, and useful also for legislators with a view to the assigning of both honours and of punishments" (NE iii.1; 1109b30–35). Quoted from: Aristotle, *The Basic Works of Aristotle*, ed. Richard McKeon (New York: Random House, 1941). Unless otherwise noted, all quotations of Aristotle will be from this source.

[3] E.g., Anthony Kenny, despite the title of his book, agrees with this statement and begins his book thus: "It is a commonplace of Aristotelian scholarship that Aristotle had no theory of the will." Anthony Kenny, *Aristotle's Theory of the Will* (New Haven, CT: Yale University Press, 1979), vii.

[4] In fact, much of first part of Kenny's book, *Aristotle's Theory of the Will,* consists in investigating the various nuanced differences between developments of voluntariness in the *Eudemian* and *Nicomachean* Ethics.

[5] It is primarily due to chap. 8 of Hardie's book that I came to this knowledge. (W.F.R.Hardie, *Aristotle's Ethical Theory*, 2nd ed. [Oxford: Clarendon, 1980]). Cf. also chap. 5 of the following: David Bostock, *Aristotle's Ethics* (New York: Oxford University Press, 2000).

[6] Analogously, the negation of *hekousion* expressed by *akousion* is ambiguous between 'involuntary' and 'unwilling.'

[7] That *hekousion* can be used in such varied ways is most easily pointed out by the observation that one can voluntarily do something and yet do it unwillingly (i.e. she would rather not do it). A prime example is that of a ship's captain throwing cargo overboard during a storm (1110a8–11). It is, as Hardie points out, because of this "unrecognized ambiguity" in *hekousion* that there are such puzzling statements as actions that are a "mixture" (Hardie, *Aristotle's Ethical Theory*, 153).

the particular circumstances of the action" (1111a21–24).[8] Or (as Kenny puts it), the voluntary is that which is *eph' hemin*, i.e. "in one's power to do and not to do," while being "performed in full knowledge of the circumstances."[9] By either definition, there are two conditions for the voluntary: (i) the act being in the agent's power in some sense, and (ii) the agent knowing the circumstances concerning that which she is doing. In the remainder of this chapter and the book as a whole, I will refer to this latter condition (which is very essential to my project) as the 'knowledge requirement.'

These two conditions naturally correspond to two ways in which an act can lose its voluntary nature and thus be non-imputable.[10] One such way is when that act is brought about by force or coercion, such as when a wind moves someone (1110a1–4). If the moving principle is truly in the agent, or if the action is indeed *eph' hemin* (up to us) to do or not to do, there is no such external compulsion. When there is such compulsion, voluntariness is removed.

Corresponding to the knowledge requirement, the other way in which voluntariness can be lost is through ignorance: "Everything that is done by reason of ignorance is *not* voluntary"(1110b17–18).[11] The relation between voluntariness and ignorance, though, is not so simple as this statement may at first seem to indicate. Let us therefore explore the intricacies of this relationship by means of making four observations regarding ignorance.

---

[8] Cf. Hardie, *Aristotle's Ethical Theory*, 159.

[9] Kenny *Aristotle's Theory of the Will*, 11–12. This is based upon his reading of *EE* and is expressed in *EN* v.8. Of course, Kenny himself believes the shared book *EN* v properly belongs only to the *EE*. The details of this dispute is irrelevant for our purposes.

[10] It should be noted that there is actually not merely a dichotomy in Aristotle's writings between voluntary and involuntary, but a *tri*chotomy between voluntary, involuntary, and non-voluntary. The distinction between the non-voluntary and the involuntary need not concern us for the purposes of this project. We are concerned only with conditions of culpability, and thus only with whether an action is voluntary or not. If some action is not voluntary, it need not concern us whether it is involuntary or non-voluntary. I will accordingly use 'involuntary' and 'non-voluntary' more or less synonymously throughout the book so as to aid clarity. Furthermore, it should be pointed out that it is possible the distinction between the latter two is largely a result of the ambiguity of *hekousion* and *akousion* that we have already discussed (cf., for example, Hardie, *Aristotle's Ethical Theory*, chap. 8, and Bostock, *Aristotle's Ethics*, chap. 5).

[11] The reader may notice that the restriction of ignorance to the *circumstances* is dropped in this statement, a qualification included in expressing the knowledge requirement in both definitions of the voluntary. This qualification will be addressed in 'Observation 4' below.

B. *The Relation Between Voluntariness & Ignorance*

1. *Observation 1: 'Lack of Knowledge' vs. 'Error'*

The first observation concerns the scope of the meaning of 'ignorance' (*agnoia*). Not only does it have the obvious meaning of "lack of knowledge," but also encompasses "positively mistaken belief." An action can be rendered involuntary on account of ignorance, therefore, even when the agent thinks she knows what she is doing but does not. It is in fact for this reason that Kenny prefers to translate *agnoia* as "error."[12]

This second meaning of 'ignorance,' however, gives rise to a problem. Consider, for example, a case in which an agent 'Billy' intends and plans to murder some other man 'Jimmy.' While attempting to commit the murder of Jimmy, Billy sees another man, 'Stephen.' Mistakenly believing him to be Jimmy, Billy kills Stephen. If positively mistaken belief counts as a form of ignorance that removes voluntariness, it would seem that Billy could claim his killing of Stephen was involuntary and therefore not imputable. It seems obvious, however, that Billy should be culpably blamed (and consequently punished) for killing Stephen. For that to be the case, though, his act of murder would have to be considered voluntary, and this possibility appears precluded if the *agnoia* that removes voluntariness can include positively mistaken belief (as posited above.) It seems then that either *agnoia* cannot be so broadly defined, or that we must reconsider our intuition of Billy's culpability.

2. *Observation 2: Ignorance is Relative to a Certain Description*

As it turns out, we need not opt for either disjunct. The reason is based upon the second ignorance-related observation that must be made: ignorance is relative to a certain description of an action. As Bostock notes, for any action there are numerous possible propositions expressing what one is doing in the form of "'what I am doing is

---

[12] Kenny *Aristotle's Theory of the Will*, 49. It has been suggested that it is incorrect for me (and Kenny too, I suppose) to identify 'error' with ignorance since the former requires a judgment while the latter does not. In response, I wish to say two things. First, I have not *strictly* identified these two concepts – I have stated that the term *agnoia* encompasses both. Second, *agnoia* understood as error does indeed imply at least a temporary lack of knowledge about what 'here and now' is the case. So far as Aristotle is concerned, therefore, I see no overriding reason to think that he would not think both understandings of *agnoia* render an action involuntary (so far as the *agnoia* itself was not voluntary – see below). Moreover, both understandings of *agnoia* are compatible with the understanding of ignorance that is relevant to NO's (see the Introduction).

such-and-such' … and for any action that I choose to do, there will inevitably be some that I do know and some that I do not."[13] If there is a certain description of an action that an agent does not know, then *ceteris paribus*[14] she will not, on account of ignorance, be considered to have committed voluntarily the action picked out by that particular description, even though she may be regarded as having done voluntarily that action considered under another description.

This observation allows us to resolve the paradox posed by the example above. Since Billy did not know that "what I am doing is killing Stephen," he cannot be regarded as having *killed Stephen* voluntarily. Yet it is beyond question that Billy was in some sense aware of the proposition "what I am doing is killing another man," whether that other man was Stephen or Jimmy. Thus, he *can* be regarded as having committed murder of *some man* voluntarily, for he certainly was not ignorant of nor in error regarding that fact. This, in turn, means that (in accordance with our intuitions), Billy can indeed be held culpable and punished for murder in an Aristotelian system, even though he cannot be regarded as having voluntarily murdered *Stephen* per se.

3. *Observation 3: Acting 'through ignorance' vs. Acting 'Ignorantly'*

I made the caveat above that ignorance of a particular description removes voluntariness from the act picked out by that description '*ceteris paribus*.' This was done in order to rule out the possibility that Billy could have been responsible for this particular instance of ignorance. If Billy was responsible for being ignorant of the fact that it was Stephen he was killing (contra my assumption[15]), then it appears Aristotle would not count that ignorance as removing voluntariness.

I say this based upon Aristotle's distinction at 1110b24–27 between "acting by reason of ignorance" or 'through ignorance' (*di' agnoian*),

---

[13] Bostock, *Aristotle's Ethics*, 107.

[14] As we will see shortly, there are some cases in which voluntariness is not removed, even if there is such ignorance.

[15] It may be thought that there is no way in which Billy could not be responsible for his ignorance of this fact. Given that Billy was performing an action as grave and serious as murder, he (at least implicitly) knew that he should *make sure* that he was killing the right person. In response, there is some truth in this, and some of the things we will later observe (especially in the material on Suárez) add credence to this belief. To have brought in such complexities at this early point would have hindered my attempt to clarify basic Aristotelian concepts. I thus wanted to assume that Billy was not in any way responsible for being ignorant of the fact that Stephen was not Jimmy. If necessary, we could posit some scenario such as Stephen, unbeknownst to anyone, was so enamored by Jimmy's looks that he had just had a plastic surgery so as to alter his appearance to look exactly like Jimmy.

and "acting *in* ignorance" or 'ignorantly' (*agnoōn*). The former case of ignorance (i.e. acting 'through ignorance') is the ignorance discussed thus far that removes voluntariness.[16] It is ignorance for which one is not responsible. By contrast, the ignorance involved in cases of one acting 'in ignorance' is ignorance for which the agent *is* responsible. Such ignorance, given that the agent is responsible for it, does not remove voluntariness from the act which that ignorance accompanies.

What counts as the kind of ignorance that does not remove voluntariness? Aristotle mentions as examples ignorance resulting from drunkenness and rage (1110b24–27). I do not believe he intends to restrict this category of ignorance to those cases resulting from voluntarily-induced altered bodily/mental states. Rather, the idea seems to be this: if the agent voluntarily acts irresponsibly in regard to the preservation of her knowledge by voluntarily doing something that could reasonably cause a subsequent ignorance of that knowledge, that ignorance would not remove voluntariness from an act it accompanies. In other words, Aristotle's point seems to concern not bodily states per se, but responsibility in the preservation of one's knowledge. When acting *di' agnoian*, the agent has no (reasonable) control over her ignorance and the act accompanying the ignorance is not voluntary. When acting *agnoōn*, she does have control over her ignorance/error. As a result, the act which this ignorance/error accompanies is not rendered involuntary.

While this distinction is initially appealing, it is far from perspicuous.[17] Let us return to Billy and Stephen and posit that Billy only attempts to commit any murder at all (whether it be of Jimmy or Stephen) because he drank a bottle of whiskey beforehand. After drinking the bottle, Billy 'just doesn't know what he's doing' and ends up killing someone. Aristotle surely would not excuse Billy's act of murder on account of his being drunk, since it was Billy's fault that he was drunk in the first place. He must be punished.

Such a conclusion seems intuitively correct. After all, Billy should not get 'off the hook' from murder because he chose to drink the whisky that led to his loss of control. There is, however, reason for doubt, as it appears the *only* thing Billy did voluntarily was drink. He did not, by Aristotle's definition of voluntary, murder anyone voluntarily. There was, in other words, never a description of his action "what I am doing

---

[16] Cf. 1110b17.
[17] Indeed, Bostock calls it "obscure" (*Aristotle's Ethics*, 109).

is killing someone" of which he was aware. And *if punishment/blame is dependent upon voluntariness*, it seems that while he could certainly be punished for getting drunk, no punishment or blame could be attached for the murder per se. There thus seems to be a mismatch between the conditions for voluntariness and certain cases in which we wish blame to be ascribed.[18]

In a way, it is understandable how this mismatch may have come about.[19] Aristotle was at pains to give the criteria for voluntariness, one of which is the absence of ignorance. Having already linked voluntariness and blame, he then noticed that his statements could be construed so as to let certain agents who are irresponsible in regard to the use or preservation of their knowledge avoid blame. It would not do simply to blame those irresponsible agents merely for failing to preserve their knowledge properly, for then a drunkard who did not commit murder would be equally blameworthy as one who did (assuming equal levels of drunkenness, ignorance, and any other potentially relevant factors). Some extra culpability must attach to any wrongful action taken as a result of, and subsequent to the cause of, ignorance. In order therefore to preserve this higher level of blameworthiness for wrongful acts resulting from irresponsible failure to preserve knowledge, he (i) distinguished between an ignorance for which one is not responsible and an ignorance for which one is responsible. Following upon this distinction, he (ii) stated that it is only ignorance of the former kind to which he referred when he said ignorance removes voluntariness and, correlatively, blame. Consequently, we must note the distinction between acting *di' agnoian* and *agnoōn* and recognize that in the former voluntariness is removed while in the latter it is not.

4. *Observation 4: Ignorance of Particulars vs. Ignorance of the Universal*

According to Aristotle, the ignorance that removes voluntariness is only "ignorance of particulars, i.e. of the circumstances of the action and the objects with which it is concerned" (1110b34–35). For example, ignorance of what exactly one is doing, or to whom one is doing it, or in what manner the action is being performed all would qualify as

[18] Bostock makes these points (*Aristotle's Ethics*, 110–111).

[19] The reconstruction offered here is ordered logically, not necessarily text-based chronologically.

cases of ignorance which excuses (as long as the agent is not responsible for that ignorance such that she is acting *agnoōn*).[20] This is contrasted with instances of ignorance, or error, which do not excuse, namely ignorance "of what is to his advantage … (it leads rather to wickedness)" and "ignorance of the universal (for *that* men are *blamed*)" (1110b30–33). What exactly, though, are these 'ignorance of what is to his advantage' and 'ignorance of the universal' that do not remove voluntariness and how do they differ from other cases of ignorance we have been discussing?

Hardie states that these are "not descriptions of different kinds of ignorance" but rather "alternative descriptions of one kind of ignorance," namely the "ignorance in respect of which a man is bad."[21] The idea is that ignorance (or, perhaps more appropriate in this context, 'error') about *general* moral directives and principles does not excuse. So, while ignorance of the fact that, say, one's touching a door knob sets off a chain reaction that results in the death of another would excuse (since this would be ignorance of a particular circumstance), ignorance of the general moral principle 'one should not kill' would neither render a subsequent killing involuntary nor preclude blame. This explanation raises the question, though, why "men are *blamed*" for ignorance of the universal but not blamed for ignorance of the particular.

One of the motivations for claiming that ignorance of the universal is blameworthy is no doubt to be able to hold agents who are 'wicked to the core,' so to speak, responsible for their actions. After all, it seems clear that someone who believes murder to be a good thing should be held accountable. It is less clear, however, why ignorance of the universal cannot, in certain cases, excuse the agent. If the agent is truly ignorant, or in error, of the fact that murder is a bad thing and inculpably so, society may be able to justify his punishment on utilitarian grounds, but it is unclear how he could be held to be voluntarily evil.[22]

One possible solution to this puzzle is to deny that an agent ever could be *inculpably* ignorant of universal moral principles. Aristotle seems to imply this at 1113b16 when he says "wickedness *is* voluntary."

---

[20] Cf. 1111a1–11.

[21] Hardie, *Aristotle's Ethical Theory*, 157. Cf. also Bostock, *Aristotle's Ethics*, 108–109.

[22] Thus Kenny is led to state that "Aristotle seems too severe on the topic of universal error" since "whether a man can be blamed for holding [evil moral principles] surely depends in part on what chances he had of acquiring better ones" (*Aristotle's Theory of the Will*, 51).

In support of this notion, it can be postulated that there is some "universal natural law ... within the grasp of all men" such that, one "could easily have known" it.[23] Such accessibility to general moral principles means that if an agent is wicked (i.e. in 'error' or 'ignorance' of universal moral principles), he is so voluntarily and thus culpably.

In a later section, I will take up again this case of being ignorant of the universal and this proposed solution so as to show how the problem of NO's lurks at the core of Aristotle's action theory. Before moving on, however, it will be useful to summarize our analysis of the voluntary and our observations of ignorance.

C. *Summary of Aristotelian Voluntariness and its Relation to Ignorance*

For Aristotle, the voluntary describes a particular description of an action in which two conditions are fulfilled: the moving principle of that action is in the agent, and the agent knows the particular circumstances that are made reference to in that particular description. Corresponding to these two conditions are two ways in which voluntariness can be nullified. The action could be due to 'force' and not thereby to the agent's own interior moving principle. Or the agent could be ignorant regarding the particular circumstances surrounding that action. There are four observations to be made about ignorance as it relates to the voluntary. First, ignorance is a broad enough term so as to include mistaken belief. There should be nothing surprising in this, since to be mistaken about something is not to know (i.e. be ignorant of) the true facts of the matter. Second, ignorance (and thus voluntariness) is relative to a certain description of the action. Aspects of the same action can be variously regarded as voluntary or involuntary depending upon the operative description. Third, ignorance only

[23] Kenny, *Aristotle's Theory of the Will*, 51, 52. Interestingly, Kenny seems to come up short of saying that *all* ignorance of the universal is blameworthy, for the whole statement (based upon his interpretation of 1114b34 ff) reads: "If so, Aristotle is now qualifying his earlier position: *not all* universal error is blameworthy, but only ignorance of what one should and could easily have known" (52, italics mine). This seems fine as an interpretation of 1114b34 ff, which seems concerned with "laws." Nonetheless, if this qualified position is to be applied to universal moral principles, it is unclear to me how it can be consistent with Aristotle's statements in *NE* iii.1. In the body, I thus state that it must be Aristotle's position that all, not only some, *general, universal* moral principles must be easily known. In any case, I do not believe much is at stake in which option is chosen for the general purpose of this thesis.

nullifies voluntariness of some action if that action is done 'through ignorance' (*di' agnoian*). If the action is done 'ignorantly' (*agnoōn*), i.e., as the result of irresponsible preservation of knowledge, voluntariness apparently remains. Finally, ignorance can only excuse from blame if it is ignorance of particulars, whereas ignorance of the universal (i.e. of general moral principles) is blameworthy.

II. Ignorance of the Universal: The Problem of NO's Already Posed

As we have observed, Aristotle apparently holds ignorance of general moral principles blameworthy on account of the fact that the general moral law is within grasp such that it could easily be acquired. This leads us to inquire under what conditions an agent would *not* grasp the moral law when she easily could.

It may be that one's social environment plays a role in failing to grasp moral principles. In *NE* x.9 (1179a34 ff.), Aristotle discusses the important role that community and social environment can play in shaping one's moral outlook.[24] Failure to acquire correct moral principles, therefore, could be traced to such factors. I mention this response merely to set it aside. First, it is not clear to me that all such failures to become moral are explicable in this sense. And if they are, it is not clear how the moral law would be within such agents' grasps such that it could be easily acquired. At any rate, such explanations of moral failure are irrelevant to the current project.

The most obvious Aristotelian answer for why an agent fails to grasp any one particular correct moral principle is that he has a bad character, i.e. because he is vicious.[25] And since one's vicious character is voluntarily acquired,[26] one is ultimately responsible for failing to know the universal in the relevant way. His failure to grasp it results from his having voluntarily formed his character in a bad way.

Even if failure to acquire knowledge of some universal moral principles is a result of one's character, problems remain. On the one hand, there is the further question as to what was that agent's guiding principle by which he formed such a character that would subsequently lead

[24] See also *NE* ii.1 (1130b22–26).

[25] Cf., for example, *NE* vii.8 (1150b30–1151a30). See also *NE* iii.1 (especially 1110b28 ff.).

[26] *NE* iii.5 (esp. 1113b30–1114a13).

to such failures. For the agent to be ultimately blameworthy for having failed to correctly grasp the moral law, that guiding principle by which one's character would have been formed must itself have been voluntarily chosen. And if a non-explanatory regress is to be avoided, there must have been at least some initial choices not formed by a prior character or guiding principle.[27] Thus, appeal to character does not necessarily solve all questions with regard to the voluntariness of being ignorant of a universal.

I thus take it that there may be some acts and failures to put oneself in a certain state of affairs (e.g. to not be ignorant of the moral law) not ultimately determined by a prior character.[28] If this is the case, though, how can those other failures not ultimately explicable in terms of character be explained?

One possibility would be that some agents intentionally refuse to acquire knowledge of certain moral laws. However, I see no reason to rule out the additional possibility that at least some such cases of failing to grasp a general precept or other of moral law not explicable by vice could result from what we would normally call negligence (or carelessness, or failing to take care). Assuming that such a failure can result from negligence, Aristotle would most likely consider it blameworthy: "and so too [we punish] in the case of anything else that they are thought to be ignorant of through carelessness; we assume that it is in their power not to be ignorant, since they have the power of taking care" (1114a1–3).[29] Yet how could Aristotle consistently maintain that such an unintended failure is blameworthy? To be blameworthy, it

---

[27] Cf. Hardie, *Aristotle's Ethical Theory*, chap. 9 for a related discussion. Cf. also Engberg-Pedersen, *Aristotle's Theory of Moral Insight* (Oxford: Clarendon, 1983) chap. 9.

[28] As just noted, at least those initial acts by which a voluntary character is formed must be, in some sense, undetermined by a prior character. I furthermore suppose it is possible that many voluntary acts and failures to put oneself in a certain state of affairs are not fully determined by one's character even after it has been previously formed. It thus seems that appeal to character (and to vice in particular) does not necessarily explain all agential failures in Aristotle's system. For a discussion of this project's relationship to virtue in general, please see the Introduction.

[29] It may be objected that the negligence referred to in 1114a1–3 is negligence resulting from one's character. Indeed, the passage proceeds in 1114a4–31 to discuss how one can be responsible for one's negligence because of one's character. It is not necessarily clear, though, that the discussion in 1114a4–31 is meant to apply to *all* cases of negligence. Instead, that passage could be read as a response to the hypothetical objection that at least those cases of negligence resulting from character should not be blamed. The objection and response in 1114a4–31, therefore, could be read as relevant only to a subset of those cases of blameworthy negligence discussed in 1114a1–3.

would need to be voluntary.[30] But it is difficult to see how such a failure could be voluntary when it was not only unintended, but the agent apparently did not even realize that she was failing to do something she ought.

Making this point, Bostock writes:

> when I am careless, inattentive, negligent, or just plain forgetful, it hardly seems right to say that I intend or choose or decide so to be. It is not (usually) that I consider whether to take care, or to remember, and decide not to, but rather that the thought simply fails to occur to me (though it should have done [so]).[31]

In other words, consider an agent *S* who lacks knowledge of the moral law on account of negligence. *S* perhaps *could* have acquired the moral law, *if* it had only occurred to her to do so. But in cases normally labeled 'negligent,' it does *not* occur to an agent to do so. If it does occur, the failure would not be considered negligent but rather willfully 'wicked.' And since *ex hypothesi* it did not occur to *S*, it appears that she, in this case, could *not* have acquired the moral law. Consequently, the proximity of general moral principles is irrelevant to her particular ability to obtain them. The question thus remains: How she can be held blameworthy?[32]

At this point, let us note that the situation before us is a NO of the type central to this book. *S* omitted to learn some general principle of moral law (or learned it incorrectly and therefore omitted to learn it correctly) and did so not intentionally, but simply because it did not occur to her to do so. Yet, she is somehow still to be held blameworthy for that omission. Aristotle thus can be read as presenting us with the problem of NO's in the heart of his ethical theory. Let us advance our understanding of the problem of NO's by asking how this particular omission might legitimately be considered blameworthy and thus voluntary.

One way to understand such ignorance of the moral law as blameworthy would be to deny the link between voluntariness and blameworthiness.[33] Aristotle never explicitly states that "culpable ignorance

---

[30] Cf. 1109b30–32.

[31] Bostock, *Aristotle's Ethics*, 110.

[32] There are similarities between the problems noted here and the problems with the 'think harder' solution I discussed in the Introduction.

[33] We mentioned this above as one possibility to help resolve the question of how the actions committed ignorantly can themselves be considered blameworthy.

is 'voluntary.' "[34] This, in turn, leaves a path open for us to assert that ignorance of the universal can still be culpably ascribed to the agent without that blameworthy ignorance being voluntary. But while some have argued against the link between voluntariness and culpability,[35] it would be preferable to maintain the link and find a way to account for the voluntariness of NO's such as the one before us.

Let us start by examining the case of thus failing to acquire a correct moral principle in light of the conditions for voluntariness.[36] Recall that voluntariness requires knowledge of what one is doing; it requires knowledge of the specific description that picks out the act to be considered voluntary.[37] From this it follows that if one omits to acquire a correct general moral principle (or, what amounts to the same thing, acquires a bad general moral principle) *voluntarily*, it would seem that the agent would have to know *at the very least* the specific circumstance that 'what I am doing is omitting to acquire a correct moral principle' or 'what I am doing is acquiring a false moral principle.' Not to know this would appear to be ignorance of a particular circumstance, i.e. ignorance of a certain description of one's current action. We thus arrive at a quandary in relation to negligently not knowing the moral law: (i) we have already seen that this specific type of ignorance (i.e. ignorance of the particular circumstance as expressed in the description of the act) *does* remove voluntariness, and (ii) it appears to be exactly this type of ignorance that the careless, negligent, yet non-wicked agent possesses. It is thus unclear how such an agent's omission can be considered voluntary. The moral law's being 'within grasp' is irrelevant to the voluntariness of not knowing it if the agent does not somehow *know* that it is within her grasp such that she should grasp it.

A solution to this quandary may, however, lie in the *di' agnoian*/*agnoōn* distinction discussed above.[38] Let it be the case that such an agent's ignorance of the particular circumstance that 'what I am doing is omitting to acquire a correct moral principle' is itself, on account of

---

[34] Bostock, *Aristotle's Ethics*, 110. Cf. also 119.

[35] Most notable is Robert M. Adams, "Involuntary Sins," *Philosophical Review* 94 (January 1985): 3–31.

[36] Please note that I am not claiming that the ensuing explanation applies to all, or even the majority of, instances of ignorance of the universal. Instead, it applies to those possible cases in which the ignorance is not the result of a prior vice and is not the result of an intentional ignorance but yet is, *ex hypothesi*, voluntary.

[37] Cf. 'Observation 2.'

[38] This was the topic of 'Observation 3.'

some reason, voluntary and culpable.[39] If so, the agent could be regarded as having subsequently failed to acquire the correct moral principle *agnoōn*. In other words, the omission of gaining a correct moral principle would in this case be performed *agnoōn* since accompanying this omission there is an ignorance, for which the agent is responsible, of the fact that 'what I am doing is omitting to acquire a correct moral principle.' Given that the omission was performed *agnoōn* and not *di' agnoian*, voluntariness is not removed from the resulting omission to gain a correct moral principle.

III. Four (More) Observations Relevant to 'Ignorance of the Universal'

This proposed solution requires four observations. (A) First, note that there are actually two 'ignorances' here. There is the ignorance ('ignorance$_1$') of the particular fact that 'what I am doing is omitting to acquire a correct moral principle,' and there is the resulting ignorance ('ignorance$_2$') of the universal moral principle. This need not cause a particular problem, as long as one recognizes that it is ignorance$_2$ that corresponds to the NO itself, and ignorance$_1$ that corresponds to the ignorance that causes the NO and for which an agent is directly responsible.[40]

(B) Per this understanding, the statement "'ignorance of the universal' does not remove voluntariness" is not to be understood in such cases as a separate, additional caveat to the knowledge requirement for voluntariness. It is instead a particular application of the one, single caveat Aristotle makes concerning ignorance which is embodied in the *di' agnoian*/*agnoōn* distinction. Thus, the knowledge requirement

[39] As pointed out above, I do not believe this ignorance would have to be a result of bodily states such as drunkenness or rage. There are no doubt several other ways in which an agent could be responsible for her ignorance, and thus subsequently act *agnoōn*.

[40] In fact, if the broader meaning of ignorance as 'error' is kept in mind, the possibilities for confusion are even less, for ignorance$_2$ would then be regarded as positively mistaken belief about a general moral principle. Then ignorance (of the fact that one is acquiring an incorrect principle) would be causing the acquisition of a misguided principle. Note that even in the latter understanding, this acquisition could still be considered an omission since the agent, at the same time, *omitted* to acquire a correct belief.

for voluntariness stands, and the only exceptions are acts performed *agnoōn*.[41]

(C) Third, if the interpretation I have given is correct, the agent under discussion is voluntarily responsible for ignorance$_1$. This means that at some point logically prior to that ignorance, the knowledge requirement must have been fulfilled in regard to *that* ignorance. In other words, given the relativity of ignorance to descriptions of actions, there must have been some action such that the agent had knowledge that "what I am doing is (at least potentially) causing a subsequent ignorance$_1$."[42]

(D) The conditions for voluntariness that Aristotle lays out concern *actions*. Furthermore, the instances of ignorance appealed to by the *di' agnoian*/*agnoōn* distinction are said to accompany *actions*. Ignorance, however, does not seem to be an action. Perhaps, then, the same conditions and distinctions do not apply to it. In other words, it may not matter if ignorance$_2$ occurs *di' agnoian* or *agnoōn*, for the ignorances described by these latter terms are relevant only when they accompany acts, and ignorance$_2$ seems not to be an act. Furthermore, ignorance$_1$ need not be an act. To regard its voluntariness in terms of those conditions necessary for acts, therefore, may not be appropriate. This concern is heightened once it is applied to the topic of this book. NO's are *omissions*, not *commissions*. Consequently, it may be a mistake to be examining Aristotle's conditions for voluntariness of *actions* in an attempt to evaluate the voluntariness of NO's.

Having made these four observations, I wish to proceed by first responding to the concern raised in (D). This will then allow me to make some comments regarding NO's in general and identify two specific tasks that must be accomplished for us to solve the general problem of NO's. We will then be in a position to discuss an interpretation

---

[41] Bostock does not quite state this point, but hints at it when he writes "then it is the same thought that lies behind both of these qualifications, namely that there are cases where I do act in ignorance [sc. *agnoōn*] of some relevant feature of my action, and so do not *intend* to do what I do, and yet I can still be blamed for it" (*Aristotle's Ethics*, 109).

[42] Closely related to this is the further point that, if all morally-relevant action requires knowledge of some universal moral premise, the agent must have had prior knowledge of *some* universal or other. In other words, ignorance of *all* universals does not seem possible if an agent is to ever be blameworthy for any instance of ignorance of a universal. Consequently, when Aristotle speaks of 'ignorance of the universal' not excusing, this interpretation holds that the agent must have, at some logically prior time, had knowledge of some universal.

of Aristotle's understanding of *akrasia* in the next chapter by which we will begin to accomplish one of those tasks.

In response to the concern expressed in (D) that ignorance is not an action, I want first to suggest that while ignorance$_1$ need not be an act, there could very well be an act by which that ignorance is voluntarily brought about. In that case, our concern over ascribing voluntariness to such ignorance should vanish. In regard to ignorance$_2$, let it be recalled that 'ignorance' for Aristotle can mean 'error.' Consequently, when one is arriving at 'ignorance of the universal,' it could be the case that one is acquiring or adhering to a false, misguided moral principle. And acquisition of principles, it seems, is act-like enough to be categorized as *di' agnoian* or *agnoōn*. Furthermore, this 'error' could at the same time be considered an omission, for by acquiring an incorrect moral principle, one is *omitting* to acquire a correct one. That is to say, in certain cases action and omission seem to be two sides of the same coin: if you do one, you are by the same token performing the other. These considerations may then lessen the concern that Aristotle's conditions for voluntariness apply to acts while 'ignorance of the universal' initially appears not to be an act.

'Ignorance of the universal,' however, is only one particular type of NO. It is not clear that the analysis in terms of action we just offered for it can be applied to all other NO's. And if it cannot, does this entail that we may be misguided in our attempt to apply Aristotle's conditions for the voluntariness of *commissions* to such *omissions*?

To respond to this concern, I first want to suggest it may be possible to define 'action' broadly enough so as to include omissions. On this understanding, an agent in a sense *commits* an omission by not performing some action. In fact, when we later encounter authors who believe in a faculty of the will, this interpretation will be even more viable. For it will then be open to them to state that in omissions the agent has an elicited *action* of the will by which they will the omission.

Nonetheless, some of the authors in this study do not insist that an elicited action of 'willing to omit' is necessary for a culpable omission to take place. What, then, if that view is correct and if there is no other way in which to understand an omission as an action? Is the examination of Aristotle's criteria for voluntariness of actions misguided? I believe not, for even if Aristotle's discussion of the voluntary is only with acts in mind, it seems reasonable to assume that the only part of his discussion specifically *act*-related is the first condition concerning motion, i.e. that the moving principle must be in the agent. The second condition, i.e. the knowledge requirement, does not seem specifically *act*-related. And since it is common intuition that voluntariness entails some kind of intention, and intention in turn requires knowledge of what one is or is *not* doing, I believe it to be a safe assumption that the knowledge requirement, at the very least, must apply to omissions if they are to be called voluntary and considered blameworthy. Aristotle's knowledge requirement, therefore, must be dealt with in some form. The concerns expressed in (D) can thus be disposed of.

We are now in a position to outline the task of much of the rest of this book. Taking my point of departure from Aristotle's discussion (and in particular from observations (A) and (B) above), I take it that the voluntariness of NO's must somehow ultimately be explained in terms of the *di' agnoian*/*agnoōn* distinction; a NO must come about *agnoōn* if it is to be culpably ascribed to an agent. This, though, leaves us with the task represented by (C): we will need to explain how the ignorance accompanying a NO can be understood to be voluntary. The forgetfulness or ignorance accompanying NO's (represented above by ignorance$_1$) does not *seem* to have come about by the agent having altered her mental state (as through drunkenness) or having purposefully caused herself to have ignorance.[43] Finding a way to ascribe voluntariness to this ignorance will thus constitute the major challenge of this book.

Although it is not *prima facie* evident, a proper understanding of Aristotle's akratic will help us begin to address the task represented by (C) and thereby help us solve the problem of negligent omissions (of which 'ignorance of the universal' can be an instance).[44]

---

[43] In fact, if this were the case, the ignorance would be of a type the medievals refer to as 'affected'ignorance, and the resulting omission would then, in that case, not be negligent.

[44] The shrewd reader of Aristotle may note that, in this chapter, I have not discussed *NE* v.8 (1135a15–1136a9), a passage in which Aristotle does discuss negligent omissions when he says that injury, understood as a "mistake," occurs when its infliction is "not contrary to reasonable expectation" but also not because of a vice. As discussed in the Introduction, I only discuss passages insofar as they advance the ultimate goal of solving the problem of NO's. This particular passage is not very helpful in that regard. It simply implies that such 'mistakes' can be voluntary but does nothing to help *explain how* they are voluntary, and it is this latter question that I am particularly concerned with.

CHAPTER 2

ARISTOTLE'S AKRATIC: FORESHADOWING A SOLUTION

I. Preliminary Remarks

We can begin the process of addressing the challenge left for us at the end of the last chapter by looking at Aristotle's *akratic* in 1146b31–1147b19. Although the akratic is not necessarily engaged in a NO, examining this passage will be worthwhile. Let me elaborate upon this claim both in general terms and in terms related to the previous chapter.

As for a general elaboration, Aristotle regards the akratic's action as blameworthy and voluntary.[1] At the same time, it is clear that there is something amiss with the akratic's knowledge at the time of the akratic act. Ignorance of some sort is involved and yet, given the presumed voluntariness, it must be the case that the akratic still somehow fulfills the knowledge requirement. Examining this passage in which Aristotle explores the various levels of relationship between knowledge and ignorance will thus give us a hint as to the threshold for knowledge at which the knowledge requirement for voluntariness can still be fulfilled.

Examining the akratic is also relevant when cast in light of the task set for us in the previous chapter, the one represented by what we called observation (C). We noticed there that 'ignorance of the universal' (referred to as 'ignorance$_2$') is itself actually a NO that arises on account of a prior ignorance of the fact that "what I am doing is omitting to acquire a correct moral principle" (i.e. ignorance$_1$). For the NO (ignorance$_2$) to count as blameworthy on account of having been committed *agnoōn*, ignorance$_1$ must itself be voluntary; there must be some other, logically prior fulfillment of the knowledge requirement related to ignorance$_1$ itself. If there can be found a way in which cases of

---

[1] A notable exception is Randall Curren who does not believe the akratic's act must be voluntary to be blameworthy. He writes with reference to akratic action that "Aristotle does not want to restrict responsibility to voluntary action, as is sometimes thought" (Randall Curren, "The Contribution of *EN* III.5 to Aristotle's Theory of Responsibility," *History of Philosophy Quarterly* 6 (1989): 261–277).

ignorance (such as ignorance$_1$) can be considered voluntary, then we will have solved both the problem of NO's in general and the problem of the voluntariness of 'ignorance of the universal' in particular. A close examination of the akratic and the relative levels of knowledge and ignorance accompanying the voluntary act of *akrasia* will constitute an important step toward ultimately accomplishing this goal.

Having said this, we now move on to the interpretation.

II. Interpretation

In what follows, I do not intend to offer a solution to the problem of *akrasia*, nor am I interested in showing how Aristotle believes himself to have solved the problem of how it is possible.[2] Instead, I aim merely to discuss an interpretation with a view toward determining how robust knowledge must be such that the knowledge requirement for voluntariness is fulfilled.

Space precludes me from engaging with all possible interpretations of this famous passage.[3] There is, however, a certain approach to this passage that characterizes many attempts which I will call a 'classical interpretation' (hereafter, 'CI').[4] I will here present a different interpretation by contrasting it with that more common one, making reference

[2] Indeed, such a task could be the topic of a whole book in and of itself.

[3] There are, after all, nearly as many different interpretations as there have been commentators. For an important recent study of this passage that somewhat agrees, but ultimately diverges from the interpretation I offer here, see: Martin Pickavé and Jennifer Whiting, "Nicomachean Ethics 7.3 on Akratic Ignorance," *Oxford Studies in Ancient Philosophy* 34 (2008): 323–371.

[4] Although I do not necessarily base my presentation of the CI upon his, Dahl devotes a chapter to presenting what he calls the "traditional interpretation" in: N.O. Dahl, *Practical Reason, Aristotle, and Weakness of Will* (Minneapolis: University of Minnesota Press, 1984). Indeed, his presentation of the traditional interpretation is much more thorough than that offered here. Let me further note that I am not hereby claiming that, as an empirical fact, the majority of all past interpretations of this famous passage necessarily follow what I am calling the CI. In a sense, it is irrelevant to my purposes whether the CI is the most common interpretation of this passage or not. Instead, I am contrasting what I call the CI to my interpretation so as to make my interpretation clearer. I am confident, however, that the reader familiar with much of the literature on Aristotle's akratic will recognize the CI as a very common way of interpreting this passage. Indeed, it seems to be something like the CI that Pickavé and Whiting have in view when they say that their interpretation will challenge the "one assumption on which otherwise divergent commentators seem to agree – namely, that Aristotle seeks to explain akratic behaviour by appeal to a failure either to have or to use knowledge of some *particular*" (Pickavé and Whiting, "Nicomachean Ethics 7.3," 324).

to variations as appropriate.[5] (Please refer to Appendix A for my full translation of this passage.) First, however, some background regarding the phenomeon of *akrasia* (or incontinence, as it is commonly called) itself and the CI is needed.

Akrasia is the putative phenomenon in which an agent voluntarily opts for and performs the action she considers to be worse in preference to one she considers better as a result of being under the influence of some passion. And she does this knowing that she is choosing the worse one. Socrates had famously denied that *akrasia* was possible, stating that all apparent instances of it were actually due to mistaken belief; an agent never willingly chooses what she believes to be the worse course of action.[6]

The problem with Socrates's position is that it contradicts common experience.[7] People do appear sometimes to act knowingly against their best interests. And, in Aristotle's mind, such apparent lapses cannot be explained by appealing to the distinction between knowledge proper and true belief. This appeal would claim that it is only when a person has true belief, but not knowledge proper, about her best course of action that she can act against her judgment as to what is best. But since belief can be adhered to as adamantly as knowledge, Aristotle states that this distinction "makes no difference to the argument."[8] Having set this distinction aside, he assumes knowledge and proceeds

---

[5] In doing so, I am following a general strategy utilized by Dahl in *Practical Reason*. As can be deduced, the interpretation offered here is different from that expressed by the CI. I should explicitly state that my interpretation is by no means the first to challenge what I call the CI. As conceded in the previous footnote, not every interpretation of Aristotle's *akratic* follows the CI. Some examples of those who have challenged the CI are Dahl (*Practical Reason*), Pickavé and Whiting ("Nicomachean Ethics 7.3") and David Charles in his *Aristotle's Philosophy of Action* (Ithaca, NY: Cornell University Press, 1984). Since the present interpretation also challenges the CI, it should only be expected that there are some similarities between it and those just listed. It should, however, be pointed out that the present interpretation was derived independently of these, or any other, interpretations which challenge the CI. So far as I can tell, the present treatment does diverge in various ways from those others. It should further be noted that my ultimate task is not to solve problems related to Aristotle's *akratic*; my discussion of it is in service to illuminating and solving the problem of NO's. Despite this limitation, I believe the interpretation and various means of argumentation offered here are interesting and thought-provoking with regard to Aristotle's understanding of *akrasia*.

[6] Plato's *Protagoras*, 352e–358d.

[7] 1145b25–30.

[8] 1146b23–30.

to determine the manner in which one supposedly "knows" when she acts akratically.[9]

> But since we call 'knowing' in two ways (for both the one having but not using knowledge and the one [having] and using are said to know) it will matter whether one has [knowledge] but is not contemplating it or [both] has and contemplates it [when one is doing] those things which one must not do. For this [i.e. doing that which one should not do when both having and contemplating knowledge] seems amazing [sc. impossible], but it is not amazing [for one to do what should not be done] if one is not contemplating [the knowledge].[10]

The CI regards the distinction between (i) merely having (possessing) but not using and (ii) having *and* using (or contemplating) as the basis for Aristotle's solution to the problem of *akrasia*. The basic idea is the following: Suppose an agent knows (i.e. possesses knowledge) that eating peanuts is bad for her. This knowledge is somewhere in the recesses of her mind. At some point, she is offered and does not advert to that piece of knowledge in the recesses of her mind. Because she does not, at that time, advert to that knowledge so as to realize that eating the peanut is bad for her, she is able to bring herself to eat it. Nevertheless, because she does have in the recesses of her mind the 'knowledge' that eating peanuts is bad for her, she can be said to have acted against her knowledge.

I think this interpretation is completely misguided. If it were correct, the phenomenon of *akrasia* that Aristotle would have to be concerned with in this passage would be the following: acting against *what would be* one's best judgment *if one considered* all relevant pieces of knowledge one possesses. I find it difficult to believe, however, that actions against such *potential,* but not *actual*, best judgments are the 'observed facts' that Aristotle devotes time and effort to explain. The *akrasia* that is commonly 'observed' occurs when an agent somehow realizes that what she is doing is an action she should not be doing. According to the CI, though, the agent would not even realize that she should not be doing the action she is performing.[11]

---

[9] Cf. J.C.B. Gosling, *Weakness of the Will* (London; New York: Routledge, 1990), 26. His treatment of Aristotle is found in chapter 3. In addition, he comments on Aristotle's *akrasia* in: Justin Gosling, "Mad, Drunk or Asleep? - Aristotle's Akratic," *Phronesis* 38, no. 1 (1993): 98–104.

[10] The translation of 1146b31 ff. is mine unless otherwise indicated.

[11] Charles seems to refer to a similar point when he states that the failure "to draw an entailed conclusion" might be "a degree of irrationality too great to be characteristic of the acratic man" (*Aristotle's Philosophy of Action,* 156).

Furthermore, what sort of puzzle does such an occurrence pose? If certain facts are not adverted to in any way, then it would be *expected* that an agent could act against this non-adverted-to 'knowledge.' To supposedly solve the problem of *akrasia* in this way would seem not to have interacted at all with what most see as the problem of *akrasia*. At the very least, such a phenomenon as acting against one's knowledge *that is not even adverted to* poses no real problem and would thus hardly seem worthy of any lengthy, serious philosophical discussion.[12]

Given these considerations, it is my conviction that in this (and the following) portion of the passage, Aristotle is not explaining *akrasia*, but doing the preparatory work of specifying what *does not qualify* as *akrasia*. And what does not qualify? Phenomena that are not 'interesting' or 'surprising' and thus need no philosophical explanation. And which are these phenomena? Those in which an agent acts against her knowledge while not thinking/contemplating it. These cases are not 'amazing' (i.e. they are very possible). Nor do they count as instances of *akrasia*, for the explanation of their possibility is obvious (despite many interpreters thinking that the whole passage is devoted to precisely the task of explaining the possibility of such instances).

If 1146b31–35 is read as Aristotle performing the 'brush clearing' exercise of ruling out phenomena that do not count as *akrasia*, that text can be seen as disqualifying two separate cases as instances of *akrasia*: [i] Cases of acting against one's knowledge that is not adverted to do not constitute *akrasia*, for such actions are not impossible or 'amazing' in any sense. On the other hand, [ii] acting against one's knowledge while contemplating it is likewise not *akrasia* (1146b31–35), for such an action cannot occur in the first place - it is 'amazing [or, impossible].'

This last point deserves attention. It might be thought that acting against one's knowledge while one is contemplating it ([ii] above) *is* the interesting, surprising phenomenon Aristotle is concerned with. If I am correct in my assertion that Aristotle does not regard *akrasia* as a case of having but not using knowledge, and does regard it as an instance of acting against one's better judgment, it would seem to follow that acting against one's knowledge while contemplating it *is* the interesting phenomenon Aristotle is searching for and wants to

---

[12] Pickavé and Whiting seem to agree when they write that "It is only to the extent that the *akratēs* acts knowing both what she does *and* that she ought not do it, that there is a real problem explaining how akratic action is possible" (Pickavé and Whiting, "Nicomachean Ethics 7.3," 326).

explain. In fact, as long as 'amazing' (*deinos*) is read not as 'impossible' but rather as 'surprising,' Aristotle even says as much.

The answer to this objection will be obvious after the remainder of the passage has been considered. Nonetheless, let me at present note the following point: since Aristotle has *thus far* only presented us with two possibilities regarding possessed knowledge, use or non-use, it seems safe to interpret contemplation here as *full* use. (As will be seen, I believe there is a third possibility of 'half use' offered at 1147a11. When it is offered, it clearly is done in contrast to what has been said before. This third alternative, then, should not be read back into this first part of the passage.) But if *akrasia* is understood by Aristotle as acting against one's fully-used/contemplated knowledge, then none of what Aristotle goes on to say in the remainder of the passage would actually bear upon his understanding of *akrasia*; none of his explanations center around the case of someone having and fully using/contemplating her knowledge. That Aristotle could commit such a mistake – namely, to devote a passage to *akrasia*, identify the phenomenon at the beginning of that passage as involving *full* use/contemplation, and then proceed through the rest of the passage without regarding that phenomenon as involving *full* use/contemplation, – would (pardon the play on words) itself seem 'amazing'/impossible.

I can only conclude, therefore, that if 'use/contemplation' implies '*full* use/contemplation' in 1146b31–35, then 'amazing' (*deinos*) should be read as impossible. Aristotle would thereby be saying, as I claim above, that it is impossible to act against knowledge that one is *fully using/contemplating*. Therefore, such a description (i.e. acting against knowledge one is fully using) cannot be that which applies to the phenomenon of *akrasia* in which he is interested.[13] Accordingly, I claim that in 1146b31–35 Aristotle is ruling out this second scenario ([ii] above) as an object for his inquiry into *akrasia*.

Let us now return to the first type of scenario ([i] above) that I claim Aristotle was attempting to rule out as an instance of *akrasia* in 1146b31–35. This was the case in which one is not adverting to any relevant knowledge possessed. One's acting against that knowledge is thus neither interesting nor philosophically puzzling and therefore not constitutive of *akrasia*. Some might argue that in my presentation above I have presented the case of acting against knowledge merely

---

[13] Interpreters typically so interpret it. Cf., e.g. Gosling, *Weakness of the Will*.

possessed too simply so as to misleadingly make it appear philosophically uninteresting. My presentation (so the objection goes) was too simple for I discussed the possession and non-use of knowledge only in relation to a potential concluding judgment regarding what one should do. Practical reasoning, however, is not so simple. There are different kinds of premises involved in reaching a concluding judgment, each of which themselves must be known and used so as to arrive at that conclusion. Perhaps, then, the distinction between merely knowing and using *would*, contra my position, create an interesting case of what is recognized as *akrasia* if we applied this distinction in light of the various premises involved in practical reasoning.

Aristotle considers this objection and (I maintain) immediately rejects its claim that applying that distinction to the various premises creates an 'interesting' case. He states that "nothing prevents one from acting against knowledge while using only the universal [premise] but not the [premise] about the part" (1147a1–2). In a sense, Aristotle is saying that appealing to premises makes no difference. If a premise is not being 'used' or adverted to, then "nothing prevents" (i.e., it can only be expected) that one could act against the conclusion that the premise, were it used and combined with the used universal premise, would yield. Acting against such a potential, but not-arrived-at, conclusion is neither unexpected nor interesting.

In my opinion, he then proceeds, in 1147a3–10, to explain this position in further detail:

> And [to help explain how this is possible and not amazing after all] there are different types of universals [in both the universal and particular premises]; for on the one hand there is (a) that which refers to the agent and on the other hand there is (b) that which refers to the object. An example [of this] is that ('A1' - the universal premise with a focus on universal term 'a') dry things are profitable to *every human being*, and that ('A2' - particular premise with focus on universal term 'a') he himself is a human being, or that ('B1' - a somewhat universal but less universal premise than the universal premise proper, with focus on universal term 'b') this such-a-thing is dry; but whether ('B2' - particular premise with focus on universal term 'b') this thing is this such-a-thing, either [the one who acts against knowledge] does not have this knowledge or does not use it. Now according to these [different premises which we have just delineated] it matters to a great extent which ways [i.e. premises] that [one knows], so that it does not seem out of place [to have acted against knowledge] when one knows in one way [i.e. when lacking 'B2'], but [to act against knowledge] when knowing in another way [i.e. 'B2'] is amazing [or impossible].

Before elaborating on how this passage supports the interpretation I am promoting, a few preliminary comments about my translation of it are in order. First, I understand 1147a3–10 as an explanation of 1147a1–2. I base this upon the fact that 1147a3–10 ends by giving a concrete example of how one can be using a universal premise but not using a particular premise (as stipulated in 1147a2). This correspondence between the general statement at 1147a1–2 and the example ending at 1147a10 is too large to believe 1147a1–10 does not constitute a single argument in and of itself. Consequently, I have added to my translation "[to help explain how this is possible]" in 1147a3.[14]

I also want to explain my translation of 1147a4 where it reads "there are different types of universals [in both the universal and particular premises]", the structure I have given to 1147a5–10 and the parenthetical explanatory notes therein. The translation is based upon Terry Irwin's notes wherein he says that "universal" here does not imply different "universal premises, but universal terms or concepts … that may appear in either the universal or the particular premises."[15] That this is the correct way to view this passage can be confirmed, I believe, by observing how well it accords with the structure able to be given to the immediately following lines,[16] in which it is shown how these universal terms can be present in both the universal and particular premises. To bring this point out more clearly, I (following Irwin) have indicated the universal term referring to the agent as 'A' and that referring to the object as 'B' and have shown in parentheses how 'A' and 'B' can be in various premises.

A final observation is this: it might be thought that my translation makes it appear as if there are one universal premise and three particular premises, one of which is itself somewhat universal (B1). This might cause confusion given the traditional understanding that a syllogism consists of only one universal and one particular premise. But as Kenny notes, there can be numerous "atomic premises" that (to preserve the traditional structure) can be combined so as to produce a single, compound particular premise (hereafter, 'pp'). Furthermore, some of these

[14] I take this as relatively uncontroversial. 1147a1–10 is often treated as a single passage. See, e.g., Dahl, *Practical Reason* and Charles, *Aristotle's Philosophy of Action*.

[15] Terry Irwin (ed. and trans.), *Aristotle; Nicomachean Ethics*, 2nd ed. (Indianapolis/Cambridge: Hackett, 1999), 258.

[16] This structure is actually that given by Fine and Irwin in: Aristotle, *Introductory Readings*, trans. Terence Irwin and Gail Fine (Indianapolis/Cambridge: Hackett, 1996), 261.

can even be somewhat "universally quantified" (such as B1), though to a lesser extent than the universal premise proper.[17] There thus need be no confusion, and the basic point of my translation can emerge: there are several particular facts which an agent can either merely have, or have and use, and these are indicated by what I have labeled as premises of one sort or another.

With these foregoing remarks in mind, we can proceed to Aristotle's explanation that it is not interesting (and thus, not the understanding of *akrasia* in which he is interested) that somebody should act against his knowledge while not using any one pp. He states that someone could be 'using' all the following pieces of knowledge: (A1) knowledge in relation to the universal agent term, 'dry things are profitable to every human being,' (B1) a premise expressing a universal fact in regard to the object term: 'this such-a-thing is dry,' and also (A2) a pp in regard to the agent term: 'he himself is a human being.' Even if the agent is 'using' all these pieces of knowledge, it would still be expected for the agent to fail to do what otherwise he would know to be best if he is *not* using (B2), the pp in regard to the object term. In other words, it is not "out of place [to have acted against knowledge]" in this situation. Failing to 'use' a pp, therefore, does not result in the phenomenon of *akrasia* Aristotle is interested in and thus cannot serve as its explanation.

At this point, a summary of the preceding is in order. The CI finds, in the portion of the passage we have discussed so far, the basic mechanics behind a case of *akrasia*. Acting against knowledge occurs when an agent does not 'use' knowledge relevant to some pp, thus precluding her from reaching the appropriate conclusion concerning what she should do. If for no other reason, I find this position difficult because, if this is the case, the putative akratic agent is *not* acting against her actual best judgment; she is instead acting against what her best judgment *would have otherwise been*. But acting against what her best judgment *would have otherwise been* is not choosing and performing the option one actually considers worse and is, furthermore, nothing to marvel at or philosophically investigate.[18]

---

[17] Kenny, *Aristotle's Theory*, 156.

[18] A proponent of the CI does have a response. Consider a putative akratic act in which the agent is using the universal but not the pp's. Let's posit the universal is simply "Do not taste sweets" and the relevant unused particular is "grapes are sweet." Given use of the universal, the agent could say and fully believe that she should not taste sweets while nevertheless tasting a grape on account of non-use of the pp. What is happening here is that the knowledge that the agent is adverting to is not fully applicable

In contrast, I see 1146b31–1147a10 as Aristotle's preparation for his constructive proposal by ruling out cases that are *not* to count as *akrasia*. Not only is not using knowledge not to count, and not only is not using knowledge in relation to a pp not to count, but also not using knowledge in regard to one pp while at the same time using knowledge in relation to another pp is not to count. In other words, he seems to be saying that *akrasia*, if it is an interesting phenomenon worthy of philosophical investigation, cannot simply be explained by saying somebody is not using a pp.[19]

This brings us to what I regard as the crux of the passage. Having eliminated the different ways of acting against knowledge that do not constitute *akrasia*, he begins to explain what does constitute it. He does

---

to her action because it needs to be complemented with use of the pp. The phenomenon is nonetheless interesting and worthy of study, however, because - at least at first glance - it certainly *appears* that the agent is willfully and knowingly acting against her knowledge (cf., for example, Kenny, *Aristotle's Theory*, 166). This interpretation furthermore has the benefit that it could make sense of Aristotle's statement in 1147b15 that "[the situation] has become like that which Socrates was seeking to bring about." In this proposal, the agent is not *actually* acting against her better, actual knowledge in any sense (just as Socrates would have liked) - she only seems to be. In other words, under this proposal *akrasia* is merely a simple paradox easily resolved once it is realized that certain universal pieces of knowledge do not, despite appearances, actually 'connect up' so to speak with one's actions.

In response, I want to make a few points. First, I believe my proposal will make at least as much, if not more, sense of the reference to Socrates at the end of the passage while, at the same time, presenting a much more compelling interpretation. After all, it is difficult to imagine that in all instances in which *akrasia* is thought to occur there exists such a disconnection between one's knowledge and use of the universal and the action. Furthermore, as William Charlton points out, it is hard to make sense of how a universal could be 'used' without the relevant particular being used (William Charlton, *Weakness of Will* [Oxford: Basil Blackwell, 1988]. Cf. also Bostock, *Aristotle's Ethics*, 133). Knowledge of universal premises seems to become 'used' only when some relevant particular knowledge brings it to mind. In other words, it is difficult to understand how the agent's knowledge that sweets are not to be tasted was brought to mind and thus used unless it was the presence of the grape and knowledge of its sweetness that aroused it. And it will not do to suggest that the knowledge represented by the universal premise could have been aroused by knowledge of some other sweet thing (such as a peach), for certainly in all cases of supposed *akrasia* the relevant universal is not brought to mind by awareness of some other object or particular knowledge that is unrelated to the akratic act.

[19] Note that, at this point, I disagree with Pickavé and Whiting who see these earlier parts of the passage as introducing "a generic sort of failure of which the *akratēs'* failure is eventually shown to be a species" (Pickavé and Whiting, "Nicomachean Ethics 7.3," 333). Dahl, by contrast, sees 1147a1–10 as referring to the impetuous, as opposed to weak, akratic (*Practical Reason*, 203). Charles allows the possibility that this section may contain references to more than one type of akratic (*Aristotle's Philosophy of Action*, 124ff.).

this by saying there is a different way of "having knowledge but not using it ... so that in a way one can both have and not have [... knowledge which is not being fully used]" (1147a12–13). Giving as examples the mental state of "the sleeper and the mad person and the drunk person," he says that this is also the state of the akratic's knowledge (cf. 1147a15). What exactly, though, is this state of having and not having, while still not using, in which the sleeper, mad, intoxicated and akratic persons find themselves?

This epistemological state has sometimes been understood as picking out a state of 'half-knowledge' that is *below* merely having knowledge. As Kenny writes, "Not having, half-having, having, and using are four points on a scale of increasing actualisation of potentiality."[20] This interpretation is supported by one manner of looking at the examples. A person merely having but not using his knowledge could easily bring that knowledge to awareness and use it. But a drunkard, mad, or sleeping person cannot simply summon his stored knowledge for use. He must first regain sobriety or wake up before being able to contemplate the intricacies of, say, the Pythagorean Theorem. Such knowledge is "not at the moment available for use" and is thus "one remove back from" merely having knowledge.[21]

Why, though, should we think that acting against one's knowledge, when that knowledge is 'one remove back' from the state of merely having knowledge, would constitute an interesting phenomenon? According to my interpretation, Aristotle has already said that the interesting phenomenon of *akrasia* he is investigating does not consist in acting against one's knowledge that is merely possessed; acting against such knowledge is only to be expected and poses no puzzle. But if that is the case, then acting against one's knowledge that is an additional 'remove back' from actuality would be even more expected and less interesting. It seems doubtful such an occurrence would interest or puzzle Aristotle at all.

Moreover, the proposed understanding of knowledge 'had but not had' does not seem to fit with our experience. When we think of someone acting akratically, we do not suppose that the knowledge against which she acted was less 'actualized' than knowledge merely possessed but not adverted to. Usually, we assume that the knowledge was *more*

---

20 Kenny, *Aristotle's Theory*, 160–161.

21 Gosling, *Weakness of the Will*, 27.

actualized than knowledge merely possessed. For (as we have already said) the phenomenon consists not in purposely choosing against the option that one *would have otherwise known* is better, but in choosing against the option that one, in some sense actively, knows is better.

Given these consideration, I take it that the state of the akratic's knowledge is not 'one remove back,' but 'one step closer' to use than mere possession. This interpretation receives support from 1147a19–20 in which Aristotle states that "saying the words which come from knowledge is no sign; for those who are in these states will recite geometrical demonstrations and say verses of Empedocles." Persons who can recite geometrical demonstrations, for example, are a long way from being at a state *further* removed from use. On the contrary, it seems as if they are, in one sense, 'closer' to using their knowledge; they are 'half-using' it. For at least the information is before their minds in some sense, however little that may be, whereas the person merely possessing knowledge does not have it present before her awareness at the moment in *any* sense.

Furthermore, interpreting the sleeper (assuming what is meant is one who talks in her sleep),[22] the mad, and the drunkard as half-using their knowledge, and stating that the akratic's state is like theirs, does indeed give us an interesting and remarkable phenomenon of *akrasia* that is worth philosophical reflection. To explain: the sleep-talker, mad and drunk are all somewhat remarkable in that they seem to know, and even seem to be in a sense 'using' their knowledge, for they can recite proofs and verses, even though it is clear that they are not fully or properly using that knowledge. In other words, it is an interesting occurrence that these three persons can appear to perform such complicated intellectual tasks while it is clear that they nonetheless do not at present have the ability actually to do so. Such a paradox is interesting and calls for some explanation.

---

[22] E.g., Kenny, *Aristotle's Theory*, 162; Dahl, *Practical Reason*, 179. Takatura Ando also refers to the sleeper as a somnambulist (Takatura Ando, *Aristotle's Theory of Practical Cognition*, 3rd ed. [Hague: Martinus Nijhoff, 1971], 249). This assumption seems safe based upon the supposed objection he addresses that people in such states, one of which is sleeping, "say verses of Empedocles." If Aristotle meant merely a sleeper, it seems as if the example may be out of place. For not only would it not fit the description of such people as speaking, but it would also be hard to see how a person sleeping and completely unconscious is in any way analogous to an akratic. A person who is simply completely unconscious knows nothing at the time, whereas the akratic knows (in some sense) she is doing something that is not the best thing to do.

Given that the akratic's state is likened to that of the three examples, the akratic's state must be similarly paradoxical. According to my interpretation, it is. The akratic is *half-using* her knowledge in a way similar to that of the sleeper, mad and drunk. Her knowledge of what is best to do is before her in a way that merely possessed knowledge is not, but is somehow 'offbeat' or clouded in that it is not being fully used[23] (similar, say, to how a drunk geometer's contemplation of a proof of the Pythagorean Theorem can be offbeat or clouded). Like those three, she currently has some knowledge that is actually before her mind - in her case, knowledge that what she is doing is wrong. And by all counts, she appears to be using it. Her actions, though, show that she is not. This kind of occurrence, then, does give rise to an interesting puzzle, and thus is the account of *akrasia* Aristotle has been trying to identify.

Of course, it might be thought that the cases of the sleeper, mad, and drunk are not all that remarkable nor paradoxical, for the solution to them is obvious: the agents are sleeping, mad, or drunk! And there are certain physiological mechanisms that can explain such events. This observation, however, does not detract from the paradoxical nature of *akrasia*; it rather adds to it. For while the akratic, similar to the drunkard *et al.*, is half-using some knowledge, there is *dissimilarly* no obvious way to solve the paradox she presents. The akratic seems to be, in a sense, in her 'right mind.' And appealing to "emotions and sexual desires and others such as these" to explain her offbeat use of knowledge (1147a16) is not as satisfying as appealing to alcohol to explain a drunkard's offbeat knowledge. In other words, "emotions and sexual desires" do not seem, on the surface, as explanatory as drunkenness or madness. Consequently, *akrasia*, precisely because it entails some half-use of knowledge, is interesting because, unlike other cases of half-use, there appears to be no clear explanation as to how it is possible.

In my view, therefore, it is not until 1147a11 that Aristotle begins to identify the understanding of *akrasia* with which he is concerned. When he does so, he identifies *akrasia* as a state in which someone acts against her knowledge that she is 'half-using' in a sense, such that the knowledge is cloudy or off-beat. This phenomenon is interesting and paradoxical because, by all counts, the agent *appears* to be using her knowledge. Given she acts contrary to it, though, she must not be using it.

---

[23] I took the terminology 'offbeat' primarily from Gosling's writings.

It might be thought that my interpretation of the drunkard *et al.* (and thus of the akratic) as being one step closer to, instead of one remove back from, use is questionable. This concern would be partially based on the observation that (as the CI asserts) the drunkard *et al.* could not, if they wanted to, even summon up their knowledge for full use as they can in the case of merely having knowledge. Their knowledge, then, must be one remove back from mere use, not one step closer.

In response, I would argue that the way in which the state of the drunkard *et al.* is understood depends upon the perspective one brings to it. Consider, for instance, two clocks, A and B. Clock A is working but is persistently a minute slow. Clock B would work perfectly if it were plugged in but is currently disconnected. The question as to which clock is closer to perfect use is ambiguous. Viewed in one way, B is because, if it were only plugged in, it would give you accurate time, whereas, if A is ever to give you accurate time, it first needs to be sent off to the shop and fixed. According to another viewpoint, however, A is closer to full use. Although it would take more effort for A ultimately to reach full use than B, at least A is being somewhat used right now, and can give *some* indication or general idea of the time, whereas B can not. The difference in the two perspectives is that the former (analogous to the CI) views the clock's nearness to 'use' in relation to how easy it would be for it to achieve perfect full use, whereas the latter (analogous to my interpretation) views nearness to 'use' in terms of how close to perfect use it is working *now*.

In like manner, it is similarly ambiguous to ask whether the akratic and the drunkard *et al.* are further from or closer to use of their knowledge. It depends on perspective. From my viewpoint, the latter option is to be preferred, for it not only fits with the interpretation I have given, but also fits with our general intuition of *akrasia* as a case of action against one's knowledge that is, in at least some sense, being used *now*.

There is, however, the following objection to my interpretation. If by this third alternative in regard to knowledge Aristotle intended 'half-use' as I have proposed, it seems Aristotle would have said "in a way one can both *use and not use*" knowledge. What he says instead, though, is "in a way one can both *have and not have*" it (1147a13). This would then seem to indicate a level below 'having,' not one below 'using.'

My response to this objection is similar to a remark I made above. Up to this point in the text, Aristotle has presented only a simple dichotomy regarding knowledge: it can be either merely possessed, or used. Given this stark, undifferentiated contrast, it is possible to interpret Aristotle as meaning 'full' or 'perfect' use by the latter option. Thus, any use of knowledge that falls short of full use (such as half-use) would not qualify as 'use' proper. It must then be initially classed as a way of having but not (fully or properly) using. There are therefore at least two ways of 'having' knowledge, thus explaining why Aristotle says there is "a split in the way of having but not using" knowledge (1147a12). And just as it would be misleading, given this stark dichotomy, to classify half-used knowledge as 'used,' it would also be somewhat misleading to describe it as 'possessed' or 'had.' For this latter description, given the same stark dichotomy, implies no use whatsoever. Half-used knowledge, then, while indeed possessed by the agent, is not 'possessed' in the sense that knowledge 'possessed' has been understood up to now (i.e. as implying no use). Half-use must therefore be seen as a way of 'having and not having' knowledge; it is possessed, but is not possessed in the simple way that most merely 'possessed' knowledge is.

Support for this assertion comes from the work of Alfred Mele.[24] He appeals to Aristotle's discussion of memory in *On Memory and Reminiscence* (449b15–23) in which Aristotle implies that knowledge remembered "is not knowledge that one is contemplating (*theōrōn*) at the time."[25] His argument is this: given that the word for "contemplate," *theōrōn*, is one of the words employed in our passage for 'use,' then knowledge remembered is not technically 'used' knowledge. It must, then, be knowledge that one 'has' but is not properly 'using.' But this knowledge that one is remembering is nonetheless being adverted to. It is, after all, impossible to remember some knowledge without being aware, in some sense, of that knowledge: "in some cases of remembering, we are *aware* of a pertinent 'scientific' fact that we know."[26] This awareness, however, does not imply 'use,' for 'use' may technically entail "something over and above the mere awareness of the known fact," such as "*focusing* … one's attention upon" it.[27]

---

[24] Alfred R. Mele, "Aristotle on *Akrasia* and Knowledge," *Modern Schoolman* 58 (1981): 137–59.

[25] Ibid., 142.

[26] Ibid., 142.

[27] Ibid., 143. Mele suggests the following possible description of the state of being aware of knowledge without 'using' it: "If this is his conception, then a person who, at a time *t*, knows that *p*, is aware of its being the case that *p*, is remembering proving that *p*, and is focusing his attention only upon his memory of proving *p*-that is, he is not contemplating this knowledge *even though* he is conscious of the fact that *p*."

Knowledge that is remembered, then, must be all of the following: possessed, not 'used,' but nonetheless *occurrent* since the agent is *aware* and *conscious* of that knowledge. To say this, however, seems to me to say that there must be "a split in the way of having knowledge but not using it" (1147a12). Some knowledge that is possessed is in the recesses of the agent's mind, while some of it *is* before her mind, but not in a way such that it can be technically considered 'used.' Given that there is some actuality in knowledge of this latter type, I describe it as 'half-used.'

My claim will be that 'half-used' knowledge is adequate so as to fulfill the knowledge requirement. As long as there is *some* level of clouded awareness by the agent that what she is doing is wrong, and this awareness is 'one step closer' to full use than is mere possession, the akratic's act can be considered voluntary and thus blameworthy. This claim will, in turn, enable us to see whether there is some analogous clouded, half-used knowledge related to cases of ignorance like ignorance_1 such that they can be voluntary and the resulting NO's be, in some sense, culpable. Before we come to that point, however, it is worth continuing through Aristotle's text to ensure that my understanding of the *akratic* is consistent with the remainder of the passage.

The largest obstacle to my interpretation is the following: The remainder of the passage is typically seen as implying that the problem in *akrasia* revolves around the pp and its use or non-use. This view based upon Aristotle's discussion of some appetite as the ultimate cause of *akrasia* and that appetite's inherent affinity to the pp. If an appetite is the cause of *akrasia*, and that appetite is linked with the pp, then it seems to follow that the appetite causes *akrasia* by means of causing non-use of the associated pp.

In contrast, my interpretation demands that the question of use or non-use (or, as it turns out, half-use) revolves not around the pp, but the conclusion regarding what one should or should not do. To demonstrate this point, recall the observation above that ignorance, and therefore knowledge, relevant to the question of voluntariness is relative to a certain description of that act. So, in the first place, if an act is to count as akratic, there must be some description of that act according to which that action is prohibited, such as "I should not do such and such." And if it is to count as voluntary, there must be (i) some knowledge that that act falls under that description by which it is prohibited and (ii) that knowledge must be at least half-used (according to my view that half-use fulfills the knowledge requirement). The description of the action in which that action is prohibited, however, cannot issue solely from the pp; pp's typically do not deal with prohibitions or permissions. Instead, prohibitions occur only in the conclusion to a piece of practical reasoning, after the pp has been joined with a universal premise in which acts of a certain type are proscribed. Since my interpretation relies upon the assertion that the agent half-uses his knowledge that what he is doing is wrong, it must then be the case that that which he is half-using is his knowledge not of the *pp*, but of the *conclusion* that he should not do such and such. My task then is to show that the rest of the passage can be read as consistent with this view. In what follows, I not only do this, but demonstrate how my interpretation is to be preferred to the CI.

Consider 1147a29 ff. According to some proponents of the CI, this passage presents us with two potential syllogisms, a 'good' one and a 'bad' one:[28]

Good Syllogism	Bad Syllogism
GU: I should not taste sweets	BU: Everything sweet is pleasant (and presumably pleasant things are to be tasted)
GP: This is sweet	BP: This is sweet
GConcl: Do not taste this	BConcl: Taste this

Before examining this understanding, one preliminary remark is in order. There is some debate in the literature over whether the conclusion to a practical syllogism is an action (as 1147a28 indicates), a command, or perhaps some other form of propositional knowledge. The details of this debate are not central to our present purposes. The point to be made is that, regardless of the position taken, there must be some form of propositional knowledge either contained within, or accompanying, a conclusion to a practical syllogism.[29] In other words, accompanying GConcl. there must be some knowledge such as "I must not taste this sweet thing," and accompanying BConcl. "I am (should) tasting

[28] Of course, not all versions of the CI accord with the exact way in which I have expressed 1147a29 ff. Unfortunately, it is beyond our scope and space to consider all possible CI variations. Nonetheless, the above is fair to most versions of the CI and will suffice for me to indicate how my emphasis on the conclusion is to be preferred to the general strategy of the CI.

[29] Cf. for example Dahl, *Practical Reason*, 194 ff., and Charles, *Aristotle's Philosophy of Action*, 89 ff.

(taste) this sweet thing." Arriving at a conclusion, therefore, entails at least knowledge of what it is one is doing by means of reaching that conclusion. To believe otherwise would be equivalent to believing practical syllogisms issue in actions the details of which agents do not necessarily know.

These remarks having been made, we are now in a position to see why my focus on the conclusion, instead of on the pp, supports my interpretation in preference to the CI. Regarding syllogism pairs of the type above, the CI's basic approach is to assert that the agent never reaches GConcl. Various ways are suggested in which this results,[30] but the usual one is to say that the agent's knowledge of the GP is not used in an appropriate way. One view, for example, suggests that since the GP and the BP are the same, desire makes the akratic properly 'use' her knowledge that "This is sweet" only in relation to the BU, thus yielding the use of BP but not of GP.[31] Regardless of the specific details in any one variation, the general approach assumes that something goes wrong with the agent's knowledge at the level of the GP, thus precluding arrival at GConcl.[32]

If the GConcl. is never reached, however, I simply fail to see how the agent's action could be considered voluntary. Let's suppose that the putative akratic act is the eating of a strawberry (i.e. the "this" is a strawberry). It is very possible that her eating the strawberry is voluntary, for she very likely is aware of the description "what I am doing is eating a strawberry," and thus the knowledge requirement for the act of 'eating a strawberry' is fulfilled. Moreover, it is probable that she knows the strawberry is sweet, as suggested in the so-called 'bad syllogism.' In that case, she also voluntarily performs the act of 'eating something sweet.' But for her voluntarily to perform an act of *akrasia*, the relevant particular detail she would need to be aware of is not that she is eating a strawberry, nor even necessarily that she is tasting something sweet. Rather, since *akrasia* is the phenomenon of doing something one

[30] For example, Aquinas's view was that the universal premise may be specific enough such that it need not match up with the pp so as to yield the GConcl. If the GU were "Don't eat sweets after hours," then it, along with the GP, would not yield GConcl. if the agent did not also know it was 'after hours.' (cf. Thomas Aquinas's *Sententia Libri Ethicorum* 7.3).

[31] Cf. Gosling, *Weakness of the Will*, 29–30 for a good discussion of this and other proposals.

[32] Proponents of the CI, of course, believe themselves further fortified in this interpretation since it appears to fit with their view of the discussion of failures to use the pp in 1146b31–1147a10.

knows she should not be doing, the relevant detail would have to be that she is doing something she knows she should not be doing. In other words, she would have to have some awareness that the description "what I am doing is tasting something I should not" is associated with her action. But if she never reaches the GConcl., then it is that description of her action knowledge of which she does *not* arrive at. How, in other words, could she know (i.e. be aware) that she is doing something she should not if she never combines the GP with the GU so as to arrive at GConcl.? She would instead be committing an akratic act unwittingly. That, however, does not qualify as voluntary (and thus not even as *akrasia* proper.)

In light of this consideration, it is somewhat puzzling that the CI has received as much credence as it has. Of course, there are no doubt attempts to rescue it from this problem. For example, one proposal holds that such an action as eating the strawberry can still be regarded as acting against one's better knowledge because one's better knowledge is embodied in the GU and it can be somewhat active in that the agent is aware of it.[33] If this were the phenomenon of acting against one's knowledge, however, it would seem to be so in a very diminished, and certainly not at all interesting, sense. More importantly, whether it counts as 'technically' acting against knowledge or not, I see no way how such a response can maintain the voluntariness of the akratic act. A GU, without an accompanying GP and GConcl., will not lead the agent to any awareness (half-use or not) at any level that the act she is performing falls under some description like "what I am doing right now I should not be." In fact, absence of the GP and GConcl. specifically preclude such awareness. And without this awareness, the act, understood by that *akrasia*-related description, cannot be voluntary.[34]

[33] I believe Kenny may have something like this in mind when he writes that "For his purpose, Aristotle does not need to spell out the universal premise in detail, because he agrees with popular opinion against Socrates that the incontinent man is aware of this principle throughout" (*Aristotle's Theory*, 160). This awareness, though, does not mean that for Kenny the universal premise is "operative"; it only becomes "operative when consequences are drawn from it" (*Aristotle's Theory*, 161). Apparently for Kenny, being in awareness and being operative are not equivalent at least so far as the universal premise is concerned.

[34] I take it that the knowledge requirement for voluntariness entails some level of awareness. To say otherwise would be to say that the knowledge requirement does not exclude cases in which agents are unaware of what they are doing. But it seems precisely so as to exclude such cases from voluntariness that the knowledge requirement exists in the first place.

The CI thus once again appears unsatisfactory. It must yet be shown, however, that my interpretation can offer a consistent reading of the rest of this particular passage such that it can be preferred. Let me start, therefore, by offering my understanding of the discussion of practical reasoning in 1147a29 ff.

In contrast to the way in which it is presented above, I follow several others[35] in positing that there is only *one* syllogism present. The phrase "everything sweet is pleasant, and … this is sweet" is the compound pp.[36] Once this move is made (and there seems to me no overriding reason to reject it), it is rather obvious that the unstated universal premise[37] is something along the lines of "Nothing pleasant must be tasted."[38] We thus have:

U: Nothing pleasant must be tasted.
P: Everything sweet is pleasant, and this is sweet
Concl: This must not be tasted

How, though, does *akrasia* occur when there is not a 'bad' syllogism to represent the akratic act and oppose a 'good' one, but only one syllogism? It can occur, according to my interpretation, because appetite affects the agent's knowledge of Concl., causing her to 'half-use' that knowledge such that she has awareness of it, but that awareness is clouded and offbeat. As such, she can act against it.

Two objections immediately suggest themselves, the first of which I hope to dispose of briefly. It wonders how the agent can even arrive at Concl. For Aristotle states that in practical reasoning, when a conclusion is drawn, the agent will then "act immediately" on it (1147a27 ff.). The akratic agent, however, by definition fails to act in accord with

[35] E.g., Irwin, *Aristotle; Nicomachean Ethics*, 260, and Kenny, *Aristotle's Theory*, 155 ff.

[36] Cf. our discussion above of Kenny's statements in *Aristotle's Theory* regarding multiple atomic pp's being combined into a compound pp.

[37] The exact form of this premise has long been a locus for debate and attempts to absolve the CI from inconsistencies in this part of the passage (cf. Gosling, *Weakness of the Will*).

[38] Irwin, *Aristotle; Nicomachean Ethics*, 260. This is his translation. It has been pointed out to me that the wording may be a bit ambiguous between "all non-pleasant things must be tasted," "pleasant things can be, but need not be tasted," and "all non-pleasant things must not be tasted." It is the latter that is intended. For simplicity's sake, I retain Irwin's wording in the text. I think it plausible to maintain that Aristotle did not spell out the exact form of the universal himself because it was so obvious. If it had been a premise as creative as that sometimes suggested, it stands to reason that, in that case, he would have definitely stated the exact form.

Concl. It thus seems she must not arrive at it. In response, I want simply to point out Aristotle's caveat that states the Concl. is acted upon if one is "not hindered." As some commentators observe,[39] the hindrance can be interior to the agent, such as her appetite and accompanying diminished use of her knowledge. Given this possibility, this objection does not speak decisively against my position.

The second objection relies on the point mentioned above that appetite seems linked more to the pp than to the conclusion (hence, the CI's emphasis on the breakdown in *akrasia* occurring at the level of the pp). We have been told, after all, that "sense perception [is already] the master [of the particular belief]" (1147a26). And given that appetite is related to, and arises from, sense perception, it appears that appetite, if it affects any part of the syllogism, would affect the pp and not the conclusion.

I do not think, however, that this poses a difficult challenge to my proposal. I am willing to concede that appetite is linked with the pp in the following sense: it initially arises when the agent arrives at the knowledge corresponding to at least one of the atomic premises in the pp. Indeed such should be expected. For example, when an agent, upon seeing a strawberry, arrives at the realization that 'this is sweet,' it is natural that an appetite for that strawberry can at that point arise. Just because appetite arises in conjunction with the knowledge corresponding to the pp, however, does not mean that it must then affect the agent's knowledge-status in relation to the pp. (In fact, it seems to me that the akratic agent, if she fully knows *anything*, must at least know 'this is sweet' in the full sense, for she does, even according to the CI, act upon that knowledge.)[40] Instead, I contend that there is no reason not to

---

[39] E.g., Dahl, *Practical Reason*, chap. 11. See also Charles, *Aristotle's Philosophy of Action*, 129.

[40] Note that an additional benefit of my interpretation is that we are not left with what Gosling refers to as the "Inconsistency" (*Weakness of the Will*, 28). By this, he means to pose the puzzle of how it is Aristotle can say at 1147a35 that "(and this latter belief is active)" by which he (and I) interpret as referring to the pp. It is a puzzle to Gosling because, according to the CI, *akrasia* occurs when a pp is somehow not being 'used' or is not 'active' while here, at this point, Aristotle is stating that in *akrasia* the pp *is active*. This issue causes no puzzle for my interpretation. I am happy to admit that the pp is *active* for, in my interpretation, appetite 'does its damage,' so to speak, not to the pp, but to the conclusion. In fact, I can even maintain that I *want* the pp to be active both so that practical reasoning continues on to the conclusion (and thereby the knowledge requirement for voluntariness can be fulfilled, as I have discussed above), and also because its activity helps ensure that appetite will indeed be present, for (as I have just mentioned), appetite is introduced along with an agent's realization/use of the knowledge corresponding to the pp.

assume that appetite, once having been introduced into the psyche of the agent by means of the knowledge corresponding to the pp, can then affect the agent's knowledge in regard to other pieces of knowledge, such as the conclusion. Just because appetite arises in conjunction with the pp need not mean that its epistemic effect is limited to, or even focused upon, the pp.

With this in mind, we can make sense of 1147a34 in which Aristotle states that "on the one hand the belief says to flee this, but on the other hand appetite leads one on." The first part of this phrase refers to the akratic actually arriving at the conclusion prohibiting the act, and can even be construed to include the possibility that the akratic is saying the words of that concluding prohibition in exactly the way a drunkard or new learner would draw a conclusion to a geometry proof and recite it without fully understanding it (cf. 1147a16 ff.). And why is the akratic drawing the conclusion in such an offbeat way? Because appetite, since

---

While we are discussing Gosling, it might be interesting to mention his solution as one example of how the CI leads interpreters to make rather counterintuitive suggestions. Recalling the earlier distinction between particular terms in reference to the object term and to the subject term, Gosling reasons that there are two pp's corresponding to these terms. There is a pp concerning the object (e.g. 'this is sweet'), and a pp concerning the agent (e.g. I am human). Both of these are needed since the universal premise refers to the prohibition of a certain type of object for a certain type of agent. Given, then, that Aristotle says here that 'this is sweet' is active, Gosling reasons that it must be the pp in reference to the agent that the akratic consequently fails to know. In other words, Gosling says desire makes "the agent 'forget they are human'" (34). This position seems (to me at least) to be unlikely. Could one really forget she is human? It seems more likely that Aristotle was convinced one could *not* fail to be aware of this fact (see, for example, 1111a6–8). In fact, he was so convinced of this that, in my opinion, this explains why he did not mention it as a possibility in 1147a1–10 when he is ruling out cases that cannot be knowledge. In other words, he considers the possibility of someone lacking "(particular b) this thing is this such-a-thing" (and, according to my interpretation, rules this out as a possible case of *akrasia*), but never mentions the case of one lacking "(particular premise a) he himself is a human being" for such would supposedly be impossible according to Aristotle. Moreover, it bears mentioning that this earlier portion, which serves as the basis for Gosling's admittedly creative solution, is actually evidence against his solution. For (i) if the CI is correct and *akrasia* results from failure of use of some pp, and (ii) if 1147a1–10 is intended to show the logical mechanics of this failure when it refers to acting against knowledge not seeming 'out of place' (i.e. this phrase is understood by the CI, contra my assertion, as indicating scenarios in which *akrasia* is possible), and furthermore if (iii) the pp which is not used in cases of *akrasia* is the one in reference to the agent, then it seems as if Aristotle would have said that it is when one lacks particular a, not particular b, that action against knowledge would not seem out of place. At any rate, I believe the case of Gosling's interpretation shows how the CI can force one into counterintuitive solutions. (Despite this particular observation, it bears noting that Gosling's discussions are very informative and insightful.)

it can "change the body" (1147a16) and "lead on" by "moving each of the parts" (1147a37) causes the akratic not to use that knowledge properly, even when she seems to be using it. It allows her to 'half-use' it, at best.[41]

We come now to the end of the passage wherein a great debate has raged over whether *teleutaia protasis*, translated as "last proposition" (1147b10), should be taken as referring to the pp or the conclusion. It is this which the akratic "either ... does not have ... when he is being affected or he has it in a way which is not knowledge but in the way of saying [words] just as the drunk person says the words of Empedocles" (1147b11–13). It should now come as no surprise that I see it as a reference to the conclusion, a minority position.[42] Proponents of the CI, by contrast, understand it as referring to the pp. They do so not only based upon their general view, but also because the passage states the *teleutaia protasis* is "of sensible things and is a lord of actions" and it is the pp that is often associated with *sensibilia* (cf. 1147a26). In response, the CI's argument is not conclusive because the conclusion of a practical syllogism itself also seems to be "of sensible things" in that it is concerned with *sensibilia* and one's response to them. Furthermore, it is the conclusion that appears to be "a lord of actions," not a pp; there is no action without the conclusion corresponding to that action.

We can now, I believe, read the remainder of the passage consistently by applying my interpretation. The akratic does not have the conclusion, or rather, has knowledge of it in the way a drunkard has knowledge of the words of Empedocles: both can somehow express the

---

[41] I should add here a grammatical comment. I have followed Irwin (*Aristotle; Nicomachean Ethics*) in 1147b2 by adding "[second]" before belief: "The [second] belief is not contrary to correct reason in itself, but coincidentally ... (for appetite is opposite to correct reason, but not the [second] belief)." By this, I am referring to the particular premise. I believe translating it in this way actually supports my interpretation that the pp only introduces appetite into the agent's psyche but is not itself affected by that appetite. My reason is as follows: since the pp introduces appetite, it might be thought (as indeed the CI maintains) that the pp is the problem in *akrasia*, despite (in my view) Aristotle's constant denials of this (cf. 1147a1–10). In order to preclude this misinterpretation, then, Aristotle wants to be clear that the problem is not with the pp (i.e. the "second belief"). Hence, his statement that the "[second] belief is not contrary to correct reason itself." It is contrary to correct reason only 'coincidentally' in that it is in relation to the pp that appetite, the actual culprit in *akrasia*, is introduced into one's psyche and subsequently affects one's use of the conclusion.

[42] Others who share this view generally are Dahl (*Practical Reason*), Charles (*Aristotle's Philosophy of Action*), and Pickavé and Whiting ("Nicomachean Ethics 7.3"). In addition, Kenny sees it as intentionally ambiguous and intended to refer to either the pp or the conclusion (Kenny, *Aristotle's Theory*, 164).

knowledge (perhaps verbally) and thereby seem to be using it, but neither is *fully* using the knowledge: the drunkard does not know what the words mean, and the akratic affirms the conclusion without *really* affirming it. She is sort of using it because she may be saying it, but sort of not because that is all she is doing - just arriving at and saying it. She can even be considered 'ignorant' in that she is not fully using the conclusion (1147b6). The conclusion is, therefore, *for the akratic*, not *fully* "expressive of knowledge" (1147b14).

This allows Aristotle to say that "even [the situation] has become like that which Socrates was seeking to bring about" (1147b15). Aristotle's position is somewhat like Socrates's because it does posit some form of ignorance, i.e. falling short of *full* use, on the part of the akratic. It is not, though, the akratic's view of the 'good' that has been changed. It is instead her *use* of the conclusion that follows from her view of the good that has been affected; it is the *use* of the conclusion that is, in a way, "drug around because of being affected" (1147b17). Consequently, while Aristotle's position is similar to Socrates's in points, it is not the same. For Aristotle, simple knowledge of what is good is not sufficient. Conclusions must flow from it, and the knowledge of these conclusions must not only be used, but *fully* used. And doing the latter is sometimes made difficult on account of the influence of appetite.[43]

There is of course much to be unsatisfied with in Aristotle's discussion. For example, he says that, as in the case of the drunkard's ignorance, to know how the akratic's ignorance is lifted one must consult the physicists (i.e. "natural scientists").[44] This seems rather uninformative. If the pp in a practical syllogism introduces appetite, how can a person faced with a practical situation expel appetite from the body in a way similar to that in which the drunkard can sober up? We are offered no answer. It may be that Aristotle did not intend to give us answers such as these. Instead, he may merely have wanted to indicate to us *what* the phenomenon of *akrasia* is, *when* and in some sense *how* it occurs, and (most importantly for our purposes) *under what*

[43] Note that my interpretation ultimately differs from that of Pickavé and Whiting ("Nicomachean Ethics 7.3") who find the failure in akrasia to be a failure to use a universal premise. On the other hand, there are unsurprisingly some similarities between the present interpretation and those offered by Dahl and Charles according to which the akratic knows the conclusion but does not properly know it. See, e.g. Dahl, *Practical Reason*, 210 and Charles, *Aristotle's Philosophy of Action*, 122 ff.

[44] Irwin, *Aristotle; Nicomachean Ethics*.

epistemic condition it comes to pass.[45] I hold that the answer to this last question is in the state of half-use, and this state of half-use is sufficient to fulfill the knowledge requirement such that the commission of *akrasia* is voluntary.

III. Summary

We undertook our investigation of Aristotle's view of *akrasia* for one purpose - we wanted to know the epistemic condition of the akratic. Given that *akrasia* is blameworthy, it must be voluntary. Voluntariness, in turn, requires fulfillment of the knowledge requirement. Given that the passage on *akrasia* discusses some form of diminished knowledge, we hypothesized it may be the case that the threshold for fulfilling the knowledge requirement may not be very high. We then offered an understanding of that passage according to which the akratic exercises what can be called a 'half-use' of her knowledge. Support for this understanding was then offered by demonstrating how the whole passage could be read consistently in light of it. This then enables us to conclude that some sort of half-use is sufficient for fulfillment of the knowledge requirement.

A few brief remarks remain to be made. First, it is at this point difficult to say exactly what this half-use consists in other than that it is analogous to the knowledge drunkards sometimes exhibit. This need not pose a problem, for it at least enables us to posit that some form of diminished knowledge/awareness may be sufficient to fulfill the knowledge requirement. If, then, we are later able to identify some form of relevant diminished awareness possessed by an agent guilty of a NO, we will then be better able to ascribe some voluntary failure to the agent at some point in the causal genesis of that NO for which she can be blamed.

This leads to the second summary point. It is sometimes thought that *akrasia* is a case of acting *agnoōn* and thus its blameworthiness and the root of its voluntariness lie in allowing oneself to get into a state in which one is affected by appetite.[46] This approach appeals to the fact

[45] This is, after all, his stated purpose: "We must consider first, then, whether incontinent people act knowingly or not, and in what sense knowingly" (1146b8–9).

[46] Cf. David Ross, *Aristotle*, 5th ed. (London: Methuen, 1949), 223. Cf. also: James Jerome Walsh, *Aristotle's Conception of Moral Weakness* (New York: Columbia University Press, 1963), chap. 4.

that drunkenness is used while explicating both concepts: acts done while drunk are acts done *agnoōn*, and the akratic's epistemic state is likened to that of a drunkard. Such an understanding might moreover seem beneficial to my project in that I want eventually to show that voluntariness of a NO lies somehow in acting *agnoōn*.

Despite these considerations, I do not believe Aristotle understands the voluntariness of *akrasia* in this way for the following four reasons: (i) If he did so understand it, he could have simply said that appetite can cause one subsequently to act *agnoōn* and, when it does, the resulting act is a form of *akrasia*. He did not, and even if he had, *akrasia* would then be just another case in which the agent is not aware of what she is doing and would pose no special puzzle. Moreover, (ii) if the voluntariness of *akrasia* were to result on account of the agent acting *agnoōn*, Aristotle need not have undertaken to see in what sense the akratic has knowledge; it would have already been clear and his whole discussion would have been to no purpose. (iii) If *akrasia* were simply a form of acting *agnoōn*, it stands to reason that when he made the analogy to the drunkard's state, he would have appealed not to how the drunkard was expressing and using (or failing to use) any knowledge she may possess, but rather to how drunkenness causes the drunkard subsequently to act *agnoōn*. And (iv) if appetite simply causes one to act *agnoōn*, then the actions would not be against one's actual better judgment at the time, but against *what would otherwise have been* the agent's better judgment. This, however, is not *akrasia*. I thus believe it is no more than a coincidence that both concepts are explained in terms of drunkenness.

As a result, I take it that the akratic act is voluntary in and of itself, not simply as a result of being committed *agnoōn*. After all, there are undoubtedly many instances we recognize as *akrasia* resulting from appetite in which we cannot hold the agent responsible for having had that appetite (as we can in the cases of drunkenness). We thus need not be tempted to think that the voluntariness of *akrasia* arises on account of some prior voluntary act of letting oneself be affected by appetite. Instead, the agent's act of *akrasia* is itself voluntary. This, in turn, means that studying her epistemic state at the time of *akrasia* can give an indication of the threshold at which the knowledge requirement is fulfilled for any voluntary, culpable act.

These last observations lead into my final point. It is true that I want to explain the voluntariness of a NO in terms of acting *agnoōn*. To do this, however, I need to accomplish the task represented by observation (C) in the previous chapter: I need to explain how the ignorance itself (analogous to ignorance$_1$ earlier) can itself be voluntary. For it to be voluntary, there must be some prior fulfillment of the knowledge requirement in regard to it. It has been in service to this task that I have explored the question of how robust one's knowledge must be in order for voluntariness to be ascribed. As we will see, the insights we have discovered here will accord well with the solution ultimately given to the problem.

CHAPTER 3

A NEGLIGENT OMISSION AT THE ROOT OF ALL SINFULNESS

ANSELM AND THE DEVIL

In this chapter, I will explore Anselm's action theory and, in particular, his understanding of the will-as-affection. This exploration will be important for a few reasons. First, doing so will set the groundwork for chapter 7 wherein we see that Scotus adopts Anselm's *affectiones* of the will. Second, this exploration will result in an important theological pay-off in regard to NO's. Anselm develops his theory of the will in parts and, upon reflection, it appears that the parts do not easily fit together. If we construct a full account of Anselm's understanding of the will, we can arrive at a consistent picture of the will but one that implies Anselm is unable to account for the origin of evil in the way he and the theological systems following him typically do. In fact, it turns out that evil and sinfulness would originally, according to Anselm's theory, have had to have arisen from a negligent omission! Consequently, this chapter will show that the thoughts of one of the most influential medieval theologians, one whose influence is still felt today in many areas of philosophy and theology, logically lead to the conclusion that the first time there was a sin, that sin was a NO. A high level of importance for theology could thus be claimed for NO's, a level of importance that implies these types of sin urgently need to be solved. If they cannot, much of contemporary theology that stems from Anselm may have to be rethought.

I. Introduction

In some of his lesser-known treatises,[1] Anselm attempts to demonstrate how it is possible that rational creatures (humans and the

[1] Anselm's writings will be referred to throughout the chapter by the following abbreviations: "*Mono*" (*Monologion*), "*CDH*" (*Cur Deus Homo*), "*DV*" (*De Veritate*), "*DLA*" (*De Libertate Arbitrii*), "*DCD*" (*De Casu Diaboli*), "*DC*" (*De Concordia Praescientiae et Praedestinationis et Gratiae Dei Cum Libero Arbitrio*). All English

angels[2]) can sin and be held accountable for their sinning. Not surprisingly, he believes that actions, such as the committing of sins, have their basis in the 'wills' of these rational creatures.[3] This fact alone, though, is not enough to show that such creatures are culpable for their actions, for Anselm believes that culpability requires that the will be somehow self-determined.[4] In order to show this, Anselm states that the will is self-moving.

This leads Anselm to a problem. Namely, how can a will's *first* self-movement toward sin be explained given the fact that the will is putatively created by God as 'good'? One response he could have offered is that it is a primitive fact about the will that it is characterized by freedom, and that this freedom entails it could move itself towards various types of actions, sinful or otherwise. This response, though, would have two undesirable consequences. First, as we shall see shortly, Anselm's peculiar understanding of freedom precludes 'an ability to sin' as being part of it. Second, it would not adequately address the fear that an unexplained first movement of the will toward sin would have to be characterized as "completely spontaneous ... entirely random and wholly inexplicable" and therefore not ascribable culpably to a subject, a concern often raised in contemporary discussions of libertarian free will.[5]

---

translations, unless otherwise noted, are from *Anselm of Canterbury: Collected Works*, 2nd American Edition, trans. and ed. Jasper Hopkins and Herbert Richards,(Toronto and New York: Edwin Mellen, 1975). The Latin quotations are from the standard: *S. Anselmi Cantuariensis Archiepiscopi Opera Omnia,* Ad fidem codicum recensuit Franciscus Selesius Schmitt (Stuttgart – Bad Cannstatt: Friedrich Frommann Verlag, 1968).

[2] I refer to angels and the devil (an evil angel) because Anselm himself does so and couches much of his discussion in the context of the devil's first sin. By using Anselm's terminology, I am making no claim as to the actual existence of such angels. Whatever is said in reference to an angel can equally be applied to humans who, according to Anselm, are similar to angels insofar as they are rational creatures.

[3] For the purposes of this chapter, I will construe 'action' broadly so as to include instances of 'willing' as themselves 'actions.' For a discussion of possible differences and similarities between 'actions' and 'willings' in Anselm, see Tomas Ekenberg, "Free Will and Free Action in Anselm of Canterbury," *History of Philosophy Quarterly* 22, no. 4 (1980): 301–318.

[4] It should be noted that in Anselm's theory the details differ when speaking of culpability for actions after a creature's first sin (actions during which a will may not be in its 'original' state) and actions when a will is in its original state. In this chapter, we will be concerned with culpability for actions when the will is in its original state.

[5] Stanley G. Kane raises this worry about such a response in his *Anselm's Doctrine of Freedom of the Will* (Lewiston, NY: The Edwin Mellen Press, 1981), 46. For an example of the contemporary expression of this problem inherent to libertarian accounts of free will, see chap. 11 of Peter van Inwagen, *Metaphysics* (Boulder: Westview, 1993).

Perhaps because of these worries, Anselm does not primarily (although there are a few exceptions) address this problem in the above manner. Instead, he tries to explain how a rational creature's first self-movement toward sin is possible by taking the devil's fall as a paradigm case of such a self-movement. His explanation is greatly dependent upon what he calls the *affectiones* of the will.[6] It is by means of a proper understanding of these *affectiones* that one is supposed to understand how the first sin of the devil or any other rational creature is possible and culpably ascribable to that agent. In order to understand the *affectiones* and ultimately see how they lead to the conclusion that the devil's first sin must have been a NO (if indeed it was a sin), we need to examine the general framework of Anselm's action theory.

II. Anselm's General Framework

Anselm's general framework begins with his notion of justice (*iustitia*). According to him, "justice is uprightness (*rectitudo*)-of-will kept for its own sake."[7] Let us examine each part of this definition separately. The first component is 'uprightness-of-will.' Anselm explains that this 'uprightness-of-will' in a rational creature consists of willing "what he ought to have willed – namely, the end for which he had received a will."[8] What, though, is this 'end?' Sometimes, Anselm discusses a proximate 'end' of ordering the various 'goods' in a hierarchy of goodness, and then willing each of those goods according to their place in that hierarchy. This proximate end, then, logically leads to the remote end of willing to love the greatest good (i.e. God) above all else,[9] an act which will make the rational creature happy.[10] In other places, the

[6] Cf. Kane, *Anselm's Doctrine*, 46–48. Any point Anselm makes in reference to the wills of angels in their original state can be taken to apply to any rational creature in such an original state and vice versa. Any particular differences that Anselm recognizes between the devil's and Adam's first sin are not relevant for the purposes of this chapter. (As Hopkins points out, a slight difference may be discussed in *CDH* II, 21, that is nonetheless irrelevant to our discussion. See p. 478 of Jasper Hopkins, "Anselm on Freedom and the Will: A Discussion of G. Stanley Kane's Interpretation of Anselm," *Philosophy Research Archives* 9 (1983): 471–494.) Consequently, it will for the most part be irrelevant whether an angel or a human is under consideration in the passages from Anselm we consider in relation to the will.

[7] Iustitia igitur est rectitudo voluntatis propter se servata (*DV*, chap. 12).

[8] Nam is quamdiu voluit quod debuit, ad quod scilicet voluntatem acceperat, … (*DV*, chap. 4).

[9] Cf., for example, *Mono*. chaps. 48–69, 74.

[10] *Mono*., chap. 69.

remote end is understood in terms of being "just and happy in order that it [the rational creature] would enjoy" God.[11] These two descriptions of the remote end are similar enough such that there is no particular need to choose between them. The important point for our purpose is that each description associates the remote *telos* with both happiness and justice. Consequently, the part of justice described as 'uprightness-of-will,' can be understood to consist in a rational creature willing to be both just and happy.[12]

The next component of the definition of justice is the characterization of this uprightness-of-will as "kept." By this term, Anselm is not referring to a mere passive action of *not losing this 'uprightness-of-will.'* Rather, he makes it exceedingly clear that it consists in *actively* 'willing' the 'uprightness-of-will;' the 'keeping' it cannot be separated from the 'willing' it.[13]

The final part of the definition is "for its own sake." Justice entails not doing what one ought to because of "external rewards," but doing it for no other reason than that one should.[14] Having examined this final component now permits us to reformulate Anselm's understanding of justice as: actual willing (from the word "kept") the end (to be just and happy so as to enjoy and love God above all) for which one received a will (from "uprightness-of-will") for no other reason except that it is the end for which one received the will (from "kept for its own sake").

---

[11] Intentio namque dei fuit, ut iustam faceret atque beatam naturam rationalem ad fruendum se (*DC* III, chap. 13). Cf. also Hopkins, "Anselm on Freedom," 476.

[12] There is, of course, a difficulty here in that 'just' is part of the definition of 'justice,' thus making the explanation seemingly circular. While this may be a problem, it should not affect our main argument if the definition is indeed circular. Nevertheless, the problem could perhaps be resolved by understanding an instance of 'just' willing in terms of the description of the various *teloi* in *Mono*. In this case, 'just' willing would be: in reference to some x of a certain nature, willing an action appropriate to the nature of that x, and willing that action to a degree which corresponds to the degree to which that x possesses goodness. Consequently, willing the love and enjoyment of God, and all which follows from that, would be the highest and most 'just' willing. If this is the way to understand 'just' willing (and I think there is reason to believe it is), then the circularity in the definition of justice is only apparent.

[13] Sicut autem simul illam [iustitiam] habemus et volumus, ita illam simul volumus et servamus; quoniam sicut eam non servamus nisi cum illam volumus (*DV*, chap. 12). In reference to the same point, Hopkins ("Anselm on Freedom," 472) agrees that an activity, though not constituting justice, is required for it. See also John R. Sheets, "Justice in the Moral Thought of St. Anselm," *Modern Schoolman* 25 (January 1948): 132–133.

[14] *DV*, chap. 12.

This idea of justice is crucial because it constitutes much of Anselm's definition of freedom. "Freedom of choice," according to him, is not "the ability to sin and not to sin."[15] Instead, "freedom of choice is the ability to keep uprightness-of-will for the sake of this uprightness itself."[16] This description from the word "keep" onwards is essentially the definition of justice. Consequently, Anselm claims that freedom is the *ability*, or power, to persevere in having justice, and does not contain as a component an ability or power to sin.[17]

As hinted at the beginning of this chapter, this distinctive definition of freedom appears to make it impossible for Anselm to assert that a rational creature sins by means of its freedom of will. And if a creature's sin cannot be traced back to the will's freedom, how can the creature be culpable? Anselm faces these questions in *DLA*, chs.1–2, where the interlocutor (the 'student') asks these same questions in reference to the first sin of the devil. Anselm's reply to the student, in short, is that the devil did indeed sin "by means of an ability to sin, as well as freely and by free choice and of no necessity."[18] How, though, can Anselm say this when his definition of freedom specifically excludes an ability to sin? To understand how, we turn to Anselm's understanding of the will.

III. The Structutre of the Will

Anselm gives his most fully developed account of the will in *DC* III, chap.11, in which he states that the term 'will' is used in three different

---

[15] Libertatem arbitrii non puto esse potentiam peccandi et non peccandi (*DLA*, chap. 1).

[16] ... illa libertas arbitrii est potestas servandi rectitudinem voluntatis propter ipsam rectitudinem (*DLA*, chap. 3).

[17] See Ekenberg, "Free Will and Free Action," 309, where the same link between freedom and justice is similarly made. For one viewpoint regarding the relationship between Anselm's definition of freedom and the "Principle of Alternative Possibilities" (PAP), see Sandra Visser and Thomas Williams, "Anselm's Account of Freedom," *Canadian Journal of Philosophy* 31 (June, 2001): 221–244. With some minor revisions, this article has been reprinted on two different occasions. The first is: Sandra Visser and Thomas Williams, "Anselm's Account of Freedom," in *The Cambridge Companion to Anselm*, ed. Brian Davies and Brian Leftow (Cambridge, UK: Cambridge University Press, 2004). See also their recent book: "Sandra Visser and Thomas Williams, *Anselm* (Oxford, New York: Oxford University Press, 2009). All subsequent references will be to the original article.

[18] Et per potestatem peccandi et sponte et per liberum arbitrium et non ex necessitate nostra et angelica natura primitus peccavit et servire potuit peccato (*DLA*, chap. 2).

senses.[19] In the first sense, 'will' refers to the "instrument-for-willing" which is the "power-of-the-soul which we use for willing."[20] Secondly, the term 'will' can refer to an "inclination (*affectio*)...of the instrument" which "is that by which the instrument is so inclined to will some given thing."[21] Finally, it may refer to the "use of this instrument" which occurs "only when we are thinking of the thing which we will."[22]

The important part of this distinction for our purposes is the will-as-inclination (henceforth referred to as 'affection'). Anselm describes an affection of the will as that which "if this thing [i.e. an object of an affection] comes to mind, then the will wills [to have] it either immediately or at the appropriate time."[23] For example, persons are so inclined to will their own health that whenever somebody thinks about being healthy, he or she wills to be healthy. The picture drawn for us is that a potential object of willing, if it represents to the agent the generic object[24] of an affection, cannot be merely 'considered' as if one were weighing the option of whether to will that object or not (unless there were simultaneously two potential objects of willing, each representing to the same degree the generic object of the same affection).[25] Rather, it seems to be the case that one has no choice but to will the generic object of an affection if some possible object of willing comes to mind that represents the generic object of that affection.[26] Consequently, it appears that Anselm is describing the operation of the will-as-affection in terms of what we will call a 'strong conditional.' This 'strong conditional'

---

[19] In *DC*, Anselm is discussing the will in reference to humans, not angelic creatures. This need not concern us, though, as he intends his general description of the will to be applicable to all rational creatures.

[20] Instrumentum volendi est vis illa animae qua utimur ad volendum (*DC* III, chap. 11).

[21] Affectio huius instrumenti est, qua sic afficitur ipsum instrumentum ad volendum aliquid (*DC* III, chap. 11).

[22] Usus vero eiusdem instrumenti est, quem non habemus, nisi cum cogitamus rem quam volumus (*DC* III, chap. 11).

[23] Affectio huius instrumenti est, qua sic afficitur ipsum instrumentum ad volendum aliquid – etiam quando illud quod vult non cogitat –, ut si venit in memoriam, aut statim aut suo tempore illud velit (*DC* III, chap. 11).

[24] For example, eating chocolate ice cream may represent happiness, the generic object of the affection-for-happiness.

[25] For example, consideration could take place if one is presented with the option of eating either chocolate or vanilla ice cream and one is equally made happy by eating either of them.

[26] Kane seems to agree when he writes that an Anselmian affection can be regarded as what is often referred to by dispositions which "have a law-like character" (*Anselm's Doctrine*, 64).

description can be formulated as follows: If one thinks about an object of an affection of the will, one has *no other option* but actually to will (understood in the sense of will-use) that object. Stated differently, an object of an affection seems to be only 'a thought away' from actually being will-used, for as soon as it is thought about, it is willed (i.e. will-used).[27]

According to Anselm, there are at least *two* different affections of the will. The first "of these is the inclination to will what is beneficial [or happiness (*commoditas*)]. The other is the inclination to will what is right."[28] A rational being has both of these affections in its original state. Why does Anselm think he needs to posit the creature having these two different affections? There are two reasons. First, recall that a creature's remote *telos* involves being both just and happy. Given that the powers of entities are to equip them to achieve their *teloi*, rational creatures would need a power adequate for helping them reach their particular *teloi*. Since the power by which a rational creature moves itself is its will, it follows that the will would be endowed by God with inclinations toward both justice and happiness; such inclinations in the will could allow a rational creature to move itself toward its *telos*.

This brings us to the second reason Anselm needed to posit at least two different affections, namely, to explain how a rational creature can *move itself* in a non-necessary manner and thereby be self-determining. Anselm is trying to demonstrate how the will can be self-determined in performing its first action. If there were only one affection of the will, the will-instrument would will-use in accordance with that affection necessarily. Every action of the will would therefore be necessary and determined. In other words, the rational creature's willed actions would ultimately be no different from, say, the action of fire. Just as it is fire's nature to burn, and it does so necessarily whenever it exists, it would likewise be a rational creature's nature to will in accordance with whichever affection it was endowed with. It would thus will in a necessary manner. And just as fire cannot be self-determining in its act of burning because doing so is its nature and its nature is not from itself,

[27] The ideas of justice being merely 'a thought away,' the 'strong conditional,' and the term 'planned ignorance' (later in the chapter) are to be attributed to conversations with Marilyn McCord Adams.

[28] ita instrumentum volendi duas habet aptitudines, quas voco 'affectiones'. Quarum una est ad volendum commoditatem, altera ad volendum rectitudinem (*DC* III, chap. 11). I will often refer to these affections as the affection (or 'will')-for-happiness and the affection (or 'will')-for-justice.

neither could a one-willed creature be self-determining since it would be doing what is in its nature to do and its nature is not from itself. If, by contrast, there were at least two affections of the will by which the creature need not will in accordance with only one disposition, then the creature would not will necessarily and could determine itself. Consequently, if a rational creature is to be self-determining it must have at least two different affections of the will.

At this point, though, an objection could be raised challenging the claim that having only one affection would result in necessary willing. It seems as if I have been describing the will as willing *only* when doing so is in accordance with an affection. Is it not possible, though, that there are acts of willing that need not be in accordance with *any* affection of the will? For example (the objection goes), let us suppose rational creatures have only one affection. Then, given the 'strong conditional' discussed above, whenever the object of that affection is 'in the mind,' the will wills it. However, could there not be other instances in which the object of the sole affection is not in mind, and the will is then free to will otherwise than in accordance with it? If so, then the presence of only one affection need not necessitate that the will's actions are determined.

In response, it is clear that Anselm wants to deny that there can be acts of willing that are not in accordance with any affection of the will. He makes this clear in *DCD*, chap.13 when he asks his student whether an angel who received only the will (i.e. affection) for happiness would "be able to move himself to willing anything else." The answer is "No."[29] In chapter 14 of the same book, Anselm makes a similar argument with regard to an angel who may have received only the will-for-uprightness. By stating that these one-willed angels would not be able to will anything else, Anselm is making clear his assumption that no willing can take place apart from an affection of the will.

There are thus for Anselm no unmotivated acts of willing.[30] All acts of willing must have some motivation that is traced back to an affection of the will. Indeed, it seems partly because of this assumption that he introduces the notion of the will-as-affection in the first place; it is

[29] In *DCD*, Anselm does not refer to the affections *per se* but does refer to the will-for-happiness and the will-for-uprightness. Nevertheless, it is clear from Anselm's writings that each of these 'wills' in *DCD* are to be understood as equivalent to the notion of will-as-affection as discussed in *DC*.

[30] Cf. also Visser and Williams, "Anselm's Account," 233.

supposed to serve as an explanation of why creatures will what they do. If there were no explanation for a creature's acts of willing, Anselm would be faced with the problem we noted at the beginning, namely, that a movement of the will would have to be characterized as "completely spontaneous," a conclusion the implications of which Anselm apparently wanted to avoid.[31] Consequently, it seems as if Anselm does indeed need to posit at least two affections of the will in order to begin to make his case that there are non-necessary acts of willing. By having two affections, the creature can determine itself.[32]

Not only do these two affections of the will supposedly rule out necessity in willing, but they also help Anselm begin to respond to a worry we had earlier, namely: How can rational creatures sin without the ability to sin being part of the definition of freedom? To understand how Anselm believes sinning is possible, we need first recall the relation of the affections to a rational creature's *telos*. Recall that above we noted these two affections (for happiness and for justice) were needed by rational creatures so that they could move themselves toward their *telos* of being both just and happy. Reaching this end, however, does not simply follow as a result of merely *having* these two affections. Rather, the creature must, in a sense, 'coordinate' them. Anselm explains:

> (1) the will-as-instrument would use the will-which-is-justice for commanding and governing (though being itself instructed by the spirit, which is also called mind and reason) and that (2) without any detriment it would use the other will [i.e. affection-for-happiness] to the end of obedience.[33]

---

[31] This is in reference to Kane (*Anselm's Doctrine*, 46) and the contemporary concern that contemporary accounts of libertarian free will ultimately end in undetermined spontaneity. Note that by "spontaneous" here I am not referring to Anselm's term "sponte," which more implies an idea of self-determination and is not intended to indicate a sense of spontaneous randomness. See the following: Stan R. Tyvoll, "Anselm's Definition of Free Will: A Hierarchical Interpretation," *American Catholic Philosophical Quarterly* 80, no. 2 (2006): 155–171; Daniel Deme, "The 'Origin' of Evil According to Anselm of Canterbury," *Heythrop Journal* 43 (2002): 170–184.

[32] Note that the options for willing are not that one can will in accord with one affection as opposed to the other. For Anselm, we always will our own happiness. The option for willing arises from the fact that we can moderate this willing of happiness with concerns for justice.

[33] Sic autem deus ordinavit has duas voluntates sive affectiones, ut voluntas quae est instrumentum, uteretur ea quae est iustitia, ad imperium et regimen, docente spiritu, qui et mens et ratio dicitur; et altera uteretur ad oboediendum sine omni incommoditate (*DC* III, chap. 13).

The idea is that, to reach its end, a rational creature cannot allow willings in accordance with the affection-for-happiness to take precedence over those in accordance with the affection-for-justice, but must rather subject the former to the latter. According to Anselm, we always will our own happiness. We can, however, moderate this willing by concerns for justice. And Anselm believes that for a rational creature to act so as to reach its *telos*, it must self-determine itself by tempering its otherwise unchecked willing of happiness by concerns for justice.

IV. The Formal Account of the Devil's Sin

With this background, we are now able to see how Anselm believes a rational creature can sin by focusing on his discussion of the devil's sin. In *DCD* chap. 14, Anselm says that God made "both wills [i.e. the affections] so agree in him [the devil] that he wills to be happy and wills justly." This agreement consisted in the will-for-justice tempering the will-for-happiness so "that its [i.e. the will-for-happiness] excesses would be checked."[34] It was not necessary, however, for the devil to choose in his willings so as to subordinate the will-for-happiness to the will-for-justice. There was instead the possibility that the devil could "desert justice by means of an immoderate will" (i.e. letting the will-for-happiness take precedence).[35] And this is exactly what the devil did! Anselm states that the devil "sinned by willing something beneficial which he did not possess and was not supposed to will at that time."[36] Namely, "he willed inordinately to be like God."[37] The devil's willing of the happiness that would ensue from being like God was a willing not tempered by the will-for-justice and was therefore a sin.

Before moving on, it is worth mentioning that the idea a rational creature could sin by willing to be like God may, at first glance, seem somewhat problematic. Anselm generally understands all created natures to be imitations of God that naturally strive to be as godlike

[34] necesse est ut sic faciat deus utramque voluntatem in illo convenire, ut et beatus esse velit et iuste velit. Quatenus addita iustitia sic temperet voluntatem beatitudinis, ut et resecet voluntatis excessum et excedendi non amputet potestatem (*DCD*, chap. 14). This accords with the way we just saw that *DC* III, 13 describes the relationship between the affections.

[35] … deseruerit iustitiam per immoderatem voluntatem (*DCD*, chap. 14).

[36] Peccavit ergo volendo aliquod commodum, quod nec habebat nec tunc velle debuit (*DCD*, chap. 4).

[37] voluit inordinate similis esse deo (*DCD*, chap. 4).

as possible by reaching toward their *teloi*. How, then, could it be a sin for the devil to strive to be as godlike as his nature would allow? I presume, given his general metaphysics, Anselm would grant that there is nothing wrong *per se* in the devil trying to be as Godlike as is appropriate to his *telos*. What was wrong in the devil's wanting to be like God, though, was that the devil was not trying to achieve this result through reaching his *telos*.

As we mentioned above, a rational creature's *telos* involves being not only happy, but also *just*. When the devil willed to be like God, he was willing to be subordinate to none and thus was willing only in accordance with the affection-for-happiness. In willing to be subordinate to none, he was actually willing to be greater than God in that his will would not be subject to God's.[38] Justice, on the other hand, dictated that a creature not attempt to be so Godlike as to be subordinate to none. The devil's willing to be like God, therefore, was a willing not in accordance with the affection-for-justice and consequently not in line with his *telos*. The devil should have tempered his willing for happiness on account of this justice-related consideration. It can thus be said that the devil's sin ultimately lay in his not properly coordinating the two affections in his will. And by placing the locus of sin in a failure to coordinate, Anselm is able to posit an ability to sin despite his distinctive definition of freedom.

V. Further Aspects of a Sinful Act

Not only does Anselm's notion of 'coordinating' the affections allow him to posit that rational creatures have an ability to sin, but he believes it also helps him explain how a creature's sin can be non-necessary and therefore culpably ascribed to the creature. This claim is based upon the idea that since a rational creature has two affections, it need not follow the inclinations of one of the affections mechanically. The presence of a second affection creates options, or alternative possibilities, for willing. Which of these alternative possibilities are willed, in turn, depends upon how the creature 'coordinates' the two affections. The creature is supposedly the one doing the actual 'coordinating' and thus

[38] For an excellent discussion of this issue, along with many others, in *DCD*, see: Marilyn McCord Adams, "St. Anselm on Evil: De casu diaboli," *Documenti e studi sulla tradizione filosofica medievale* 3 (1992): 423–451.

the 'coordinating' is *a se*. As such, the creature can be culpable for failures to coordinate properly.

This claim, though, raises a problem which can be seen by comparing the angels who did not sin to those who did. The angels who did not sin must have 'persevered' in coordinating properly, while those who sinned must not have so 'persevered.' The difference between these two groups, then, can be characterized in terms of the quality of 'perseverance,' the former having it and the latter not. But how, the student wonders in *DCD*, chap.2, can the devil be held accountable for his sin when God gave the good angels perseverance and presumably did not give it to the devil? Anselm's answer is that, even though God gave the devil "the ability and the will to receive perseverance," God did not give perseverance itself to him because "he did not receive it."[39] The offer of perseverance itself was not received. And since the devil did not receive it, then God cannot be held accountable for the devil not having it.

This response, though, begs the question as to why the devil did not receive this perseverance when he had the ability and will to receive it. To answer this, Anselm explains that persevering in willing is simply "to will completely" (*pervelle*). 'Perseverance' itself, then, is not some quality *added on* to an act of willing, but is rather the act of willing itself continually performed. And since the devil had the ability to keep continually a good (i.e. properly coordinated) will as long as he willed to keep it, then the devil had the ability to receive perseverance. The fact that he did not continue to will to keep the good will, therefore, is supposed to suffice to explain why he did not receive perseverance even though he had the ability to.

This line of argumentation does not seem to be very helpful, for it just pushes the issue at question back to another level. Namely, how could the devil not have continually willed to keep a good will while the good angels did? Or, as the student asks, "Why did [the Devil] not will to keep what he was keeping except because God did not grant him to will [to keep it]."[40] If perseverance ultimately comes down to 'keeping' a good will, and if some of the angels did that while others did not, then there must be a difference in the 'ability to keep a good will' between those two groups. And if so, God actually does seem culpable

---

[39] Deus dedit illi voluntatem et potestatem accipiendi perseverantiam. … Non accepit et ideo non habuit (*DCD*, chap. 3).

[40] … quare tenere non voluit quod tenebat, nisi quia deus non dedit velle (*DCD*, chap. 3).

in that the evil angels' abilities to 'keep,' which were given by God, were evidently somehow deficient in comparison to those of the good angels.

Anselm challenges the student's argument by stating that it is false simply to say that the devil did not 'will to keep' the good will; to the contrary, the devil "freely lost the will which he had" because he willed to desert it.[41] In order to understand what Anselm is getting at here, we need to discuss his distinction between two ways that will-acts can result in the loss of some possession. One is when 'not-willing-to-keep' takes precedence over a 'willing-to-desert,' and the other is when the latter takes precedence over the former. Anselm explains this difference as follows:

> When you do not will to keep a thing for its own sake but will to desert it for its own sake (for example, a lighted coal placed in your bare hand), then perhaps not-willing-to-keep precedes willing-to-desert, and you will to desert because you do not will to keep. … But when you have a thing which only on account of something else you do not will to keep and which only on account of something else you will to desert, and when you prefer this other thing which you cannot have unless you give up what you do have, then willing-to-desert precedes not-willing-to-keep.[42]

Anselm illustrates the latter concept of willing-to-desert taking precedence with the example of a miser. A miser has the will to keep all the money he can for its own sake. However, a miser also needs to eat, and acquiring bread for nourishment requires money. When a miser, then, buys bread and thereby parts with some of his money, it is not that the miser is actually willing not-to-keep his money. Rather, the miser wills to lose his money only as a result of the external factor of his wishing to eat and stay alive. Thus, the miser's willing to spend the money is, since he is *not* not willing 'to keep [it] for its own sake,' a case where willing-to-desert takes precedence over not-willing-to-keep.

According to Anselm, the devil's not keeping a good will can be similarly characterized. It is not that the devil did not will to keep a good

[41] Sponte dimisit voluntatem quam habebat (*DCD*, chap. 3).

[42] Quando aliquam rem propter se non vis tenere sed deserere, ut carbonem ignitum positum in nuda manu: tunc forsitan prius est non velle tenere quam velle deserere, et ideo vis deserere, quia non vis tenere. … Cum autem tenes quod non nisi propter aliud non vis tenere, nec nisi propter aliud vis deserere, et magis vis aliud quod non potes habere nisi deseras quod tenes: tunc velle deserere prius est quam non velle tenere (*DCD*, chap. 3).

will for its own sake. Rather, the devil willed to lose the good will only as a result of his willing a separate, incompatible object, namely, to be like God. His act of willing, then, was one in which the willing-to-desert took precedence. As a result, Anselm believes he has neutralized the student's charge. By ultimately locating the devil's lack of perseverance in an act of willing-to-*desert*, God cannot be charged with failing to give the devil a deficient ability of 'willing to *keep*' a good will. As such, God cannot be held accountable for the devil's sin; the sin is to be ascribable to the devil.

VI. The Problem

In what we have seen above, Anselm has tried to argue for a two-pronged thesis. First, by defining sin in terms of letting the affection-for-happiness take precedence over the affection-for-justice, he has been able to posit an ability to sin in the devil and other rational creatures, even though that ability to sin is not part of the definition of freedom. Second, he has tried to secure the notion that God is not in any way to be held culpable for the devil's first sin by describing that sin as an instance of the devil 'willing to desert' the good will. In order for this two-pronged thesis to hold, though, the further notion that the devil is culpable for his 'willing to desert' must be secured, a task which Anselm does not do.[43] Can this be done?

It is my contention that Anselm could *not possibly* accomplish this task in light of his overall theory of the will. To argue this, I will first need to show that the devil did, at some point, perform an act of upright willing. To do this, let's begin by noticing that nothing said in the interchange in *DCD*, chapters 2–3 implies that the devil *never* willed correctly. In fact, the student suggests that the devil *did* in fact, at some point, perform some act of correct willing when he says the following:

> ...it is as if you were saying that what he *willed at first*, he did not will afterwards. Therefore, when he *no longer willed what he willed at first*, why did he not will it except that he did not have the will [for it]? I am not talking about *the will which he had at first when he did will*...(italics mine).[44]

[43] For a good discussion of some ways in which it is problematic to impute 'willing to desert' as blameworthy to the devil, see Adams "St. Anselm" (esp. 445 ff.).

[44] ... tale est ac si dicas: Quod voluit prius, postea non voluit. Quando ergo non voluit quod prius voluit: quare non voluit, nisi quia non habuit voluntatem? Non dico voluntatem quam prius habuit cum voluit (*DCD*, chap. 3).

Anselm never disputes the implication of the italicized phrases, leading us to believe that Anselm would grant that the devil may have, in fact, at some point performed an act of correct willing.

Further support for the claim that the devil must have once willed uprightly rests upon one detail of the affections not yet discussed. In *DC* III, chap.13 Anselm states that "the will [i.e. affection]-for-justice is itself justice."[45] By substituting the definition of 'justice,' examined at the beginning of this chapter, for the term itself, this statement can be rephrased as "the affection-for-justice is itself 'uprightness of will *kept* for its own sake.'"[46] If we recall our earlier examination of the word 'kept' in relation to Anselm's definition of justice, we remember that the term implies an *active* willing of the 'uprightness-of-will' ("the receiving, having, and willing" of the uprightness which is part of justice "*occur simultaneously*").[47] Consequently, the devil, in virtue of having an affection-for-justice, must have, at some point, willed justly.[48] This progression can be expressed as follows:

(1) The devil received an affection-for-justice (*DCD*, chap.14).
(2) The affection-for-justice is justice itself (*DC* III, chap.13).
(3) Therefore, the devil actually received justice (1,2).
(4) Receiving justice entails having willed uprightness-of-will for its own sake when it is received (*DV*, chap. 12).
(5) Consequently, the devil, at one time, actually *will-used* uprightness-of-will for its own sake (3,4).[49]

From the above considerations, it seems that we are safe to conclude that the devil did, in fact, at one time, will justly. The question now arises as to whether the devil could have 'deserted' justice while he was actually *will-using* justice. The answer to this appears to be "No." If the devil is willing justice, and if letting the will-for-happiness take

[45] Voluntas quidem iustitiae est ipsa iustitia (*DC* III, chap. 13).

[46] Note that this definition of justice helps explain a distinctive viewpoint Anselm has. According to Anselm, once one sins one no longer has the affection-for-justice. This claim makes sense in light of the definition of the affection-for-justice as 'uprightness *kept*.'

[47] *DV*, chap. 12, italics mine. Cf. also Sheets, "Justice in the Moral Thought," 132 and 136.

[48] Of course, the devil did not *per-velle* justly – he did not persevere in willing justly. But one need not persevere in a willing to have done it at all. And Anselm only says the devil did not *pervelle*, not that he did not *velle*.

[49] We could further ask if the initial will-use was also self-determined. I do not think, however, that much rides on the answer to this question for present purposes.

precedence over the will-for-justice is injustice, then it is impossible that the devil could will-use unjustly while also willing justice.

> (6) The devil is willing justice (5).
> (7) Justice entails willing what one ought to will for the sake of itself (*DV*, chap. 12).
> (8) Injustice, conversely, entails willing what one ought not to will or willing what one ought for the wrong reason (7).
> (9) Consequently, the devil cannot be willing what he ought not or for the wrong reason when he is willing justice (6,7,8).

The conclusion is that the devil was not will-using justice when he sinned. Anselm's theory of the affections, however, does not merely imply that the devil could not be willing justice when he sinned, but also the much stronger claim that the devil must have somehow simply *forgotten* about doing a just act when he sinned.

To see this, recall that Anselm characterizes the affections in terms of what we called the 'strong conditional' ("if one thinks about the object of the affection, one has *no other option* but actually to will (i.e. will-use) it"). Now, consider the time *t* at which the devil deserted justice (i.e. sinned). Since the devil had *ex hypothesi* not already committed a sin, the devil still had the affection-for-justice at *t*. And in light of (5) above, the devil had at least at one point prior to *t* (call it *t*') willed justly and was, up until *t*, just.[50] Given the strong conditional, therefore, if the devil thought of justice at *t*, he would have willed justice: "Likewise, in a just man the instrument-for-willing is so inclined [*affectum*] to will justice (even when a man is asleep) that when he thinks of justice he wills [to have] it immediately."[51] Willing justice, however, would preclude deserting it. Since the devil deserted justice at *t*, the devil therefore could not have even been considering doing a just act at *t*. Justice was not even in his thoughts, so to speak. Given, moreover, that the devil did previously will justly at *t*', it follows that the devil

---

[50] *DCD* makes it clear that the devil was no longer able to will justly after his first sin. His just willing must therefore have occurred before his sin.

[51] In iusto quoque homine similiter est affectum idem instrumentum ad volendum iustitiam – etiam cum dormit -, ut cum eam cogitate, statim illam velit (*DC* III, chap. 11). The context seems to make clear that the *velit* here is to be understood not merely as a desire, but as an actual will-use. See also Tyvoll, "Anselm's Definition," 159. For a view that seems somewhat opposed, cf. Robert Brown, "Some Problems with Anselm's View of Human Will," *Anselm Studies* 2 (1988): 333–342.

was also thinking about justice at t'.[52] Therefore, if the devil was thinking about justice at t', and was not thinking about justice at t, his sin ultimately seems to be a result of simply 'forgetting,' or not happening to think, about justice at t.

The conclusion to this line of reasoning, then, is that the devil must have willed what was unjust without consciously thinking of it as such at the time. This follows, of course, from the fact that if justice had been in the mind of the devil, he would have willed justice in accord with the strong conditional characterization of the affection-for-justice. In a sense, then, it could be said that justice was merely 'a thought away' from being will-used. But if justice was merely 'a thought away' when the devil deserted it, then culpability must ultimately somehow lie in the fact that the devil did not continually think about justice with the aim that the affection for it would govern his will-for-happiness. It seems, therefore, that he would need some sort of 'will to persevere in thinking consciously at all times about justice' so that he would properly coordinate the affections and not fall into sin.[53] How, though, was the devil to be expected to have this 'will-not-to-forget justice'?[54]

Before answering this question, it is worth considering an objection to the preceding analysis that gave rise to it. Instead of the devil not thinking about justice at the time of his sin, why could it not be that the

---

[52] Kane notes that Anselm makes this explicit in *DC* III, chap. 11, where Anselm writes: "the use of the will is the willing which occurs only when we are thinking of that thing which we will." As Kane notes, for Anselm "a volition in every instance involves conscious thought of what is being willed" (*Anselm's Doctrine*, 18).

[53] It has been objected that this is an exceedingly demanding condition. Indeed it is. Nonetheless, this exceedingly demanding condition is required based upon Anselm's analysis. A less demanding condition would not necessarily suffice. Consider a so-called 'will-not-to-desert-justice'. Such a will would supposedly be a will to think about justice not at all times, but only at those times when a choice is to be made. (Hoffman, "Intellectual Determinism," argues that Aquinas held a position resembling this condition.) The only way that an Anselmian agent could ensure he did not forget about justice at the time a choice is to be made, however, would be to think about it all the time. Otherwise, the possibility of not thinking about justice at an appropriate time would exist. It thus seems that a will-not-to-desert-justice would, if truly held, be no less demanding. At any rate, I am not convinced much hangs on this issue so far as the purposes of this chapter are concerned. It will turn out that, regardless of whether the condition is as demanding as I think it is or not, the sinning agent would ultimately have sinned because he committed the NO of not thinking about justice when he should have.

[54] Throughout the remainder of this chapter, I will use the concepts of 'the will to persevere', 'the will-not-to-forget about justice', and 'the will always to coordinate the affections' interchangeably to refer to the aspect of the will currently under consideration.

devil was simply mistaken about what justice required? In other words, maybe the devil abandoned justice because he mistakenly thought that justice required immoderately desiring to be like God. This objection, however, cannot hold for a number of reasons. If the devil really did think that, then he thought that either inculpably or culpably. If inculpably, no sin would ensue. If culpably, then justice would have already been abandoned. More importantly, Anselm's general train of thought rules out the possibility that the bad angels could have made such a mistake. According to Anselm, God's point in granting dual affections was to enable self-determination via a choice between alternatives. If, at the pivotal moment of self-determining choice, it were possible for an angel to mistakenly think that the object of the affection-for-justice was the same as that of the affection-for-happiness, no alternatives would have existed. Self-determination would not have been possible, thereby contradicting God's purposes in granting dual affections to begin with. Contra the objection, therefore, the devil's sin cannot be explained by a simple mistake regarding the actual object of the affection-for-justice. We can thus return to wondering how the devil was to be expected to have a 'will-not-to-forget justice.'

One reply could be that he was to have this will-not-to-forget as a result of the affection-for-justice. The idea behind this proposal is that the affection-for-justice, once invoked through an action of just willing (such as the devil had at *t*'), should have caused him to realize that he could not quit thinking about justice lest he fall into sin. This response, however, is problematic. If the devil were to have this will somehow as a result of the affection-for-justice, then the devil, when he first received/will-used in accordance with the affection, would have willed that he continuously think about justice. In other words, when the devil willed justice at time *t*', the devil would have willed at *t*' to continue thinking about justice after *t*'. But if such a willing at *t*' were sufficient to bring it about that the devil would think about justice after *t*', then the devil would have thought about justice immediately after *t*' and at every subsequent moment, including time *t*. The devil, though, sinned at *t*. We have shown that the devil could *not* have been thinking about justice at *t*. Consequently, a willing to continue thinking about justice in this case cannot be sufficient to bring it about that the devil actually continues to think about justice, and the suggestion seems to fail.

One might defend the proposal that the will-not-to-forget can be traced back to the affection-for-justice in the following manner: maybe it is the case that the devil's willing at *t*' to continue thinking about justice after *t*' was not sufficient for him to do so because he had a lesser degree of the affection-for-justice. If so, the argumentation I offered immediately above would not necessarily dispute the claim that he was to have this will-not-to-forget as a result of initially willing in accordance with the affection-for-justice.

There does, at first glance, seem to be some textual support for this suggestion. The idea that the affection-for-justice comes with different degrees is suggested by a section in *DC* III, chap.3, which indicates that justice can be *restored* by degrees: "But if by free choice the will keeps what it has received and thereby merits either an *increment of received justice*..."[55] If justice can be restored by degrees, then it stands to reason that there may indeed be degrees within justice and its affection.

Upon closer examination, though, there is no reason to believe that this passage is relevant to our consideration of the devil's sin. To begin with, the passage is referring not to the devil, but only to human beings. While it is true that Anselm's general discussion of the will can be applied to all rational creatures (angels and humans) alike, he is here referring only to human beings after they have committed their first sins. For Anselm, humans and the evil angels are alike in that they lose their affection-for-justice after they have sinned. They are different, however, in the status of that loss. Unlike humans, the evil angels are unable ever to reacquire their affection-for-justice.[56] Since (i) what is being discussed here is justice being *restored*, and (ii) the evil angels are unable ever to reacquire justice, then (iii) this passage must be referring only to humans. Furthermore, the use of the term *restore* implies that justice must have once been had and then lost. In our discussion of the devil, though, we are concerned solely with the state of the devil before he had sinned and lost any endowments. Consequently, this passage in *DC* cannot support the suggestion that the devil may have had a lesser degree of the affection-for-justice when he first willed justice.

The suggestion that the devil may have had a lesser degree of the affection-for-justice would not be tenable at any rate. Anselm's attempt to absolve God from responsibility for sin in chapters 2 and 3 of *DCD* is ultimately based on the assumption that both the good and bad angels were originally *identically* endowed. If there were different degrees among the *original* affections-for-justice, Anselm would defeat his purpose of trying to trace the origin of sin back to created self-determined choice by leaving open the possibility that God is partly

[55] Si autem voluntas, per liberum arbitrium servando quod accepit, meretur aut augmentum acceptae iustitiae (*DC* III, chap. 3, italics mine).

[56] Cf. *DCD*, chap. 17.

culpable for the devil's sin. God would be responsible because in that case he would have given the devil a 'lesser affection-for-justice' which, as opposed to a 'greater affection-for-justice,' could not bring it about that a willing-to-continue-doing-some-x is sufficient for the continuance of doing that x. We can thus conclude that the devil did not receive a lesser or inadequate affection-for-justice but received one in all ways identical to those of the good angels. Given this, the will-not-to-forget cannot be traced back to a willing in accord with the affection-for-justice.

Where, then, in the rational creature should we locate this ability to will-to-think-continuously about justice if not in the affection-for-justice? The most plausible answer seems to be that Anselm recognized the agent as being capable of making some sort of executive decision as to how to use one's will-instrument. Under this understanding, it would simply be up to the devil's executive power to *continuously* decide to think about justice.

To buttress this suggestion, let us turn to *DLA*, chap.7. There, the student asks the teacher how temptation is ever succumbed to "if the will-to-keep-uprightness were stronger than the force of temptation," a claim Anselm had just made in chapter 6 of *DLA*. In order to answer this query, Anselm asks the student to consider the case of a strong man who has enough strength to hold a "wild bull" but from whom a ram was able to shake "itself loose" (*DLA*, chap.7). Can this phenomenon be explained by saying that the man actually had less strength in the case of the ram than he did in the case of the bull? The answer, of course, is "No." Rather, the man only used less strength in the case of the ram. But this only raises the question of how can the man's use of less strength than he had be explained?

The answer given is that using less strength was 'chosen.' But what entity did the choosing? At this point, Anselm is a bit ambiguous. In one sense, he suggests that it is simply the agent who chose. Alternatively, he seems to imply that the locus of choosing is to be found in the will-instrument, for it is the will-instrument that has "the inalienable strength which cannot be overcome by any other force. And in willing, the will [referring to the instrument] uses this strength *now more, now less*" (italics mine).[57] What Anselm apparently means is that the

[57] Sic intellige voluntatem quam voco instrumentum volendi, inseparabilem et nulla alia vi superabilem fortitudinem habere, qua aliquando magis, aliquando minus utitur in volendo (*DLA*, chap. 7).

agent's executive decision is carried out by the will-instrument; the will-instrument can be seen as representing the agent. Since the agent has this executive power as represented in the will-instrument, the agent has the privilege of choosing what it wills more or less strongly and employing the use of the will to that purpose.[58] Given this, it can be said that the creature's responsibility to coordinate the affections falls to the will-instrument (or, rather, the agent's employment of the will-instrument). And if so, then it is the executive employment of the will-instrument that is ultimately responsible for the devil's first sin by means of its failing always to make the agent think about justice.

VII. Can We Explain the Fall of the Devil in the *DCD* Account?

Anselm's account of the actual circumstances in which the devil sinned is interesting. He states that the devil's sin arose from a situation in which the devil and the good angels did not know that they would be punished if they committed an act forbidden them by God. This ignorance, since it was required for the angels to perform a non-necessary act of willing, was necessary; it was a "necessary ignorance."[59] If the angels did know they would be punished, considerations of happiness would have told in favor of not disobeying God: since disobeying God would eventually issue in punishment, the affection-for-happiness would have prompted the creature to avoid such punishment by obeying God. In addition, given that obeying God is a just act, the affection-for-justice would equally have prompted the creature to obey God. But if both sets of motivating considerations would issue in the creature obeying God, there would have been no possibility of moral conflict for the creature and, accordingly, no non-necessary choice or self-determination. Conversely, if there is 'necessary ignorance' such that the angels would not know they would be punished if they disobeyed God, considerations of happiness would then tend in favor of disobeying God (given that disobeying God seems to bring about some *commodum*, as it does in the *DCD* account). In this case, moral conflict would be real, and a non-necessary choice could be made. As a result,

---

[58] For a somewhat related discussion of this passage, cf. Brown, "Some Problems," 333–342.

[59] See Adams, "St. Anselm," 441 ff.

'necessary ignorance' was necessary if the creature was to be self-determined and thus culpable for its sin.

This ignorance, though, was only an ignorance of the results. The angels were *not* ignorant of what they were supposed to do. Anselm writes "[the evil angel] knew that he ought not to will what he willed in transgressing."[60] But if doing what one is supposed to do is just, then (and this is the important point) this implies that the devil and the evil angels *must* have known about the demands of justice.

This observation, though, presents a problem. We demonstrated above that since the affections are characterized by the 'strong conditional,' the devil could only have sinned when he had 'forgotten' about justice; he would have had to have been, in a sense, unconscious or *ignorant* of justice at the time of his sin. If the devil's 'knowledge' of what he must do was before his mind, then we seem unable to understand how the devil could have culpably sinned. If the devil was considering justice, and if one cannot sin while thinking about justice, we have no way to explain the devil's sin. It seems as if, under the assumption that that knowledge was in the devil's awareness, there is no possibility that the devil could have sinned. If the devil sinned, it must consequently be the case that he was not actively aware, at the time at which he sinned, of the requirements for justice. His 'knowledge' of what he must do must have been non-occurrent and merely in the recesses of his mind.

An objection remains. Recall Anselm's discussion of the strong man in *DLA*, chap.7. There we saw that the responsibility to coordinate properly the affections seems to lie in the will-instrument (as it represents the agent's executive power). If the instrument has this responsibility, though, does it not follow that it could intentionally shirk this responsibility and coordinate them improperly, even if the agent were thinking about the demands of justice? It may seem so, for Anselm writes that the instrument can decide "what it wills more strongly; and when it is offered what it wills more strongly, it immediately abandons what it [i.e. the instrument] wills less strongly."[61] The picture drawn for us is that the instrument apparently has the ability to override the tendency of any one affection. As such, it seems that even the devil could

[60] ... scivit se non debere velle quod praevaricando voluit (*DCD*, chap. 22).

[61] Unde quod fortius vult, nullatenus deserit oblato eo quod minus fortiter vult; et cum offertur quod vult fortius, statim dimittit quod non pariter vult (*DLA*, chap. 7).

still sin while thinking about justice because his will-instrument could 'override,' so to speak, the dictates[62] of the affection-for-justice.

Does this portrayal of the instrument's strength contradict our contention that the devil could not have been actively thinking about justice when he sinned? I believe a closer reading of *DLA*, chap. 7 provides an answer of 'No.' When Anselm speaks of the instrument having ultimate control over the 'will-to-keep-uprightness,' Anselm is contrasting the will-as-instrument with the will-as-use. He is *not* referring to the will-as-affection. In fact, when he wrote *DLA*, he had not yet even developed the concept of the will-as-affection; this was not done until he wrote *DCD*. Much less, then, had he created the concept of the 'strong conditional' which has been causing the problem in his account. It was not introduced until he wrote the even later *DC*. If we are to take his mature discussion of the will in *DC* as normative, it seems we must conclude that Anselm's discussion in *DLA* cannot be used to support the idea that the will-instrument could prevent the affection-for-justice causing justice to be willed if justice is thought about.

As a result, we appear unable to explain how the devil could sin by willing to be like God *unless* it was on account of a simple forgetfulness of the demands of justice. If the devil did indeed sin, then it must be that he was temporarily not mindful of justice's requirements. His sin consisted in the fact that he *omitted* to uphold justice because *he just happened not to think* about justice and its demands. In other words, he committed what can be called a negligent omission, and it is not clear how he can ultimately be held responsible for it.

VIII. Conclusion

As Kane remarks, "Anselm never satisfactorily explains how the interplay of the two affections in beings created perfect can develop into a full-fledged moral conflict between them."[63] Although Kane approaches this issue much differently, our consideration of the implication of Anselm's *affectiones* supports this conclusion.

If the devil did indeed sin, then Anselm would have to admit that this occurred on account of a simple forgetting about the demands for

---

[62] Although the term 'dictate' can signify a cognitive act, I use it here to express the directive that would result from using a particular affection.

[63] Kane, *Anselm's Doctrine*, 86.

justice despite the fact that he otherwise knew them.[64] The devil *omitted* to will uprightly because he just did not happen to think about the demands of justice. According to Anselm's theory, therefore, the devil's first sin could be regarded as a type of sin of negligent omission; he would have fulfilled his moral obligation to uphold justice if he had only thought about it – it just so happened that he must not have thought about it.

This is most likely not the conclusion Anselm desired. One can be fairly certain that Anselm did not foresee that his statements on the will led to it. In fact, given the strong conditional, self-determination is still not possible for, if the generic object of the affection-for-justice is thought about, the agent must will it.[65] It was for the purpose of self-determination, however, that Anselm posited two affections of the will in the first place.

It may be objected that Anselm did not intend the strong conditional to be understood so strongly, for it is the strong conditional that has caused all the problems. No doubt that is true, which makes its presence in the midst of his most mature reflections on the will in *DC* all the more puzzling. Anselm would have been better off positing a 'weak conditional,' a conditional along the lines of: "if a *telos*-relevant choice is to be made, the agent can consider the generic objects of each of the affections and can decide whether to perform a willing either in accordance only with the promptings of the affection-for-happiness, or in accordance with the promptings of the affection-for-happiness as moderated by considerations of justice." But in that case, we would be left in the position Anselm was presumably trying to avoid: having to accept a completely indeterminist, non-explanatory account of the first self-movement toward sin by the devil or any other rational creature.[66] Some philosophers and theologians find that the inexplicability of such sin is theologically apt and/or intended, in which case one may well

---

[64] As we said above, Anselm's statements to the effect that the devil knew what he should do must be interpreted as taking 'knowledge' in the sense that facts in the recesses of one's mind but not before one's mind can be understood as 'knowledge' (i.e. the first, but rejected understanding of knowledge I discussed in the Introduction to the book).

[65] Interestingly, Brown ("Some Problems," 339–341) also points out that Anselm's statements inadvertently make self-determination difficult, but he does so along different lines.

[66] Hopkins ("Anselm on Freedom," 478) claims that Anselm intended the devil's sin, and perhaps that of Adam's, to indeed be indeterminist accounts, while all other accounts are not indeterminist.

wonder why Anselm devoted so much of his writing to trying to explain such sins. [67] For those who desire some sort of rationale for any type of 'original sin' or first self-movement towards sin, such indeterminism may not suffice. The alternatives, unfortunately, are not much better. For many (and, as Schedler shrewdly points out, for Anselm) "fully knowledgeable and voluntary wrongdoing does not seem conceivable" either.[68] It would in that case remain that all initial self-movements towards sin must result from some form of negligent omission, the culpability of which is itself unclear and thus constitutes the topic of this book.[69]

When we come to chapter 7, we will see that Scotus does indeed adopt Anselmian *affectiones* in such a way as to avoid the strong conditional. In the meantime, however, it is interesting to have noted that one of the earliest, and most distinctive, thinkers on the will and its relation to the intellect could not avoid the logical implication that the first rational creature's sin must have been some form of a NO. Consequently, if NO's cannot be solved, a significant portion of Anselm's theology is undermined.

---

[67] Deme, "The 'Origin' of Evil," 173–182. See also Hopkins, "Anselm on Freedom," 479.

[68] George Schedler, "Anselm and Aquinas on the Fall of Satan: A Case Study of Retributive Punishment," *Proceedings of the American Catholic Philosophical Association* 56 (1982): 61–69 (quotation is from p. 68). Schedler does not focus on the *affectiones* as this study does but instead assumes that the devil's sin cannot be negligent. He then demonstrates that other statements Anselm makes precludes him from being able to assert the devil could have sinned given this initial assumption.

[69] How, for instance, can a non-intended, non-desired (otherwise, the agent would already be sinful) initial instance of 'not-thinking-about' be blameworthy.

CHAPTER 4

NEGLIGENT VS. NON-NEGLIGENT

A THOMISTIC DISTINCTION DIRECTING US TOWARD A SOLUTION

Along with Suárez, Aquinas is one of the only two in this study who explicitly address the problem of negligent omissions. Indeed, he devotes a whole question to the problem of negligence in general in IIa-IIae, q.54. As I have already indicated in the Introduction, however, that discussion and those that surround it are irrelevant for the purposes of this book. The discussions in that part of IIa-IIae (specifically qq. 47–56) are couched in terms of virtue (and prudence in particular). Since this book's focus is more act- (as opposed to character-) based,[1] these passages will not be discussed in this chapter.

Fortunately, some of Aquinas's discussions outside of IIa-IIae do directly relate to the problem of negligent omissions. I will accordingly focus on them. By doing so, we will ultimately arrive at the surprising conclusion that Aquinas would have to admit that the locus of culpability, and therefore of voluntariness, in NO's such as we are interested in lies in a non-negligent omission. I will further explain that this fact need not destroy the distinction between negligent and non-negligent omissions; the distinction can still be regarded as valid within Aquinas's framework. At the end of the book, I will show how the insights gained from attempting to render Aquinas consistent by means of this conclusion can be regarded as agreeable with and somewhat prescient of our own ultimate solution to the problem of NO's. Before I do any of this, I must give a brief overview of Aquinas's action theory.

I. The Structure of Human Action

A. *The Voluntary*

For Aquinas, an act is voluntary when two conditions are met: the principle of the action must be internal to the agent, and the agent must

[1] Please see the thorough discussion about the orientation of this book in the Introduction.

be able to move itself by this inner principle. This latter criterion, in turn, can only be satisfied by the agent having "some conception of an end" such that it acts "on account of the end."[2]

Describing the 'voluntary' in this way, though, appears to cause a problem for Aquinas: it seems to allow the possibility that the actions of brute animals, which have an inner principle of action and "some knowledge of the end," could also be classified as voluntary.[3] Given that Aquinas does not want to describe the actions of brute animals as 'voluntary' in the same sense as are the actions of rational agents, he proceeds to offer a distinction between *imperfectly* and *perfectly* voluntary actions. This distinction is itself further based upon different ways of having "cognition of the end," namely, "partial" and "full."[4] Knowledge of an end is to be considered 'partial' when the agent merely apprehends the end but does not recognize the end *as an end* nor think about how it may need to act in order to achieve that end.[5] The acts of agents, such as brute animals which possess only such 'partial' knowledge of the ends of their acts, can thus be called voluntary only *imperfectly*.

In contrast, an action is *perfectly* voluntary when the agent has 'full' knowledge of the end in that it recognizes the end *as an end* and moves itself purposely, through its inner principle of action, so as to attain that end. Such 'full' knowledge can be present only in agents endowed with 'reason.' Consequently, only rational beings, in contrast to brute animals, can act *perfectly* voluntarily, a notion which can be expressed by the following criterion:

> (V1) The perfectly voluntary consists of an act in which there is (a) 'full' knowledge of the end by a rational agent along with (b) an inner principle of action by which it moves itself towards that end.

---

[2] Quae vero habent notitiam finis dicuntur seipsa movere, quia in eis est principium non solum ut agant, sed etiam ut agant propter finem (*ST* Ia-IIae q.6, a.1). As already mentioned in the Introduction, all Latin text of Aquinas is from the Leonine edition found at www.corpusthomisticum.org. English translations, unless otherwise noted, are mine.

[3] ad rationem voluntarii requiritur quod principium actus sit intra, cum aliqua cognitione finis (*ST* Ia-IIae, q.6, a.2).

[4] Est autem duplex cognitio finis, perfecta scilicet, et imperfecta (ibid.). In using the terms 'partial' and 'full,' I follow the practice of the Blackfriars translation. See: St. Aquinas Aquinas, *Summa Theologicae*, ed. Blackfriars. (London: Eyre & Spottiswoode, and New York: McGraw-Hill, 1970).

[5] Imperfecta autem cognitio finis est quae in sola finis apprehensione consistit, sine hoc quod cognoscatur ratio finis, et proportio actus ad finem (ibid.).

B. *The Relation between the 'Voluntary' and the 'Will'*

This brings us to the next important point. Aquinas believes that rational creatures possess a faculty of the 'will.'[6] He further seems to hold that any action ultimately issuing from the will is to be considered voluntary. This latter claim seems to be the background assumption throughout *ST* Ia-IIae, q.6, a.4, in which he denies that any violence can be done to the will properly speaking.[7] The claim becomes almost explicit when, in the same article, his description of what an action of the will consists of seems to include the description of the voluntary I discussed above: "an act of will is … a certain inclination proceeding from an inner principle (thus satisfying condition (b) of the voluntary) with awareness (thus satisfying condition (a))."[8] If the will acts, then it must of necessity do so voluntarily.[9]

II. Voluntariness without Action and Sins of Omission

With these initial considerations out of the way, we are now ready to consider the problem of how Aquinas believes "negligent omissions (where one does not decide on and choose inaction)"[10] can be culpable and therefore sinful. For clarity's sake, let's quickly recap the puzzle surrounding NO's: the problem arises because sins must, of necessity, be

---

[6] Cf. *ST* Ia-IIae, q.6, a.2 *ad*.1: the 'will' is a "rational appetite and for that reason is not able to be in those things which lack reason." The same point seems to be made at *ST* I, q.82, a.1, *arg*.2. In that passage, Aristotle is interpreted as stating in *De Anima* iii, 9 (432b3) that "the will is in the reason." As is widely thought, Aristotle himself had no faculty psychology of the 'will' and any attribution of one to him would be technically incorrect. Nevertheless, the wording of the objection lends support to the idea that, for Aquinas, there is some connection between having a 'will' and 'reason.' Of course, showing that the possession of a 'will' requires 'reason' does not entail that all rational creatures possess a 'will' simply in virtue of the fact that they have 'reason.' Nevertheless, Aquinas does seem to assume that rational creatures do indeed have 'wills.' At the very least, it is clear that for Aquinas *some* rational creatures (sc. humans) have wills, and this concession will be enough for us to proceed.

[7] Note that violence *can* be done to "acts ordered by the will" such as those which are to be "exercised through the medium of another power." For example, I may 'will' to move my arms but, because someone much stronger than myself is restraining my arms, I may be unable to do so. In such a situation, there is violence done to my willed action (moving my arms), but there is still no violence done to my will itself or its *interior* act in that, despite outward restraints, I can still internally 'will' to move them.

[8] Et huius ratio est quia actus voluntatis nihil est aliud quam inclinatio quaedam procedens ab interiori principio cognoscente (*ST* Ia-IIae, q.6, a.4).

[9] To see the point made in similar terms, see: Stump, *Aquinas*, 285.

[10] Hause, "Voluntariness and Causality," 59.

voluntary in order to be so classed.[11] Negligent omissions, on the other hand, seem not to be voluntary by virtue of the fact that the supposed sinful inaction is not chosen or planned by the agent. If a negligent omission is not voluntary, then how can it be a sin?

In order to begin examining this issue, we need to look at *ST* Ia-IIae, q.6, a.3 in which Aquinas discusses whether there can be voluntariness without an act. He asserts that there can be voluntariness without an act via the example of a ship's pilot who caused a shipwreck when he or she did not act, but could have acted, to save the ship. Because the pilot did not act but could and should have, he or she voluntarily caused the shipwreck precisely through not acting and can thus be held responsible and blameworthy.

At first glance, this example of a shipwreck does not necessarily seem relevant to our discussion because the omission in it need not be considered negligent if that which is omitted is merely an external act and not an interior one of the will also. For example, let us suppose that the pilot knew that the ship was about to wreck but said to himself or herself something like the following: "I am not going to act so as to save this ship, even though I know that I can and should" and thus willed not to save the ship. In such a situation, it seems clear that voluntariness and blame should be ascribed to the pilot. After all, the specific Thomistic conditions for voluntariness are clearly fulfilled by the pilot in this example: an end was apprehended (for example, letting the ship wreck) and the inner principle of self-movement (the will) did the act of *willing* not to perform an external act so that the apprehended end would be achieved.[12]

---

[11] Cf. Aquinas's *De Malo* (*DM*) q.2, a.1, *arg*.2.

[12] It may be thought that this way of ascribing voluntariness to the pilot's action is problematic in that 'letting the ship wreck' could only be considered an end if it somehow appeared 'good' to the pilot (since, for Aquinas, an end can only be willed *sub ratione boni*). An alternative formulation of this scenario that may seem more reasonable is thus the following: The end of saving the ship presented itself and the pilot voluntarily willed not to take action so as to save it. The reason I prefer phrasing the 'end' as I do in the body of the chapter is that the Thomistic conditions for voluntariness (as expressed in (V1)) are fulfilled in it. In the alternative version presented in this note, on the other hand, it is difficult to understand how the act of *willing* not to take action so as to save the ship can be considered 'voluntary.' To be voluntary, the non-action would have to be willed in service to some end. It certainly could not be willed in service to the end of saving the ship, for willing not-to-take-action-so-as-to-save-the-ship is not a means toward achieving the end of saving the ship. Consequently, it would have to be willed in service of some other end. If it were willed in service to some other end, however, then such willing would not aptly be described as a willing not to take action

If this were the only point Aquinas were trying to make in this article (namely that voluntariness can happen without an *external* act as long as there is still an *internal* act of willing), this discussion would indeed have no relevance to the topic of negligent omissions. Aquinas, however, makes it clear that he intends the example of the pilot to show that there can be voluntariness when there is both a lack of an *external* act and a lack of an *internal* act such as the act of the will itself: "There is able to be voluntariness without an act. Sometimes this voluntariness occurs without an exterior act although there is an interior act. *Moreover, voluntariness can occur sometimes even without an interior act, such as when one does not will to act*" (italics mine).[13] As such, what Aquinas says here may, after all, be applicable to cases of negligent omissions in which there is no internal act (either positive or negative) of the will.

Leaving aside the further question as to whether it is plausible to assert that the pilot could have had no internal act of the will at all in such a situation,[14] this brings us to the problem as to how Aquinas thinks voluntariness can be ascribed to an agent when the agent's will performs no internal act of willing at all. For example, would not the lack of any internal act of the pilot's will in the example above imply that part of condition (b) for voluntariness (that is, that there be

so as to save the ship. Rather, it would probably better be described as a voluntary willing of *something else*, a side-effect of which is that action is not taken so as to save the ship. Such a voluntary willing would thus be related to the end of saving the ship only accidentally, a situation which entails a host of other problems that I discuss later. For this reason, therefore, I phrase the situation as I do in the text. Nevertheless, at this point of the investigation the reader need not be concerned with these details. Either formulation of the scenario is sufficient, for my only point is simply to describe a situation in which voluntariness and blame are naturally ascribed in response to a case of actual internal *willing*, and to point out that such cases are unproblematic.

[13] Et sic voluntarium potest esse absque actu, quandoque quidem absque actu exteriori, cum actu interiori, sicut cum vult non agere; aliquando autem et absque actu interiori, sicut cum non vult (*ST* Ia-IIae, q.6, a.3). The distinction is that between *vult non agere*, in which there is an act of the will, and *non vult agere*, in which there is not even an internal act of the will (*absque actu interiori*).

[14] It may seem plausible to suppose that one must have some positive act of the will through which one wills not to have a further or external act of the will when faced with such a situation. Suárez, for example, seems *somewhat* sympathetic to such a position (see his *De Vitiis et Peccatis*, disp. iii, sec. ii, n.5–6). Others deny this claim, as Scotus famously does by stating that one can simply intentionally *non velle* as opposed to positively *nilling* (cf. for example, his *Ord.* II, d.6, q.2, n.34, and *Ord.* IV, suppl., d.49, qq.9–10). This issue, however, need not detain us at present since it will ultimately have no bearing on this line of reasoning.

self-movement by means of an inner principle) is not fulfilled? And would this not further entail that the pilot's omission is *not* voluntary?

The resolution to this problem ultimately lies in the fact that Aquinas believes he has given two seemingly equivalent characterizations of the voluntary. The first characterization is the notion we have already discussed and designated as (V1).

> (V1) The perfectly voluntary consists of an act in which there is (a) 'full' knowledge of the end by a rational agent along with (b) an inner principle of action by which it moves itself towards that end.

The second characterization is derived from the following observation: since any act of the will is, by definition, self-movement through an inner principle toward an apprehended end, it follows that any act of the will is voluntary.[15] This naturally leads to what appears to be a second, equivalent characterization of the voluntary that can be expressed as:

> (V2) The perfectly voluntary consists of that which is 'from the will' (*a voluntate*)[16]

Having established that whatever proceeds 'from the will' is by definition voluntary, Aquinas can then posit a distinction between two different ways something can be 'from' something else (*ab aliquo*).[17] Something is from another *directly* when the latter causes the former by acting, while something[18] is from another *indirectly* when the former proceeds from the latter "from the fact that it does not act." For Aquinas, then, something (namely, a lack of willing) can be 'from the will' *indirectly* by virtue of the will not doing what it is its nature to do, namely perform an internal act of willing. Nevertheless, such a non-willing (as in the case of the pilot) may still be voluntary via (V2) because that non-willing is 'from the will,' albeit indirectly. And it is thus by means

---

[15] This was discussed above under the section titled "The Relation between the 'Voluntary' and the 'Will.'"

[16] Dicendum quod voluntarium dicitur quod est a voluntate (*ST* Ia-IIae, q.6, a.3).

[17] Ab aliquo autem dicitur esse aliquid dupliciter. Uno modo, directe, quod scilicet procedit ab aliquo inquantum est agens, sicut calefactio a calore. Alio modo, indirecte, ex hoc ipso quod non agit. (ibid.).

[18] I intentionally modify voluntary and involuntary of the general, unspecific term 'something' as opposed to another term so as to avoid confusion since Aquinas believes these adjectives can apply to acts and non-acts alike.

of the directly/indirectly distinction that Aquinas can assert the pilot's complete lack of an internal act of willing to be fully voluntary.[19]

At first glance, it appears that the distinction between being directly and indirectly 'from the will' does indeed help explain how a non-action of the will can be considered voluntary. The issue as to how a lack of internal willing can be voluntary, however, is still not yet solved, for the directly/indirectly distinction is applicable only in light of (V2), for only (V2) is phrased in terms of 'from the will.' By contrast, (V1), which is supposedly equivalent to and the foundation for (V2), lacks any reference to being 'from the will,' and thus the distinction cannot be applied in light of it. A lack of internal willing, then, would still seem to be non-voluntary by means of (V1), despite the possibility of such a lack being deemed voluntary by virtue of (V2). The question that arises at this point, then, is how two supposedly equivalent characterizations of the voluntary can deliver different judgments regarding a lack of internal willing.

One way to answer this question would be to say that this apparent inconsistency arose because Aquinas, after having arrived at (V2), simply worked with (V2) and reified it in such a way that he drew implications from it without checking to make sure that such implications were consistent with (V2)'s basis in (V1), thus unwittingly violating the latter. In other words, perhaps the notion of something being 'from the will' was used in a very technical, univocal sense when (V2) was derived from (V1); namely, it implied there need be a true act of the will in which there is some actual *movement* or *action* directed toward an end. After having established (V2), however, Aquinas then used 'from the

[19] It is important to note that I am discussing Aquinas's case of being indirectly from the will but supposedly voluntary as it relates to a *total* lack of an internal act of the will. If there were an internal act of the will in which the will *wills* not-to-act (*vult non agere*), there would be no problem in describing the resulting non-action as voluntary (as is discussed above.) Furthermore, there would be no problem in describing even one type of internal lack of willing as voluntary. This would occur when the will had actually *willed* not to will some action. In such a situation, the resultant non-action could still be considered to be from the will indirectly by virtue of the fact that there is a non-willing of that action. Nevertheless, it could still be considered voluntary by virtue of the fact that the non-willing would itself be from the will *directly* in that the will 'willed' this non-willing. The initial 'willing' not-to-will would be clearly voluntary because an end would be apprehended (not-to-will) and the agent would actually move itself through an inner principle to achieve this end (that is, the agent would *will* not-to-will). In the case under consideration in the body of the chapter, though, Aquinas does not hint that there is even this initial internal act of willing not-to-will. Every aspect of the case under consideration, then, must be considered as coming *indirectly* from the will, thus giving rise to the problems we are facing.

will' in an equivocal sense, one aspect of which (the indirect aspect in which there is no actual *moving* toward an end by the will) was no longer consistent with the univocal sense initially intended when (V2) was inferred from (V1). As a result, some of the deliverances of (V2) are illegitimate and should thus be subordinated to those of (V1).

I find this way of resolving our problem, however, problematic. Aside from the general unlikeliness that such a systematic thinker as Aquinas would have thus illegitimately conflated an equivocal meaning in (V2) with a univocal meaning in (V1), he seems fully aware of some of the conditions of (V1) in *arg* 3 and *ad* 3 of the article in which he develops the directly/indirectly-from-the-will distinction. *Arg* 3 asserts that there must be some 'action' in something called 'voluntary' based upon the fact that condition (a) of (V1) requires there to be knowledge of the end and of the means to attain that end and such knowledge "involves activity." Drawing upon his argumentation in the *responsio*, Aquinas replies by saying that just as there can be voluntariness without an act of the will, there can even be voluntariness without "an act of cognition."[20] Setting aside the issue of whether knowledge involves activity, this reply shows that he has gone so far as to state almost directly that something can be considered voluntary even when it apparently conflicts with condition (a) of (V1). The apparent inconsistencies between (V1) and his description of non-actions as voluntary in q.6, a.3, therefore, cannot simply be traced back to an unwitting denial of condition (b), for here he directly says that the other condition of (V1) can be violated without precluding voluntariness. If Aquinas had simply neglected the requirements of (V1), certainly this objection would have reminded him of them and he would have answered differently. As a result, it seems clear that Aquinas regards (V1) as somehow consistent with the possibilities of not-willing and even not-cognizing being described as voluntary. (Please note: His reply to this argument seems to make his position on the 'voluntary' even more problematic than originally thought since it leads us to assume that he believes either of the two conditions of (V1) can be violated without the act becoming involuntary.) And since negligent omissions are basically those omissions in which the agent just happens not to 'think' or 'have cognition of' his or her duties, and accordingly does not perform any action of the will in regard to them, this reply leaves open the possibility that

[20] The quotations in this paragraph are from the Blackfriars translation.

Aquinas believes voluntariness can be ascribed in cases of negligent omissions.

Despite Aquinas's assertion that such cases can be voluntary, it is still unclear exactly how (V1), if it is a criterion for voluntariness at all, is consistent with the asserted possibility of not-willing and not-cognizing being voluntary. Perhaps one way to reconcile (V1) with these possibilities is to say that the not-willing and the not-cognizing are due to an earlier voluntary act of willing and cognizing that are fully in accord with (V1). In order to illustrate this, let us posit the following:

> Example 1: A person is supposed to go to Mass (to use a Thomistic example of a morally required action) in an hour. Knowing that she would prefer to play chess than go to Mass, she begins playing a long, intense chess game on the internet instead of making plans to go to Mass. She does this even with the knowledge that most likely she will become so engrossed in the game that she will not think about going to Mass. It is not the case that she is necessarily intending to miss church or that she wills not-to-will to go to church. Rather, she just knows she likes chess better than Mass and wills the conditional 'if playing chess causes Mass to be missed, then so be it.' At the time to go to Mass, she is indeed so engrossed in her game that she does not even think about going; it does not cross her mind.

In this example, if we only focus on the exact moment when she was supposed to go to Mass but did not, it seems as if her not going was non-voluntary and non-culpable because she honestly, at that moment, did not think about going to Mass and consequently did not will it. Nevertheless, when the larger time frame is examined, it becomes clear that she is culpable and did, in a sense, voluntarily not-think-about, and thus not-will, going to Mass because earlier she voluntarily, in full accordance with (V1), thought about and willed to play chess knowing it may ultimately be incompatible with going to Mass. In this case, it becomes clear how an act of not-cognizing and not-willing are voluntary and consistent with (V1); they are due to earlier intentional, voluntary acts of cognizing and willing that are obviously incompatible with that which is not-willed and not-cognized.

Aquinas discusses a situation like this in *De Malo* q.2, a.1 where he is wondering whether sins of omission require an act.[21] His ultimate

[21] English translations of *De Malo* (*DM*) will be, unless otherwise noted, from: St. Thomas Aquinas, *On Evil*, trans. Jean Oesterle (Notre Dame, Indiana: University of Notre Dame Press, 1995).

answer is yes: "for omission a voluntary act is required as a cause."[22] As part of his reasoning for this conclusion, he gives an example similar to the one we just posited where somebody voluntarily wills and does something which she knows will ultimately cause her to omit doing what she ought. Aquinas says that in this type of omission, a voluntary act causes the omission and the omission is apparently culpable and voluntary in virtue of the fact that "the will is moved to" do the fully voluntary act "with foresight of the consequent omission."

If this were all that were said, it would seem as if we had solved the problem of how omissions characterized by non-willing and non-cognizing could be voluntary per (V1). They could be voluntary by virtue of the fact that in them another fully voluntary act is willed with the knowledge that such willing would, or at least could, cause the non-willing and non-cognizing that comprise the resulting omission. This resolution, however, does not help us explain how a *negligent* omission is voluntary and sinful. In the above example the omission cannot be called negligent because the voluntary act was done *with the knowledge* that it could cause the omission. The real problem remains, then, as to whether a negligent omission, where somebody "simply forgets" what she is supposed to do, can be voluntary and sinful in the Thomistic framework.[23]

In order to answer this, let us return to *DM* q.2, a.1. Aquinas posits another kind of omission which occurs when "someone engrossed in some activity, does not think about what he is bound to do" but, as opposed to Example 1, is engrossed in that activity without having had the foresight that it would cause an omission. This type of omission is indeed what we have been calling a negligent omission and can be contrasted to the previous type of omission by the following illustration:

> Example 2: A person would go to Mass, but she just happens to be playing chess at the time of Mass and going to it never occurs to her; she did not, however, plan to play chess with the knowledge that doing so may cause her to forget to go to Mass (as in Example 1).

What is important to realize here is that Aquinas makes it clear that he still regards this latter type of omission (namely, a negligent omission)

[22] ... quod ad omissionem requiritur actus voluntarius ut causa (*DM* q.2, a.1). It is worth noting that in half of this article Aquinas considers "what is required for sin as being of the essence of sin" and says that in relation to this an act is not required. We, however, are discussing the sin of negligent omission as to its *cause*, which is the topic of the other half of this article. Consequently, we will focus on that part.

[23] Cf. Hause, "Voluntariness and Causality," 61.

as voluntary and therefore sinful (given, of course, the assumption that going to Mass is morally/theologically obligatory). In other words, it is clear that Aquinas believes there are sins of negligent omission similar in structure to Example 2, although we have still yet to discover how negligent omissions can be considered voluntary given (V1).

It has been suggested to me that one way of answering this question is to attribute a sense of alternate possibilities as a requirement for voluntariness – something that was not explicitly done in either (V1) or (V2). By virtue of calling 'voluntary' an omission such as that discussed in Example 2, Aquinas supposedly implies in *DM* q.2, a.1 (so the suggestion goes) that the agent *could have* thought about her duties and thus *could have* acted with knowledge from her inner principle. In other words, this suggestion reads Aquinas as stating an agent can omit voluntarily at some time t_2 (despite not necessarily having taken special precautions at a previous time t_1) in virtue of the fact that she had the alternative possibility of thinking about her duty and fulfilling it at t_2.[24] Moreover, such a solution purportedly solves the problem of NO's. NO's can presumably be voluntary because a negligently omitting agent has an alternative possibility by virtue of the fact that she *can* think about her duty and fulfill it.

The question of the relationship between Aquinas's theory of freedom and the principle of alternative possibilities is a contentious one that cannot be solved here.[25] And neither am I taking, nor do I have to take, a stand on that issue for present purposes. First, it is not at all clear to me that *DM* q.2, a.1 implies that voluntariness requires synchronic

---

[24] Tobias Hoffmann argues that such an understanding underlies Aquinas's explanation of the devil's sin. See Hoffmann, "Aquinas and Intellectual Determinism."

[25] A significant amount of scholarship on Aquinas has been devoted to this issue. For some sampling of the literature, see: Eleonore Stump, "Intellect, Will, and the Principle of Alternate Possibilities," in *Christian Theism and the Problems of Philosophy*, ed. Michael D. Beaty (Notre Dame: University of Notre Dame Press, 1990), 254–285; Stump, *Aquinas*, chap. 9; Stump, "Aquinas's Account of Freedom; Scott MacDonald, "Practical Reasoning and Reasons-Explanations: Aquinas's Account of Reason's Role in Action," in *Aquinas's Moral Theory*, ed. Scott MacDonald (Ithaca, NY: Cornell University Press, 1998), 133–160; MacDonald, "Libertarian Account," Lee, "Relation Between Intellect and Will"; Hause, "Thomas Aquinas and the Voluntarists"; Colleen McCluskey, "Happiness and Freedom in Aquinas's Theory of Action," *Medieval Philosophy and Theology* 9 (2000): 69–90; McCluskey, "Intellective Appetite"; John H. Wright, "Human Freedom and Divine Action" in *Human and Divine Agency*, ed. F. Michael McLain and W. Mark Richardson (Lanham, New York and Oxford: University Press of America, 1999), 41–47; Thomas J. Loughran, "Aquinas, Compatibilist," in *Human and Divine Agency*, ed. F. Michael McLain and W. Mark Richardson (Lanham, New York and Oxford: University Press of America, 1999), 1–39; Kevin M. Staley, "Aquinas: Compatibilist or Libertarian?" *The Saint Anselm Journal* 2, no. 2 (2005): 73–79.

alternate possibilities in a case such as Example 2. Such a reading seems to be more a result of a prior preconception that voluntariness requires such alternative possibilities than it is a result of that particular text. More importantly, imputing alternate possibilities to the agent in Example 2 would not actually help explain anything with regard to the voluntariness of NO's. Even if Aquinas were implicitly asserting that such an agent *could have* thought about her obligation at the time of her omission in Example 2, it is still not clear *how* she could have done so. Merely asserting that there must be such an alternative possibility open to the agent is no different, and no more helpful, than simply asserting the 'think harder' solution.[26] Indeed, it may be that Aquinas did not even intend to explain *how* such an NO could be voluntary in *DM* q.2, a.1. Instead, he may have only been concerned to make it clear *that* such a NO could be voluntary.

Since our task is to determine *how* NO's can fulfill the requirements for voluntariness, we cannot simply conclude the investigation with a simple assertion of the putative existence of alternative possibilities existing at the moment of the omission. Instead, if such presence of alternative possibilities does indeed ground the voluntariness of NO's, then we must press on to ask how such alternative possibilities exist at the moment of the omission – an explanation not provided by the text of *DM* q.2, a.1. A simple assertion (whether correct or not) that voluntariness requires alternative possibilities does nothing to explain the problem with which this book is concerned. Since the NO's under discussion in this book are *ex hypothesi* blameworthy and voluntary, and if voluntariness did always require alternative possibilities, then it would be a trivial fact that NO's are voluntary by means of alternative possibilities. Such a trivial fact, though, would not lessen the puzzle of NO's. Consequently, it is best to proceed by abstracting from the issue of alternative possibilities and taking Aquinas's descriptions of voluntariness in (V1) and (V2) as they are. Given this, we can return to our earlier question of how an omission like the one in Example 2 can fulfill the conditions in (V1).

Perhaps one way of trying to answer this last question is to specify how the locus of culpability for the sin of the omission in Example 1 differs from that in Example 2. In Example 1, sinfulness seems to lie in the fact that one knew that willing to play chess ('C') might cause one

[26] See the discussion of this in the Introduction.

to omit doing 'D' (which is obligatory) and willed C anyway. In other words, culpability lies in the fact that one willed against one's better knowledge. In what we have been calling a sin of negligent omission, as exemplified in Example 2, the structure of the act is generally the same: a person wills to play chess ('C'), and willing C causes one to omit doing D (which is obligatory). The difference, though, is that in the latter, there is no foresight that willing C would cause the omission; thus, the locus of culpability in sins of negligent omission cannot lie in willing against one's better knowledge. Consequently, if there is to be culpability in negligent sins of omission, it seems that culpability, and therefore voluntariness, must lie somehow in the failure to have the foresight or knowledge that doing C precludes D. This can be stated in terms of a formal conclusion as follows:

> (C1) In sins of negligent omission, culpability seems to lie somehow in the failure to have the foresight or knowledge of the subsequent omission. It seems not to lie in willing against one's better knowledge.[27]

III. Clarification of Terminology and Concepts

Before we proceed further, it is necessary to address a terminological problem regarding "directly" and "indirectly" that arises when looking at the two accounts in *DM and ST*. In the *ST* account, the Latin terms Aquinas uses are *directe* and *indirecte*. There, for something to be from the will *directe* means that the will actually does act in a way that is concordant with (V1), (that is, an agent does perform an act of the will) while something is said to come from the will *indirecte* by virtue of the will not acting. In *DM*, omissions such as are exemplified in Examples 1 and 2 are also described in terms of being caused 'directly' and 'indirectly' respectively, but the contexts, terms, and meanings are slightly different. Here, the context is not how an omission is voluntary but how an omission is caused. The term translated as "directly" in *DM* is *per se* and is used in the context not of how something "from the will" as in *ST*, but in the context of how a separate voluntary act causes an omission. The omission is said to be caused 'directly' (*per se*) by a separate voluntary action because the voluntary act was done with the

[27] Please note that I have used the word 'seems' here because ultimately I will reject some of the implications of (C1). I will readdress (C1) specifically under the section "Possible Objections to the Argument."

foresight that it would cause the omission. Please note that in such direct, *per se* causation there is still an act coming directly (*directe*) from the will in the *ST* sense in reference to the separate voluntary act (such as willing to play chess or willing C).

On the other hand, sins of negligent omission (Example 2) are said to be caused "indirectly" (*per accidens*, not *indirecte*) in the *DM* account when a separate voluntary action causes an omission in the absence of any foresight that the omission would be thus caused. Nevertheless, it is important to note that even in this indirect causation of an omission, there is still a voluntary act springing directly (*directe*) from the will in the *ST* sense as we have seen. For example, in Example 2 the omission is indirect (*per accidens*) as a result of the agent directly (*directe*) willing to play chess without the foresight that doing such would cause her to omit going to Mass. The important point to be made is that in both sinful omissions caused directly (*per se* - Example 1) and indirectly (*per accidens* - Example 2) in the *DM* sense of the terms, there is always some action coming directly (*directe*) from the will in the *ST* sense of the term. This can be stated as an assumption with which it is obvious Aquinas is working:[28]

> (A1) In all instances of sinful omission, there is some act springing directly (*directe*) from the will (*a voluntate*), in the sense of *ST* Ia-IIae, q.6, a.3, in reference to a separate voluntary act.

IV. A Potential Resolution?

We can now try to answer the question we posed earlier. With respect to the *ST* account we wondered how Aquinas could assert that internal non-willings and non-cognitions in negligent omissions could be voluntary given that (V1) seems to call for exactly the opposite conditions for something to be called voluntary. In light of the *DM* account, it now appears as if our initial intuition was correct in that the conditions of (V1) *do* have to be satisfied for something to be called voluntary. That is, there does have to be an actual act of willing and an actual act of apprehending an end. What the *DM* account has clarified for us,

---

[28] Cf. *DM* q.2, a.1. Various statements throughout the article support this assertion. For example: Si autem consideretur id quod requiritur ad peccatum ut causa peccati, sic oportet quod ad quodlibet peccatum, etiam omissionis aliquis actus requiratur.

though, is that those actual, direct acts of willing and knowledge do not have to be directly related to the omission in question; they can be related merely indirectly (*per accidens*) in the *DM* sense of a voluntary act indirectly causing an omission. In other words, internal acts of not-willing A and not-apprehending A are voluntary not simply because it is in the power of the will to will A and of the intellect to apprehend A as the *ST* account seems to suggest. Rather, such an instance of not-knowing and not-willing can be called voluntary because the not-apprehending and not-willing of A are ultimately caused by a separate, fully voluntary act in which there is an apprehension and willing of B (even though it is performed without the knowledge that doing B will result in the not-willing and not-apprehending of A).

While the *DM* account thus suggests a way in which we can regard a negligent omission as voluntary, it nevertheless seems initially unsatisfying. To say that an omission which is unintended can be classed as voluntary just because the agent is performing a different type of act, which is fully voluntary per (V1), hardly seems justified. For instance, let us posit another example:[29]

> Example 3: An agent really plans to go see a movie tonight at 9:00 and has the time, means and money to do so. Furthermore, let us assume for the sake of argument that attending this movie is a morally obligatory action (for example, she made a promise to a friend to go). At 7:00, however, she starts writing a philosophy paper. At 8:30 while in the midst of writing, she has a breakthrough in her thinking, becomes excited, and begins typing her ideas furiously while concentrating on nothing else but the logic of her argument. When she finally finishes writing down her thoughts, she just happens to glance at the clock and notices that it is now 9:30. She then realizes she has missed her movie and becomes very upset, especially given the fact that she has plenty of time tomorrow to work on her paper! She could have easily gone to the movie tonight and finished writing down her thoughts tomorrow, if she had only not forgotten about going to the movie.

I suspect that this person would hardly call her omission of going to the movie voluntary. To the contrary, she would probably say that it was involuntary by virtue of the fact she did not plan to miss it nor did she take steps with the purpose of attempting to miss it. Indeed, it seems as

---

[29] As the reader will notice, Example 3 is largely similar to Sample 2 that is used to demonstrate Type-2 NO's in other parts of this book.

if she had even fulfilled the conditions for voluntarily planning to go to the movie: she had apprehended the end of going to the movie, and had moved herself through the intention of her will to take steps so as to see the movie (for example, she willed at 6:30 that at 8:45 she would shut off her computer, walk to the cinema, buy popcorn, and take her seat in the back row of the theater). I doubt she would take much solace in hearing that her omission could be characterized as voluntary, indirectly or not, just because she was performing a completely different act (working on her paper) that was voluntary. Working on the paper may have been voluntary, but missing the movie was not! To call this omission voluntary on account of a separate voluntary act, as suggested by *DM*, seems to be nothing more than a semantic ruse. While one may persist in *calling* such an omission voluntary, it is done so in such an extended sense that none of the characteristics, obligations, and consequences that a normal voluntary act entails apply to it. As such, it would seem that such omissions as the one here should not be able to fulfill the voluntariness requirement that is normally required for something to count as a sin.

Despite these observations, it is clear from *DM* that Aquinas believes negligent omissions, such as in Example 3, *are* voluntary such that sin can be imputed to the omitting agent. Furthermore, I believe that something similar to the rationale offered above in regard to Example 3 does play a role in his asserting such. Nevertheless, as it now stands the explanation is unsatisfactory and must be supplemented by many details if it is to be at all credible. In order to do this, let us look again at Example 3. It seems that the reason the agent missed the movie was a lack of knowledge, lack of intellectual awareness, or *ignorance* of what time it was at the exact moment when she should have quit writing her paper and left her desk to go to the movie. If she had only known the time, she would have quit writing and gone to the movie. This leads us to turn to Aquinas's discussion of 'ignorance as a cause of sin' in order to explore how a sin of negligent omission, which happens when the omitted action just does not even come to mind, is caused.

V. Ignorance as the Cause of Sin

In both *DM* q.3, a.6 and *ST* Ia-IIae, q.76, a.1, Aquinas states that ignorance can be a cause of sin in the sense that it removes the knowledge that would otherwise be an impediment to sin.[30] This is consistent with our description of the causes of the sin in Example 3. The agent was deprived of the knowledge of the time when it was time to go. Had she not been deprived of this knowledge, the omission would have been prevented (for she then would have known that it was time to go when it was indeed time to go [for example, 8:45] and she would have gone). As a result, her sin of omitting to go to the movie can be sketched as follows: (i) a voluntary act (writing her paper) directly from her will (ii) caused a (temporal?) ignorance of the time, which (iii) served as the cause of her omission of attending the movie.

Although this observation broadens our description of the genesis of her supposed sin, the problem does not lie in simply finding a cause for her not-going to the movie. What is needed in order to ascribe culpability for the sin is some voluntariness in the cause, a voluntariness that is more immediately related to the omission than that of the voluntariness we observed in *DM* q. 2, a.1 where an otherwise unrelated act, which indirectly causes the omission, is voluntary.

Perhaps Aquinas may be able to assert that a negligent omission is voluntary if the ignorance, which is the cause of the omission, is itself somehow voluntary and not merely an unintended byproduct of a separate voluntary act. In other words, as it stands now, the voluntariness of (i) unintentionally causes (ii) which, in turn, leads to (iii). If we could ascribe immediate voluntariness to (ii) in isolation from (i), however, then (iii) could be considered voluntary given the close and obvious causal connection between (ii) and (iii). Furthermore, if (ii) is going to be the locus of the voluntariness of (iii), and if (iii) can be considered a sin as directly following from (ii), then it stands to reason that the ignorance expressed in (ii) may itself also be sinful. Consequently, we are left to consider whether ignorance itself can be a sin.

In *ST* Ia-IIae, q.76, a.2 and *DM* q.3, a.7, Aquinas begins stating that ignorance can be a sin by distinguishing between ignorance (*ignorantia*) and not-knowing or nescience (*nescientia*). Nescience occurs

---

[30] For example, *DM* q.3, a.6: Ignorantia ergo, quae huiusmodi scientiam tollit, recte dicitur esse causa peccati sicut removens prohibens. It is worth mentioning that Aquinas, drawing upon Aristotle's discussion of movers in the *Physics*, calls this type of cause an indirect (*per accidens*) cause as opposed to a direct (*per se*) cause. However, the context and connotation of direct and indirect are different here from the use of those terms in the passages considered earlier and are not pertinent to our discussion. Hence, I have refrained from discussing this distinction with regard to ignorance so as to not needlessly complicate the topic.

simply when someone does not have knowledge. An omission resulting from it is not considered sinful. In contrast, ignorance implies an absence of knowledge "which a person is designed by nature to have."[31] Only the latter can be considered a sin, which means it must therefore also be voluntary "since it is of the nature of sin that it is voluntary."[32] Nevertheless, not all ignorance is sinful. Aquinas recognizes one class of ignorance as "invincible" and thus not voluntary.[33] Aquinas's thought is that there are cases in which one is, by nature, supposed to have certain knowledge (which means it cannot be classified as nescience) but, because of circumstances completely outside of one's control, she has been unable ever to attain that knowledge, thus rendering the ignorance involuntary and sinless.[34] Therefore, only in those cases in which one is supposed to have knowledge and has been able to attain such knowledge are voluntariness and sin to be imputed to the ignorant agent.

These observations, though, lead us to the need to specify exactly in what way such sinful ignorance is voluntary per (V1). Aquinas makes it clear that the voluntariness involved in a case of sinful ignorance

---

[31] Ignorantia nihil est aliud quam carere scientia quam qui natus est habere (*DM*, q.3, a.7).

[32] Quod cum de ratione peccati sit quod sit voluntarium (*DM*, q.3, a.8). It should be pointed out that this distinction between *nescientia* and *ignorantia* is not without its problems due to the vagueness of the concept 'designed by nature to have.' If agents are only 'designed by nature to have' knowledge of general things such as the general precepts of the divine law, then it seems as if very few cases of ignorance which would normally be regarded as blameworthy (such as, say, the ignorance that this book should be turned in by such and such a date) would not be. Nevertheless, we need not pursue these issues further for the purposes of this chapter.

[33] Cf. *DM* q.3, a.8 and *ST* Ia-IIae, q.76, a.3.

[34] While I have given an interpretation of how invincible ignorance differs from nescience, it is still possible to question whether it is actually different. This is based upon the intuition that it is inconsistent to say that one is supposed to have a piece of knowledge while at the same time asserting that it is impossible for a person ever to have acquired this piece of knowledge. Indeed, it seems possible that Aquinas himself may have conflated the two concepts. This becomes especially apparent in *ST* q.76. After introducing the distinction in a.2, he proceeds in a.3 to discuss ignorance alone and says it can be voluntary when one is not required to have some piece of knowledge, a description which sounds strikingly similar to the way nescience is described in a.2. This inconsistency may perhaps be avoided if Aquinas is operating with an idea of obstructable natures. In this case, a person would be 'designed by nature' to know something simply in virtue, say, of being a human being but would be unable to know it because of circumstances outside of his or her control (for example, if he or she were born with a brain lesion). Being of a human nature would fulfill the 'apt by nature' requirement, while the brain lesion would nevertheless be a prohibiting circumstance outside of one's control. There is no need to resolve this issue here since all we need presently to focus upon is ignorance of the type that is voluntary.

actually precedes the ignorance: "... ignorance can take away the subsequent but not the preceding voluntariness."[35] It is clear, then, that the agent, at a preceding moment, must have done a voluntary act that immediately prevented her from having the knowledge she should have had.[36]

Perhaps what Aquinas has in mind here is the idea that such ignorance is voluntary per (V1) in virtue of the fact that it is directly willed (as in the case of an agent seeing the end of being ignorant and taking steps so as to become ignorant). While such a description of ignorance as voluntary would impinge directly on step (ii), it is not relevant to sins of *negligent* omission like Example 3 because in these latter sins the ignorance is not directly willed. What we need is an ignorance that is not desired or willed but nevertheless voluntary. (Furthermore, please note that it is not enough to say simply that the ignorance itself may be considered voluntary simply in light of the fact that it is a result of another willed voluntary act.[37] If this were the response, then we would be left right back where we began in Example 3. Namely, we would be left wondering whether calling the ignorance voluntary in virtue of another voluntary act is simply a semantic ruse similar to calling the resultant omission voluntary in virtue of another voluntary act.

---

[35] quod ignorantia voluntarium sequens tollere potest, non autem voluntarium precedens (*DM*, q.3, a.8).

[36] It has been objected that Aquinas's discussion of ignorance as a cause of sin is irrelevant to the problem of NO's. The objection is based upon Aquinas's *De Veritate* q.8, a.6, *ad* 7 in which Aquinas refers to knowledge *in potentia essentiali* (characterizing a not-yet-learned item of knowledge) and *in potentia accidentali* (characterizing knowledge once learned but not currently being considered). According to the objection, when Aquinas is discussing ignorance, he only has in mind ignorance that corresponds to knowledge *in potentia essentiali* whereas, in a NO, the agent supposedly does have knowledge but is merely not adverting to it, thus making it *in potentia accidentali*.

The distinction between these two types of knowledge *in potentia* will be discussed later. For now, I simply want to claim that the objection does not hold. The texts of *DM* q.3, a.6 and *ST* Ia-IIae, q.76, a.1 do not explicitly indicate that Aquinas has in mind only knowledge *in potentia essentiali*. But even if he does only have that concept in mind, that does not mean those texts are irrelevant to NO's. The type of ignorance ultimately relevant to a NO could be characterized as knowledge *in potentia essentiali*. For the ignorance ultimately at the root of a NO is not ignorance of one's obligations, but rather ignorance of the fact that it is *now* TEF. And *that* piece of knowledge, namely, the knowledge that "It is now time for me to fulfill my obligation," given the temporal indexical in it, cannot be learned prior to the NO. Such knowledge, therefore, could conceivably be considered to be *in potentia essentiali* so far as the agent is concerned. And if so, then these texts are relevant. See also my discussion of ignorance and non-consideration in the Introduction.

[37] Cf. *DM* q.3, a.8.

In other words, such a response would not directly fulfill our requirement of addressing step (ii) in isolation from step (i).[38])

Another way in which Aquinas explains how ignorance can be voluntary does impinge on step (ii) and is more pertinent to our investigation of sins of negligent omission. He says ignorance can be called voluntary when "a person does not make an effort to know, and this is ignorance from negligence."[39] Consequently, the ignorance involved in a negligent omission is itself a negligent, but voluntary, ignorance. It is clear by the way the contrast has been drawn between the various types of ignorance that Aquinas does not believe that in negligent ignorance the ignorance is directly willed. A person negligently ignorant does *not* decide that she wants to be ignorant and take steps to accomplish that. Rather, negligent ignorance occurs when an agent "fails to apply his mind to know those things he ought to know."[40] Aquinas's example is

---

[38] Here in *DM* q.3, a.8, Aquinas discusses another way the ignorance could be considered voluntary: it could be voluntary in virtue of the fact that someone, as opposed to taking a separate action that causes ignorance, does not take an action which would otherwise prevent the ignorance. This description of ignorance as voluntary, though, does not help our investigation for it forces us to ask why the person did not perform the act so as to prevent ignorance. If he did not perform the act with the purpose of causing the ignorance, then the ignorance is, in a sense, intended and as such is irrelevant to sins of negligent omission. If he willed not to perform the act without the knowledge that such refraining from action would cause the subsequent ignorance, then the whole process of not-performing-the-action itself becomes a negligent omission and we would be back where we started. Namely, we would be left asking what is the cause of the initial lack of knowledge or ignorance of the fact that not performing the act would cause the subsequent ignorance. In other words, explaining ignorance in this latter way sets up a non-explanatory regress.

[39] Secundo ignorantia dicitur voluntaria indirecte quia non adhibet studium ad cognoscendum; et haec est ignorantia negligentiae (*DM* q.3, a.8). Similar to the objection noted above in n.36, it has been objected that this discussion of negligent ignorance is irrelevant to our problem of NO's. The objection is again based on the claim that Aquinas has in mind not simply the non-consideration of some piece of knowledge that one possesses, but rather the non-possession (due to negligence) of some piece of possible knowledge that one has never learned in the first place. The response is similar to that given in n.36. The agent in Example 3, for instance, has not yet learned that "It is *now* time for me to stop writing and go to the movie." The ignorance involved in a NO is not ignorance of an obligation per se. Instead, it can be regarded as an ignorance that it is now time to fulfill some obligation. Indeed, that is one piece of knowledge that a negligently omitting agent, by definition, lacks (otherwise, she would not negligently omit). Therefore, objections that claim "Aquinas's discussions of ignorance cannot be applied to NO's because in a NO, an agent has at least learned her obligation" cannot be sustained; such objections underestimate the different potential pieces of knowledge that must be known and adverted to in order to avoid a NO. See also my discussion of ignorance and non-consideration in the Introduction.

[40] Si non applicet animum ad cognoscendum ea quae cognoscere debet (*DM* q.3, a.8.).

the law. Everyone ought to know the law; hence, anyone who does not take the necessary steps to learn the law is voluntarily negligent. This description of negligence, however, assumes that the agent *knows*, at the very least, that she ought to know the law. Otherwise, it would be a case of invincible ignorance which, as we have seen, is involuntary and therefore non-sinful.

In order to explore this latter point, let us posit an admittedly extreme but apt example:

> Example 4: A person is born into a society structured by laws.[41] Nevertheless, this person is extremely sheltered by her parents; she is never allowed out of her house, to watch television, to read newspapers, or to listen to the radio. She has absolutely no contact with the outside world. Furthermore, her parents have never told her anything about society, its structure, or its laws. One day, she just happens to leave home and wanders into a grocery store. Hungry, she sees an apple, picks it up, walks out of the store and begins eating without paying for it just as she would do at her parents' house.

While the agent in Example 4 may have broken a law, it is difficult to characterize her breaking of the law as voluntary. She did not know there was such a thing as shoplifting and that it is wrong. Furthermore (and more pertinent to the present point), it would be difficult to say her ignorance of the law of shoplifting was voluntarily negligent simply because she did not apply herself to learning about the law and which actions were acceptable and unacceptable under it. She did not even know that such a thing as a law existed! How, then, could she have applied herself to know about it? She would have first had to have known that there is such a thing as a law and that she is obliged to know about it. As the example now stands, her ignorance would most appropriately be called invincible, not negligent, for there was no way for her to have known what things she ought to try to know.

The point being made is that even in negligent ignorance, some knowledge is required; namely, the knowledge that one is obliged to know something! In order for there to be negligent ignorance, there must have been some point at which the agent knew and was cognizant of the fact that she should know something and, in spite of

[41] The context makes it appear as if Aquinas is referring to societal laws. Even if he is not, the example is sufficient to make my point.

this knowledge, decided to do something other than learn the things she should.[42] Thus, we discover another conclusion:

> (C2) Negligent ignorance requires that there must be some time when the agent actually, actively knew that she should attempt to know those things of which she is now negligently ignorant of.

This observation, though, just pushes the issue back one step further. Namely, how do we explain that a person *knows* that she should know something, yet does not take steps so as to know it?

To answer this question, we need first to return to Example 3 and diagram the agent's omission of going to the movie (while still assuming that attending the movie is a morally obligatory act) in light of what we have now learned about negligent omissions.

> (1) The agent omitted going to the movie.
> (2) This omission was due to her ignorance of the time at 8:45. This is the time when, had she been cognizant of it, she would have quit writing her paper to attend the movie.
> (3) Since the ignorance was the cause of her omitting to attend the movie, if her omission is to be called negligent, so her ignorance is to be called negligent (cf. our discussion above regarding *DM*, q.3, a.8).
> (4) Ignorance is negligent when one does not apply one's mind to know that which one should know.
> (5) In this case, step (4) would mean that she did not apply herself in some way so that she would be certain that, at 8:45, she would know that it is in fact 8:45 and would not be ignorant of that fact.
> (6) Given (C2), the agent must have *known*, at some time, that she should apply herself so as to be certain that, at 8:45, she would indeed know that it was 8:45. For example, she may have known that she should take steps such as set an alarm clock so that at 8:45 she would not be ignorant that it was 8:45.
> (7) Despite the knowledge that she should take some steps, such as set an alarm clock, to prevent her ignorance of the time at 8:45, she omitted taking any such step.

It is clear that the real, ultimate locus of responsibility in this sin of negligently omitting to go to the movie lies in (7). The question, though, is how do we explain the fact that she did not act in (7) so as to prevent

[42] Please note that this conclusion stands even if the above example were to be objected to on the basis that a 'divine law' is in some way or other 'stamped on all hearts' preventing her from being invincibly ignorant. In fact, this objection would support my ultimate point that, for culpability, knowledge must, somewhere along the way, be present.

the subsequent ignorance of the time when the clock strikes 8:45. In response, let us point out that the failure to act in (7) is itself an omission in virtue of the fact that she omitted to take steps so as to make sure she would have the knowledge she should have by which she could avoid the subsequent negligent ignorance. Namely, she omitted acting so as to insure she would not be ignorant of the time at 8:45. In addition, since this subsequent negligent ignorance of the time would lead to the sin of omitting going to the movie (still assuming, of course, that going to the movie is a morally obligatory act), the omission in (7) is a *sin* of omission. Furthermore, in accordance with (C2), because the ignorance involved in omitting going to the movie must be negligent and not invincible, we must assume that the agent in (7) of necessity *knew* that she should apply herself so that she would know what she should know at the time that she should know it. In other words, she knew that she should make sure she was not ignorant of the time when the clock struck 8:45. It was with the knowledge of what she should do that she refrained from doing that which she should do. But why would she refrain from acting in spite of having that knowledge?

To answer this, we need first to recognize that in Example 3 the agent did not directly will the omission in (7). Indeed, since we are assuming that the omission in this case is sinful,[43] the omission cannot directly be willed. This is based on *DM* q.2, a.1 where Aquinas makes it clear that such a sinful omission cannot be directly willed because "non-being and evil are contrary to the intention and the will."[44] Consequently, and in full accord with what we observed earlier in *DM* q.2, a.1 and in (A1), the omission must be the result of her willing something else which caused the omission. For instance, she may have willed to continue taking her shower instead of pausing her shower in order to set her alarm. If so, it is important to realize that she willed to continue taking her shower *with the knowledge* that her taking this shower was causing her to omit, at least for the time being, setting her alarm or taking other such steps.

---

[43] Recall that for the sake of this chapter, we ascribed a moral obligation to attend the movie. Therefore, the omission of going to the movie and of not taking steps so as not to be ignorant of the time at which it is necessary to go to the movie are sinful.

[44] quia non ens et malum est praeter intentionem (*DM* q.2, a.1). No doubt this assertion is further based on Aquinas's assumption that all things are willed *sub ratione boni* and that there is no *bonum* in an omission *per se*.

Characterizing her omission in (7) in this way, though, is similar to the way we saw Aquinas characterize a sin of omission caused *directly* (*per se*) by a voluntary act, for in (7) her "will is moved to something positive [for example, taking a shower] with foresight of a consequent omission [she knew taking the shower was preventing her from setting the alarm]." The problem is that a sin of negligent omission, such as Example 3 is intended to illustrate, is supposed to be a case where the sin is caused by a voluntary act of the will not directly (*per se*), but rather indirectly (*per accidens*). What our investigation is beginning to show, though, is that just as (7) is the ultimate cause for (1), so also in cases where there is a negligent sin of omission, the *ultimate* cause of the sin would have to be traced, in a Thomistic framework, to a voluntary act of the will that is a *per se*, not a *per accidens*, cause. Consequently, every sin of negligent omission should ultimately be able to be traced back to an action of the will which directly (*per se*) causes an omission (although it is a separate omission) as discussed in *DM* q.2, a.1. This can be demonstrated by the following:

> (8) Any sin of negligent omission requires negligent ignorance, for a negligent omission occurs just when something which one should do just happens not to come to mind.
> (9) Ignorance, if it is to be called negligent, requires at least the knowledge that one should apply oneself to gain the other knowledge of which one is in danger of being ignorant of (per (C2)).
> (10) The failure to acquire the knowledge that one knows one should acquire is itself a sin of omission.
> (11) This sin of omission, then, is committed with the knowledge that one is omitting the act of acquiring such knowledge.
> (12) Since there is the knowledge that one should takes steps so as to prevent the subsequent ignorance, the sin of omitting to take such steps must be characterized as a sin of omission coming directly (*per se*) from a voluntary act, not indirectly (*per accidens*) as a sin of negligent omission is said to, per *DM* q.2, a.1
> (13) Consequently, every negligent sin of omission has its ultimate cause in another sin of omission which is *not* negligent.

These observations help us resolve a puzzle we had before. We wondered earlier how, in light of *ST* Ia-IIae, q.6, a.3, the absence of even an internal act of the will could be called voluntary in light of (V1). We found an initial answer based upon the account in *DM* q.2, a.1 and the accompanying (A1). Namely, our answer was that such lacks of action and knowledge are called voluntary in virtue of another action which is voluntary and in full accord with (V1). We then pointed out, though, that such a resolution was unsatisfying and seemed to be nothing more than a semantic ruse because, while voluntariness perhaps could be ascribed to the incompatible act, it was still difficult to ascribe voluntariness directly to the omission; the subsequent omission seemed not to have been foreseen, so how could it be considered truly voluntary? We posited Example 3 in order to demonstrate this. Now, however, in light of (C2) and (8) - (13), we can posit the following possible resolution on behalf Aquinas that is a little more satisfying and seems less like a play on words.

The ignorance involved in a sin of negligent omission is itself a sin of omission and it is not caused by a voluntary act *indirectly*, but *directly*, because the agent knows that she should apply herself to avoid the subsequent ignorance but does something else with the foresight that doing so will cause her to omit taking actions so as to prevent that ignorance. Since there is no problem ascribing voluntariness to omissions which are caused by voluntary acts directly (*per se*), then there is no problem in ascribing voluntariness to the subsequent negligent ignorance and therefore also to the accompanying negligent omission.[45]

[45] The approach outlined in this chapter seems to me to help complete Hause's suggestions and make up for potential deficiencies. Hause's general suggestion ("Voluntariness and Causality," 63–66) for asserting that negligent omissions can be voluntary appears to be the argument that the first precepts of the moral law are imprinted naturally upon on all persons as "*directive*" and the rest can be figured out with a little reflection. Because human actions are planned, if an agent makes plans while ignoring what the imprinted moral law and its easily-drawn inferences *direct* one to do, the omission of an act which is directed by this law is voluntary and imputable: "this failure or fault is imputable to her as a planning agent." Apparently his picture is that humans, while making plans, always have the moral law, in a sense, 'whispering in their ears' and saying something like "you know you should consult me when making these plans so as not to overlook something you are supposed to do." So far as I can tell, Hause does not explain how someone could thus ignore the moral law whispering in the ear. In light of what we have said, though, we can make more sense out of Hause's suggestion. Someone may be able to ignore the whispering by virtue of the fact that they will something else with the foresight of the consequent omission of listening to the whispering. In other words, the omission of listening to the whispering could itself be a sin of omission analogous to the sin of negligent ignorance, and it would be a sin of omission caused by another voluntary act directly (*per se*) in accord with the account in *DM* q.2, a.1. His proposal could be restated in such a way as to assert that every sin of negligent omission ultimately stems from the sin of knowing that one should listen to the moral law and *non-negligently* omitting to do so. Consequently, Hause's suggestion could be conceived as compatible with our own. Of course, there are ways to challenge Hause's proposal. For example, it may be possible to challenge the idea that the moral law is always 'whispering in the ear' (if that indeed is his picture), in which case,

This leads us, though, to another problem. It appears as if we have discovered that there is truly no such thing as a sin of negligent omission stemming from the will *per accidens*. The cause of an omission in what appears to be a sin of negligent omission can ultimately be traced back to an omission that is caused by a voluntary act directly (*per se*). It seems as if Aquinas has invented a category that ultimately has very little explanatory power since, in the end, the cause of a negligent omission is a type of non-negligent omission and the validity of (C1) is thus denied. Why did Aquinas not just simply assert that all sins of omission are caused by voluntary acts of the will directly and thus avoid the problems we have been dealing with in this chapter? Before I attempt to answer this question, let me first explore possible objections, made in support of (C1), to the notion that a negligent omission does not differ from other sins of omission insofar as the locus of culpability is concerned.

VI. Possible Objections to the Argument

As the argument stands, it seems as if I have simply asserted that a sin of negligent omission is really just a sin of non-negligent omission in disguise, so to speak. Is there not, however, still a real, qualitative difference between the omission in Example 3 and that in, say, Example 1?

For example, it could be objected that Example 3 differs from Example 1 in that the locus of culpability nevertheless seems to differ in them, and this in full accordance with (C1). In Example 3, the agent did *not* realize that writing her paper would so engross her so as to cause her to omit going to the movies, or that continuing to take her shower would cause her to forget to set her alarm, whereas in Example 1 the agent *was* fully aware that her addiction to chess is so engrossing that it may very well cause her to omit attending church. In other words, in Example 3 the action of writing the paper was willed *without* "foresight of the consequent omission" of going to the movie as opposed to the situation in Example 1. Given (C1), the locus of responsibility in

the explanation of some sins of negligent omission would be more difficult. These issues, however, are outside the scope of this chapter. My point in this note is merely to show how the schema presented in this chapter is consistent with, and can add to, Hause's own proposal. For a discussion related to this suggestion, see: Robert Pasnau, *Thomas Aquinas on Human Nature* (Cambridge, UK: Cambridge University Press, 2002), 244, 442 n. 14.

Example 3 would lie in lacking that positive foresight, whereas in Example 1 the locus would be in willing against one's better knowledge. Is it not possible, then, to distinguish these two types of sin simply based upon this difference of locus of culpability as outlined in (C1)?

I believe that it is because Aquinas *did* recognize a difference between these two types of situations that he made the distinctions he did. It must be remembered, though, that the putative 'lack of foresight that the consequent omission would happen' in a negligent omission cannot be classified as a case of invincible ignorance.[46] If it were so classified, the omission would be completely excused – a result unacceptable to Aquinas since he clearly thinks an agent can be held responsible in cases of negligent omission where there is such a lack of foresight.[47] Consequently, if we are to say that sins of negligent omission differ from other sins of omission because their loci of responsibility are different (as (C1) seems to indicate), we will have to find a way to ascribe culpability to a lack of foresight without appealing ultimately to a sin of non-negligent omission.

How can a lack of foresight, however, be voluntary to the extent that culpability can be ascribed to it? Since lacking foresight is a type of ignorance, one way to ascribe voluntariness to it might be through a means similar to the way we just saw in which ignorance can be voluntary. In other words, the lack of foresight could ultimately be traced back to being caused by a direct voluntary act being willed with the knowledge that willing such an act may result in the lack of foresight that one knows one should obtain. If this were how we were to answer the question, though, we would simply be positing another causal act merely one step back in which there *is indeed* foresight of the consequent omission. As a result, we would be led once again to our conclusion above, namely that there would be ultimately no difference between omissions being caused by the will *per se* and omissions being caused by the will *per accidens* (as is the case in negligent sins of

[46] Please note that this ignorance here is a different ignorance than that which applies to not knowing that it was 8:45 when it was indeed 8:45 and time to go to the movie. Nevertheless, were this type of ignorance consisting of a lack of foresight to be invincible, the agent would still apparently have been completely excused from willing the incompatible act which caused the omission, just as she would have been excused from the omission if the ignorance of the time at 8:45 were invincible, because there was no way for her to know that willing such a thing is incompatible with the omitted act.

[47] Cf. *DM* q.3, a.8.

omission) as to their ultimate cause because all omissions could ultimately be traced back to *per se* causes. Hence, (C1) would still seem to fail as a valid means by which to distinguish sins of negligent omission from other types of sinful omissions.

VII. A Possible Solution

Here I would like to offer one possibility that may help Aquinas assert the voluntariness of a 'lack of foresight' and thus support the distinction between negligent and non-negligent omissions as asserted in (C1). We noted at the very beginning that Aquinas states there is such a thing as an imperfectly voluntary act.[48] This, he says, occurs in brute animals that only partially apprehend the end. An end is fully apprehended when (1) the end itself is apprehended, and (2) the end is viewed as attainable by some means or other (which, in turn, prompts deliberation about what those specific means may be). On the other hand, partial knowledge of the end occurs "when the end having been apprehended, the end is moved toward immediately without deliberation." The animal perceives the end, but does not think about how that end is to be achieved through means.[49]

Perhaps one could offer the possibility that in sins of negligent omission in which there is a 'lack of foresight of the consequent omission' something similar takes place. Let us return one last time to Example 3. The agent's end of attending the movie was apprehended by her. However, in light of *ST* Ia-IIae, q.6, a.2, perhaps we could regard her as having only partially apprehended the end in that she *did not adequately perceive the means* needed for her to attain that end (that is, she failed condition (2) of apprehending an end). In this case, 'lack of foresight of an omission' could thus be an expression of the fact that she did not fully apprehend that accomplishing the end required certain necessary means.

---

[48] Perfecta quidem finis cognitio est quando non solum apprehenditur res quae est finis sed etiam cognoscitur ratio finis, et proportio eius quod ordinatur in finem ad ipsum … Imperfectam autem cognitionem finis sequitur voluntarium secundum rationem imperfectam, prout scilicet apprehendens finem non deliberat, sed subito movetur in ipsum (*ST* Ia-IIae, q.6, a.2). The translation is mine. However, use of the terms "partial" and "full" derives from the Blackfriars translation.

[49] Cf. also Aquinas's *De Veritate* q.24, aa.1–2.

Such means may have included not merely planning to set the alarm when she got out of the shower, for she could have easily forgotten to do that even if she had planned to, just as she forgot to go to the movie as she had planned to. Perhaps in her particular case the correct means toward that end would have been to get out of the shower and set her alarm because she is the type of person who may forget to set the alarm if she waits until she gets out of the shower. Or, alternatively, perhaps the proper means that should have been taken in her case was for her to repeat over and over "set my alarm for 8:45, set my alarm for 8:45" and so on until she got out of the shower and actually set it, so that she did not forget to do so in the intervening time. The fact that she did not think about and act upon these or other means needed to ensure that she did not omit going to the movies could be viewed as somehow equivalent to a 'lack of foresight' of the consequent omission in the absence of those means and could be interpreted (along the lines of q.6, a.3) as her having only partial apprehension of the end. And just as the actions of brute animals can be called voluntary with only a partial apprehension of the end, so can her omission be called voluntary because of her partial apprehension, although it can thus be called voluntary only "imperfectly."[50] In this case, the difference between sins of negligent and non-negligent omission asserted in (C1) might still stand because the responsibility for her omission in this would be because of the 'lack of foresight' of the necessary means, and this lack of foresight would be voluntary in some sense.

This solution does have some intuitive appeal, largely because it accords well with the following Thomistic belief: Since ignorance typically lessens the severity of sin,[51] and since in sins of negligent omission there is (at least) some ignorance of the subsequent omission, sins of negligent omission are typically less sinful than sins of non-negligent omission. Certainly, by stating that a negligent omission is voluntary only imperfectly, we have found a way in which culpability for such omissions may be lessened, for it would seem that the less voluntariness there is, the less culpability there can be. The above proposal to retain (C1), therefore, seems consistent with the Thomistic framework.

---

[50] Ibid.

[51] Cf. *ST* Ia-IIae, q.76, a.4

Upon closer examination, though, it becomes clear that Aquinas could not accept this proposal that sins of negligent omission can be distinguished by (C1) through an appeal to voluntariness being diminished in the way just described. The way voluntariness is diminished in the current proposal is that it is diminished from a state of "perfect" to a state of "imperfect" voluntariness. Aquinas, however, states in *ad* 3 of q.6, a.2 that "Praise and blame follow upon acts that are voluntary according to the perfect sense of voluntary"[52] Any omission that is to be considered a sin, as negligent omissions apparently can be, must therefore be voluntary in the 'perfect' sense; an attempt to retain voluntariness in sins of negligent omission by likening that voluntariness to those of brute animals must fail. Consequently, the argument made in support of (C1) fails, and our main proposal still stands: in every sin of negligent omission, the voluntariness and culpability present must ultimately be traced back to a separate sin of non-negligent omission.[53]

---

[52] Ad tertium dicendum quod laus et vituperium consequuntur actum voluntarium secundum perfectam voluntarii rationem; qualis non invenitur in brutis (*ST* Ia-IIae, q.6, a.2, *ad* 3).

[53] It has been suggested that I am wrong in rejecting this possible solution. The suggestion goes as follows: There is a form of imperfect voluntariness to which praise and blame do apply – the form according to which agents act from routine without deliberating about their actions (such as brushing their teeth) although they *could* deliberate about those actions. Praise and blame could attach to this so-called 'privative' (as opposed to 'negative') sense of imperfect voluntariness and *ST* Ia-IIae, q.6, a.2 *ad* 3 should be read as allowing this possibility. Moreover, doing so would supposedly solve the problem of NO's. For example, suppose somebody tripped and needed help from one brushing his teeth. The one brushing his teeth, however, did not help but continued brushing his teeth without thinking about whether he should continue this routine activity. The one brushing his teeth could be blamed for neglecting to help and continuing to brush his teeth because, although he did not deliberate about continuing to brush his teeth, he *could* have reconsidered brushing his teeth in light of the person tripping. In this case, his privative imperfectly voluntary act of brushing his teeth would be blameworthy.

There are many problematic aspects with this suggestion. First, *ST* Ia-IIae, q.6, a.2 *ad* 3 does not warrant the attachment of praise and blame to privative imperfectly voluntary acts; the latter category is not even mentioned. Nor is there any reason, based upon the surrounding text, to 'read' it as doing so. Moreover, more would need to be said regarding the sense of 'could' when it is said that agents are not deliberating about their routine actions but they 'could' deliberate. Suppose the idea is that he 'could' deliberate because his seeing the person trip prompts him to reconsider whether he should continue brushing his teeth or not. In this case, the subsequent failure to help the tripped person would not constitute a NO in the sense under question in this book. He may be 'neglecting' to help the person in one sense of the word 'neglect,' but he would not be

VIII. Final Resolution

Despite the failure to ascribe voluntariness to sins of negligent omission without ultimately having to appeal to a sin of non-negligent omission, the discussion of different levels of sinfulness perhaps helps provide an answer to a question I posed earlier, namely: Why did Aquinas not just simply assert that all sins of omission are caused by voluntary acts of the will directly without positing a category of negligent omission and thus avoid the problems we have been dealing with in this chapter? The answer lies in his desire to ascribe different levels of culpability based on the amount of ignorance present in the omission.

In order to explain this, let me first point out that he could not maintain the distinction between negligent and non-negligent omissions simply by stating that negligent omissions are non-culpable. For instance, consider his example of a helmsman of a ship in *ST* Ia-IIae, q.6, a.3. If he were to hold that negligent omissions are non-culpable, he would be forced to say that a helmsman to whom the idea of saving the ship just happened not to come to mind is not culpable. Nobody, including Aquinas, would say that. It is the helmsman's job to guide the ship safely. It is his or her responsibility that the idea of saving the ship *does indeed* come to mind. Consequently, Aquinas has to find some way to describe negligent omissions as voluntary and culpable; otherwise, we are left in counterintuitive situations such as excusing this helmsman completely.

On the other hand, Aquinas (along with most persons, I suspect) recognizes some difference between a helmsman to whom the idea of saving the ship *just simply* does not come to mind, and a helmsman

---

neglecting to fulfill an obligation in the sense that it did not come to mind. His seeing the person trip and being prompted to consider whether he should help or not constitutes an awareness of the situation. His subsequent failure to help would then be either a result of some sort of malice (he did not want to help) or miscalculation (he did not think the person needed help such that he should stop his routine). In either case, the omission to help (even if it is blameworthy) would not be a true NO. Suppose alternatively that the idea is that he 'could' deliberate about continuing his routine without having been prompted to reconsider whether to continue brushing his teeth. In this case, it is unclear what is meant by the claim that he 'could,' in the here and now, reconsider his routine. To simply assert (as so many have done in conversation with me) that he 'could' is not a solution to a problem, but rather a statement of it! Indeed, determining in what sense agents 'could' think about their obligation at the appropriate time is the primary task of this entire book!

who decides to leave the deck with the full knowledge that doing so will lead to a shipwreck. It seems that most persons would agree that this latter helmsman is more blameworthy than the former while still asserting that the former deserves some blame. It is thus my suggestion that it was Aquinas's recognition of these two facts (negligent omissions cannot be completely absolved, but non-negligent omissions are worse) that led him to create the distinction between sins of negligent and non-negligent omission. Even though the cause and voluntariness of a negligent omission ultimately lies in a non-negligent omission, this does not mean that the former necessarily collapses into the latter. A sin of negligent omission is still different from a non-negligent one in that a sin of negligent omission has both an omission which is foreseen and one which is not, whereas a sin of non-negligent omission only has an omission which is foreseen.

This, though, leads to the question as to why a sin of negligent omission is not as culpable as a sin of non-negligent omission since both sins of negligent and non-negligent omission involve situations in which the agent omits to do something she knows she should do (for the negligent omitter at least *knows* that she should apply herself to know the things she needs to know in order to avoid negligent ignorance). In fact, why is not a sin of negligent omission even more, instead of less, blameworthy than other sins of omission since it actually involves two sins: the sin of omitting to prevent the subsequent negligent ignorance, and the negligent omission itself?

Aquinas actually offers an answer to this question when he states that sometimes "the first lessens the second sin, with the result that both together do not have as much weight as one alone would have."[54] The picture is the following: Consider an omission 'O' which has what we will call a 'blame level' of 10. Now, imagine the same omission but committed as a result of negligent ignorance. This addition of negligent ignorance drops the level of blame from 10 to 3. In addition, the negligent ignorance itself has a blame level of 5. As a result, the complete sin of negligent omission has a blame level of only 8, which is still less than 'O's original blame level of 10 without the negligent ignorance.

A question that arises is why negligent ignorance (which is itself ultimately rooted in a sin of non-negligent omission) would have a lower blame level than the original non-negligent omission 'O'? While some

[54] Et potest contingere, si primum diminuat secundum, quod ambo simul non habeant tantam gravitatem quantam unum solum haberet (*ST* Ia-IIae, q.76, a.4, *ad* 2).

possibilities suggest themselves,[55] it is not necessary at this point to worry about or answer this question. All that is needed for present purposes is to acknowledge that Aquinas assumes some sins are considered worse than others.[56] This would then make it possible for him to assert that some types of sinful omission may be worse than the sin of omission known as negligent ignorance.

Before concluding, I must address one final objection to the resolution. I have based the 'Final Resolution' on Aquinas's desire to lessen the severity of some sins on account of ignorance. This lessening is proportionate to the extent that ignorance "takes away the voluntariness."[57] We saw above, however, that Aquinas states that praise and blame can only be ascribed to actions that are fully voluntary. This was why the 'Possible Solution,' which posited a partial voluntariness, was unacceptable. The question, then, is how Aquinas can state that blame is lessened, but not removed, through a decrease in voluntariness while also maintaining that blame can only be applied to actions that are fully voluntary?

Once again, we need not be overly detained by this question. Aquinas's answer seems to be that even though voluntariness is decreased by the ignorance in the actual negligent omission, there is still full, perfect voluntariness present in the process of a negligent omission considered as a whole because the sin of negligent ignorance, which leads to the negligent omission, is fully, perfectly voluntary.[58] In virtue of this instance of perfect voluntariness, praise and blame can be attached to an omission of which the voluntariness, considered in

---

[55] While I cannot say with certainty why this is the case, perhaps an answer lies in the possibility that blame is proportionate to the specific thing omitted. In negligent ignorance, the specific thing that is omitted is simply knowledge, the omitting of which considered in and of itself may not be that bad due to the fact that a lack of knowledge does not, of necessity, lead to any other omissions or specifically bad consequences. For example, ignorance of how to steer a ship, considered in and of itself, may not be very bad because such ignorance may not necessarily lead to a shipwreck. On the other hand, the omitting to steer the ship clear of an iceberg non-negligently could be considered very bad because omitting to steer clear will definitely lead to a shipwreck.

[56] Indeed, without such an assumption the whole distinction between mortal and venial sins would seem to make no sense.

[57] in tantum ignorantia habet excusare peccatum in toto vel in parte, in quantum tollit voluntarium (*DM* q.3, a.8, cf. also *ST* Ia-IIae, q.76, a.4).

[58] Quando autem aliquis indirecte vult ignorare quia negligit addiscere, vel etiam quando per accidens ignorantiam vult, dum vult directe vel indirecte aliquid ad quod ignorantia sequitur, talis ignorantia non totaliter causat involuntarium in actu sequenti; quia actus *sequens ex hoc ipso quod procedit ex ignorantia, quae est voluntaria, est quodammodo voluntarius* (*DM* q.3, a.8, emphasis mine).

relation to the actual omission itself, can nevertheless be somewhat decreased as illustrated above. As a result, the 'Final Resolution' can still stand.

IX. Concluding Thoughts

The overall focus of this book is to discern how a negligent omission could ever be voluntary and therefore sinful. In this chapter, we have shown that Aquinas would need to solve this problem by stating that the ultimate cause of every sin of negligent omission must be a sin of non-negligent omission that is unquestionably voluntary. We have furthermore demonstrated that this fact does not necessarily mean that, for Aquinas, sins of negligent omission do not simply collapse into sins of non-negligent omission; there is still a real difference between the two and the distinction is useful.

There are many questions that remain unanswered. For example, how does one come to know that she should apply herself to learn certain other things so as to avoid negligent ignorance in moral matters? Or, supposing someone has learned such things, is it really reasonable to expect that person to keep all those things in mind at all times so as never to commit a sin of omission negligently? For example, is it not possible that someone who has applied her mind so as to prevent negligent ignorance could still, upon waking up one morning, just happen not to think about those things she has learned and consequently commit a negligent omission despite possessing the requisite knowledge?

In response to this latter question, some may appeal to Aquinas's understanding of the devil's sin and the notion of knowledge *in potentia accidentali*.[59] Such knowledge is knowledge that is "habitually present to the intellect."[60] As Hoffmann has argued, the sin of the devil (for Aquinas) lay not in failure to possess any knowledge, but rather in a failure to use such habitual knowledge that was *in potentia accidentali*. He states that even though "all the relevant factors to make the decision [were] in the angel's reach"[61] in virtue of their being *in potentia accidentali*, the angel sinned by simply not bringing those factors to full consideration. Specifically, the devil did not consider "the rule of

[59] See n.35 above. Cf. Aquinas's *De Veritate* q.8, a.6 *ad* 7.
[60] Hoffman, "Aquinas and Intellectual Determinism," 148.
[61] Ibid., 149.

action" by which his choice should have been governed even though that rule was 'within his reach.'[62] Similarly, some may think it possible that a negligently omitting agent may have knowledge related to her obligation habitually present to her intellect and, as such, is to be held blameworthy for not considering that which was 'within her reach.'

In response, it first ought to be noted that one cannot simply equate the cognitive state of the devil, who is said to have had knowledge *in potentia accidentali*, to that of negligently omitting humans. As Aquinas himself notes, the intellects of angels and humans are different in virtue of the fact that the latter, but not the former, reason discursively.[63] Such a difference in reasoning could mean that what is 'within the reach' of one may not necessarily be 'within the reach' of another. In other words, the nature of the reasoning (discursive versus non-discursive) may have an effect on the degree to which some particular piece of knowledge is 'within reach' of an agent. If one need not reason discursively so as to make a judgment, then it stands to reason that particular pieces of knowledge may be more 'within reach' for that agent than they would be, *ceteris paribus*, for one who must reason discursively before making a judgment.

Second, even if the negligently omitting agent *is* presumed to have habitual knowledge, or knowledge *in potentia accidentali*, of her obligation, it is (as I stated in the Introduction) unclear exactly *what* that would mean! To simply say that an agent is blameworthy because she ignored habitual knowledge is really to restate the question at issue instead of to answer it; it is simply a reassertion of the 'think harder' solution. Is a putative piece of habitual knowledge actually present before the agent's mind or not? If so, then it would seem to be more actual and the omission would not be negligent in the sense intended in this book. If the knowledge is not actually present, then in what sense is it 'within the reach' of the agent's intellect in the here and now?

---

[62] Ibid., 152. For Aquinas's discussion of failing to adhere to a rule of action, see both *Summa Contra Gentiles* 3.10 and *DM* q.1, a.3. Jacques Maritain emphasized these texts. See the following three works, all by Maritain: *St. Thomas and the Problem of Evil* (Milwaukee: Marquette University Press, 1942); *Existence and the Existent* (Garden City, NJ: Doubleday, 1948), chap. 4; *God and the Permission of Evil* (Milwaukee: The Bruce Publishing Co., 1966). See also: Gallagher, "Free Choice and Free Judgment," 260; and Lawrence Dewan, "St. Thomas and the First Cause of Moral Evil" in *Les philosophies morales et politiques au Moyen Âge*, ed. C.B. Bazán, E. Andújar, and L.G. Sbrocchi (New York-Ottawa-Toronto: Legas, 1995), 1223–1230.

[63] See *DM* q.16, a.4.

It is in an attempt to address this and related questions that we now turn to Scotus in order to begin constructing a model that will provide a more complete solution by addressing some of these issues. By doing so, we will eventually come to a way in which to understand *how* knowledge of one's obligations is 'within the reach' of the agent's intellect. We will thereby solve not only the problem of NO's, but also offer a possible, and substantive, understanding of so-called 'habitual knowledge.'

CHAPTER 5

CAN I HAVE YOUR *DIVIDED* ATTENTION?

SCOTUS, INDISTINCT INTELLECTIONS, AND TYPE-1 NEGLIGENT OMISSIONS ALMOST SOLVED

As we have seen, if a NO is to be blameworthy, the ignorance accompanying that NO must itself be voluntary. In this chapter, I will offer a way in which to understand as voluntary the ignorance accompanying Type-1 NO's, instances of NO in which the agent could reasonably have been expected to keep in mind continuously her obligation until it was fulfilled.[1] The proposal will rely on certain elements in Scotus's thought. We will, therefore, first discuss a few aspects of his general action theory. His 'doctrine of indistinct intellections' will then be presented, after which we will nearly be in a position fully to understand how such ignorance can be voluntary. Only one problem will remain, and we will conclude with a brief discussion of it and an indication that its resolution will occur after we have examined Suarez's writings.

Before diving into Scotus's theory, a few quick words about his writings need to be said. Unlike other significant medieval philosophers, the manuscript tradition for Scotus's writings is very complicated.[2] First, not all of Scotus's works are in critical editions. When I quote the Latin from a passage that is so included, I use the critical

---

[1] For the sake of clarity, I repeat Sample 1 from the introductory chapter here. It will also be restated in the text at a later point in this chapter.

> Sample 1: At 6:55 p.m., John promises, and is thus morally obligated in some sense, to pick up his friend Des at the airport, for which he will need to leave at 7:00. At 6:56, a mere one minute after promising Des, John begins watching television and subsequently forgets to leave at 7:00 to pick Des up. It is not until 9:00, when Des calls John to ask him where he is, that John realizes he has omitted to fulfill his obligation.

[2] For an overview, see Thomas Williams, "Introduction," in *The Cambridge Companion to Duns Scotus*, ed. Thomas Williams (Cambridge, UK: Cambridge University Press, 2003), 1–14.

edition.[3] Latin passages that are not included in critical editions will come from various texts; these will be indicated as appropriate.

More importantly, many of the passages I will refer to that are not from the critical edition are not necessarily from Scotus himself, even though they appear in the Wadding-Vivès edition of Scotus's *Opera Omnia*.[4] This is especially the case with important passages from the so-called *Opus Oxoniense* II, d.42. Many of them seem to be part of the *Additiones magnae* of Scotus's companion, William of Alnwick.[5] Therefore, it is possible that some of the discussion that follows is technically not derived from Scotus's own. Nonetheless, it is thought that Alnwick attempted to stay true to Scotus's own thoughts.[6] Since these passages had been traditionally attributed to Scotus, and since they are thought to be at least representative of his thoughts, I will for the sake of simplicity treat them as if they are Scotus's. The very conscientious reader, however, is warned that some such passages may ultimately be from Alnwick's *Additiones*. In the end, it really will not matter for the purposes of this book who is ultimately responsible for the thoughts. The important point is what the thoughts are and if they can (as I believe they do) help us solve the true problem facing us – that of negligent omissions.

---

[3] Passages from Scotus's commentary on Aristotle's Metaphysics (*QMet*) will be from: John Duns Scotus, *Quaestiones super libros Metaphysicorum Aristotelis: Libri VI-IX*, vol. 4 of *Opera Philosophica*, ed. G. Etzkorn, R. Andrews, G. Gál, R. Green, F. Kelly, G. Marcil, T. Noone, and R. Wood (St. Bonaventure, NY: The Franciscan Institute, 1997). Other Latin passages from the critical edition will be from various volumes of the Vatican edition: John Duns Scotus, *Opera Omnia*, 21 vols. to date (Città del Vaticano: Typis Polyglottis Vaticanis, 1950-). I make reference to the critical edition whenever it is available. For passages not available in the critical edition, I indicate the source of the Latin being used.

[4] Duns Scotus, *Opera Omnia*, editio nova / juxta editionem Waddingi XII tomos continentem a patribus franciscanis de observantia accurate recognita. 26 v. (Westmead, Farnborough, Hants: Gregg International, 1969).

[5] See, for example, Wolter, *Will and Morality*, 38.

[6] Wolter, for example, states of d.42 in particular that "the material in the present selection seems to represent the mind of Scotus, if not his actual words" (*Will and Morality*, 38). While dealing with a different part of Book II, Stephen Dumont similarly expresses that "Available evidence, however, gives every indication that the Additiones are faithful to Scotus." See Stephen D. Dumont, "Did Duns Scotus Change His Mind on the Will?" in *Nach der Verurteilung von 1277. Philosophie und Theologie an der Universität von Paris im letzten Viertel des 13. Jahrhunderts. Studien und Text*, ed. Jan. A. Aertsen, Kent Emery Jr., and Andres Speer (Berlin and New York: Walter de Gruyter, 2001), 719–794. The quotation is from p. 767.

I. A Few General Aspects of Scotus's Action Theory: 'Will' & Voluntariness

A. *Nature and 'Will:' Scotus's Account of Voluntariness*

Before I begin my account, I must make one brief remark regarding the relationship between the agent and that agent's faculties of the will and intellect so as to avoid creating a misleading impression throughout this chapter. As Richard Cross points out, Scotus does not regard the agent's soul as *really* different from the will and intellect.[7] This means that it is always ultimately the soul that performs actions. The will and intellect do not perform actions in their own right, and to speak as if they do is misleading. They are instead the soul's causal powers. Nonetheless, Scotus himself often speaks, out of a concern for simplicity, as if the will and intellect do perform actions of themselves. I will thus follow his (and Cross's) lead and do the same. The reader need only be mindful that whenever it is said, for example, that "the will acts," what is actually meant is that the soul of the agent acts by means of her volitional causal power. Having made this clarification, we can now proceed.

Scotus's action theory begins with a basic distinction between two types of active potencies: those characterized as 'natural,' and those by the 'will.' Their distinction arises from the "radically different way in which they elicit their respective operations."[8] A natural potency is one that "of itself is determined to act, so that so far as itself is concerned, it cannot fail to act when not impeded from without." By contrast, the will is a potency that is not so determined to act, but can "perform either this act or its opposite, or can either act or not act at all."[9] This

[7] Richard Cross, *Duns Scotus* (Oxford: Oxford University Press, 1999), 83–84. For Scotus, they are only 'formally,' not 'really,' distinct. The points brought out in this paragraph are from Cross, and I follow his practice of speaking as if they really are different for the sake of simplicity.

[8] De primo sciendum est quod prima distinctio potentiae activae est secundum diversum modum eliciendi operationem (*QMet* IX, q.15, n.21). All English translations from *QMet* will be from: Allan B. Wolter, *Duns Scotus on the Will and Morality* (Washington, DC: Catholic University Press, 1986). The present quotation is from p. 151. In many cases (such as this one), Wolter's translations are based upon Latin texts that have subsequently been published in a critical edition of Scotus's texts. I will often nonetheless use Wolter's translation because, in these instances, the non-critical text Wolter used and the text of the critical edition do not substantively diverge. The only substantive divergence occurs in chapter 7 and I fully discuss it there in n. 40.

[9] Aut non est ex se determinata, sed potest agere hunc actum vel oppositum actum; agere etiam vel non agere (*QMet* IX, q.15, n.22; Wolter, *Will and Morality*, 151).

indetermination of the will is not to be understood as implying that the will is only in general undetermined with respect to different actions and that, before performing one as opposed to another of them, it must somehow be determined to perform it. Instead, the will can elicit any of these acts or non-acts with "no change in its nature."[10] It requires no specific determining influence.

If a variety of results are possible for the will with no change in its nature, it may be wondered how the potency of the will is ever reduced to one particular act as opposed to another. Typically, an indeterminate power is reduced to a determinate action by means of some external explanatory factor that determines it in that particular way. This, however, is not what Scotus understands as happening in the case of the will. The will is not determined from without, but determines itself. It is, in other words, an uncaused cause with respect to its own actions and non-actions. Thus, when asked why the will wills one act instead of refraining from willing or willing another act, Scotus replies it is simply because "The will wills."[11] The will is sufficient to determine itself. Its indeterminacy is "that of a superabundant sufficiency."[12] The will need not be determined from without, but possesses unlimited actuality such that it can determine itself with respect to its own act or lack thereof. It is, in other words, a self-determining power for opposites.[13]

---

[10] Illa ergo potentia activa dicitur esse oppositorum - sive contrariorum sive contradictoriorum - productorum quae, manens natura una, habet terminum primum sub quo potest utrumque oppositum aeque cadere (*QMet* IX, q.15, n.11; Wolter, *Will and Morality*, 147).

[11] Similiter ista 'voluntas vult' et 'voluntas non vult determinate, determinatione necessaria ex se' (*QMet* IX, q.15, n.25; Wolter, *Will and Morality*, 151).

[12] Responsio: est quaedam indeterminatio insufficientiae, sive ex potentialitate et defectu actualitatis, sicut materia non habens formam est indeterminata ad agendum actionem formae; est aliae superabundantis sufficientiae, quae est ex illimitatione actualitatis, vel simpliciter vel quoadammodo (*QMet* IX, q.15, n.31; Wolter, *Will and Morality* 153). For a discussion, see Allan B. Wolter, *The Philosophical Theology of John Duns Scotus*, ed. Marilyn McCord Adams (Ithaca, NY: Cornell University Press, 1990). Cf. especially chapter 8.

[13] In explicating his notion of the will as such a self-determining power for opposites that can perform opposites with no change in its nature, Scotus maps his understanding of 'will' as opposed to 'nature' onto Aristotle's distinction between 'rational' and 'irrational' powers (*QMet* IX, q.15). As Wolter points out, by doing so Scotus actually twists the wax nose of authority (cf. Wolter, *Philosophical Theology*, ch. 7). Aristotle had understood as the rational power the intellect, a power which for Scotus is 'natural' and would thus, when mapped onto Aristotle's distinction, be considered 'irrational.' The specifics of this discussion need not detain us, as they are not directly relevant for this book, and the description of Scotus's understanding of the will given above is

As such, an agent is culpable for how she uses her will. Scotus's account of the will is thus, at the same time, his account of voluntariness.

B. *A First Constraint on the Will & the* Velle/Nolle *Distinction*

Despite the will's inherent freedom for opposites, there are two important constraints on its activity. To understand the first, we must introduce Scotus's understanding of the distinction between willing (*velle*) and nilling (*nolle*). While etymologically 'nil' can be interchangeable with a simple lack of willing (*non velle*), Scotus does not so regard it. In his view, just as willing is a positive act of the will "whereby it receives some agreeable object" or action, nilling is a substantive, positively elicited act of the will whereby it shuns: "for 'to nil' is a positive act of the will by which it flees from something disagreeable, or rather by which it recoils from a disagreeable object."[14]

This distinction forms the basis for the first constraint on the will's freedom. Scotus does not believe the will's ability to determine itself entails that it can will evil under the aspect of evil. Willing is only possible in regard to some object or action when the latter is viewed under the aspect of some goodness in it. Likewise, nilling is the only elicited action possible when an object or action is regarded under the aspect of evil: "... when evil is shown to me I am able to elicit an act of nolition only, just as when offered some good, if I elicit an act, it can only be one of volition."[15] Nothing can be willed *because* it is evil; if it is willed, it must be willed because the agent sees some good in the object of that willing. Likewise, a good cannot be nilled because of some goodness it contains. If an object of the will is to be nilled, the agent must do so on account of some evil seen in it. The will is thus constrained as to under what aspects it can either will or nil.

It might be thought this first constraint actually determines a will's act in certain cases and thus deprives it of its freedom to determine

---

sufficient. Let it simply be noted that the distinction arises in the midst of Scotus's attempt to find truth in Aristotle's original distinction, although he does not necessarily preserve the distinction in the way Aristotle would have himself done.

[14] est enim 'nolle' actus positivus voluntatis, quo fugit disconveniens sive quo resilit ab obiecto disconveniente; 'velle' autem est actus quo acceptat obiectum aliquod conveniens (*Ord.* II, d.6, q.2, n.34; VIII, p.39, translation mine). All texts of *Ord.* II, d.6 are from the critical (Vatican) edition.

[15] tamen sicut circa malum ostensum non possum elicere actum voluntatis nisi nolle, ita circa bonum apprehensum et oblatum non possum elicere actum voluntatis nisi velle (*Ord.* IV, suppl., d.49, qq.9–10, Latin text and translation from Wolter, *Will and Morality*, 192 and 193).

itself. Consider, for example, some object of the will in which the agent sees only goodness and no evil. Nilling it is not possible. It may, then, seem to follow that the agent is constrained to will it, which in turn would entail that the will lacks a power for opposites in that case. This conjecture, however, overlooks the possibility that the will can simply refuse to act at all. While the agent could not nil such an object, she does have open to her the option of *refraining* from willing it.[16] She can either will or not will (*velle* or *non-velle*) it. Likewise, if only evil is seen in an object of the will, the agent is not necessitated to nil it; she can either nil or not nil (*nolle* or *non-nolle*) it.[17] By its ability either to will or not will, or to nil or not nil, the will retains its power for opposites: "However, this concern with opposite actions or action should be understood to include the negation of action [i.e., the ability deliberately not to act when all conditions for acting are present]."[18] At all times, the will retains its power for opposites and thus the freedom to determine itself.

C. *A Second Constraint on the Will: Scotus's Knowledge Requirement*

The second constraint concerns the intellect. Despite the will's freedom, it is not the case that the will can just simply will, or nil, anything whatsoever. For any willing or nilling (or intentional refusals to do either of these), the agent must have the object of the will in mind; some sort of knowledge of the object of the will is required for the will to be regarded as having determined itself with respect to that object. In short, Scotus also recognizes a 'knowledge requirement' for willing.[19]

---

[16] Recall that 'to nil' is a positive, elicited act of the will for Scotus, and is not interchangeable with a simple 'lack of willing.' Hence, inaction (i.e. lack of either willing or nilling) constitutes a third option for Scotus.

[17] "... if it [the will] should elicit some act with respect to these objects, it is limited and has to elicit an act of willing in regard to happiness and an act of nilling as regards misery. *Nevertheless, it is not absolutely determined to elicit either the one act or the other.*" [... quia si eliciat aliquem actum circa obiecta ista, necessario et determinate elicit actus volendi respectu beatitudinem et actum nolendi circa miseriam. Non tamen absolute determinatur ad unum actum eliciendum nec ad alium (*Ord.* IV, suppl., d.49, qq.9–10, Latin text and translation from Wolter, *Will and Morality*, 192 and 193, italics mine).]

[18] Hoc autem debet intelligi quod potentia sit oppositarum actionum, seu actionis et negationis eius (*QMet* IX, q.15, n.12; Wolter, *Will and Morality*, 147).

[19] Note that for Scotus all instances of 'willing' proper are voluntary. Because of its freedom, any true act of the will is by nature voluntary. Consequently, a 'knowledge requirement' for willing is equivalent to a knowledge requirement for voluntariness.

(SKR) "every volition necessarily requires an intellection naturally prior, although simultaneous in duration."[20]

The object of willing or nilling must be, at the time of the will's action, 'intellected'; the agent must have some intellection of that which she is willing or nilling.

Simply to say that an intellection is needed for an elicited action, however, is to neglect much of the complexity in Scotus's understanding of the intellect and its relation to the will. For not only are there different types of intellections, but the will itself interestingly has some control over which intellections are present. To explore these details, we now turn to what I call Scotus's 'Doctrine of Indistinct Intellections.'

II. Doctrine of Indistinct Intellections

A. *General Overview of the 'Doctrine of Indistinct Intellections'*

Scotus's doctrine of indistinct intellections can be briefly summarized by the following points: All intellections are not equal. They consist of various strengths, or levels of 'distinctness.' The more distinct an intellection is, the more focused is one's intellect on the object of that intellection. In addition, different intellections of varying strengths can exist in an agent's intellect at the same time. While an agent's intellect is focused on the object of one particular intellection, it is possible that other, weaker intellections coexist in what he calls an *indistinct* way.

---

[20] ... quia omnis volitio requirit necessario intellectionem naturaliter priorem, licet simul duratione (*Opus Oxon.* II, d.42, q.2, n.3; XIII, p.451a). Unless otherwise indicated, all Latin text from the so-called *Opus Oxoniense* (hereafter, '*Oxon.*') are from the Wadding-Vivès edition of Scotus's Opera Omnia and thus may not be authentically from Scotus (see comments at the beginning of this chapter). All translations of texts from this passage, unless otherwise indicated, are mine. See also p.99 of: Bernadine M. Bonansea, "Duns Scotus' Voluntarism" in *Studies in Philosophy and in the History of Philosophy, Vol. 3: John Duns Scotus, 1265–1965*, ed. John K. Ryan & Bernadine M. Bonansea (Washington DC: Catholic University Press, 1965), 83–121. One could also consult *Lectura* II, d.25 and *Reportatio* II, d.25 in which the intellect's role in willing is discussed and explained in two different ways. Indeed, these passages have led to much controversy with regard to the question of whether Scotus changed his mind on the will. For an extremely thorough discussion of these issues, see Dumont, "Did Scotus Change His Mind." The issues surrounding this controversy need not detain us. In both positions that Scotus putatively took (the intellect as a co-cause of willing, or as a *sine qua non* cause of willing), it is nonetheless the case that the intellect is needed for willing and thus ought to be consistent with SKR.

Indistinct intellections are important because their 'indistinct' status is sufficient such that the will can, in some way, "take pleasure" (*complacere*) in the objects of those indistinct intellections and in those intellections themselves, thereby strengthening the latter. This strengthening, in turn, makes those intellections more distinct. Correlatively, intellections can become more indistinct if the will does not take pleasure in them or their objects.

The payoff from this doctrine is it affords a way in which to understand the will as having some power over the intellect; the will can control which intellections are distinct and indistinct. By doing so, the will can control the primary focus of an agent's cognition, for the more distinct an intellection, the more that intellection constitutes one's cognition.

B. *Detailed Exposition of the 'Doctrine of Indistinct Intellections'*

In order to explicate this doctrine Scotus advances three propositions that we will consider in detail.

> (P1) "It being the case that one perfect and distinct intellection exists in the intellect, many indistinct and imperfect intellections are able to inhere [in the intellect]."[21]
>
> (P2) "It being the case that one intellection is inhering in the intellect but is not being cognized as an object, the will is able to will and take pleasure (*complacere sibi*) in the object of that intellection, and in that intellection, and it is able not to take pleasure."[22]
>
> (P3) "It being the case that the will is taking pleasure in an intellection, the intellection is made stronger and intensified; it being the case that the

---

There may be a further question as to why I refer to this as Scotus's version of the 'knowledge requirement' when the 'knowledge requirement' was initially introduced in Chapter 1 as a condition for voluntariness, not willing per se. In response, Scotus's understanding of voluntariness is captured by his understanding of willing. Anything an agent wills, that willing is imputable to her because the will does not will unless it freely does so. In other words, Scotus's account of the will as a free power is his account of voluntariness.

[21] Prima, quod una intellectione perfecta et distincta existente in intellectu, multae intellectiones indistinctae et imperfectae possunt inesse (*Oxon.* II, d.42, q.4, n.10; XIII, 460b).

[22] Secunda propositio est (b) quod intellectione inexistente, licet non cognita, ut objectum, potest voluntas velle et complacere sibi in objecto illius intellectionis, et in illa intellectione, et non complacere sibi (ibid.; 460b).

> will is not taking pleasure in or nilling [an intellection], the intellection is weakened in intensity and set aside (*remittitur*)."[23]

Scotus defends (P1), the claim that there can be both distinct and indistinct intellections coexisting in the intellect, by means of an analogy to vision. When someone is looking directly at some object *x*, it can be said that she sees *x* without precluding the possibility that those objects close to *x*, objects *w* and *y*, fall within her peripheral vision. For example, presently while sitting at Starbucks I am looking directly at my computer screen. I can nevertheless see, out of the corner of my eye, both a man in a red coat stand up to grab a newspaper and a car drive by the window. They are still in my peripheral vision. Focusing one's vision on one object, as I am doing now with regard to the computer screen, need not rule out sight of other things.

In addition, let it be noted that seeing other objects in my peripheral vision does not entail any deficiency in my sight of my computer screen. My vision is not currently 'split' between the computer screen and those things in my peripheral vision such that I do not see the screen as well as I could. Instead, I see the screen completely and 'perfectly,' so to speak, despite the fact that I can also see other objects less perfectly.

The discussion of *visibilia* allows Scotus to explain what he means by distinct and indistinct intellections. A distinct intellection is to be understood as analogous to an object seen directly and perfectly. Indistinct intellections, meanwhile, are comparable to objects viewed peripherally. We are thus led by this comparison to regard the mind as having some sort of eye that 'focuses' on one intellection or another while it can, at the same time, 'see' some other intellections contained within the mind peripherally, i.e. indistinctly.

Up to this point, all Scotus has done is affirm a comparison between vision and cognition. What reason, though, do we have to believe that cognition is in fact structured analogously to vision such that it similarly accommodates both distinct and indistinct intellections? Scotus's answer to this question is the following: "if this is possible in a [bodily] sense" (i.e. if it is possible for one of the five senses to be such that there is peripheral access to items not being directly focused on by that

[23] Tertia propositio est, (c) quod voluntate complacente intellectioni, intellectio firmatur et intenditur, ipsa autem non complacente vel nolente, infirmatur et remittitur (ibid.; 461a).

sense), "then much more is it possible in the intellect."[24] This response makes use of two premises. First, Scotus believes that whatever possibilities apply to a lower power of the soul apply even more fully to a higher power. Second, the intellect is a power superior to that of any of the senses. It thus results that whatever possibilities apply to any of the senses, those possibilities apply more so to the intellect. Since the visual sense has this ability to focus on one thing while still having access to, or registering, others, so does the intellect have this ability and has it to a greater degree.

While most medievals (and many contemporary thinkers, I assume) would agree that the intellect is a power superior to the senses, the first premise is open to objection. A power can be considered 'higher' than another in virtue of some quality or characteristic unrelated to particular possibilities applicable to a lower power. Without some further assumption that higher powers can do all things lower powers do in the same general way (abstracting from the particular actions of those powers), there is no reason to accept the first premise, and thus the argument.

This instance of inadequate argumentation, however, need not deter us from accepting the intended conclusion. Common experience confirms that our intellects can be aware of more than one thing at a time and can be aware of those several items to varying degrees. For example, when one is auditioning for a teaching job, her cognition is doubtless focused on the material that she is teaching. This intellectual focus upon the material, however, does not preclude her from also being aware and actively cognizant of the additional fact that she is currently being evaluated, nor from even being somewhat aware of the fact that a student may be sleeping in the back row. She is moreover aware of these different facts to various degrees at the same time.

Consider furthermore my earlier illustration of peripheral *visibilia* while sitting in Starbucks. If I am aware of the different objects or events that I am seeing to the extent that I can write about and describe them, it seems likely to be the case that I have processed those peripheral images mentally, i.e. I have formed intellections corresponding to those

[24] Patet in exemplo in visu, qui in pyramide et infra basim videt unum punctum in cono distincte, et tamen in eadem pyramide, et infra eamdem basim videt multa imperfecte et indistincte, et tamen una est tantum visio perfecta istius, scilicet super quod cadit axis pyramidis; si hoc est possibile in sensu, multo magis in intellectu (ibid.; p.460b).

images. Moreover, those intellections corresponding to objects seen peripherally are no doubt less distinct in my cognition than is the intellection corresponding to my sight of the computer screen. In other words, sight requires some corresponding form of cognition or intellection. (It thus turns out that Scotus's appeal to vision to make his point regarding indistinct intellections may be particularly apt.) In light of these considerations, we can proceed having accepted (P1)'s claim (if not Scotus's argumentation for it) that indistinct intellections can accompany distinct ones.

We come now to what I regard as the crucial step in Scotus's doctrine of indistinct intellections, (P2). Recall that (P2) states:

> (P2) "It being the case that one intellection is inhering in the intellect but is not being cognized as an object, the will is able to will and take pleasure in the object of that intellection, and in that intellection, and it is able not to take pleasure."

To parse this proposition, let it be the case that I have a distinct intellection *a* of the paragraph I am currently writing, and an indistinct intellection *b* of my dogs I just left at home. The first portion of (P2) speaks of intellections inhering in the intellect but not being "cognized *as an object*." What does this mean? Namely, that I am not cognizing the fact *that* I have an intellection *a* or *b*; the intellection *itself* is not being cognized, or, say, reflected upon.

Scotus then proceeds to say that the will can "take pleasure" (*complacere*) not only "in the object of that intellection," but also "in that intellection" itself. This last claim is initially puzzling based upon the first part of (P2). If an intellection is itself not being cognized, it is unclear how the will could perform any action upon that intellection *per se*. To solve this puzzle, we need first to understand what Scotus means by the will "taking pleasure" (*complacere*) in something.

For Scotus, *complacere* is a specific action of the will, the free action of liking, approving, or, at the very least, freely acquiescing to some object or action of which the will itself is not necessarily the efficient cause. To illustrate: this is the term Scotus uses in his discussion of the Trinity to refer to the Divine will's action in response to the Father begetting the Son. In Scotus's understanding, the Divine intellect is the principium of the Son within the Trinity; it is the Divine intellect that performs this role. Nonetheless, the divine will is engaged in the process insofar as it approves and is pleased with (*complacere*) this begetting. And on account of this liking, the will permits the process of the

Father begetting the Son to continue.[25] When, therefore, Scotus writes in (P2) that the will takes pleasure (*complacere*) in an object of an intellection, he means that the will somehow approves of, or at least acquiesces in, that object.

Taking pleasure in the object of an intellection, in turn, has certain implications for the intellection itself. If I, for instance, approve of or acquiesce in some object of thought, I must also approve of/acquiesce in/take pleasure in (*complacere*) the very thought itself by which I am able to think of that object. For example, let it be the case that I start to enjoy thinking of the object of indistinct intellection *b*, my dogs I just left at home. As I am glad to think about them, I am, at the same time, enjoying not only them, but the very thought/intellection of them by which I am able to think about them. In other words, by approving or enjoying my dogs in thought, I also approve of or enjoy the thought itself by which I enjoy or approve of my dogs. And it is this phenomenon (i.e. the taking pleasure in some object of an intellection *spilling over*, so to speak, into a taking pleasure in that intellection itself) Scotus is referring to in the latter part of (P2). The will can perform an action of *complacere* on an intellection "not cognized as an object" by performing *complacere* on the object of that intellection.[26]

Approving of or acquiescing in the object of an intellection does not simply result in taking pleasure in the intellection itself. According to Scotus, such *complacere* has the further effect of intensifying that thought. This is the point expressed by (P3):

> (P3) "It being the case that the will is taking pleasure in an intellection, the intellection is made stronger and intensified; it being the case that the will is not taking pleasure in or nilling [an intellection], the intellection is weakened in intensity and set aside (*remittitur*)."

There is a spectrum of distinctness and indistinctness along which intellections fall. When any particular intellection is 'taken pleasure in,' that intellection is strengthened, by which Scotus means it becomes more distinct and less indistinct. The converse also obtains.

(P3) is a reasonable inference. By liking/approving of my dogs, I think of them more intensely. Because I think of them more intensely, the intellection *b* of which they are an object and *by which* I think of

[25] Cf. *Ord.* I, d.6, q.1.

[26] How the will can perform *complacere* on the object of such an indistinct intellection will be discussed shortly.

them must accordingly be more intense. What else could thinking of an object more intensely mean other than that the intellection by which one thinks is stronger and more intense? Consequently, the overall picture is that whenever one takes pleasure in an object of an intellection, the corresponding intellection itself is intensified and thereby becomes more distinct within the agent's intellect. By the same token, whenever an object of an intellection, and thus the intellection itself, is not taken pleasure in, the intellection loses strength and becomes less distinct and more indistinct.

Putting these three propositions together, Scotus arrives at the conclusion that the will, and thereby the agent, can control cognition; our intellect is within our own power.

> I say therefore that while one intellection exists perfectly in the intellect, many confused and imperfect intellections can be there, unless the former intellection is perfect and actual to such an extent that it does not allow any other with it; therefore, it being the case that those confused and imperfect intellections existing, the will, according to the second proposition, can take pleasure in any one of them it pleases, even if that intellection had not been cognized actually as an object, and from the third proposition it being the case that the will is taking pleasure in some intellection, it confirms [that intellection] and intends it. Therefore, that intellection, which had been neglected and imperfect, becomes perfect and strengthened through that act of taking pleasure, and in this way [the will] is able to order thought and convert the intellect to that thought.[27]

The will can act on the intellect by means of its ability to take pleasure in certain intellections or not. Given that there is a range of distinct and indistinct intellections within one's intellect, the will can thus determine, on account of this ability to perform *complacere*, one's current cognition. The will can strengthen or weaken any of them to such a point that their objects either become the content of cognition (if strengthened) or are no longer the content of cognition (if weakened).[28]

---

[27] Dico igitur quod una intellectione intellectus existente perfecta, possunt ibi esse multae confusae et imperfectae, nisi illa intellectio esset ita perfecta et actualis, quod non pateretur secum aliam; illis ergo confusis et imperfectis ibi existentibus, potest voluntas, secundum propositionem secundam, complacere in qualibet earum, etiamsi illa intellectio non fuerit cognita, ut objectum actualiter, et ex tertia voluntate complacente in aliqua intellectione, confirmat illam et intendit. Illa igitur, quae fuit remissa et imperfecta, fit per istam complacentiam perfecta et intensa, et sic potest imperare cogitationem et convertere intellectum ad illam (*Oxon*. II, d.42., n.11; XIII, p.461a–b).

[28] Note that for Scotus only a distinct intellection is technically *cognized*. 'Cognition' per se is thus comprised of one's distinct intellection. This will be discussed below.

C. *Relevance of the 'Doctrine' for Scotus's Knowledge Requirement*

Scotus's doctrine of indistinct intellections is very important, for it provides an as-yet-unseen means by which to fulfill the knowledge requirement. A recurrent theme in this book has been that for a voluntary, culpable action or omission to take place, there must be in the intellect some active knowledge corresponding to the object of that action or omission; the agent must know and be aware of that which she is doing. The impression may have thus been given that the relevant required knowledge or awareness must be at the forefront, so to speak, of one's mind. This, however, is not the case for Scotus.

To see why it is not, recall SKR, Scotus's understanding of the knowledge requirement for willing: "every volition necessarily requires an intellection naturally prior." Note that SKR says that merely an *intellection* is 'required' (by which is meant 'adequate') for the will to perform a volition, such as *complacere* is.[29] It does not say that full-blown *cognition* (a mental activity analogous to knowledge being at the forefront of one's mind) is required. Consequently, the knowledge requirement for an act of *complacere* can be fulfilled by an indistinct intellection; the presence of an indistinct intellection is adequate such that the will can perform an act of *complacere* with regard to either the object of that intellection or the intellection itself (cf. (P2)). Given, moreover, that any act of the will is imputable to the agent (otherwise, it is not the will that causes the act) we can thus derive the following important conclusion regarding the 'fulfillment of Scotus's knowledge requirement.'

> (FSKR) That an intellection be of some imperfect/indistinct status is adequate such that the will can culpably perform, or fail to perform, some act of *complacere* related to that intellection.

One might object to FSKR by claiming that it is based upon an overly-literal reading of SKR. Even though SKR is stated in terms of

---

[29] It is unclear to me whether an intellection, as opposed to a full cognition, is sufficient not just for acts of *complacere* but for any act of the will whatsoever. If SKR is taken literally, then it seems as if the latter is the case. For SKR states that intellection is required (by which it is clear he means it is 'sufficient' in the sense that no more robust cognitive activity is needed) for 'volition' and does not specify that it is required for only certain types of volition (one of which is *complacere*). I, however, consider this a bit inconclusive because the context in which this passage is found is concerned solely with acts of *complacere*. By *volitio*, therefore, Scotus may have intended us to understand *complacere* and not any act of willing whatsoever. At any rate, nothing essential in my argument turns on one understanding or another. My argument depends on what is required for an act of *complacere*, and either understanding of *volitio* is compatible with only an intellection being required for an act of *complacere*.

'intellection' instead of 'cognition,' it is possible (so the objection goes) that Scotus is speaking loosely here. In light of this possibility, it is ill-advised to derive FSKR and affirm that indistinct intellections are sufficient to fulfill the knowledge requirement.

When the context of the SKR is looked at more closely, however, the objection cannot be sustained. That context is one in which Scotus's primary aim is to show how sinfulness in *cognition* is possible. It becomes clear upon examination that Scotus believes intellections form the content of cognition *per se* only when they become distinct. One therefore controls whether she sins in 'cognition' or not by virtue of strengthening certain indistinct intellections to distinctness, or weakening certain distinct intellections such that they no longer are distinct. The difference between an intellection and 'cognition' per se is thus at the forefront in this passage. It is for this reason doubtful that Scotus would have mistakenly used the non-modified 'intellection' if he meant 'cognition/distinct intellection.' Moreover, (and more importantly) Scotus's whole idea of being able to control one's thought by means of strengthening an intellection rests upon the very idea that an indistinct status of an intellection is adequate for the will to act in regard to either that intellection or its object. If FSKR is false because it is based on an overly-literal reading of SKR, it is difficult to see how the doctrine of indistinct intellections accomplishes its purpose in the first place: to provide a way to understand the will as able to control thought.

D. *A Few Implications of the 'Doctrine'*

While SKR does not state that full cognition is required for an act of *complacere*, some attention should nevertheless be drawn to the fact that it does state an intellection is required. But if an act of the will requires an intellection, then it seems the will cannot be in control of that very intellection by which it begins to will; otherwise, a circle is set up. Recognizing this, Scotus distinguishes between a first and second thought. There must be some 'first thought' (*prima cogitatio*) preceding all acts of willing, and this cannot be in our power for reasons just mentioned.[30] Having had this first thought, however, the will does have the ability to act or not act upon it by means of performing *complacere*.

[30] Such a thought could arise, say, from normal experience. Seeing something, for example, could impose a thought involuntarily. After the thought is present, the will can then strengthen or weaken it and thus control it in that way.

The resulting thoughts, i.e. 'second thoughts,' are thus the ones that are in our power.[31]

The restriction just noted implies one further fact. Given the doctrine of indistinct intellections, changing one's cognition consists in converting it from one intellection to another by weakening the current cognition/distinct intellection while strengthening an indistinct one. This means there must be at least an indistinct intellection in addition to and coexisting with the distinct intellection/cognition for a change of cognition to take place. Without any alternative intellection, the will has no control over thought.

It might be objected that under Scotus's distinctive action theory, the will would have control over a distinct intellection without indistinct intellections being present to the following extent: it could actively nil the intellection (assuming it could be regarded under some aspect of *malum*) in which case the intellection would weaken, lose its status as distinct and the content of cognition, and perhaps even leave the mind entirely (per (P3)).

In response, common experience testifies that it is difficult to make oneself stop thinking about something. Consider the familiar scenario I call the 'Pink Elephant Consideration.' We have no doubt heard of someone telling someone else "Don't think about a pink elephant." Invariably, the listener can then not help but to think about a pink elephant, and the more he tries *not* to think about a pink elephant, the more he in fact does so. It does not seem possible simply to nil one's thought of a pink elephant. To stop thinking about it, or anything, it often seems the case that something else must be thought of.

This is in fact the tactic Scotus takes, for he denies that an act of nilling, although it itself is a positive act of the will, can occur apart from a separate act of *velle*:

> And among those 'acts,' a certain order is clear, *because every act of nilling (nolle) presupposes some act of willing (velle)*. For there is no act of shunning (*refugio*), unless it is as a result of not being able to stand together with something which has been accepted as agreeable.[32]

---

[31] Dicitur igitur quod aliqua intellectio vel cogitatio est a voluntate imperata; et cum possit distingui cogitatio generaliter in primam et secundam, de prima probo quod non potest esse in potestate voluntatis, quia aliqua cogitatio praecedit necessario omne *velle*, (saltem natura); sed quod praecedit omne *velle*, et est prius, natura saltem, non est in potestate nostra (*Oxon*. II, d.42, q.4, n.5; XIII, p.454b).

[32] Et istorum 'actuum' patet ordo, quia omne nolle praesupponit aliquod velle: a nullo enim refugio, nisi quia non potest stare cum aliquo quod accepto tamquam

In other words, although an act of *nolle* is a positive, elicited act of the will, it cannot take place in a vacuum; it requires for its performance a separate act of *velle*.

Why does Scotus believe that any act of *nolle* requires a separate act of *velle*? The answer seems to be found in his reliance upon Anselm. Recall from Chapter 3 Anselm's example of the miser in *DCD*, c.3. A miser wants to keep all his money. He needs to eat, however, and thus sometimes must spend some of the money he otherwise would keep so as to buy bread. Scotus appeals to this example in order to make his case that "every act of nilling presupposes some act of willing." Scotus intends for us to understand the miser giving up his money as an act of nilling, one that depends on his separate act of willing to buy bread.[33]

conveniens, et hoc dicit Anselmus *De casu diaboli* cap. 3, ponens exemplum de avaro, nummo et pane (*Ord.* II, d.6, q.2, n.35; VIII, p.40, italics and translation mine); cf. also ibid., n.36.

[33] Appeal to this example to make his point does not seem to serve Scotus particularly well. It is clear that Scotus regards the decision to part with some possession as analogous to an act of nilling. In the passage under question, however, Anselm discusses *two* different ways in which an agent may come to decide to part with some possession, and distinguishes them through precedence relations between "not willing to keep" and "willing to desert." The example of the miser is intended as a case in which "willing to desert" takes precedence over "not willing to keep." It is not as if the miser does not will to keep the money; rather, he wills to desert it and does so because of his desire to eat. Consequently, when "willing to desert" takes precedence over "not willing to keep," Anselm does want us to understand that something is deserted, or lost, or fled from, only as a result of some other willing (such as eating bread).

In the same breath, however, Anselm makes it clear that sometimes the reverse is the case: someone can give up some possession not as a result of wanting something else, but simply because the agent wants to flee from that which he or she has for its own sake:

> When you do not will to keep a thing for its own sake but *will to desert it for its own sake* (for example, a lighted coal placed in your bare hand), then perhaps not-willing-to-keep precedes willing-to-desert, and you will to desert because you do not will to keep ... [Quando aliquam rem propter se non vis tenere sed deserere, ut carbonem ignitum positum in nuda manu: tunc forsitan prius est non velle tenere quam velle deserere, et ideo vis deserere, quia non vis tenere... (*DCD*, chap.3, italics mine)]

In other words, Anselm makes it explicit that something can be fled from, shunned, or deserted *for its own sake* and not as a result of some other willing of which the desertion is only a double effect. This, in turn, implies that the loss of some possession (i.e. the analogue to Scotus's act of nilling) need not, in Anselm's mind, be willed simply as a result of another willing; the loss can be willed directly without the necessity of another act of will intervening.

Given this is the case, Scotus's selective appeal to Anselm as support for his claim that "*every* act of nilling presupposes some act of willing" is somewhat puzzling. It is

He makes it clear that unlike acts of *velle*, all acts of *nolle* require a correlative, yet separate act of *velle*. This means, as far as thought is concerned, that if an agent is to be able to control his cognition by means of *nolle*, he must have more than one intellection in his intellect.

Control of cognition, therefore, requires that one has alternate intellections cognitively available to oneself.[34] One way in which to help ensure such alternate intellections is to avoid engaging in what I call 'intellectual tunnel vision.' To explain what I mean by this latter concept, consider again our sense of vision. In vision, one can focus one's sight upon a particular object so intently that peripheral objects fall completely out of view.[35] Scotus states that the same can happen in thought. One's thought of a particular object can be so intense (i.e. the intellection can be so distinct) that no other potential object of the intellect can simultaneously exist with it (i.e. there are no indistinct intellections present). This is, coincidentally, the phenomenon Scotus

---

not even clear why Scotus would have desired to characterize *nolle* as dependent on *velle* in the first place. Why, after all, cannot a *malum* be shunned or fled from (i.e. nilled) on account of the very fact that it is a *malum*, just as a *bonum* can be willed on account of the very fact that it is a bonum? Why, in other words, is there such an asymmetry?

There are some potential answers to this question. Perhaps he posits the asymmetry on account of common observations, such as the Pink Elephant Consideration. Or, it may be the case that he just simply disagrees with Anselm's view that something can be fled from for its own sake. Consider the example of the burning coal in a bare hand. Scotus could reply that the coal is shunned not for its own sake, but rather on account of a separate willing to have one's hand feel no pain or something similar. Consequently (Scotus could reply), Anselm does not convincingly show that the desire for the loss of some possession is not always in virtue of a separate act of *velle*. Scotus could even go so far as to reply that this is why he selectively used Anselm, i.e. that he only appealed to the examples of Anselm which he thought were valid. Despite these worries, it is nonetheless clear that Scotus claims that an act of *nolle* requires a separate act of *velle*.

[34] I suppose it would be possible to reject this claim by asserting that the intellect could have control over a distinct intellection, no other intellections being present, by simply refusing to continue to will (*non velle*) to perform *complacere* on that intellection. The distinct intellection would thereby cease and the agent would thus exhibit control over her cognition. Though theoretically possible, I do not find this suggestion plausible. Taken to its extreme, it would entail a blank, contentless intellect – an occurrence that seems nearly impossible to occur. Something is almost always present to our minds. Even if such control were possible, it would be rare and would not, in any case, be relevant to the point currently being made so far as NO's are concerned.

[35] This phenomenon occurs relatively often in our day-to-day affairs. For example, sometimes we can be so focused upon looking at something ahead of us that we do not even notice when a friend walks by us. When the friend points out to us that we ignored her, our response is commonly something along the lines of "I didn't even see you. I was so focused on something that I didn't notice anything else." In other words, we seem capable of something commonly referred to as 'tunnel vision.'

refers to in the extended passage quoted above where he states that an intellection can exist perfectly (i.e. distinctly) "to such an extent that it does not allow any other [indistinct intellections] with it." If one wants to be able to control her cognition, then resisting intellectual tunnel vision, which would drive out alternative intellections, is required. The concept of intellectual tunnel vision will become important as we proceed.

III. Application to Type-1 NO's

Having made the above observations, it will be relatively easy to demonstrate how the ignorance in Type-1 NO's can be voluntary and the agent considered culpable. Stated briefly, an agent will ultimately be culpable because she will have failed to have freely performed *complacere* continuously on the obligation-related intellection when she is near the time of expected fulfillment (TEF).

Recall that Type-1 cases are those in which the agent is aware of her obligation at a point of time suitably near enough TEF such that she can reasonably be expected to keep that obligation in mind continuously until it is to be fulfilled. For ease of exposition, we will repeat the prototypical Type-1 case here:

> Sample 1: At 6:55 p.m., John promises, and is thus morally obligated in some sense, to pick up his friend Des at the airport, for which he will need to leave at 7:00. At 6:56, a mere one minute after promising Des, John begins watching television and subsequently forgets to leave at 7:00 to pick Des up. It is not until 9:00, when Des calls John to ask him where he is, that John realizes he has omitted to fulfill his obligation.

We first need to be clear on exactly what is meant when it is said that John 'forgot.' It might be tempting to equate forgetting with not *cognizing*, i.e. the relevant intellection no longer being distinct. According to this understanding, John would be said to have 'forgotten' because he now had a distinct intellection of that which he was watching on TV and no longer a distinct intellection regarding his obligation to pick up Des.

Given, however, Scotus's robust understanding of indistinct intellections and the will's relation to them exemplified by FSKR, mere demotion of a cognition to the status of an indistinct intellection cannot be the kind of 'forgetfulness' we are concerned with in NO's. FSKR entails that indistinct intellections are adequate such that the will can freely, no other condition needing be fulfilled, perform an act of *complacere* on their objects and the intellections themselves. The indistinct intellection itself serves to fulfill the knowledge requirement. As a result, an obligation-related intellection being present as an indistinct intellection entails not forgetfulness, but some awareness of that obligation. If John is truly to have 'forgotten' his obligation, it must be the case that the obligation-related intellection ceased to exist *even as an indistinct intellection* in the intellect.

In light of this, why is it that John can be blamed for his current ignorance/forgetfulness? Because it was in his power to prevent that obligation-related intellection from ceasing as an intellection. An intellection ceases, per (P3), when the agent either nils or fails to perform *complacere* (a form of *non velle*) on that intellection. And either of these options are within the voluntary control of the agent and thus are to be ascribable to the agent.[36] Why? Because, per FSKR, the actual presence of that intellection (whether distinct or indistinct), before the agent permits it to cease, fulfills the knowledge requirement for actions or non-actions of the will regarding it. And since the knowledge requirement is fulfilled, the will's action or non-action in regard to that intellection is free and thus imputable. If John, therefore, fails to perform *complacere* continuously on the obligation-related intellection or its object to the extent such that the intellection persists as *at least an indistinct intellection* until the time of expected fulfillment (TEF), 7:00, then that failure, which entails ignorance regarding his obligation, is imputable to him. John could have performed *complacere* at least to the extent that it continues as an indistinct intellection but freely did not.

Before entertaining an objection to the preceding claim, I want to make one further point. Note that for John to have avoided forgetting, and thus culpability, in a Type-1 scenario, the intellection would have had to have *continued* from the 6:55 until TEF, 7:00. How could he have assured that an intellection continue? By *continuing* to perform *complacere* on either it or its object. Of course, an intense level of *complacere* need not be performed continuously, for the intellection need

[36] Of course, 'nilling' is only within the power of the will if the agent perceives some *malum* in it. The present point is that whichever option is appropriate, *non-velle* or *nolle*, in the situation, that option (or both, if both are possible depending upon the intellection being viewed under different aspects) is available to the agent's will. As it turns out, I discuss below whether the agent could 'nil' an obligation-related intellection and still commit a *negligent* omission.

not be continuously distinct. It does, however, need to be continuously present, and for this, continual *complacere* is required.[37] Per (P3), if an agent performs no act of will (*non velle*, one species of which is *non complacere*) in regard to an intellection, that intellection weakens and is "set aside [*remittitur*]." Constant performance of *complacere* on the obligation-related intellection is thus called for so as to avoid sinfulness in Type-1 scenarios.

It is important to note that we have, earlier in this book, already seen a precedent for this understanding. In Chapter 3 we noted that Anselm says the devil ultimately sinned because he did not *pervelle* to receive a persevering good will. Perseverance of the good will was continually offered to the devil and other evil angels, but they did not receive it because they did not *continually* will to receive it. Their sin, therefore, could be traced back to a failure to continuously will, according to Anselm. Now, in the light of the doctrine of indistinct intellections, Anselm's view receives some support and elaboration.

There remains an objection to my method for claiming John is culpable for his ignorance. I claim that it is in the power of his will to continue the intellection, for the presence of the intellection fulfills the knowledge requirement with regard to actions or non-actions of the will regarding it, and its ceasing is the result of either an action (*nolle*) or non-action (*non complacere*) of the will. Note, however, that it cannot be the case that John actively nils the obligation-related intellection. *Ex hypothesi*, John's omission is negligent. If he actively nils the intellection regarding his obligation, the resulting omission would seem more intentional as opposed to negligent. If his omission is negligent, then, it must be that he simply fails to perform *complacere* on it. But (so goes the objection) there are some instances of 'failures to perform' that decidedly are not voluntary, and for a couple of reasons this seems to be one of them.

First, consider the details of the scenario. It is not as if John decided 'not to perform *complacere*.' He simply decided to watch TV, and that simply had the side-effect of his ceasing to pay attention to, and thus to perform *complacere* on, his obligation-related intellection. Watching TV drove the intellection out of his mind, so to speak. Given that the

[37] In the next chapter which concerns Type-2 NO's, I make great use of this idea of continuing *complacere* on an intellection. I refer to the process of continuing *complacere* as performing 'ContinualComp.'

intellection's ceasing was a side-effect and not intended, it does not seem right to charge him with having done it voluntarily and thus culpably.

Note that the objection implicitly appeals to the concept of 'intellectual tunnel vision' I discussed above: the extent of John's intellectual focus on the television is such that the corresponding intellection is so perfect/distinct as not to allow any other intellections (or at least some other ones) to coexist with it. I want to begin my response by claiming that engaging in intellectual tunnel vision is itself voluntary, for the will is in control of how much *complacere* it performs on any one intellection and intellectual tunnel vision only occurs as a result of extensive *complacere*. And since performing intellectual tunnel vision is voluntary, one can be held liable for engaging in it.

This response, though, brings up the second reason for the objection that not all 'failures to perform' are voluntary. Although it can be the case that engaging in tunnel vision is voluntary (so goes the objection), that does not mean that its side-effects are. Recall the discussion of voluntary in Chapter 1. It was noted there that voluntariness is relative to a certain description of an act. Consequently, John may have been somewhat aware of the fact that <what I am doing is performing tunnel vision on the television-related intellection> without knowing that the same act could be described by <I am causing my obligation-related intellection to cease when I should not as a result of performing tunnel vision on the television-related intellection>. But if he did not know this latter description, then the act referred to by it (i.e. causing the obligation-related intellection to cease) should not count as voluntary.

This last point, in fact, can be made without appeal to a separate act of tunnel vision. If an agent does not realize that there is an applicable description such as <what I am doing is failing to perform *complacere* upon an obligation-related intellection when I should, the result of which is that it ceases>, the occurrence specifically referred to by that description seems not to be voluntary. As long as John was not mentally entertaining such descriptions while watching TV, it is unclear how the ceasing of his obligation-related intellection can be voluntary. Therefore, the presence of the indistinct intellection may suffice for fulfilling the knowledge requirement in regard to acts of the will in general upon that intellection, but it is not clear that it suffices to fulfill the knowledge requirement for the act of acting *appropriately* or non-sinfully in regard to that intellection.

The intuition underlying the objection is this: for an agent to be blameworthy for failing to keep an obligation continuously in mind, she must at least know that she needs to keep it in mind. This sets up a dilemma, however, for if an agent fails to keep it in mind while knowing she should, failure to keep it in mind would seem to be intentional. Any resulting omission would thus appear not to be *negligent* per se, but somehow intended. We thus have a two-fold task ahead of us. We must (i) give some account of how the agent knows she should keep an obligation continuously in mind until TEF in Type-1 scenarios, and (ii) make sure the account of that knowledge does not cause the class of putative negligent omissions to collapse into that of intentional ones.

Despite these remaining issues, we have nonetheless in this chapter made great strides toward the solution of Type-1 NO's. As it turns out, the presence of the intellection as indistinct will indeed help fulfill, in a distinctive way, the knowledge requirement pertaining to the requirement that the agent knows she should keep that intellection continuously in mind. It will not be until we have covered the material on Suárez, though, that this will become clear. Once we do that, the problem of culpability for Type-1 NO's will be solved.

CHAPTER 6

I CAN'T GET YOU OUT OF MY MIND

SCOTUS, LINGERING INDISTINCT INTELLECTIONS, AND TYPE-2 NEGLIGENT OMISSIONS

In the preceding chapter, we used the doctrine of indistinct intellections to take significant steps toward solving Type-1 NO's, NO's in which the agent is reasonably expected to keep in mind her obligation continuously until TEF. What, though, about Type-2 NO's, cases in which the relevant time lag is long enough such that the agent could not reasonably be expected to keep in mind her obligation continuously until TEF, but short enough such that there is no expectation for her to 'write notes to herself' or do something along those lines? Is the doctrine of indistinct intellections useful for explaining their culpability?

In this chapter I will demonstrate how it can be so applied by proposing a significant development of Scotus's machinery, a development I will call 'Lingering Indistinct Intellections.' Moreover, I will show that there are two variations of Type-2 NO's and that my proposal helps explain culpability in both of them. I will end by acknowledging a task similar to that expressed after we discussed Type-1 NO's remains. Namely, there will still be a question as to how the agent is to have knowledge of certain relevant descriptions of her action or non-action. The answer to this will ultimately come in the chapter on Suárez. Nonetheless, the work done in this chapter will be indispensable for the resolution of Type-2 NO's.

I. Type-2 NO's: Special Challenges Posed

Given the longer time-lag in Type-2 cases, NO's of this type pose some particular challenges not presented by Type-1 cases. These particular challenges, in turn, make Type-2 NO's the most challenging to solve. For ease of exposition, I repeat the basic example of a Type-2 case here.

> Sample 2: John arrives at his apartment at 4:30 and, at that time, makes a promise, and is thus morally obligated in some sense, to pick up his friend Des at the airport tonight. He will need to leave at 7:00 in order to do this. Knowing that he has two and a half hours, he begins watching TV. As it turns out, he becomes so engrossed in the show he is watching that he forgets to pick up Des. It is not until 9:00, when Des calls John to ask him where he is, that John realizes he has omitted to fulfill his obligation.

We need to find a way to ascribe voluntariness and blameworthiness to John's ignorance, at 7:00, of the fact that it was then time for him to quit watching TV and leave. This is especially challenging, for it is difficult to specify any point in the example at which John may have done something unacceptable.

It may be suggested that one point in which culpability can ultimately be placed is John's watching TV. Why? It is clear that John did not have present in his mind an intellection of his obligation at 7:00; otherwise, the omission would not be negligent, but rather intentional (since an indistinct intellection implies some awareness on the part of the agent). And since John was watching TV, one can perhaps conclude that this obligation-related intellection is absent (and thus John's ignorance is present) on account of John performing intellectual tunnel vision on what he was watching. In such a case, blameworthiness is traced back to his performance of intellectual tunnel vision.

As it is, this suggestion does not initially carry much weight. Let us posit for sake of argument that John did indeed perform intellectual tunnel vision (hereafter, 'ITV') and did so at 5:00. There seems to be nothing wrong with his performing ITV at that time. He is *ex hypothesi* not required to keep the obligation in mind continuously (as in Type-1 cases). Furthermore, he need not have the obligation-related intellection in mind until 7:00, and performing ITV at 5:00 does not necessarily entail that the obligation-related intellection will be absent at 7:00. There thus appears to be no direct incompatibility between performing ITV at 5:00 and recalling or fulfilling his obligation.

The defense for the permissibility of performing ITV just offered, however, is itself questionable. It may be conceded that performing ITV at 5:00 is not, in and of itself, incompatible with recalling one's obligation at 7:00; only performing ITV at 7:00 would be. However, once ITV is begun, there is no guarantee that one will happen to recall one's obligation. Therefore, if John is about to perform ITV at 5:00, he has the further obligation to take steps (such as set an alarm) so as to help 'bring him out of tunnel vision,' so to speak, and remind him of his obligation to pick up Des. If he does not, then his subsequent ignorance can be traced back to his failure to take these steps when he is about to perform tunnel vision. In this way, one could continue to trace John's culpability back to his performance of ITV at 5:00 since he did so without taking additional steps.

Although this last objection is appealing in that it preserves performance of ITV as a cause of subsequent ignorance, it has the following drawback: it regards the resulting NO more in terms of a Type-3 NO, one in which either the time lag, seriousness of the matter, and/or particular circumstances call for additional preventative measures to be taken (such setting an alarm or tying a string around the finger) so as to ensure recalling one's obligation. The main challenge of Type-2 NO's, on the other hand, is to explain culpability when these extra precautions are *not* reasonably expected. If, then, John is to be blameworthy for a Type-2 NO, it seems not to be because of his starting ITV.

In light of this, one may try to hold John blameworthy not on account of hypothesizing that he performed ITV, but simply because he let the obligation-related intellection cease at some point (whether as a result of ITV or a simple absence of *complacere*) while watching TV. In this case, John would be blameworthy for failing to continue that intellection. This suggestion, however, fails because *ex hypothesi*, Sample 2 is a Type-2, not a Type-1, scenario. As such, John is under no obligation to maintain the obligation-related intellection in his mind continuously until 7:00; he cannot reasonably be expected to do so. To pin the blame on account of his failure to continue the obligation-related intellection runs the risk of treating Type-2 NO's as if they were those of Type 1.

These observations leave us in a tenuous position with regard to Type-2 NO's. We cannot solve them by requiring additional precautions such as writing oneself notes; that would collapse them into Type-3 NO's. At the same time, we cannot require the agent continuously to maintain the obligation-related intellection. That is a defining characteristic of Type-1 NO's. But if we both (i) affirm that the agent can permit the obligation-related intellection to cease before the time of expected fulfillment (TEF) and (ii) can do so without taking any supplemental precautions to remind herself of her obligation before TEF, culpability becomes very difficult to ascribe. For it will then seemingly be just a matter of chance whether an agent happens to recall her obligation or not, and she cannot rightly be blamed if the obligation-related intellection just happens not to come back to mind.

I will suggest throughout the remainder of this chapter that the resolution to Type-2 NO's does indeed depend on an agent being required to maintain an intellection continuously.[1] The intellection that must be maintained, however, is not the obligation-related intellection. There is no need to assume (as is implicitly done above) that the full obligation-related intellection is the only intellection an agent could cause to continue so as to make sure she fulfills her obligation. There is another type of intellection, one which I call a 'Lingering Indistinct Intellection' (hereafter 'LII') that the agent must continue so as to avoid committing a NO in Type-2 scenarios. In what follows, I will explain the concept of a LII and explain how the agent's continuing it does not entail Type-2 scenarios collapsing into those of Type-1. In the midst of this discussion, I will show that there are two variations of Type-2 NO's, each of which calls for a slightly different, yet LII-related, account of voluntariness for the NO. I will then conclude by noting the issues yet to be resolved in regard to Type-2 NO's and indicate that they will be after we have covered the material on Suarez.

II. Lingering Indistinct Intellections (LII's)

A. *General Description of LII's & Their Importance*

In many ways, what a 'lingering indistinct intellection' is can be derived from its name: it is an intellection that both is indistinct and lingers *as an indistinct intellection* in the agent's intellect. To say simply this, though, is not to recognize the way in which I regard LII's as substantially differing from other indistinct intellections. Allow me, therefore, to expound the concept by means of the analogy to vision.

Consider the fact that objects in one's peripheral vision not subsequently directly focused upon are, in general, in the periphery only briefly. Or, if they do remain peripherally-viewed objects for a longer time period, they do so often not because of any characteristic they themselves possess (otherwise the agent would probably look at them directly on account of that characteristic), but merely by happenstance. To explain: an agent, if not intrigued by a particular object x in her peripheral vision, generally lets that object fall out of her peripheral vision very quickly. She will either change her line of sight on account

[1] This means that ultimately the agent is not permitted to perform ITV in Type-2 cases also.

of following some other object *y* that does intrigue her especially, or (if she need not change her line of sight) will often perform visual tunnel vision on *y* to such an extent that *x* falls away from view. Of course, there are times at which one neither changes her line of sight nor performs visual tunnel vision and *x* remains in her peripheral view. In these latter cases, however, *x* generally remains in peripheral view by mere chance and could easily depart from view if the agent were either to focus more on what she is looking at or decide to change her line of sight. Objects viewed peripherally, therefore, are usually transitory and, at the very least, their existence as peripherally-viewed objects is extremely tenuous.

I argue that most indistinct intellections likewise do not linger as indistinct intellections but typically exist in the intellect only briefly. An intellection that is indistinct metaphorically presents itself to the agent as an alternative for cognition, just as peripherally-viewed objects present themselves as alternatives for direct vision. If the agent is interested in a particular intellection, she strengthens it so that it will comprise the content of cognition (i.e. she makes it distinct through *complacere*). If she is not interested, she subsequently ignores it and its object, a process that, per (P3), weakens and vitiates the intellection to non-existence. This is confirmed by experience. When alternative intellections present themselves to our intellect, we typically make a decision regarding those intellections: we will either focus on them, or dispose of them entirely from our cognitive view.

On the other hand, there do seem to be a few cases in which an intellection does persist indistinctly, and does so not by chance, but precisely because of some characteristic of that intellection itself. Consider again the analogy of vision. Let us imagine that peripherally-viewed object *x* and directly-viewed object *y* are both stationary such that the agent does not change her visual field. All things being equal, the agent would overly-focus on *y* to such an extent that *x* would drop from the periphery. However, let it furthermore be the case that *x* is the sort of object that flashes brilliantly in such an intermittent pattern that the agent is not able to habituate to its flashes. Because of the inability to habituate, the agent cannot focus fully on *y*; *x* continues to intrude upon her visual field, causing her to give *some* attention, however slight, to it. In other words, *x* lingers in the agent's peripheral view on account of some characteristic *x* possesses (brilliant intermittent flashing). This lingering of *x* in the peripheral visual field, in turn, creates some sort of disturbance or annoyance for the agent and her vision.

I want to suggest a similar phenomenon can occur in the intellect. Analogous to a flashing peripherally-viewed object, I will give reasons to support the possibility of an indistinct intellection that persists, or lingers, in the intellect as an indistinct intellection and does so not merely by chance or happenstance. Moreover, the lingering of this indistinct intellection gives rise to a certain 'feeling,' so to speak, of cognitive dissonance or annoyance, thereby disrupting the cognitive state of the agent to a degree.[2]

Having described a LII in general, I should briefly mention what I mean by the state of cognitive dissonance or annoyance caused by a LII and how this is related to solving Type-2 NO's. Consider the somewhat common phenomenon in which an agent realizes she has some nagging thought that she must be forgetting about something, or feels unsettled, or has some sort of 'cloud hanging over her head,' so to speak. Such descriptions correspond to what I take to be an agent's experience of cognitive disturbance or dissonance resulting from a LII. It is the LII's continuous presence that causes this feeling. This feeling, in turn, is to serve as a reminder to the agent that she must remember to do something. Stated very generally, therefore, Type-2 NO's occur when the agent either fails to heed (i.e. *neglects*) the reminder embodied by this feeling of dissonance, or either fails (i.e. *neglects*) to have a LII that would cause the cognitive dissonance that serves as a reminder to fulfill some obligation.

This is the basic outline of my proposed solution to Type-2 NO's. Before it can be elaborated upon, however, I must first discuss how a LII is formed in the first place, and why I think intellections of that type cause cognitive annoyance with the result that the agent is warned not to forget her obligation.

B. *The Formation of LII's, Part I: 'ContinualComp'*

Before discussing the content of a LII, I first want to examine how an intellection can be continued as merely an indistinct intellection over a

---

[2] My use of the term 'feeling' here may seem incorrect to some since what I am describing is an intellectual phenomenon, whereas feelings are technically emotional states involving physical changes. I do not believe this concern need detain us. If one wanted to persist in objecting to this terminological use, I could reply that an intellectual disruption may cause physical changes that could manifest themselves as feelings. But I am inclined to think that such argumentation is unnecessary. My main point is to discuss the commonly-experienced state of cognitive dissonance. I trust that this main point is grasped by the majority of readers.

period of time such that it can be characterized as 'lingering.' We have, in fact, already seen in the previous chapter how an intellection in general can be continued: for continuance of an intellection, *complacere* must be continually performed on an intellection to such an extent that that intellection does not cease to exist. What I want to do now, however, is elaborate a little more fully on what is involved in maintaining an intellection specifically at an indistinct level.

Performing *complacere* could be viewed as an exercise of 'psychic power.' The more strongly *complacere* is performed, the more psychic power one commits to the object of the intellection and thus to the intellection itself. For ease of exposition, therefore, let us assume that the relative strength of any intellection can be measured in terms of such psychic power, and let one unit of such power be called a 'complac.' Furthermore, let the level of psychic power above which an intellection is distinct and thus forms the content of cognition *per se* be 20 complacs; intellections with fewer complacs, yet more than 0, are correlatively indistinct.

With the above in mind, there seem to be two ways in which an intellection can be understood to linger indistinctly. First, the strength of the intellection could waffle up and down within the indistinct range. To explain: let intellection *q* be an indistinct intellection at a strength of 10 complacs. Per (P3), if *complacere* is not performed, *q* will begin to diminish and will eventually cease. If too much *complacere* is performed, *q* will strengthen and become distinct. Intellection *q* would therefore linger if *complacere* and *non-complacere* were performed alternately on the intellection or its object.[3] For example, let us suppose we want *q* to remain at the 10-complac level. If, as a result of not receiving any psychic power (i.e. *non-complacere*), the intellection were to diminish down to a level of 9 complacs, *complacere* must be performed on it just enough so that it returns to the 10-complac level.[4] This process could then be repeated over and over so as to reach a sort of stasis.

---

[3] Performing *complacere* on the object of the intellection is fine because, as mentioned in the previous chapter, that *complacere* 'spills over,' so to speak, into the intellection itself.

[4] Of course, the reverse demonstration can be done if an intellection becomes too strong and the agent wants it to remain at a lower level: she would cease performing any *complacere* or nil it to such an extent that it would decrease. I do not discuss this possibility in the text, however, for (as will become apparent by the end of the book), there is no problem with any obligation-related intellection becoming too strong. Becoming too weak is the major pitfall that must be avoided so as to avoid NO's.

There is another way in which such a stasis could be achieved. Instead of depending upon an alternation between *complacere* and *non-complacere*, this way assumes that *complacere* can be performed at different levels of intensity. One can 'take pleasure in' something more or less intensely. Given this, a *continual* but less intense performance of *complacere*, analogous to the idling of an engine, on either the intellection or its object would result in a lingering of an intellection.

I do not believe it ultimately matters which of these two options we pick. In the first place, depending upon how quickly the alternation of short bursts of *complacere* occurs in the first suggestion, maintaining a LII by that means would closely resemble the continual *complacere* of the second. Moreover, in both scenarios, some level of constant vigilance is called for. Such need is obvious in the second way, for how else can a constant willing (of which *complacere* is a form) come about. In the first, one must always beware of the imminent dissipation of a neglected (i.e. *complacere*-not-performed-on) indistinct intellection. For ease of explanation, I will use the term 'ContinualComp' to refer to either of these processes by which an intellection is caused to linger at an indistinct level.

C. *The Formation of LII's, Part 2: 'Mere Obligation Intellections' (MOI's)*

Based upon what has been said so far, it may be wondered how my solution for Type-2 NO's differs from that for Type-1 NO's. Both require continuance of an intellection by means of *complacere*, and it is compatible with the solution for Type-1 NO's that the intellection be continued as indistinct. The answer is that the two scenarios call for different intellections to be continued. In Type-1 scenarios, it is the full obligation-related intellection one is expected to continue so as to avoid culpability. In Type-2 scenarios, a slightly different intellection is involved.

Consider the intellection John has of his obligation upon initially undertaking it. Its content is something like <I am promising to pick up Des from the airport at 7:00 this evening>. Note that there are two different types of content contained therein. On the one hand, there is the content relevant to what exactly it is he must do, namely "pick up Des from the airport at 7:00." This description of the action under question entails nothing regarding John's obligation to perform it. It could follow any number of phrases that do not imply an obligation, such as

"I am permitted, but do not need, to," "I am not allowed to," "Nobody will." The fact that John is placing himself under an obligation, or is obligated, is thus conceptually different from the action to which he is obligated.

Given there are at least these two different concepts in the initial intellection, there seems no reason why an intellection of the fact that one is obligated to do *something at all* could not be psychically separated from the idea of *what exactly* it is one is obligated to. For example, it may be the case that there are actually two different intellections initially, each corresponding to one of the concepts. Or perhaps the content corresponding to one of the concepts eventually drops out of the intellection. Or maybe the agent can simply psychically separate them by performing *complacere* on one concept contained in the intellection and not on the other. I do not believe it is very important to stipulate an exact process; my only aim is to state that there seems to be no reason some such process could not exist. Consequently, I want to posit its possibility and affirm that whichever concept survives as an intellection does so on account of the agent performing *complacere* on it.

It is possible, therefore, that an agent, after having undertaken an obligation, could eventually come to have an intellection corresponding to the mere fact that she has an obligation. That is, there can be an intellection with the content <I must do something> without it being the case that a description of what that 'something' is be contained in that intellection. Common experience supports this assertion. We often have intellections, whether distinct or indistinct, concerning the fact that there is something we are to do without it being the case that we know what that something is. I want to call such an intellection, i.e. one regarding merely the fact that one must do something, a 'Mere Obligation Intellection' (hereafter, 'MOI'). It is, in my proposal, the MOI that is to become the LII and be the recipient of ContinualComp. The content of the intellection that lingers is hence something to the effect that one must do something.

III. How the LII/MOI Concepts Help Explain Culpability for Type-2 NO's

A. *The Overall Picture & Two Variations of Type-2 NO's*

We are now in a position to understand how one can be expected to recall an obligation in a Type-2 scenario. I will begin by presenting the general picture and subsequently address particular details. Consider John at 4:30 in Sample 2. At that point, he undertakes the obligation. The time lag between undertaking and TEF is *ex hypothesi* too long for him reasonably to be expected to keep his obligation in mind continuously so as to make sure he remembers it. Alternatively, the time lag is too short, nor do the particular circumstances warrant, that he set an alarm, take extra precautions, etc. He must, however, make sure to recall his obligation. As a result, he psychically separates out from his initial intellection the MOI, an intellection of the mere fact that there is something he needs to do. It is this MOI that will help him recall his obligation.[5]

Since he is depending upon the MOI to remind him of his obligation, he cannot let it slip from his intellect. He accordingly performs ContinualComp on this MOI, causing it to become a LII. The presence of the MOI/LII and the fact that he is performing ContinualComp so that it continues as a LII cause a feeling of cognitive dissonance, annoyance, or unsettledness. This annoyance or unsettledness, in turn, serves as a constant reminder to John that something is amiss. It 'casts a cloud over his head,' so to speak. As a result, he comes to have what we often call the 'sneaking suspicion' that he is forgetting something. This sneaking suspicion, or feeling of unsettledness, is to serve as a warning to John not to forget something. In other words, it places him in a constant 'on-guard' status against not failing to remember his obligation.[6]

At or near 7:00, he is to heed the warning presented by this 'on-guard' or unsettled status. Given that he is experiencing such cognitive dissonance caused by the result of a LII, and basically contributing to that dissonance by means of his performance of ContinualComp, it would certainly seem appropriate to inquire about the source of this

---

[5] It has been suggested to me by Edward Waggoner that this 'psychic separation' is equivalent to setting an alarm clock, just an internal one. In a sense, this is correct. This, however, need not mean Type-2 NO's are collapsible into those of Type-3. My position is that there are situations in which setting such an internal alarm clock is called for and more plausible than taking extra steps such as setting an actual alarm, etc. Moreover, I maintain that there is a time span over which we are able to maintain this internal alarm clock.

[6] Why exactly the MOI/LII is to be experienced as a warning will be taken up near the end of the chapter. For now, consider the fact that by being aware of a MOI, the agent knows she must do something but does not know what that something is. To know one must do something but not know what that something is, however, seems inherently to 'call out' to, or rather 'warn', the agent to find out what it is she is forgetting.

dissonance. When he does, he *ideally*[7] recalls that he is to pick up Des; it is 'picking up Des' that he has been 'on-guard' not to forget. The combination of the LII and ContinualComp are thus to help prevent John's ignorance of his obligation at 7:00.

We can now return to Sample 2 and begin to explain how it is that John does not recall his obligation at 7:00 and can be blamed for it. In fact, there are two possible explanations, and it will be easier to elaborate upon these explanations by appeal to the following two variations of Sample 2.

> Sample 2, Variation A: When John receives the phone call from Des at 9:00, his first reaction is to exclaim (either aloud or silently to himself), "I knew I was forgetting something!"
>
> Sample 2, Variation B: When John receives the phone call from Des at 9:00, it 'hits him out of the blue,' so to speak. His first reaction is *not* "I knew I was forgetting something!" but rather, "I *completely* forgot."

I believe Variations A and B accurately depict two different reactions often experienced as a result of finding out we omitted to fulfill an obligation. Sometimes, we *knew* we were forgetting something, and somewhat chastise ourselves for going ahead and doing whatever we did instead of thinking some more about what it is we might have forgotten. At other times, finding out we omitted an obligation we had previously undertaken completely surprises us. Now that we are reminded of it, we can of course recall having undertaken it, but any thoughts of the obligation had meanwhile slipped completely from our minds. There were no thoughts to the effect that we must be forgetting something running up to the time of expected fulfillment.

I believe the omissions in both variations can be considered culpable NO's.[8] Moreover, the voluntariness by which they are culpable can

---

[7] I say 'ideally,' for we can all easily imagine cases in which someone does try to remember her obligation and just cannot. Is this a problem for my interpretation? No. Issues surrounding this question will be discussed later in the book. Suffice it to say for now, however, that if an agent does all she should so as to remember her obligation (i.e. she was supposed to create a MOI/LII, and she heeded it as a warning and thus 'racked her brain' in order to find out what it was) and she just cannot remember her obligation, her ignorance would in that case be what the medievals called 'invincible' and thus not-voluntary. In response, it may be suggested that the full obligation-related intellection instead of the MOI should be continued. I discuss this later in the chapter.

[8] There are certain additional circumstances that could make the omissions in either case non-culpable. These will be discussed in the conclusion. My point here is that culpability can theoretically be ascribed to scenarios resembling either Variation A or Variation B.

ultimately be explained by appeal to the concept of a MOI/LII and ContinualComp. In Variation A, John is culpable for voluntarily ignoring the warning given him by the feeling of unsettledness. He experiences this feeling of unsettledness or cognitive dissonance and, in the face of that warning, nonetheless refuses (*ex hypothesi*) to inquire into its source.[9] He does something else instead of pay more attention to that warning – he continues watching TV and, as a result, remains ignorant of the fact that he is supposed to fulfill his obligation. The *neglectfulness* in a NO of this type and variation, therefore, consists in the fact that he *neglects* (does not heed) the warning he is being issued by the LII. Moreover, it will eventually become clear that he voluntarily neglects this warning, for the presence of the MOI/LII implies awareness of the fact that <he should do *something*> (that, after all, is the content of the MOI). And knowing that one should do something, but not knowing what that something is, should be experienced as a sign or warning to investigate what exactly it is that one must do.[10]

In Variation B, he does not have a warning in the form of unsettledness to heed. How, then, is he to be held blameworthy in this case? Precisely *because* he has no warning to heed. Upon undertaking an obligation in a Type-2 scenario, one has the further obligation to psychically create a MOI and perform ContinualComp on it so that it becomes a LII and subsequently causes some form of cognitive annoyance/unsettledness by which the agent is to be warned. If this warning is missing, it is because either (i) the agent began the process, but at some point before TEF did something else instead of continue to perform ContinualComp, leading to the cessation of the MOI/LII as an intellection, or (ii) the agent *neglected* to create the MOI and begin ContinualComp in the first place but did something else instead. He

[9] Of course, there are cases in which an agent in a Variation A scenario does attempt to inquire into the source for the unsettledness and fails to find out, just as we often sometimes know we are forgetting something and just cannot remember, however hard we may try, what it is. In such cases, the omission may indeed be non-culpable and involuntary (assuming that the circumstances were not such that it should have been a Type-3 scenario in which the agent writes herself a note, etc.). We will be able to comment more on this in the concluding chapter. The present point is that there are cases in which an agent either does not, or at least does not adequately, probe into the cause of her unsettledness. Such cases are culpable for reasons I am about to explain.

[10] Particular questions concerning the ascription of voluntariness to such acts will be discussed near the end of this chapter. At the present, it is enough to recognize that in such actions, the will refuses (*non velle*) to heed the warning and inquire into the details of one's obligation. Since this refusal results from the will's freedom, the refusal is voluntary and can be ascribed to the agent.

treated his obligation flippantly. I will briefly comment on each of these possibilities.

Type-2/Variation B (i)

If a Type-2/Variation B NO ultimately occurs because the agent failed to perform ContinualComp on the MOI and thus cause it to persist as a LII, the agent is culpable and neglectful in a way analogous that which occurs in Type-1 NO's. The neglectfulness consists in the agent's *neglecting* to continue the MOI. Since it is within the agent's power of the will to continue performing *complacere* on that MOI, such neglect is also voluntary and culpable.

Type-2/Variation B (ii)

Identifying the exact instance of *neglectfulness* is even easier in those cases in which there is no MOI, and thus no warning mechanism in place. It lies in the agent's *neglecting* the task of creating the MOI and beginning to perform ContinualComp on it in the first place. Allow me to elaborate by means of an analogy.

Consider the common situation of being introduced to several new persons upon entering a room. One of two different phenomena typically ensues: either we immediately forget the name of (nearly) every person we just met, or we actually do recall several of their names. I suggest that that when we do remember names, it is because we have in some sense mentally 'processed' those names differently than we do whenever we do not remember. Perhaps, for example, we paused (albeit imperceptibly) to repeat the name in our head. In any case, when we remember, it is likely that we psychically did something with the intellection of the new person's name such that the information would be affixed to a longer-term memory. Correlatively, this distinctive act of mental processing is absent in those instances in which we do not remember the names.[11]

I understand an agent to be, at the time of initially undertaking an obligation in a Type-2 scenario, in a position analogous to that of the person walking into a room full of new faces. If she takes her obligation seriously, she mentally 'processes' the intellection regarding that obligation in a way qualitatively different from how she would if she did

[11] The analogy to remembering names was suggested to me by a professor from Southern Illinois University-Edwardsville during an interview at the Eastern APA in Boston (Dec. 2004). I unfortunately do not know her name.

not take it seriously, just as a person meeting new people 'processes' the names of those she wants to be sure to remember differently. And in terms of the framework presented here, I understand the 'processing' to consist of separating out a MOI and beginning ContinualComp on it. If performing this process is *neglected*, the resulting omission can ultimately be traced back to this instance of neglect.

Having presented the overall picture and introduced the two variations, I will now address several questions that have no doubt arisen in the reader's mind. By doing so, the overall picture of culpability for Type-2 NO's will be more fully developed.

B. *How Type-2 NO's Differ From Those Of Type-1*

Type-1 and Type-2 scenarios differ on the basis of some qualitative difference in their respective time lags between undertaking an obligation and TEF. Wherein, though, lies that qualitative difference? In response to an earlier concern that Type-2 NO's may collapse into those of Type-1 on account of both scenarios requiring continuance of an intellection, I indicated that they are nevertheless different because the two types of scenario call for different intellections to be continued. In Type-1 cases, the full intellection regarding one's obligation is to be continued; in Type-2 cases, it is only the MOI. The qualitative difference, therefore, arises in virtue of the fact that the different time-spans call for different intellections to be continued.

Despite this clarification, it may be wondered why continuance of the full obligation-related intellection, instead of only the MOI, is not called for in Type-2 cases. If continuance of an intellection is required anyway, why not simply posit that the agent is required to maintain the more complete intellection?

Asserting that one may need continue only the MOI instead of the full obligation-related intellection is all the more puzzling in light of the following consideration: even if a MOI is continued until TEF, there is still the possibility for ignorance regarding one's obligation at that time. For it may happen (and often does) that one specifically recalls "I am supposed to do *something*" and, despite her best efforts, cannot recall exactly what it is she is to do. If, on the other hand, the original, complete obligation-related intellection is continued, the agent will be unable to recall the fact that she has an obligation without, at the same time, recalling what specifically it is. Since she is required to continue some intellection anyway, she might as well be required to continue the intellection that is less likely to lead to failure of recalling her obligation - namely, the full obligation-related intellection. As a result, it is difficult to imagine a scenario in which one ought to continue only a MOI.

This last consideration, if valid, would imply that there is no basis by which qualitatively to distinguish Type-1 from Type-2 scenarios. The only difference between them would be one of degree: the continuance is to be longer in one than in the other. The solutions to NO's of each type would correlatively be the same, for scenarios of both types (per this objection) call for the same process by which the same intellections are continued.

One attempt to preserve a qualitative difference between the two scenarios might be this: grant the point about what intellection must be continued, but insist the two types nonetheless differ on account of the fact that in Type-1 scenarios, the intellection must receive *complacere* to such a degree that it remains distinct, i.e. forms the content of cognition. For Type-2 scenarios, however, the intellection can remain indistinct. Stated differently, Type-1 scenarios call for a lingering *distinct* intellection instead of a lingering *indistinct* one.

This argument in support of a difference does not ultimately stand. In light of the specifics of the doctrine of indistinct intellections, there is no reason why the intellection in Type-1 cases need be distinct. As long as an intellection is indistinct, the agent has some level of cognitive awareness of it. Recall that the level of cognitive awareness present by means of an indistinct intellection is such that the will can freely and voluntarily decide either to perform *complacere* or not on the intellection and/or its object. This is on account of the fact that the presence of that indistinct intellection fulfills Scotus's knowledge requirement for voluntariness (SKR) with regard to actions concerning that intellection or its object. Given that the simple presence of an indistinct intellection implies a robust-enough level of awareness such that SKR is fulfilled, a level higher than indistinctness need not be required in Type-1 cases for the agent to fulfill her obligation. Maintenance of the obligation-related intellection at the level of distinctness, therefore, is not required in Type-1 scenarios.[12] This attempt to distinguish Type-1 from Type-2

---

[12] Indeed, Sample 1 did not posit that John ought to keep the intellection of his obligation *distinct*. It fully allowed that he may be permitted to watch TV for a few minutes, and thereby make the intellection corresponding to that action distinct. The only expectation expressed was that the full obligation-related intellection not cease and thereby depart from his intellect.

cases on the basis of the strength of the intellection-to-be-continued accordingly fails.

As opposed to the just-discussed attempt to preserve a qualitative difference between the two types, I continue to maintain their distinction on account of the specific intellection to be continued: the full intellection in Type-1 cases, and the MOI in Type-2 cases. I do so because I reject the assumption, expressed in the objection above, that if one must continue an intellection, one might as well continue the full obligation-related intellection. I say this based on the possibility that continuing a fuller intellection is psychically more difficult and strenuous than is continuing a less full one, such as a MOI. The more content contained in an intellection, the more difficult it is to maintain that full intellection. If this is so, it only makes sense to think that an agent cannot reasonably be expected to keep a fuller intellection in mind for a long time, but perhaps can reasonably be expected to continue a less full intellection for a longer time period. It is on account of this possible phenomenon that the difference in time-lags gives rise to the qualitative difference between Type-1 and Type-2 scenarios, a qualitative difference based upon the specific intellection that is to be continued.

Support for the possibility underlying this defense is to be found in common experience. Very rarely, I suggest, are agents easily able to keep in mind or stay aware of all the specifics regarding some obligation, even if they attempt to. They can only do so for short time spans. On the other hand, we often do seem to go for longer periods of time with the constant, nagging suspicion or awareness of the fact that there is something we are forgetting to do. (In fact, far from being hard to maintain, it is often hard to get rid of such suspicions and thoughts once we begin to have them.) I propose this difference in the ease of these intellections' persistence is a function of the complexity of their content: the more content-full, the more difficult to maintain; the less content-full, the less difficult. If I am correct in this, my conjecture that longer time-spans reasonably call for continuances of MOI's while shorter ones call for continuances of the full obligation-related intellections is buttressed.

C. *When Type-2 Becomes Type-1 & Knowing When To Recall the Specifics*

As just observed, I maintain that there is a qualitative difference between Type-2 and Type-1 scenarios based upon the specific intellection needing to be continued. Despite this difference, there remains the possibility that an agent could initially be in a Type-2 scenario upon undertaking the obligation but at the time of TEF be in a situation such that if a negligent omission occurs, it is classed as a Type-1 NO. To explain how this is possible, I want to entertain a concern regarding Type-2 NO's that calls into question my entire MOI/LII-based solution.

1. *The Problem of a Constant Warning: It cannot constantly be heeded*

The concern to be addressed is this: My proposed solution for Type-2 NO's is based upon the presence of a MOI/LII that is to serve as a warning to the agent that she is forgetting something. If at the time of expected fulfillment (TEF) she neglects this warning and proceeds to do whatever else it is she is doing at that time, she is blameworthy for the resulting omission. In order for her to be warned at TEF by the LII, however, she must perform *complacere* upon the MOI continuously (i.e. engage in ContinualComp) from the instant of undertaking the obligation until TEF. It is, after all, by this very act of performing ContinualComp on a MOI that the MOI becomes a LII and thus serves as a warning to the agent that she need inquire into the specifics of what it is she is being warned not to forget. It follows, therefore, that if the agent is given a warning at all on account of there being a LII, she is being warned continuously (from the point of undertaking the obligation until TEF) to inquire into the specifics.

It is unreasonable, however, to expect an agent constantly to heed this warning (i.e. 'rack her brain' so as to try to recall the specifics) over the entire time-lag in a Type-2 scenario.[13] If she were to constantly heed it, she would in effect be attempting to maintain the full obligation-related intellection continuously. The point of saving psychic energy by creating a MOI would thus be lost. My solution, on the other hand, appears to hold that the agent need only inquire into the specifics *when TEF approaches* so as to avoid engaging in a Type-2 NO. This, however, brings us to the crux of the problem. How is the agent supposed to know that TEF is approaching if she is not aware of the specifics regarding the obligation she has?

---

[13] As Tobias Hoffmann has pointed out to me, it can be not only unreasonable but even blameworthy to do so if doing so were to cause one to neglect other duties one has during that time span.

Suppose in Sample 2/Variation A that 4:30 is t_1 and 7:00 (TEF) is t_8. John need not heed the warning before t_8. How, though, is he to know at t_8 that he is indeed at t_8 if all he need be aware of is the MOI (as a LII) that contains the simple content that one must do something? There seems to be no reason for John to treat t_8 any differently from t_5 if he is only (indistinctly) aware of the fact that he must remember *something*, and not aware of the time at which he must remember that something. Given that we cannot create the unreasonable expectation for an agent to heed constantly the LII as a warning, it appears to be no more than a matter of chance as to whether the warning will be heeded at the appropriate time. The adequacy of a LII-based approach for understanding Type-2 scenarios is thus called into question.

2. *How to know when exactly to heed the warning – Semi-MOI's*
There are two responses that will help salvage a LII-based approach from such charges. First, it is possible that the agent somehow incorporates a time into the MOI, thus building into the MOI/LII at least one specific detail regarding the obligation. (Call it a semi-mere obligation intellection, if you like.) The intellection receiving ContinualComp so as to become the LII would in that case not have the mere content <I must do something> but rather <I must do something at 7:00>. Alternatively, if the agent is not normally sensitive to the particular time of day, perhaps an activity the agent knows she will be doing at TEF can be placed into the content of the MOI. Suppose, for example, John happens to know at 4:30 that he will start watching the big ballgame on TV at 6:55. Watching the game can, as a result, serve as a marker to him that he should heed the LII as a warning. The associated content in the semi-MOI would thus be <I must do something around the time I start watching the ballgame>. Adding such specifics to an intellection that will linger indistinctly in the agent's awareness is thus one way in which to address the objection above.

I think there is some intuitive support for this solution, especially as it is expressed in terms of associated activities. Many of our everyday cases of omission center on our forgetting to bring or do something when we leave, for instance, our homes or offices. For example, while sitting at home, we may be indistinctly aware that we must remember to do something as we go about our daily affairs. But as we are about to leave the house we experience this indistinct awareness as a warning. At such times, we often have the unsettled feeling expressed by the statement "I know I'm forgetting something." Per the current suggestion, the warning is experienced at this time because the underlying semi-MOI making up the LII has the content <I must remember to do something *when I leave my house*>. Because of the presence of this additional detail in the indistinct intellection, the agent is (indistinctly) aware of the fact that, upon leaving the house, she must remember something. She thus experiences the LII as a warning at the appropriate time.

There is one drawback to this solution. If what I posited earlier regarding the relation between psychic energy and content-fullness of intellections is correct, it will be somewhat more difficult to maintain a semi-MOI than a normal MOI over a period of time. It is unclear how large a problem this presents, for it may be the case that the amount of extra energy required is small enough such that an agent can still reasonably be expected to continue it over the time-lag appropriate to Type-2 scenarios. Or, it may be that the time-lag we typically recognize as appropriate to Type-2 scenarios is accordingly less than it otherwise would be if only a MOI, as opposed to a semi-MOI, need be continued. In either case, by means of the assumption of a MOI with a TEF-related detail added, we have one response to the problem of how the agent is to know when she should and should not heed the LII as a warning and inquire into what specifically she is to do.

3. *How to know when exactly to heed the warning – Periodic Heeding*
There is in addition a second way to respond to the worry above and preserve the original understanding of a MOI. Let it be the case that a TEF-related detail is not added to the MOI, and the presence of the MOI as the LII is indeed continuously experienced as a warning by the agent. I noted above that it is unreasonable to expect the agent to inquire continuously into the specific details of what it is she must remember. To do so would be practically equivalent to placing the same expectations upon an agent in a Type-2 scenario that are in effect in Type-1 cases. However, it may not be unreasonable to expect an agent, in a Type-2 scenario with a MOI/LII continuously being experienced as a warning to heed, to inquire *periodically* into the specific details of what it is she must remember.

To demonstrate the utility of this suggestion, let us again return to Sample 2/Variation A and posit that John can reasonably be expected to keep a full obligation-related intellection in mind for five minutes. Any length of time remaining to TEF longer than five minutes results for him in a Type-2 scenario. Having set these parameters, suppose that

John feels constantly warned from 4:30 on by the presence of a bare (i.e. no specific detail added) MOI serving as a LII. As a result of experiencing this LII as a warning, John heeds it by inquiring into the details of his obligation at, say, 4:33 and quickly realizes that that which he must do is pick up Des at 7:00. Since he still has time, he goes about his business. Soon, the specifics of his obligation slip from his mind again. At 4:36, he is again experiencing the unsettledness caused by the LII as a warning. At this point, however, he is aware, or no doubt quickly and easily becomes so,[14] of the fact that he just inquired into the specifics concerning that warning three minutes ago at 4:33. If three minutes ago (when John inquired into the specifics) he had discovered that TEF was near enough so that he could keep the full obligation-related intellection in mind (i.e. within five minutes), he would probably not have gone about his business as he has been for the last three minutes while continuing only the MOI. He most likely would have kept the full obligation-related intellection in mind so as to be sure to fulfill it. In other words, the time remaining to TEF in that case would have been short enough so as to enable him constantly to preserve the full intellection.[15] Since both he did not so preserve the full obligation-related intellection, and the time lapsed since his last inquiry (three minutes) does not exceed the time span within which he would have decided to keep the full obligation-related intellection in mind (five minutes), he can feel comfortable deciding not to heed the warning and can hence refrain at this time from inquiring into the specifics of his obligation. It will not be until, say, 4:39 that he will be expected to heed the warning

[14] This occurs no doubt by means of a separate intellection. Given that, it may be wondered why, if I am calling for a separate time-related intellection, the current response does not simply collapse into the first response I offered in terms of semi-MOI's. In other words, if an intellection regarding 'how long it has been since one last heeded the warning' is required, it seems as if that detail is just built into the MOI, thus turning it into a semi-MOI. But if it is so built into the MOI, this response ultimately does not differ from that offered specifically in terms of semi-MOI's.

While I concede that creating a semi-MOI by adding a detail to the intellection regarding the length of time since the warning was last heeded is possible, I deny that the present response must necessarily assume this. It thus does not collapse into the former. It may, for example, be the case that the detail regarding 'length of time since the warning was last heeded' need not be continued as, or in, any intellection, but is just simply easier to recall from the recesses of our mind for some reason when one begins wondering whether she should heed a warning. Such indeed often seems to be our (or at least 'my') experience. Given this possibility, the current response can be regarded as different from the former.

[15] Indeed, he actually would be required to do this so as to be sure not to culpably omit his obligation. Why this is the case will become clear soon.

and inquire into the specifics of his obligation. For (assuming he has not already engaged in a NO) it will only be at that time that there exists the possibility that the TEF is at hand or approaching without his being presently aware of that fact. This process is expected to continue until TEF or some instant within five minutes of TEF, at which instant the agent will be expected to bring to mind and maintain specifics of his obligation (or rather, the entire obligation-related intellection) so as to help ensure he does not engage in an omission.

The point of the example is that even if an agent experiences a MOI/LII as a constant warning, it does not necessarily follow that she must continuously heed it by inquiring into and explicitly bringing to mind the specific details of her obligation. An agent need only heed it and inquire into the details periodically. Moreover, we can give an indication as to how long the periods between inquiries should be: they should be the smallest amount of time greater than the longest amount of time one can reasonably be expected to keep a full obligation-related intellection in mind. For example, in the case above, John *ex hypothesi* can reasonably be expected to keep in mind a full obligation-related intellection for only five minutes. As a result, he is expected to heed the warning and inquire into the specific details every six minutes.

The present response has the downside that it supposes a lot of self-knowledge and self-awareness on the part of the agent. The agent must know how long it has been since she last heeded the warning and inquired into the details. She must also know how long a time period she can reasonably be expected to keep something continuously in mind. These suppositions, however, are not particularly problematic. Most of us have a general idea or 'feeling' as to over how long a time period we can reasonably be expected, or expect ourselves, to keep something continuously in mind. Moreover, it does not seem excessive to think that we are often aware, in the face of a constant warning, of whether it has been too long or not since we last explicitly brought to mind the specific details regarding some obligation. In fact, it seems as if we often do such calculations nearly automatically or (to speak in contemporary, but not medieval, language) subconsciously.

The picture of Type-2/Variation A scenarios I have just presented may be objected to on the following basis. It appears as if one must nevertheless heed the warning (by which I mean inquire into the specific details of what it is one ought to do) very often. In the example above, for instance, one must do so every six minutes. This requires an excessive amount of psychic energy and vigilance. The point of maintaining a MOI/LII instead of the full obligation-related intellection in the first place, however, is to save psychic energy for longer time spans. The understanding presented here, therefore, seems to contradict the intended purpose of the MOI/LII proposal.

In response, I first want to say that the numbers above are arbitrary, and it may be the case that many of us can be expected to keep a full obligation-related intellection in mind for more than five minutes. Second, even if it is the case that a lot of energy is expended because the warning must be often heeded, I still posit that in some cases this is more reasonably expected of an agent than is continuing the full obligation-related intellection. Finally, it may even be the case that when an agent last heeded the warning, she realized that it would be *a long* time until TEF. In that case, she need not heed the warning as often as she otherwise would, but can wait for whatever is *a long time* for her.[16] The charge that periodic heeding requires an excessive amount of energy and vigilance consequently does not stand.

To take stock of where we are, we have finished elaborating on the second way in which to respond to the initial question as to how an agent is supposed to know that TEF is approaching if she is not aware of the specifics regarding the obligation she has? The first answer was based upon the proposal of a semi-MOI; it could be the case that the TEF-related detail is added to the MOI, and it is this semi-MOI that is the LII. The second answer suggested it may be the case that the agent need only periodically heed the warning.

4. *When a Type-2 scenario becomes a Type-1 scenario: Why it is not a problem*

The argumentation in support of the second response brings up a further point regarding the relation between Type-1 and Type-2 scenarios. I indicated that if an agent heeds the warning and realizes that the time until TEF is less than that time span over which she can reasonably be expected to keep a full obligation-related intellection in mind, she must continue that full intellection constantly until TEF in order to help prevent herself from engaging in an omission. But to maintain a full obligation-related intellection continuously until TEF is characteristic

[16] Of course, this entails that upon further instances of being warned, she is aware of the fact that, at her last inquiry, she realized TEF was a long time away. This awareness itself would require an intellection. This fact, in turn, gives rise to several concerns similar to those I addressed in the previous footnote. Please see my comments there.

of Type-1, not Type-2 scenarios. Does this mean, therefore, that Type-2 scenarios can turn into those of Type-1?

The simple answer is yes. The time-lag difference between the two scenarios has been generally expressed in terms of the time-lag between the initial undertaking of the obligation and TEF, but this has been done mostly for the sake of clarity. As we pointed out in the introduction to the book, the relevant time-span by which to distinguish scenarios is that between the *latest point before TEF* that the agent has had full awareness (in the sense of being aware of all the details) regarding her obligation and TEF. The initial undertaking is no doubt the first point before TEF that the agent has such awareness. Sometimes it is also the last and only, but it need not be. If an agent has awareness of all the details of her obligation at a point suitably close to TEF such that she should keep that fuller intellection constantly in mind, then that is exactly what she is required to do. It does not matter whether she has the awareness at that time as a result of initially undertaking the obligation at that point, or arriving at that point by means of a MOI/LII. She is, at that point, no longer in a Type-2 (if she had been before), but rather in a Type-1, scenario.

The fact that a Type-2 scenario can sometimes lead into a Type-1 scenario does not lessen the distinction between those scenarios nor between the corresponding types of NO's. The two scenarios call for different intellections to be continued, and which intellection is called for is a function of how long the time span is from one's latest awareness of the specifics until TEF. The possibility that one can be in different scenarios over the course of time between the initial undertaking of the obligation and TEF only means that at different points in the time span running up to TEF, one's latest awareness of the specifics may be at first farther from, and then closer to, TEF. In order to fulfill any one particular obligation, therefore, it may be the case that different intellections need to be continued at different points.

If one fails to fulfill her obligation as a result of negligence and is initially in a Type-2 scenario, the type of NO that emerges will then be based upon what scenario she was in (i.e. what intellection she was at that time required to maintain[17]) at the time the subsequent ignorance relevant to the obligation was caused. It will be a Type-1 NO if the

---

[17] And this, of course, is based upon how long the time-span is between the last point at which she had been aware of the specifics of her obligation and TEF.

ignorance is caused by not continuing a full obligation-related intellection at some point. It will be a Type-2 NO if the ignorance results from failing either to continue a MOI or to create it in the first place (Variation B), or from failing to heed the warning issued by the MOI/LII when one should (Variation A).[18]

D. *Relative Levels of Blameworthiness as Support for the Distinction Between Types*

Having more fully discussed Type-2 NO's and their distinction from those of Type-1, I want to add support for the overall framework being presented here by considering levels of blameworthiness. *Ceteris paribus*, we typically hold agents more blameworthy for failing to fulfill an obligation when the time span between awareness of their obligation and TEF is very short than when it is a little longer (yet not so long as to call for extra precautions as in Type-3 scenarios).[19] For example, Des would no doubt be more irritated, and place a higher level of blame, on John in Sample 1 than in Sample 2. Why do we recognize such a difference in blameworthiness? I believe the answer can be phrased in terms of the current proposal.

Psychically creating a MOI, performing ContinualComp on it for a longer period of time, recognizing and heeding it as a warning, and then attempting to try to remember the specifics of one's obligation is all a very complex process. Many possibilities for failure exist in it. Given this treacherous path toward obligation fulfillment in Type-2

[18] Note that a similar demonstration can be made for how Type-3 scenarios may ultimately result in a Type-1 NO. If the agent sets an alarm and is reminded two minutes before TEF, and in those two minutes ceases to have that intellection, her NO would be of Type-1, even though she began in a Type-3 scenario. More discussion of these issues will take place in the conclusion of the book.

[19] It has been suggested to me that we sometimes hold agents more blameworthy when the time span is much longer than when it is somewhat shorter, for in longer time spans the obligated agent has had 'plenty of advance warning.' In response, I believe that when we blame an agent more because the time-span is longer, we are addressing a Type-3, not a Type-2 scenario. In other words, in cases in which there is such 'plenty of advance warning,' the time span is such that the obligated agent should have taken special precautions. Because there are fewer chances for mistake in taking an early special precaution (e.g. all one has to do is 'set an alarm' or write a note in her calendar), NO's arising in Type-3 scenarios would be more blameworthy than those arising in Type-2 scenarios. The further fact nonetheless remains, however, that Type-2 NO's are generally less blameworthy than Type-1 NO's, for in a Type-1 NO the time span is so short that there is just no excuse for the agent to have done anything that would have caused her to lose any awareness of any aspect of her obligation.

scenarios, blame can be lessened. Over a shorter time period, as in Type-1 scenarios, these more complex and longer-lasting measures which produce more possibilities for failure are not needed. To have failed, then, in a Type-1 scenario in which one does not face additional possibilities for failure is relatively more blameworthy.

In other words, there are fewer mitigating circumstances in Type-1 than in Type-2 NO's, and it is for this reason that we ascribe more blame to the former than the latter. And the fact that these mitigating circumstances can be expressed in terms of the framework presented here adds credibility to my application of the doctrine of indistinct intellections to the problem of negligent omissions.

E. *Recognizing the LII as a Warning, and the Problem of Voluntariness*

I want to lead into my discussion of voluntariness by bringing up an issue we have not yet resolved. My solution to Type-2/Variation A NO's is largely based upon the fact that the presence of the MOI as a LII on account of ContinualComp produces an experience of cognitive dissonance or unsettledness that the agent should recognize as a warning. It is not yet clear, however, *why* an agent can be expected to pay special attention to that instance of cognitive dissonance as a warning. One way to answer this question would be to assert that cognitive dissonance is inherently a warning signal that something is amiss or wrong and that the agent should inquire into why she may be having this experience. More specifically, it could be posited that the precise kind of dissonance caused by a MOI being a LII has some special affinity to states of apprehension and warning. After all, to have an intellection that one has to do something without an accompanying intellection or awareness of what that something is seems implicitly to 'call out to' or 'warn' the agent to find out what it is she must do. When it is further considered that the agent is maintaining, through ContinualComp, this relatively nonspecific intellection so that it lingers, it stands to reason that she might ask herself why she is maintaining this intellection. She would thus would be prompted (i.e. warned) to inquire into the details surrounding it.

I believe the reasoning just presented is indicative of the correct way in which to understand an agent to be expected to recognize the MOI/LII as a warning. More, however, needs to be said in support. For despite the fact it seems reasonable that the agent would 'ask herself' why she is maintaining that intellection, she may not. And if she does not, it is unclear how her failure to perceive the unsettledness as a warning can be ascribable to her. For if an agent is to be blameworthy on account of failing to heed the warning, she must *voluntarily* fail to heed the warning. Based upon the understanding of voluntariness given in Chapter 1, this entails she must have some knowledge such as <what I am doing is failing to heed a warning I should heed>. She cannot have this knowledge, however, if she does not experience the unsettledness as a warning. Furthermore, even if she does experience it as a warning, it is not clear that she would necessarily be aware of the fact that she is failing to heed it. Consequently, one issue yet to be resolved (similar to the remaining issue in regard to Type-1 NO's) is how to understand that such an agent has this particular knowledge.

We are in a similar position with regard to Type-2/Variation B NO's. In those cases, the agent either fails to continue some MOI as a LII, or fails to create a MOI/LII in the first place. These failures are supposedly voluntary and thus blameworthy because it is 'in the power of the will' to do these actions or not. But to be in the power of the will, Scotus's knowledge requirement (SKR) must be fulfilled. The knowledge required for these particular failures is either <what I am doing is failing to continue a MOI as a LII though I should so continue it> or <what I am doing is failing to create a MOI/LII though I should create it>. We have seen no reason, however, to suppose the presence of an intellection corresponding to either of these descriptions in cases in which we hold the agent to have acted voluntarily and culpably. It is thus not yet clear how these failures in Type-2/Variation B NO's are in the power of the will and voluntary.

We do, on the other hand, know some intellections the agent must have. She must initially have possessed the obligation-related intellection; otherwise, she would not be under an obligation in the first place.[20] And if she began ContinualComp on a LII but did not continue it, she must also have had the MOI. Since it does not matter whether an intellection is distinct or not so as to fulfill Scotus's knowledge requirement, the voluntariness of these failures can be demonstrated if (i) the MOI/LII somehow imparts awareness that one must continue the MOI as a LII, and (ii) the obligation-related intellection somehow imparts

[20] If she had no awareness that she was undertaking an obligation, she cannot be held as having ever been under obligation. One cannot be involuntarily (understood not in the sense of 'against one's will,' but rather in the sense of not fulfilling the conditions for voluntariness) under an obligation; to be obligated means one at least knows she is obligated.

awareness that one should create a MOI/LII. It is only if awareness of these requirements is imparted will it be the case that the agent can know she is failing to fulfill them. The general strategy for the rest of this book will be to demonstrate that these intellections we know to be present *do indeed*, contrary to initial perceptions, impart such knowledge to the agent.

IV. Summary

Despite the tasks yet to be fulfilled, much has been accomplished in this chapter. We have seen that Type-2 NO's admit of two variations, A and B. In Variation A cases, the agent ignores a warning at TEF. The warning is a warning for the agent to inquire into why she feels unsettled. Or rather, since the intellection causing the unsettledness has the content <I must do something>, if the unsettledness is experienced as a warning at all, it must be experienced as a warning that one must find out what that 'something' is. Ignoring the warning will thus result in a voluntary ignorance: the agent was aware she must know 'something' more on account of receiving this warning, but freely did some other activity (i.e. whatever else she was doing at the time, such as watching TV, etc.) instead of willed to inquire into what the 'something' is.

In Variation B cases, there is no warning at TEF for the agent to ignore. She is culpable, however, because the lack of warning is ascribable to her. She may not have created a MOI that would ultimately create the warning and was thus flippant in initially undertaking the obligation, or she may have failed to continue the MOI as a LII.

To finish solving the problem of culpability in Type-2 NO's, we now only need explain how the agent can be reasonably expected to experience the unsettledness as a warning she should heed, or how she can be expected to know that she should create and maintain a LII to serve as a warning. The ultimate explanations will come from Suárez's writings. In the meantime, however, an alternative solution to the former question can be found within Scotus's action theory itself. This solution depends upon subscribing to his *affectio*-based understanding of the will. In the next chapter, we investigate this aspect of Scotus's action theory, show how his version of the *affectiones* corrects many of the problems found in Anselm's, and provides one answer to how the agent can be expected to recognize the unsettledness resulting from the LII as a warning.

CHAPTER 7

SCOTUS'S *AFFECTION*-ATE CORRECTIVE

A POSSIBLE FINAL SOLUTION TO A TYPE-2 VARIANT

At the end of the last chapter, we noted that one important issue in regard to Type-2/Variation A NO's remained to be solved. Given that the agent experiences some sort of cognitive dissonance and unsettledness as a result of the MOI lingering by means of one's performance of ContinualComp on it, how is she to recognize that unsettledness specifically as a *warning* that needs to be heeded. If she does not so recognize it, it is not clear how she can be regarded as having voluntarily *neglected* the warning. Any consequences, such as the NO, would thus seem not to be imputable.

In chapter 3, we saw how Anselm's understanding of the *affectiones* of the will led to certain problems in his understanding of initial sin. In particular, his overall understanding of the will and the devil's sin led to the logical conclusion that the devil's initial sin had to be some form of NO. We further observed that it was his characterizing the *affectiones* in terms of what is called a 'strong conditional' (if the object of an affection comes to mind, then the will wills to have that object either immediately or at the appropriate time) that caused much of the problem.

In this third chapter on Scotus, I will use his distinctive adaptation of Anselmian *affectiones* to accomplish two tasks. First, I will show that although Scotus follows Anselm by adopting the *affectiones* doctrine, he does so in such a way as to avoid the negative implications we observed in Chapter 3. By Scotus's understanding of the affections, it may, but need not, be the case that the devil's first sin was a NO. Moreover, it will be indicated how, even if the devil's first sin was a NO, subscription to the dual-affection doctrine can be consistent with ascribing blame for that first sin.

Second, I will offer an *affectio*-based answer to the question of how an agent can be expected to recognize the unsettledness caused by a MOI/LII as a warning to be heeded. This will solve the one remaining issue related to Type-2/Variation A NO's. Of course, this solution is based upon assuming a theory of action that incorporates *affectiones* of the will. Since many do not share this notion, I will subsequently offer an alternative answer in the final chapter and conclusion to the book. Nonetheless, I point out a different solution here to note that Scotus has, within his own writings, the resources with which to deal with one important type of NO.

I. Scotus's Adaption of Anselm's 'Will as *Affectio*'

A. *General Description: The Affections and 'Will' vs. 'Nature'*

Like Anselm, Scotus believes the will can be understood as having two *affectiones* or inclinations/dispositions for willing: the *affectio commmodi* (AC) and the *affectio iustitiae* (AI). His understanding of them begins to depart from that of Anselm, though, and more puzzles begin to arise when he maps these two affections onto his distinction between 'nature' and 'will.'

Recall that Scotus sharply distinguishes between potencies characterized as 'natural' and those characterized by 'will.' A natural potency is one that "of itself is determined to act, so that so far as itself is concerned, it cannot fail to act when not impeded from without."[1] 'Natural' potencies are thus not free; they act deterministically in service to an individual's or specie's perfection. By contrast, the 'will' is free. It is a self-determining power for opposites on account of superabundant sufficiency.

Given that 'will' is contrasted with 'nature,' one would not expect to find a 'natural' appetite per se in the will. In Scotus's description of the will's *affectiones*, however, this is precisely what is found. Following Anselm, Scotus says that according to the AC "nothing can be willed save with reference to self." Although this limitation on the AC's influence alone does not entail that it is 'nature,' he goes on to imply that the AC, of itself, does not impart any power for opposites. Instead of freely choosing, an agent with only the AC would follow the dictates of the intellect's decision of what is most advantageous just as "sense appetite follows sense cognition."[2] Viewing the AC in terms of 'nature' instead

---

[1] aut enim potentia ex se est determinata ad agendum, ita quod, quantum est ex se, non potest non agere quando non impeditur ab extrinseco (*QMet* IX, q.15, n.22; Wolter, *Will and Morality*, 151).

[2] Secundum autem affectionem commodi, nihil potest velle nisi in ordine ad se, - et hanc haberet si praecise esset appetitus intellectivus sine libertate sequens cognitionem intellectivam, sicut appetitus sensitivus sequitur cognitionem sensitivam (*Ord.* III, d.26, n.110, translation from Wolter, *Will and Morality*, 179). All texts of *Ord.* III, d.26 are from the critical (Vatican) edition.

of will is even more apparent when he later writes that there "is a twofold appetite or 'will': one, namely that is *natural*, another that is free. For the will can be considered as a certain kind of nature …"[3] It is thus clear that in some sense Scotus equates the AC with 'nature' as opposed to will, despite the fact the AC is an *affectio* of the will.[4]

Scotus is keenly aware of the apparent contradiction entailed by this description of the AC. Referring to the AC as a 'natural will,' he writes that such a will "is really not will at all, nor is natural volition true volition, for the term 'natural' effectively cancels or negates the sense of both 'will' and 'volition.' "[5] Furthermore, the natural will of itself cannot even "tend, but is the tendency itself by which the will as an absolute or nonrelative entity tends." In other words, Scotus is saying that the AC, considered alone, is not a will. There must be something else in addition for a freely elicited act to occur.

It might be thought that what has been said thus far is not that different from Anselm's view. Although Anselm was not working with the distinction between will and nature, it was nonetheless true for him that either affection alone was insufficient for free self-determination (equivalent to Scotus's freedom).[6] Neither the AC nor the AI could, according to Anselm, impart the ability to have a free, self-determining action. Self-determination was possible only as a result of their combination, for their joint presence gave the agent choices in how to coordinate them. Consequently, one may be tempted to suggest that although Scotus's likening of the AC with 'nature' is new, his denial that the AC

---

[3] Respondeo ad primam quaestionem, quod duplex est appetites sive voluntas, naturalis scilicet et liber. Potest enim voluntas considerari ut est quaedam natura in quantum habet inclinationem et appetitum naturalem ad suam propriam perfectionem (*Ord.* IV, suppl., d.49, qq.9–10, Latin text and translation from Wolter, *Will and Morality*, 182 and 183, italics mine).

[4] Wolter affirms this position when he writes that the AC discussed in *Ord.* III, suppl., d.26 is to be equated with the natural will of *Ord.* III, d.17 (Wolter, *Will and Morality*, 39).

[5] Tunc dico quod sic est de voluntate, quia voluntas naturalis non est voluntas, nec velle naturale est velle, sed ly 'naturalis' distrahit ab utroque et nihil est nisi relatio consequens potentiam respectu propriae perfectionis (*Ord.* III, d.17, n.13, translation from Wolter, *Will and Morality*, 183). All texts of *Ord.* III, d.17 are from the critical (Vatican) edition.

[6] And, of course, our point was that given the specific way in which he characterized the affections, more than one affection was also inadequate for self-determination. Note that I refer to 'self-determination' as opposed to 'freedom' with regard to Anselm, since Anselm has a distinctive view of freedom. For Scotus, one determines oneself by means of one's freedom, so the terms are interchangeable in his case.

alone is a will (i.e. a free power enabling self-determination) is not substantially different from Anselm's position.

When we turn to his particular thoughts on the AI, however, we will see that Scotus does indeed have a picture different from Anselm's in mind. For Anselm, the affections play an equal role in granting the agent freedom since the presence of each provides the agent some alternative to willing solely in accord with the other affection. For Scotus, however, the two affections' roles in imparting freedom are vastly unequal. In his view, freedom is particularly tied to the AI in a way it is not to the AC. Note, for example, the quotation above in which he says there "is a twofold appetite or 'will': one, namely that is natural [the AC], another [the AI] that is *free*."[7] It is specifically the AI that is referred to as free.

This idea that the AI imparts freedom in a way the AC does not is especially evident in one notorious passage in which he replicates half of Anselm's thought experiment concerning the one-willed angel.[8] Referring to an angel endowed with only an AC, he writes it would not have a 'free appetite.' The angel becomes free only with the addition of the AI. But its freedom is not because both are present thus presenting the agent with options (as was the case with Anselm). Instead, while appealing to the genus/differentia distinction, Scotus writes that "the *affectio iustitiae* is the ultimate specific difference of *free appetite*." Specifically the AI is the *differentia* of freedom. Of course, how exactly a natural inclination can be differentiable into a free one is unclear.[9]

---

[7] *Ord.* IV, suppl., d.49, qq.9–10. Translation from Wolter, *Will and Morality*, 183, italics mine.

[8] The passage is *Reportata parisiensia* II, d.6, q.2, n.9. Translations from this text, unless otherwise noted, will be from John Boler's translation in: John Boler, "An Image for the Unity of the Will in Duns Scotus," *Journal of the History of Philosophy* 32, 1 (1994): 23–44. *Rep. par.* II, d.6, q.2 is an unedited text and, though it is included in Wadding-Vivès XXVII, may not be authentically from Scotus (see my comments about Scotus's manuscript tradition at the beginning of Chapter 5). Since Boler's article, Tobias Hoffmann has transcribed this text from a manuscript at Merton College, Oxford: John Duns Scotus, *Reportatio* 2A.6 Oxford, Merton College, MS 61 (=M). The relevant passage is at fol. 145r. Hoffmann has graciously allowed me to use his transcription. When I offer the Latin, I will use Hoffman's transcription of M 145r. Nonetheless, I will use Boler's translations (based upon the Wadding-Vivès text) so as to be fair to the argument he presents in the body of his article. This should cause no substantive problem due to the fact that the Merton manuscript is very similar at this point to that used by Boler.

[9] Boler addresses this issue in "An Image for the Unity of the Will in Duns Scotus." It has also often been remarked that Scotus repeats only half of Anselm's thought experiment in that he does not consider a one-willed angel possessing only the AI. It is

The point nevertheless remains that Scotus views the AI, elsewhere described as the will's "congenital liberty,"[10] as especially linked to an agent's freedom.

It consequently turns out that not only was Scotus aware that he was characterizing one affection of the will as 'nature' as opposed to will, but was also discussing 'freedom,' primarily in reference to only one of the will's affections. Does this mean, therefore, that the AI *alone* is free and comprises by itself the 'will' potency that is opposed to 'nature'? The answer is resoundingly, "No." The AC, despite its earlier characterization as 'nature,' is nonetheless part of free will. He makes this clear when he writes "the *affectiones commodi* and *iustitiae* are not [distinct] from free will and, as it were added to it ... the *affectiones* are not distinguished from the will in reality."[11]

If the AI and AC are not separate from free will, however, two problems arise. Despite our recognition that Scotus was aware of the problem, it is still not clear how the AC can be "not [distinct] from free will" when Scotus explicitly characterizes the AC not as will, but as 'nature.' Second, given the claim that the AC is part of free will, how can that claim be reconciled with the viewpoint that it is the AI, not the AC, that particularly imparts freedom to the agent?

It could be suggested that part of the confusion surrounding the discussion of freedom as it relates to the affections lies in the fact that we have not adequately recognized Scotus may be concerned with different notions of freedom in different contexts. In other words, maybe the freedom vs. nature distinction discussed in reference to the AI and AC is not the same sort of freedom vs. nature distinction referred to in the *QMet* IX discussion. If this is the case, it would then be permissible to say that the AC and AI are not distinct from free will (freedom being understood in one sense) while, at the same time, the AC is not 'will' or free while the AI is (freedom being understood in a different sense).

---

possible that the explanation of why this is the case rests upon his understanding of the AI as the specific differentia of freedom. If the AI is a differentia, it can serve as a differentia only to certain differentiables. It may turn out, then, that the differentiable the AI can differentiate can only be the AC. To speak of an angel with only an AI without an AC, then, would be to contradict his understanding of the AI as the differentia of freedom.

[10] *Ord.* III, d.26.

[11] Ad primum horum dico primo praemittendo quod affectiones commodi et iusti non sunt aliud a voluntate libera, quasi superaddita; sed affectio iusti est quasi ultimata differentia ... non tamen distinguuntur re istae affectiones ab ipsa voluntate (*Rep.* IIA, d.6, q.2; M 145r, translation from Boler, "An Image for the Unity," 30).

B. *One or Two Notions of Freedom? Boler vs. Lee*

There has, in fact, been some debate in the literature over this particular issue. John Boler seems not to assert that 'nature' is used any differently across contexts. Consequently, his views may not speak to the question as to how the AC can both be and not be 'nature.' (We will deal with that subsequently.) He does, however, believe Scotus can be read as discussing two separate notions of freedom in the two contexts, in which case at least part of the confusion will be mitigated (namely, how both the AI alone is linked with freedom, and the will as a whole is free).

According to Boler, there is on the one hand a "metaphysical freedom" corresponding to the power for opposites mentioned in the *QMet* IX discussion. On the other hand, it is a "moral freedom" in view when the conversation turns to the *affectiones*.[12] This latter freedom refers to the fact that the agent, by acting in accordance with the nobler AI, can transcend "the sort of operation involved in realizing the potential of a nature" represented by the AC.[13] In other words, the freedom represented by the AI is the freedom not to be restricted to willing the *bonum sibi* and simply pursuing the perfection of one's *nature* as represented in the tendencies issuing from the AC. The agent can instead *transcend* her 'nature' (represented in the will by the AC); she can will the *bonum in se* by willing in accordance with the AI. The freedom represented by the AI, then, is a freedom from willing solely with a view toward perfecting one's (Aristotelian) nature.

This freedom to transcend one's nature and to will in accordance with the AI is a 'moral' freedom because being moral consists just in transcending the natural concern for one's own benefit and willing the *bonum in se*: "… moral action (good or evil) [is] the possibility of 'tempering' (or failing to temper) our inclination for the *commodum* precisely with respect to the 'just.'"[14] Just as we observed in Anselm's theory,[15] being moral consists of the agent not letting concern for her

[12] John Boler, "Transcending the Natural: Duns Scotus on the Two Affections of the Will," *American Catholic Philosophical Quarterly* 67 (1993): 109–26. In describing Boler's position as contrasting a 'metaphysical' with a 'moral' freedom, I am following: Sukjae Lee, "Scotus on the Will: The Rational Power and the Dual Affections," *Vivarium* 36, no. 1 (1998): 40–54.

[13] Boler, "Transcending the Natural," 117–118.

[14] Boler, "Transcending the Natural," 119.

[15] Cf. Chapter 2.

own happiness or benefit take precedence, but subordinating that concern to considerations of justice.

The moral freedom to transcend one's own selfish desires for happiness is thus, for Boler, different from the metaphysical freedom consisting of the power for opposites. The fact that these notions are different, however, need not entail they are completely unrelated. For Boler, the will's description as metaphysically free is independent of and prior to any consideration of the freedom discussed in reference to the *affectiones*.[16] There is a one-way dependence relationship of moral upon metaphysical freedom, and thus metaphysical freedom can be affirmed apart from any considerations provided by the *affectio*-doctrine.

Sukjae Lee will ultimately object to Boler's claim that there are two types of freedom in view. To see why, we first need to go into some detail regarding Boler's argument that metaphysical freedom is dependent in no way upon the affections. Recall from Chapter 3 and earlier in this chapter that Anselm motivates his doctrine of *affectiones* by claiming that (at least) two *affectiones* are necessary such that a rational agent be self-determined. To support this claim, he performs two thought experiments[17] in which he considers an angel endowed with only an AC, and then one endowed only with an AI. In each case, the angel is unable to will except in accordance with the *affectio* under question. Self-determination (equivalent to 'metaphysical freedom' for Scotus) and culpability thus require two affections of the will.

As already mentioned above, Scotus replicates this thought-experiment, but *only in part*. He only considers an angel with only an AC. Given its importance, I will quote this passage at length.

> And if there were an angel, who had a cognitive appetite apart from an *affectio justitiae*, it would lack justice and it would not be a free appetite. Whence, if [this intellective agent] were to lack an *affectio justitiae*, it would thus naturally seek what is suited to intellect, just as the sense appetite [seeks] what is suited to sense; nor would it be any more free than the sense appetite. Therefore, the *affectio justitiae* is the ultimate specific difference of *free appetite*.[18]

---

[16] "... it [metaphysical freedom as superabundant sufficiency] is not really significant for the theory of dual *affectiones* – that is, if the theory simply presupposes the 'metaphysical' freedom of the will rather than contributing to its explanation" (Boler, "Transcending the Natural," 115–116). This point was brought to my attention by Lee, "Scotus on the Will," 45.

[17] *DCD*, chs.12ff.

[18] This translation is from Boler, "An Image for the Unity," 30–31. The Latin from the Merton manuscript (which, as I note above, is slightly different from that used by

Boler will appeal to this thought experiment to make his claim that metaphysical freedom can in no way depend upon the *affectio*-doctrine and any freedom the affections may impart. Recall that Scotus's understanding of the power for opposites referred to in *QMet* IX (and, in the current discussion, captured by the term 'metaphysical freedom') consists not in an ability to *velle* as opposed to *nolle*, but rather in the capacity to *velle* or *non-velle*, or alternatively, to *nolle* or *non-nolle*. The agent, in Scotus's mind therefore, is not restricted to willing either in accordance with justice or with happiness. Instead, the agent's freedom for opposites entails that the agent can either *velle* or *non-velle* happiness. But, as Boler states, "If such a refusal [i.e. *non-velle*] is possible at all … there seems to me no reason why it would not be possible for a will with a single basic inclination." The one-willed angel with only an AC, therefore, should have the freedom for opposites in that it can either *velle* or *non-velle* some particular object of happiness. Given this, it then follows that "dual basic inclinations are not necessary for [metaphysical] freedom of the will."[19]

Not only are the dual affections not necessary for metaphysical freedom, they are also not sufficient according to Boler. If, say, an agent were "schizophrenic" such that only one of her *affectiones* were "operative," her "actions could still follow non-freely (and 'naturally') from" that operative affection.[20] The point I believe Boler is making is this. It might be thought (à la Anselm) that metaphysical freedom can be guaranteed by endowing the agent with two separate dispositions for willing in that the dispositions give the agent a choice in her willing. This fact alone, however, is not enough to secure this ability.

If metaphysical freedom is to arise not from a prior power to *velle* or *non-velle*, but solely on account of the fact that having two affections gives the agent options for willing, then it must be the case that both dispositions are somehow active in the volitional life of the agent at any one time. In other words, it must be the case that there are objects of both affections competing to be the object of the will's action. Why?

Boler) is as follows: et si esset unus angelus qui haberet appetitum cognitivum absque affectione, careret instrumento, et non esset appetitus liber. Unde non est liber unde intellectivus, quia si caret <careret T> affectione iusti, ita naturaliter appeteret conveniens intellectui sicut appetitus sensitivus conveniens sensui, nec esset magis liber quam appetitus sensitivus; ideo affectio iusti est ultimata differentia specifica appetitus liberi (*Rep.* IIA, d.6, q.2; M 145r).

[19] Boler, "Transcending the Natural," 115.

[20] Boler, "Transcending the Natural," 115.

Because given no prior ability to *velle* or *non-velle* (i.e. no prior metaphysical freedom), if there are possible objects of only one of the affections available for willing at any one time, it would seem that the will must will that object; she has no inclination or affection to do otherwise.

There seems to be no reason to rule out the possibility that only one affection could be thus 'active' at any one time. (Indeed, such a situation is exactly what we posited in Chapter 3 regarding the devil's sin: if the strong conditional holds, it must be the case that for the devil to sin there was no object of justice in mind for the devil to consider and be inclined toward by his AI.) But if only one affection can be active in this way (i.e. the only object for willing corresponds to only one affection), it then follows that there are no options for willing arising simply from the fact that the agent is *endowed* with more than one affection. Having dual affections, then, is also not sufficient for metaphysical freedom.

Boler thus concludes that dual affections are neither necessary nor sufficient for metaphysical freedom. Since he maintains that they are, however, necessary for moral freedom, Lee aptly (I believe) interprets Boler as claiming that metaphysical freedom has no dependence upon moral freedom: "it would follow that the conditions for metaphysical freedom are independent from those for moral freedom. This would in turn imply that one could have superabundant sufficiency without possessing the dual affections."[21] Let's call this (B1):

> (B1) An agent can be metaphysically free (i.e. possess superabundant sufficiency) without possessing dual affections.

The majority of Lee's article is devoted to refuting (B1). He does this in several ways. By (B1), Boler must grant that the one-willed angel *could* be metaphysically free.[22] This, however, creates a problem. The passage quoted above describes the angel's appetite as not free. If the angel is metaphysically free independently of the affections, then this reference to a lack of freedom, coming as it does in the midst of an elaboration upon the affections, must be in Boler's mind a reference to moral freedom only. Lee points out that holding this position is untenable for it leaves two unviable options. Either (i) the freedom in view when the analogy is made to the sense appetite in the same passage ("nor would

[21] Lee, "Scotus on the Will," 46.

[22] This possibility of course comes directly from Boler's claim that dual-affections are not necessary for metaphysical freedom.

it be any more free than the sense appetite") would likewise have to be moral freedom, but it makes no sense to speak of sense appetite being morally free; or (ii) different notions of freedom are being appealed to in the same paragraph, for which there is no textual support.[23]

Lee further objects to (B1) based on the following observation: if the one-willed angel were metaphysically free, then its actions can be imputed to it "since it is within the Angel's power to do otherwise." But given it lacks dual affections, and if dual affections are needed for *moral* freedom, then the one-willed angel's action would have no moral import, but be amoral. (B1) thus leads to the (in Lee's mind) awkward assertion that there can be imputability without morality. In other words, it seems odd to assert that "the ability to do otherwise is not sufficient for morality even though it is sufficient for imputability."[24] These considerations lead Lee to subscribe to the opposite of (B1), namely:

> (RB1) An agent cannot be metaphysically free (i.e. possess superabundant sufficiency) without possessing dual affections.

At this point, let us make a comment on the structure of Lee's counterargument thus far. The reasons he has offered for opposing (B1) have been largely exegetical and based upon the one-willed angel passage. Boler supposedly endorses (B1), however, not primarily upon exegetical grounds, but upon his claim that dual affections are neither necessary nor sufficient for metaphysical freedom. Lee thus needs to address this claim.

He begins to do so by disputing Boler's contention that there can be a 'schizophrenic' angel. He writes, "It is crucial that the dual affections specified by Scotus, are not both 'generic' affections on par with one another. Agents with the dual affections are not schizophrenic."[25] By this he means to deny that only one affection can be operative. He then believes this denial allows him to make his own positive proposal,

---

[23] Lee, "Scotus on the Will," 48–49.

[24] Lee, "Scotus on the Will," 49. Of course, there is no reason why imputability need be tied to morality. There are many morally neutral acts that are imputable. For example, the choice of chocolate over vanilla ice cream can be imputed to me but is morally irrelevant. It is thus not obvious how much weight this particular objection carries, unless one is working with the underlying assumption that imputability is only worth mentioning or present in morally-relevant cases. As it indeed turns out, Lee believes freedom, and thus imputability, is only present in moral cases. I ultimately challenge this assumption.

[25] Lee, "Scotus on the Will," 51–52. Given that Scotus recognizes the AI as the differentia of the AC, they (at least in this sense) are not on par with one another.

namely that "the freedom expressed in our superabundant sufficiency consisted exclusively in the possibility of restraining the *affectio commodi* with the *affectio iustitiae*." In other words, Lee rejects the suggestion that there are two different notions of freedom in Scotus's text; metaphysical freedom *is* moral freedom and coextensive with it: "The range of free actions would in this case coincide with the range of moral phenomena."[26]

How, though, does Lee think the denial of the possibility of a 'schizophrenic' agent permits him to suggest that moral and metaphysical freedom are identical? I believe the rationale may be something like the following: By denying the possibility of *affectio*-schizophrenia, he is attempting to deny Boler's claim that the dual affections are not sufficient for metaphysical freedom. That they do suffice for metaphysical freedom, therefore, is a possibility. This possibility is strengthened in light of Lee's exegesis of the one-willed angel (which we saw above) wherein he observes that the freedom under discussion, and which comes about as a result of the AI, cannot be merely moral.[27] It must, then, be a metaphysical freedom that arises from the AI's addition to the AC. (I thus take it that he hereby implicitly asserts contra Boler the *necessity*, in addition to the possible *sufficiency*, of dual affections for metaphysical freedom.)

For Lee, then, the freedom imparted by the AI is metaphysical. The freedom imparted by the AI to a creature already having an AC, however, must also enable morality, i.e. it must be somewhat a moral freedom also. For it is not disputed by anyone that being able to will the *bonum in se* (through the AI) in preference to the AC's inclination for the *bonum sibi* just is what it means to be morally free. If the AI, though, imparts both moral and metaphysical freedom to someone already having the AC, then (in my reading of Lee) the two freedoms must be identical. This leads Lee to make the following bold statement: "Rather, all free actions have moral character. Why? Because the ability to transcend the affection for advantage through the affection for justice is precisely where the power of freedom has its source."[28] One cannot thus perform a [metaphysically] free act without it also being a moral act.

---

[26] Lee, "Scotus on the Will," 52.

[27] Recall he made this point by asking how "sense appetite" could be *morally* free, which would have to be the reading if only moral freedom were the type of freedom under consideration.

[28] Lee, "Scotus on the Will," 54.

I believe there is a seed of truth in Lee's conclusion, and one that will become important for our project. But as it stands, I think it may go too far, for surely it cannot be the case that *every* free act is a moral act.[29] Why, for instance, cannot a choice between two *commoda* be a completely amoral decision and yet free? I see no reason why Scotus should want to deny that I have the metaphysical freedom to perform the indifferent act of choosing between eating chocolate or vanilla ice cream.[30] Why would our agential decisions be completely determined in all our normal, day-to-day, morally-irrelevant acts while free only in the moral ones? Or rather, what would be lost for Scotus (other than a particular way of reading his one-willed angel passage) if he were to allow the possibility of freedom in our non-moral as well as our moral actions? If our freedom were so restricted, it is furthermore likely that he would have mentioned it when discussing superabundant sufficiency and the power for opposites in the first place. As far as I can tell, he did not. Given these considerations, I believe it is open for us to explore an alternate interpretation of the relationship between the metaphysical freedom and the dual affections.

C. *Two Freedoms, But Semi-Reciprocally Dependent: Combining Boler & Lee*

I want to suggest that there is an element of truth to both Boler's and Lee's excellent expositions, but that each slightly misses the mark. In agreement with Boler, I will claim that there are two freedoms. I disagree with Boler, however, by claiming there is a sense in which metaphysical freedom can be regarded as dependent upon moral freedom. In fact, I claim that the metaphysical freedom of the will as a whole is logically dependent upon a mechanism initially in place on account of moral freedom (the AI). There will thus be a sense in which I also agree with Lee's claim that the addition of the AI to a creature already endowed with an AC imparts metaphysical, in addition to moral, freedom. As opposed to Lee, however, I deny that the two freedoms are the same. It is possible to act freely in a metaphysical sense without thereby performing a moral act.

---

[29] The converse, of course, does not hold. Every moral act must, by definition, be a free act.

[30] For a discussion of the possibility of indifferent acts in both Scotus and Aquinas, see Klaus Hedwig, "Actus indifferens: Über die Theorie des indifferenten Handelns bei Thomas von Aquin und Duns Scotus," *Philosophisches Jahrbuch* 95 (1988): 120–131.

In sum, my proposal is that the AI brings, along with the possibility of transcendence over 'nature' (i.e. moral freedom), a metaphysical freedom that subsequently affects both *affections*.[31] I further believe there is a way to achieve a consistent reading of the one-willed angel passage by assuming my interpretation. The upshot of this proposal will be to enable us to answer some of the questions we had earlier; namely why is the AI more linked to freedom when the AC is part of free will and why is the AC called 'nature' when it is part of the 'will,' a potency contrasted to nature. Answering these questions will then, in turn, enable us to show how Scotus's doctrine of the affections avoids many of the problems in Anselm's account.

Allow me to explain my position by positing hypothetical steps in Scotus's consideration of how to construct his theory of the will. I will call these 'instants of considering the will' (IW's):[32]

> IW1 - There needs to be some sort of liberty to free a rational agent from nature; otherwise, it is not a moral creature.
>
> IW2 - It is recognized that willing in accordance with justice is one way to free an agent from nature; thus, it is concluded that there is an AI in addition to the 'nature' (i.e. AC).
>
> IW3 - It is realized that this AI, although able to free an agent from willing maximum advantage necessarily, should not force one to will justice necessarily either. Otherwise, such acts would not be free and thereby 'just,' thus contradicting the goal of imparting an AI in the first place (i.e. so as to create a moral creature).[33] Consequently, the AI's addition imparts some sort of ability to elicit acts 'freely.'
>
> IW4 - We need some way to explain how choices are made in regard to two opposing just acts or between doing a just act or not.

---

[31] I am in part following Marilyn McCord Adams's suggestion that the will's "distinctive capacity for opposites should infect each *affection*, taken separately." [Marilyn McCord Adams, "Duns Scotus on the Will as Rational Power" in *Via Scoti: Methodologica ad mentem Joannis Duns Scoti*, ed. Leonardo Sileo (Roma: PAA-Edizioni Antonianum, 1995), 839–854. The quotation is from p. 845.] The earlier reference to the choice between chocolate and vanilla was inspired by this same reference.

[32] I am, of course, playfully trying to parallel the Scotist idea of 'instants of nature' which are relevant in discussing other aspects of Scotus's action theory.

[33] After all, what is the point of permitting one to will what is just without thereby being just. Just as the point of endowing the creature with two affections was, for Anselm, so that the creature could self-determine itself toward justice (i.e. be 'just') or not, so for Scotus. There is no point giving an AI if, by using it, one cannot thereby be just.

IW5 – A choice between such just acts or between doing a just act or not would need to be freely elicited for the creature to be self-determined. If the agent automatically chooses the act characterized by the most 'justice,' or cannot refrain from doing a just act at all, she does not determine herself to be 'just.'

IW6 - We have already seen in IW3 that the AI brings along a power to elicit acts freely in that it allows us to transcend our nature and not necessarily will maximum advantage.

IW7 – Given this, there is no reason to preclude the possibility that the AI, the addition of which enables one freely to determine oneself, also brings along with it a more metaphysical 'power for opposites' in regard to opposing just acts or in regard to performing or refraining to perform some just act.

IW8 – Since sometimes two *commoda*, as opposed to two acts of justice, must be chosen between, and since there is a metaphysical power for opposites in regard to opposing just acts, it is only a small step to asserting the following: the same power for opposites which enables the agent to choose between two just acts or between doing a just act or not also enables the agent to choose between two *commoda* or between choosing a *commodum* or not.

IW9 – Since *commoda* are the object of the AC, this affection must itself be separately infected by this metaphysical 'power for opposites.'

IW10 - If IW8 is correct in that it is the same power for opposites that infects the AC and the AI, and since the power for opposites arises initially from the AI, it can be said that the AI brings along a power for opposites to the will that subsequently infects the AC separately. This claim is plausible since the AI is that which enabled any free acts (in the sense that it provides an alternative to 'nature') in the first place.

I am, of course, not suggesting that the above was Scotus's actual thought process. Indeed, it probably was not, for the idea of the will as a 'power for opposites' could be seen as a separate development preceding any discussion of the affections. Nevertheless, there is nothing to preclude this interpretation as a way consistently to understand the relation between the *QMet* IX and *affectio*-based accounts of the will. It is the AI that brings along with it not only the possibility for acts of willing not dictated by the AC, but also a metaphysically free power for opposites which it subsequently imparts separately to the AC. As a result, both affections, and therefore the entire will, are characterized by a metaphysical power for opposites.

This understanding that the AI brings with it a metaphysical freedom that subsequently imparts a power for opposites to each affection separately furthermore allows the freedom referred to in the one-willed angel to be understood throughout as metaphysical (such as when the AI is called "the ultimate specific difference of a *free appetite*") without denying that the AI also serves a function relevant to moral freedom. As a result, we easily avoid some of Lee's earlier criticisms of Boler. Recall that Lee wondered how the one-willed angel's appetite could be described as 'not free'? If 'free' refers to metaphysical freedom (as I maintain), and if my interpretation is right, then it is so described as 'not free' because the one-willed angel's appetite cannot be (metaphysically) free before the addition of the AI. The AC is characterized by metaphysical freedom (i.e. a power for opposites) only after the AI has separately infected it with that power for opposites. Furthermore, since all references to freedom in the one-willed angel passage are, according to me, references to metaphysical freedom, I need not be faced with the unhappy prospect of choosing between the two unviable options Lee pointed out if the freedom in view is moral.[34]

D. *Answering the Initial Questions and the 'Formal Distinction'*

Having given my interpretation of the relation between metaphysical freedom, moral freedom, and the AI, we can now return to the questions that caused us initially to wonder whether there were more than one understanding of freedom being discussed. This worry arose in part because the AI, as opposed to the AC, seemed particularly linked to freedom. If my interpretation is correct, why this is the case is now obvious. It is the AI that brings the metaphysical power of opposites to the will in the first place. Not only does it permit freedom from 'nature,' but it even imparts a freedom with regard to the ability to choose between two or more *commoda*. In a sense, we could say that the AI imparts a freedom of opposites with respect to the AC. Because such metaphysical freedom with regard to *commoda* would not be possible without the AI's role as the initial 'bearer of a power for opposites,' it is not surprising that the AI would be more linked with freedom than the AC.

[34] Recall from above that Lee charges if the freedom in view with regard to the angel's appetite is moral, then either (i) the freedom in view when the analogy is made to the sense appetite in the same passage ("nor would it be any more free than the sense appetite") would likewise have to be moral freedom, but it makes no sense to speak of sense appetite being morally free; or (ii) different notions of freedom are being appealed to in the same paragraph, for which there is no textual support.

The second worry wondered how the AC is at the same time described as 'nature' and as "not [distinct] from free will." It should now be clear how the AC is part of free will. Not only is it a part of the will as a whole, but there is a freedom of opposites with respect to the AC. Nonetheless, the AC can still be called 'nature' because, considered of itself and in isolation from the AI, it would be a 'natural' potency as opposed to one characterized by 'will.'

Despite this explanation, it may be thought that Scotus calling the AC 'nature' is nonetheless inappropriate. Since the AC is (by his own admission) 'not distinct from free will,' and since the will is free only in virtue of the AI, there is never a situation in which the AC exists alone and apart from free will. Given that an AC could never thus exist alone, what justification is there for ascribing some sort of essence to it that it never, in reality, has?

An answer to this question may be found by appealing to a distinction for which Scotus is particularly infamous: the formal distinction. In addition to *real* distinctions (distinctions between 'things' [*res*]) and distinctions of reason (distinctions that are simply the product of the conceiving intellect and not present in reality), Scotus recognized a distinction midway between these two. Although his view of what he meant by this distinction may have changed over time, the basic idea is that there can be in "what is really one and the same thing (*res*), a plurality of entities or property-bearers whose nonidentity in distinction in no way depends upon the activity of any intellect."[35] This is the basis of his formal distinction.

It appears that, in Scotus's opinion, there is a distinction 'out there' in the will between the AC and the AI, and even between the AC and the will as a whole itself, even though these are all really one and the same thing (*res*). These distinctions thus seem to be 'formal' and, if so, the

[35] Marilyn McCord Adams, *William Ockham* (Notre Dame, IN: University of Notre Dame Press, 1987), 22. Adams has a good discussion of Scotus's account of the formal distinction on pp.16–29. See also her "Ockham on Identity and Distinction," *Franciscan Studies* 14 (1976): 5–74. The interested reader may also consult the following: Peter King, "Scotus on Metaphysics," in *The Cambridge Companion to Duns Scotus*, ed. Thomas Williams (Cambridge, UK: Cambridge University Press, 2003); Allan B. Wolter, "The Formal Distinction," in *John Duns Scotus 1265–1965*, ed. J. K. Ryan and B. M. Bonansea (Washington DC: Catholic University of America Press, 1965), 45–60. For a very thorough discussion about texts that underlie some of the controversies surrounding the formal distinction, see Stephen D. Dumont, "Duns Scotus's Parisian Question on the Formal Distinction," *Vivarium* 43, no. 1 (2005): 7–62.

puzzle is solved.[36] Even though the AC would never exist without the will as a whole or without the AI, we would be permitted to talk about the AC in terms of itself and as apart from the AI and the will since it would be formally distinct. And when we do this, it is clear that the AC, in itself, is more characteristic of 'nature' than 'will.' Nonetheless, in reality the AC is never separate (i.e. never *really* distinct) from the will, nor from the AI whence it receives a power for opposites. As a result, the AC is *really* the same as free will, even though it, as formally distinct from the AI and from the will, is nature. In light of the formal distinction, therefore, Scotus's statements are consistent.

We have now explored the notion of nature, will, and freedom in relation to the affections. Having done this and having absolved Scotus from internal inconsistency in regard to them, we will now see (i) how his doctrine of the affections enables him to avoid many of the problems facing Anselm, and (ii) how it offers an understanding by which to regard the agent as experiencing the unsettledness arising from the MOI/LII in a Type-2/Variation A scenario as a warning.

II. Correction to Anselm's Formulation

It is perhaps already obvious that Scotus denies Anselm's 'strong conditional.' His basic commitment to a metaphysically free power for opposites already entails that the will is never necessitated to will in one way or another. It may, then, be wondered why I devote a separate section to Scotus's correction of Anselm's formulation. The reason is that I want to make some specific comments on how he adopted the *affectio*-doctrine without abandoning his commitment to metaphysical freedom. It is one thing to say that one believes in metaphysical freedom and that one adheres to an *affectio*-doctrine.[37] It is another, however, to show how one's understanding of the affections maps onto one's understanding of freedom and does not contradict it. And although the explanation to this latter issue is implicit in what has been said above, it will nonetheless be interesting to explore some specific details with regard to Scotus's *affectiones* and their relationship to metaphysical freedom and Anselm's strong conditional.

---

[36] I owe my recognition of this insight to conversations with Marilyn McCord Adams.

[37] After all, it is very probable that Anselm thought his doctrine of the affections was consistent with some form of metaphysical freedom.

Recall that for Anselm the affections were superadded to the will and, correlatively, the AI is a separable affection for him: an agent loses it upon sin and regains it in merely piecemeal fashion. Given that for Scotus the AI is essential for any freedom, and therefore, for there to be a 'will' properly speaking at all, the affections are *not* separable for him.[38] If they were separable, he could not write that "the *affectiones commodi* and *justitiae* are not [distinct] from free will [and], as it were, added to it. Rather the *affectio justitiae* is, as it were, the ultimate difference."[39]

The inseparability of the AI and the fact that it brings along with it a metaphysical freedom for the power of opposites is fortuitous for it helps Scotus avoid the destructive results of Anselm's strong conditional. Because of the special role of the AI in relation to freedom and its inseparability from the will, it is never the case (for Scotus) that whenever an object of an affection comes to mind the will wills to have it either immediately or at its appropriate time (as was the case with Anselm). Instead, the metaphysical freedom for opposites possessed by the AI and imparted to the AC by the AI always permits the agent not to will the object of an affection even if it comes to mind. Moreover, on account of this power for opposites separately infecting each affection, the agent can refrain from willing an object of an affection even when there is no object of another affection providing alternative objects for willing. The agent can simply refuse to will (*non-velle*) the object. Scotus's *affectiones* are therefore not characterized by a strong conditional. They can be viewed as no more than tendencies and in no way restrict metaphysical freedom.

In fact, he makes this last point explicitly even in regard to the AC. He writes that it "is neither a will nor a potency, but refers to the inclination the potency has to *tend* towards its proper perfection, *not the inclination to act in this way*."[40] What Scotus has done here is remove

---

[38] It goes without saying that the AC is not separable. It was not for Anselm, and for Scotus it plays the role of 'nature.'

[39] Ad primum horum dico primo praemittendo quod affectiones commodi et iusti non sunt aliud a voluntate libera, quasi superaddita; sed affectio iusti est quasi ultimata differentia ... non tamen distinguuntur re istae affectiones ab ipsa voluntate (*Rep.* IIA, d.6, q.2; M 145r, translation from Boler, "An Image for the Unity," 30).

[40] Dico quod voluntas naturalis, -ut sic et ut naturalis - non est voluntas ut potentia, sed tantum importat inclinationem potentiae ad recipiendum perfectionem suam, non ad agendum ut sic (*Ord.* III, d.17, n.18, translation from Wolter, *Will and Morality*, 183, second italics mine). It is worth noting that the text Wolter used (*Will and Morality*, 182) is slightly different than the Latin in the susbsequently published critical edition.

any idea of a strong conditional from the AC. By being careful to say that the natural will (i.e. AC) is "not the inclination to *act* in this way" and does not, even of itself, actively (as opposed to passively) 'tend,' Scotus has eliminated any necessity of willing advantage, even when a *commodum* is thought of.[41]

Interestingly, the Latin word underlying the word Wolter italicized (tend) is different ("*tendendum in propriam perfectionem*" in Wolter's text was replaced by "*recipiendum perfectionem*" in the critical edition). Not much hangs on this difference. The critical edition does proceed to make the same point made by Wolter's translation by using *tendentia* and *tendo*. Moreover, if the change were meaningful, it would all the more support the point being made here since 'receiving' can be even more passive than 'tending.'

There may arise a question here in that Scotus is speaking of the AC considered as nature. It would seem that, considered as nature, the AC would cause an act. In other words, if *per impossibile* the AC were alone without the AI, it seems as if the AC would, as nature, issue in certain acts – namely, those that would result in maximizing one's *commoda*. It is thus a little unclear why he says the AC considered *as nature* would not be an inclination to act. My guess is that when he refers to 'act' here, he is referring to a 'free' act. And the AC, as present in a free will, of itself does nothing but incline the will as a whole toward its objects. To say it is the inclination to act in a will characterized by freedom would perhaps run the risk of giving the impression that there is a civil war in the will without any executive power, a civil war in which the stronger tendency would win and thus action would issue forth immediately (similar to how *akrasia* is explained in a Platonic tri-partite view of the soul.) At any rate, if the AC is a mere tendency even when considered of itself, it certainly is when considered as part of the will. The quotation thus supports my claim that Scotus is denying any idea of a strong conditional characterizing the AC.

[41] A further explicit denial of any intellect-dependence of the will, and thus of any strong conditional, comes when Scotus states that a "lesser cause [intellect] cannot determine the mode of action of the superior cause [will] any more than it can force it to act" (quia causa inferior non potest determinare modum agendi causae superioris, sicut nec ipsam potest determinare ad agendam [*Ord.* IV, suppl., d.49, qq.9–10, Latin text and translation from Wolter, *Will and Morality*, 188 and 189]). In sum, Scotus here rejects the strong conditional because it would necessarily entail that the intellect is superior to the will, a belief he rejects. He demonstrates this point through the following illustration. Suppose, he says, that the will were necessitated to will something. Given that it is a superior cause, "this necessity would pertain to it of its very nature and not from some other inferior cause" such as the intellect. Further, if this superior cause needed an inferior cause to complete its act, it [the will] would "move the inferior cause to act by the same necessity," and not vice versa (si ergo voluntas habeat necessitatem ad volendum aliquid, illa necessitas convenit ei ex ratione sui et non ex alia causea inferiori. Et tunc ulterius arguo: causa superior, si necessario agat, eadem necessitate movet causas inferiores ad agendum, quarum actiones necessario requiruntur ad actionem sui [*Ord.* IV, suppl., d.49, qq.9–10, Latin text and translation from Wolter, *Will and Morality*, 188 and 189.]). In sum, Scotus is saying that even if there were necessity involved in will-acts, the strong conditional has described this necessity in the reverse. Instead of an action of the intellect necessarily causing the will to act in a certain way (as the strong conditional would seem to imply), the will would of necessity force the intellect to act in a particular way.

In summary, we have seen that Scotus denies any sort of strong conditional as applied to the will. In the first place, his basic view of the will as having a metaphysical power for opposites entails this. What we have furthermore discovered in this chapter is that his adaptation of Anselm's *affectiones* can be done in such as way as to preserve this basic commitment to metaphysical freedom. The AI brings along with it a metaphysically free power for opposites which is then imparted to the AC, and thus to the will as a whole. A commitment to *affectiones* of the will and metaphysical freedom are compatible.[42]

The interpretation offered here has the further advantage in that it provides, in addition to the basic denial of the strong conditional, a specific way in which to explain the devil's first sin in a way Anselm's theory could not. Even if no object of the affection-for-justice were present for the devil, the devil would not have had to will in accordance with the AC. Since the metaphysical power-for-opposites infects each affection separately, there would always be the *possibility* for the devil simply to *non-velle* his maximum advantage, even in the absence of alternative considerations. Consequently, there are several resources in Scotus's *affectio*-doctrine with which to avoid many of the problems discussed in chapter 3.

Scotus, of course, does not think there is any necessity in willing, and therefore no necessity in the intellect. The above illustration is really the argument flowing from a contrary-to-necessary-fact condition he posits. In that argument, he is trying to disprove that the will, of necessity, always has to will happiness, whether in general (which could be under the aspect of the AC) or in particular (which apparently could fall under the aspect of the AI if one understood happiness as that "beatitude [which] consists in the fruition of the divine essence shared by the three [divine] persons"). As he states, if the will necessarily always wills happiness, then the will [superior cause] would force the intellect [inferior but still necessary cause] "to continually consider happiness." From experience, we know that the conclusion is false; consequently, the premise that the will must always will happiness does not hold. (Cum ergo in actione voluntatis in volendo requiratur apprehensio in intellectu, sequitur quod si voluntas necessario velit beatitudinem, quod necessario determinaret intellectum ad semper considerandum de beatitudine, quod falsum est [*Ord.* IV, suppl., d.49, qq.9–10, Latin text and translation from Wolter, *Will and Morality*, 188 and 189]). There is, then, for Scotus, no necessity in willing, not even in willing that the intellect consider some particular thing or another. Much less is there a necessity arising from the intellect and imposed upon the will (as the strong conditional seems to imply).

[42] It is, of course, no surprise that Scotus endorses metaphysical freedom. He is indeed famous for this position and expresses it throughout his writings. The point currently being made is that he is able to adopt Anselmian *affectiones* into his action theory in such a way that does not compromise his position on metaphysical freedom while also avoiding some of the problems in Anselm's theory of the *affectiones*.

To say, however, that the devil possessed the *possibility* to *non-velle* his maximal happiness is not to make it likely that he would not. This is especially the case given the assumed absence of an object of the affection-for-justice (such as God's command). In the absence of such an alternate consideration or object for willing (as we posited in chapter 3) what reason would he have for not willing his maximal happiness? It seems none, and thus it is difficult to understand how he can be blamed - unless his ignorance can be traced back to negligence, in which case his sin was a NO.[43]

Of course, in chapter 3 it was only because of the strong conditional that we had to assume the devil had no consideration of any object of the AI. Under Scotus's scheme, on the other hand, there is no strong conditional. Consequently, for Scotus the devil's first sin need not have been a NO. The problem discussed in the preceding paragraph hence need not *necessarily* face Scotus.

Even if that problem need not *necessarily* face Scotus, it yet may. The devil's first sin, even assuming a Scotist understanding of the affections, may nonetheless have been a NO if there were no consideration of an object of the AI? And there seems to be no reason to rule out that possibility altogether. Can the *affectio*-doctrine help explain its culpability? I believe it can, if it were a Type-2/Variation A NO. We saw in the last chapter that the only issue not yet resolved regarding Type-2/Variation A NO's is how the agent can be expected to recognize the unsettledness arising from a LII as a warning that needs to be heeded. I will now offer a brief suggestion as to how Scotus's *affectiones* can provide an answer.

III. Type-2/Variation A NO's: One Answer for Recognizing the Warning

We posited in the last chapter that MOI/LII's may have some special affinity to states of apprehension and warning. The fact that an intellection has the mere content of <I must do something> without specifying what that something is, along with the fact that the agent is causing that relatively uninformative intellection to 'linger' on account of performing ContinualComp, seem to call out to the agent to inquire into it. It is

[43] That is to say, unless his sin is a NO. Of course, this would bring up the further problem of how his first sin was the NO itself. It would seem that his first sin would consist in the negligence by which he did not ensure that he would remember God's command.

only reasonable that she would ask herself 'Why am I continuing to perform ContinualComp on this intellection that does not tell me much.' That should then lead to her to at least consider stopping what she is doing and try to remember exactly what it is she is supposed to do. In other words, it should lead her to experience the LII as a warning to prevent subsequent ignorance of her specific obligation.

Type-2/Variation A NO's result, we pointed out, when the agent *neglects* some such warning and does not attempt to recall the specifics. In such cases the resulting temporary ignorance of her obligation is voluntary: she knew she should try to know something (i.e. she was warned that there were some details which she should remind herself of or not be temporarily ignorant of) and, despite knowing this, proceeded to do whatever else it was she was doing. We then worried about cases in which the agent does not experience the LII's presence as a warning against ignorance of certain details. How can such an agent's ignorance be voluntary? In light of Scotus's doctrine of the affections, I want to offer one suggestion according to which the agent cannot fail to recognize the MOI/LII as a warning.

We saw above that the will can never be without the AI. For Scotus, the AI is not superadded to the will, but is instead the *differentia* of a free will. It is hence the AI that makes the will a will, since for Scotus a will is no will at all unless it is free. In addition, the AI is that affection which, in addition to bringing along a power for opposites, inclines the agent toward willing justice-related objects of the will.[44]

It follows whenever the will is active in any sense (e.g. whenever the agent is not asleep), the agent is inclined by the ever-present AI toward any justice-related objects she may be aware of. It is further the case that when one has a MOI/LII, the will must be active, for such an intellection does not persist without the will's performance of continual *complacere* (ContinualComp). Consequently, whenever there is a MOI/LII, the agent will be inclined toward any justice-related object.

The distinctive claim I wish to make in support of my position is that the MOI/LII itself presents a justice-related object of the will and, consequently, the agent is inclined toward the MOI/LII by her AI. Recall

---

[44] Given that the purpose of the affections in the first place is to provide dispositions for willing, the AI is that disposition by which agent inclines toward justice-related willings, just as the AC is that disposition by which the agent inclines toward *commoda*.

that the MOI has the content <I must do something>. The object that the MOI/LII is presenting, therefore, is 'something' that one must do. If one 'must do' that 'something,' it would be unjust not to do it. Therefore, the 'something' that one 'must do' has to be related to justice. Given that, the AI must be inclining the agent toward willing 'something' which one must do. But I see no way to be inclined toward willing a 'something' about which I know not what without, at the same time, being inclined toward finding out what exactly that 'something' is. In other words, to be inclined toward willing a bare 'something' is to be, at the same time, alerted or warned that one should find out what that 'something' is.

I am, of course, not claiming that the AI makes one actually try to find out what that something is. As has been stated, the agent has a freedom for opposites and can thus refuse to heed (i.e. neglect) this warning. My only point is that the agent experiences the MOI/LII as a warning on account of the AI's inclining the agent toward that 'something' of which she knows not what. If she then does not inquire into the details of what it is she is obligated to do, we can nevertheless assert that she (in some sense) knew that she should so inquire because she had to have experienced the LII as a warning to so inquire. She can thus be held to have voluntarily *neglected* to prevent the subsequent ignorance of her obligation.

Before closing this chapter, I will address one potential objection. It could be stated that it would not be unjust *per se* not to do 'something' that one 'must do.' In other words, 'must do' need not be read as justice-related, in which case my proposal fails. In response, I admit on the one hand that the objection may have weight if the 'must' is hypothetical. For example, the must in "I must go to the water fountain if I want to get a drink of water" is not justice-related because the must is only present on the hypothesis that I want to do the justice-unrelated act of getting a drink of water. Hence, 'must' is not always relevant to justice.

Despite this concession, I consider the current objection weak since there is no justice-unrelated end specified for which the required action is a means. As stated, the 'must do' is, if anything, categorical and not hypothetical. Furthermore, given that the agent is *ex hypothesi* not aware of what it is she must do, she also is presumably not aware of whether the 'something' that she must do is a means to a justice-related or justice-unrelated end. And since it is at least *possible* that the end is justice-related, it seems that the agent should consider the 'must' as having some justice-related import.

If the objector were to persist in claiming that 'must' carries no justice-related import on its own, I would in that case simply modify the MOI. If (i) 'must' does not carry moral import of its own, and (ii) since all cases of NO are presumed to be moral, then (iii) the MOI that an agent must separate out in a Type-2 scenario has the content of not <I must do something> but of <I must *in a moral sense* do something>. Such a move is permissible, for the italicized phrase could easily have been understood as implicit in the 'must' when I initially discussed the MOI. The objection is thus obviated.

We have consequently just observed one way in which to understand an agent as blameworthy for her ignorance at TEF; she voluntarily failed to heed a warning, of which she was aware, to inquire into the specifics of her obligation. This particular solution, however, depends upon one's subscription to an *affectio*-doctrine and, even if one does, only applies to Type-2/Variation A NO's. How are such NO's to be explained, though, if one does not subscribe to *affectiones* of the will? And how are the other types of NO's to be ultimately explained? To answer these issues, we now turn to Suárez.

CHAPTER 8

NEGLECTED TREATISES HELP SOLVE NEGLIGENCE

THE ACTION THEORY OF FRANCISCO SUÁREZ

At this point in the book, we have presented most of the elements needed for a solution to Type-1 and Type-2 NO's. Nonetheless, a few problems remain, all of which can basically be reduced to the following question: How is an agent, at the time she causes the subsequent ignorance, to be understood as knowing the description of her action by which the ignorance itself can be considered voluntary? Finding a way to ascribe knowledge of such descriptions is essential to solving these NO's, for (as we saw in Chapter 1) voluntariness is relative to a certain description of an action or omission. If an agent is not aware of a description of her action by which she is causing subsequent ignorance, it therefore seems she can be held culpable for neither the ignorance nor the NO.

Another task remaining is to approach Type-3 NO's. Recall from the introduction that these are cases in which the time-span to TEF and/or circumstances are such that the agent is reasonably expected to take extra precautions so as to avoid ignorance.

In this chapter, I will explore Francisco Suárez's writings in order to address these final issues. As it turns out, the ways to resolve the questions remaining with regard to Type-1 and Type-2 NO's and the way to ascribe culpability in Type-3 NO's can all be found in two related concepts: Suárez's understanding of virtual deliberation/reflection and the associated idea of voluntariness *in alio*. By integrating these concepts into our evaluation we will have the means by which to explain culpability for all three types, and all variations within those types, of NO. In order to understand these concepts, however, we must present some basic details of Suárez's understanding of voluntariness.

I. The Directly vs. Indirectly Voluntary

A. *General Description*

The first overarching distinction between types of voluntariness is that between direct and indirect voluntariness, a distinction we saw Aquinas appeal to in Chapter 4 so as to characterize non-actions of the will as voluntary. The distinction basically lies in whether there is an elicited action of the will or not. 'Directly voluntary' describes actual *actions* of the will that are voluntary: "[the directly voluntary] is that in which the will directly exerts itself through its own act."[1] Corresponding as it does to the normal understanding of the voluntary as whatever comes from the will as free, there is as Suárez says "no difficulty in explaining" this concept.

By contrast, the indirectly voluntary (*voluntarium indirectum*) is that type of voluntariness ascribed to a lack of an elicited action of the will. In his words, it is "that which is morally judged to be from the will, as if the will expressly wills it, although the will does not elicit a proper act by which it wills."[2] The indirectly voluntary therefore describes not a willing not-to-act, but rather a non-willing altogether.

This understanding of the indirectly voluntary should pose no particular problem in light of Scotus's view of the will. Just as for Scotus the will has the ability either to *non-velle* some perceived good or *non-nolle* some perceived *malum* and do so freely, so Suárez is here stating that an agent can refrain from willing altogether and that the lack of willing can be voluntary and ascribable to the agent. There is, however, one worry in this regard that I want to quickly set aside.

It can seem somewhat odd to say that a particular absence of willing is voluntary because it can be "judged to be from the will, *as if the will expressly wills it*" when the will wills nothing. Of course, it makes sense to say a lack of an *external*, ordered action of the will can be voluntary if the will *wills* not to do something. Even a lack of a further internal act of the will could be voluntary if the will had earlier willed not to have

[1] *Directum* est illud, in quod directe tendit voluntas per actum suum, et ideo in eo explicando nulla est difficultas (*De Voluntario et Involuntario* [*DVI*], d. 1, sec. iv.13: IV, 176). All translations of Suárez are mine. All Latin is from: Francisco Suarez, *R.P. Francisci Suarez ... Opera Omnia*, 28 vols. in 30, editio nova, a D.M. André ..., juxta editionem venetianam XXIII tomos in-f° continentem, accurate recognita, reverendissimo ill. domino Sergent ... ab editore dicata (Parisiis, apud Ludovicum Vivès, 1856–78). Abbreviations to works contained in this collection are as follows: *De Voluntario et Involuntario* (*DVI*), *Commentarii et Disputationes in Tertiam Partem D. Thomae* (*CDTP*), *De Voto* (*DV*), *De Oratione, Devotione, et Horis Canonicis* (*DOD*), *De Vitiis et Peccatis* (*DVP*). After noting the work and the place within that work from which a citation comes, I will make reference to the volume number and page number in that volume relevant to the citation.

[2] *Indirectum* vero quadam generali significatione dici solet omne illud, quod moraliter censetur esse a voluntate, ac si illud expresse vellet, quamvis ipsa non eliciat proprium actum, quo illud velit (*DVI*, d.1, sec. iv.13: IV, 176).

any further elicited acts of the will. But in the absence of such a scenario, why judge a lack of an *elicited* act of the will to be *from the will*?

A similar question came up in Chapter 4. In reference to Aquinas's (V2), ["the perfectly voluntary consists of that which is 'from the will' (*a voluntate*)"], we wondered how a lack of action could be 'from the will.' His answer was that lack of willing can be 'from the will' by virtue of it being the case that the will is not doing what it is its nature to do. Suárez has a slightly different answer. Suárez places particular emphasis on the will's quality or power of *libertas* as opposed to the will itself and seems to understand this quality as somehow 'in' or as a constitutive power of the will. This *libertas*, moreover, includes for him (as for Scotus) a freedom not-to-act. Whenever, therefore, there is a lack of willing arising on account of the will's *libertas*, it can be said that the lack comes 'from the will' since the *libertas* is a constitutive power of, or 'in,' the will.

He makes this explicit when he gives his own full description of the voluntary, similar to that of Aristotle's definition[3] or Aquinas's (V1).[4] Suárez, though, makes one significant change. Instead of referring to an "inner principle" by which Aquinas clearly meant the will, Suárez writes that the voluntary is that which "arises from an intrinsic *power* of the will with cognition."[5] It is not from the will *per se*, but from the will's power of *libertas* that the voluntary arises.[6] For Suárez, the relevant internal principle is the *libertas* of the will instead of the will itself. Since, however, this *libertas* is in the will, it is acceptable to say lacks of willing are 'from the will.'

Note furthermore that for Suárez, we do not need to reconcile any definition of the voluntary in terms of 'from the will' with another

---

[3] "The moving principle is in the agent himself, he being aware of the particular circumstances of the action" (1111a21–24).

[4] (V1): The perfectly voluntary consists of an act in which there is (a) 'full' knowledge of the end by a rational agent along with (b) an inner principle of action by which it moves itself towards that end.

[5] ... libertas voluntatis includit potestatem agendi et non agendi: ergo cognito objectio, quod necessitatem illi non inferat, potest non operari ex vi suae libertatis: ergo illa carentia actus est in voluntate ex libertate eius: erit ergo voluntaria: tum quia est libera, et liberum supponit voluntarium: tum quia eo modo, quo est, oritur ab intrinseca potentia voluntatis ex cognitione: ad huiusmodi autem suspensionem actus, non requiritur actus, sed satis est carentia influxus: non ergo ad omne voluntarium est necessarius actus. (*DVI*, d.1, sec. v.2: IV, 177).

[6] There are points at which Suárez is not so careful as to make this fine distinction. It is nonetheless implied at those points, or should be given his focus upon 'libertas.'

definition in which some knowledge requirement is referred to (as we did for Aquinas).[7] Being 'from the will' has already been explained, and Suárez is furthermore careful always to state that there must be some 'cognition' (understood thinly)[8] or advertence of the intellect toward that which is voluntarily done or omitted. In other words, Suárez is clear in positing a 'knowledge requirement' in the sense used throughout this book.

Moreover, there is no doubt that Suárez's knowledge requirement must be fulfilled for instances of non-willing to be voluntary (i.e. for the indirectly voluntary). In regard specifically to the indirectly voluntary, he writes, "it is necessary that there be some cognition, or advertence on the part of the intellect."[9] If the relevant cognition (again, understood thinly) is present, a lack of willing can be voluntary; if absent, there is no voluntariness: "and henceforth it turns out that not every lack, or negation, of a free act should be judged to be voluntary, because it does not fall under cognition, nor do we always have in mind those acts."[10]

This last observation gives rise to a particularly thorny problem for our project. Recall that our task is to show how the ignorance accompanying a NO must itself be voluntary. Moreover, the ignorance in such NO's cannot arise from an elicited act of the will in which the will wills to be ignorant. Such ignorance would be intentional, or, as the medievals called it, 'affected.' Any omission resulting directly from such ignorance would not be considered 'negligent.' If the ignorance involved in a NO is to be voluntary, therefore, it must be *indirectly* voluntary: it must arise from a lack of action of the will, and that lack of action must be accompanied by some advertence of the intellect toward that ignorance.

---

[7] Recall we were concerned to reconcile the requirements listed in (V1) with (V2).

[8] Suárez often uses the term *cognitio* but by this does not necessarily mean, as opposed to Scotus, a more distinct, intensive kind of intellectual activity. Suárez does not necessarily recognize a difference between 'distinct' and 'indistinct' intellections, and therefore the technical meaning Scotus attributes to 'cognition' can not be applied to his use. In general, the 'cognition' Suárez requires for voluntariness appears to be equivalent to basic intellectual awareness.

[9] Et imprimis conveniunt omnes necessarium esse aliquam cognitionem, seu advertentiam ex parte intellectus ... (*DVI*, d.1, sec.v.2: IV, 177).

[10] atque hinc fit, ut non omnis carentia, seu negatio actus liberi censeatur voluntaria, quia non cadit sub cognitionem, nec de illa semper actus cogitamus (*DVI*, d.1, sec.v.2: IV, 177).

B. *Ignorance as Indirectly Voluntary? Suggestion 1*

Let us begin by asking the general question of how *any* case of ignorance can be indirectly voluntary. Upon asking this, a problem arises in that it is not immediately clear how ignorance can arise from a lack of an elicited act of the will. As mentioned above, many medieval (and contemporary) thinkers believe that ignorance can arise on account of an elicited action of the will. One can actively will to make oneself subsequently ignorant by a variety of means[11] and thereby cause affected ignorance. What, though, about a lack of willing? How can one make oneself ignorant by not willing?

We saw one way to do this in the chapters on Scotus. One can lose awareness of some knowledge (i.e. become temporarily ignorant) by not performing *complacere* on the related intellection or its object. Since intellections cease as a result of not having *complacere* performed on them, and since *complacere* is an action of the will, the lack of this particular act of the will would result in ignorance. Moreover, it may seem that such a lack of *complacere* is *ex cognitione* (cognition being understood in a thin, not Scotus's, sense).[12] Given that the presence of the intellection itself implies some awareness or intellectual advertence toward the object of that intellection, and given that there must be present an intellection for the will to fail to perform *complacere* on it, there must be some level of awareness of the object of an intellection whenever the will refrains from performing *complacere*. The subsequent ignorance of that object is thus brought about both as a result of a lack of willing (i.e. lack of *complacere*) and with some awareness of that object. Such ignorance thus satisfies the criteria for the indirectly voluntary.

The explanation just given seems to be a way in which to explain the indirect voluntariness of certain cases of ignorance, assuming subscription to the Scotist theory of indistinct intellections (which Suárez apparently does not). Nevertheless, such indirectly voluntary ignorance does not help explain the culpability of NO's. Why? Because the knowledge that is present in a situation such as that just described does not

---

[11] For example, one can will to get drunk, or to engage fully in some other thought-absorbing pursuit.

[12] Cf. *DVI*, d.4, sec.iii.3: IV, 224: "for it is the same to be actively cognized and actively considered" where considered is opposed to the complete absence of awareness, inconsideration (idem autem est esse actu cognitum, et esse actu condideratum).

necessarily satisfy the knowledge requirement insofar as NO's are concerned, and maybe not even as far as ignorance itself is concerned.

Recall that voluntariness is relative to a certain description of an action or omission. For an action or omission described in one particular way to count as voluntary, knowledge of that particular description is required so as to fulfill the knowledge requirement. If the agent is not aware (i.e. has no knowledge) of a particular description, then a corresponding knowledge requirement is not fulfilled and the action or omission picked out by that particular description is not voluntary. It is thus not the case that any knowledge whatsoever related to some action or omission satisfies the knowledge requirement for any one particular understanding of that action or omission.

In order to explain this point, assume that the relevant intellection above is John's intellection *d* <I must pick up Des at 7:00>. If John fails to perform *complacere* on that intellection, it will (according to the doctrine of indistinct intellections) cease and John will subsequently be ignorant of the fact that he must pick up Des at 7:00. It is not clear, however, that the *ignorance itself* is in any way voluntary. For the ignorance itself to be voluntary, John would need to know not simply *d* <I must pick up Des at 7:00> but rather something like *d'* <what I am doing is causing ignorance of the fact that 'I must pick up Des at 7:00'> while refraining from performing *complacere* on the former intellection *d*. In other words, it is *d'* that is the relevant description of the current omission in relation to causing ignorance of *d*. And it is not clear that awareness of *d'* follows from awareness of *d*. If not, then it is difficult to say how the explanation offered above explains how the ignorance of *d* itself is voluntary. The earlier presence of an intellection of which one is subsequently ignorant, therefore, does not necessarily satisfy the knowledge requirement for the *voluntariness* of that subsequent ignorance or non-awareness.

It may be objected that Scotus must have believed the presence of some intellection *i* itself satisfies the knowledge requirement such that acts of *complacere* or lacks thereof upon it could be considered voluntary. He did not require, for example, that there be a separate intellection <what I am doing is performing an act of *complacere* on intellection *i*> or <what I am not doing is performing an act of *complacere* on intellection *i* and thus am causing subsequent ignorance of its object> present such that acts of *complacere* or lacks thereof on intellection *i* be culpable (and thus voluntary). Instead, it appears from his writings that the presence of only intellection *i* is adequate. It must then be the case for him that when one freely performs *complacere* on some intellection *i*, the presence of *i* alongside the performance of *complacere* makes the agent implicitly aware that she is performing *complacere* on it. Or, alternatively, the presence of *i* while one is freely omitting to perform *complacere* on it implicitly makes the agent aware of the fact that she is omitting to perform *complacere* and thus causing subsequent ignorance. The knowledge requirement for acts or omissions of *complacere* on some intellection can thus be fulfilled by the presence of the intellection itself.

I am willing, for argument's sake, to give Scotus the benefit of the doubt and assume the suggestion just made is reasonable enough.[13] Even given this concession, however, it is not yet clear that the knowledge requirement relevant to the particular understanding of ignorance we are concerned with is fulfilled by the initial presence of an intellection *i*, the object of which one is subsequently ignorant. For we are not particularly concerned with how 'ignorance' *in abstracto* can be voluntary, but rather with how '*blameworthy* ignorance' can be voluntary. In other words, it is not enough for our purpose to show that the ignorance leading to the NO is voluntary, for that does not necessarily entail that it is blameworthy. For the agent ultimately to be held accountable for the NO (i.e. for it to be a *negligent* omission, as opposed to just an omission in the first place), the ignorance leading to it must be blameworthy, which means the agent must know she should not permit such ignorance.

For example, if John voluntarily permits ignorance of his obligation to pick up Des but does not know that he should not allow such ignorance, it is difficult to say how he can be blamed for that ignorance (and

[13] In one sense, it seems to be. Otherwise, for example, how could it be that one ever freely causes oneself to begin performing *complacere* on some intellection without assuming that, upon doing so, the agent also causes a separate intellection related to the performance of *complacere* per se? To assume this would run the risk of multiplying intellections to what some may think is an unreasonable degree. Nonetheless, I acknowledge the point could be debated. At present, however, I do not desire to enter the debate and I am not taking a particular stand on the issue as to what Scotus himself must have assumed regarding the relationship between the intellections and fulfillment of the knowledge requirement so far as performances of *complacere* or lacks thereof upon intellections are concerned. On the one hand, it makes no difference to the present point. Even if we grant Scotus this point, the underlying suggestion still seems insufficient for our purposes (as I am about to make clear in the text.) And on the other hand, (as will become apparent) some of Suárez's concepts will enable some sort of important, implicit knowledge to be assumed present in intellections, regardless of what Scotus himself may have thought.

thus for the subsequent NO). It may be voluntary, but not blameworthy. As we pointed out in the first chapter on Scotus, to qualify for blameworthiness he must first know *that* he should not let that obligation cease. In other words, it will not suffice for fulfillment of the knowledge requirement for '*blameworthy* ignorance' that an agent knows he is causing ignorance. He must instead know that he is causing ignorance *and that he should not be causing that ignorance.* For 'blameworthy ignorance' to be voluntary, therefore, the relevant description of the non-action, knowledge of which fulfills the knowledge requirement, is not <what I am doing is failing to perform *complacere* and thus causing subsequent ignorance of the object of this intellection>, but rather <what I am doing is failing to perform *complacere* and thus causing subsequent ignorance of the object of this intellection *even though I should not be causing such ignorance*>. Consequently, even if it is the case that the presence of intellection *d* <I must pick up Des at 7:00> can imply knowledge of the content of *d'* <what I am doing is causing ignorance of the fact that 'I must pick up Des at 7:00'>, it does not yet appear to follow that it also implies knowledge of the content of *d''* <what I am doing is causing ignorance of the fact that 'I must pick up Des at 7:00' *even though I should not be causing such ignorance*>.[14]

There is a further problem (similar to one we have pointed out before). Assume that the presence of *d* does somehow impart knowledge of *d''* such that John can be blamed for his ignorance. In this case, it is difficult to understand how John's omission to pick up Des could be *negligent.* If John permitted knowledge of his obligation to cease while knowing that he should not, it seems the resulting omission would be more aptly characterized as intentional instead of negligent.[15] *Ex hypothesi*, however, John's omission is negligent.

We should now recap where we are. We began by wondering how ignorance can be 'indirectly voluntary,' i.e. how ignorance can result from a lack of an elicited act of the will and yet be voluntary. We then noted that Scotus's doctrine of indistinct intellections affords one way in which ignorance can be considered voluntary. Ignorance can come about voluntarily on account of the will's refusal to perform *complacere* on some intellection. Despite the possible adequacy of this framework

[14] Note that I say 'yet' because my ultimate solution will say that it in fact does. It remains to be explained, however, how it does. Nothing we have seen thus far would lead one already to assume that *d* imparts knowledge of *d''*.

[15] Cf, for example, 'Example 1' used in Chapter 4.

to explain the voluntariness of ignorance, however, there remain the just-mentioned inadequacies for explaining the voluntariness of *blameworthy* ignorance.

As it turns out, our ultimate solution to the problem of NO's will largely depend upon the framework just presented. Before we can understand its utility for us, however, we must first explore another suggestion as to how ignorance can be indirectly voluntary.

C. *Ignorance as Indirectly Voluntary? Suggestion 2*

1. *Some Basic Assumptions*

From what I have observed, Suárez does not overtly appeal to a doctrine of indistinct intellections similar to the way in which Scotus does. Accordingly, he has no concept such as 'omitting to perform *complacere* on an intellection' to which to appeal. As a result, the task of showing how ignorance can be indirectly voluntary is especially challenging for him.

Suárez approaches this task by discussing 'inconsideration' (*inconsideratio*), an instance of not-thinking-about, or 'ignorance' (as it has been used in this book). In order to understand when, and under what conditions, inconsideration can be deemed voluntary for Suárez, it will first be helpful to discuss what counts as making a case of inconsideration non-voluntary.

As already pointed out, Suárez along with nearly every other medieval philosopher/theologian endorses:

> Invincible inconsideration/temporary-ignorance is not voluntary.

This assumption, of course, merely raises the question as to what the circumstances are that render any case of inconsideration invincible and thus involuntary. Suárez answers this question with:

> (A2) "Whenever the intellect is in such a disposition concerning some object or condition of an object, such that from the force of it the will is not able to apply the intellect to the proper consideration of that object or condition, then the inconsideration of it is altogether involuntary."[16]

[16] quandocumque intellectus in ea dispositione circa aliquod objectum, vel conditionem objecti, ut ex vi illius non possit voluntas applicare intellectum ad propriam considerationem illius objecti, seu conditionis, tunc inconsiderationem illius esse omnino involuntariam (*DVI*, d.4, sec.iii.18: IV, 228).

From (A2) we can derive that a necessary condition for voluntariness of inconsideration is that the intellect be in a disposition regarding some thing *x* such that the will can cause the intellect to consider *x* properly. How, though, does the intellect gain such a disposition? Suárez's writings indicate that either *x* or something concerning *x* must propose itself, or be proposed, to the intellect in such a way that the disposition follows: "therefore in the same way a similar effect, or condition of the act is able to be involuntarily not considered, *if nothing is actually offered, which is sufficient for exciting the mind, or will,* with the result that it applies the intellect to consideration of this type of thing" (italics mine).[17] Consequently, it appears that in order for it even to be possible that a case of inconsideration is voluntary, there must be something actually proposed to the intellect such that the intellect is in such a disposition in which the will can cause the intellect to perform proper consideration. Let us call this (A3).

> (A3) A necessary condition for the voluntariness of inconsideration is that, in some way or other, something be actually proposed to the intellect with the result that the intellect is in such a disposition that the will could cause the intellect to perform an act of consideration.

2. *Potential Problem with (A3) & One Solution Proposed*

For Suárez, 'consideration' can refer to an intellectual activity as thin as mere awareness.[18] Understood in this way, a quick perusal of (A3) may lead one to assert it is self-contradictory: if something is proposed to the intellect with the result that the intellect is in such and such a disposition, it would stand to reason that 'consideration' is already taking place. There would thus be no need for the will to cause the intellect to perform consideration; it already is. But if consideration has already occurred, how can there be inconsideration?

> (PA3) How can there be inconsideration (either voluntary or involuntary) in a case in which something has been offered to the intellect and has caused a certain disposition in it, given that this created disposition implies some form of consideration?

---

[17] ergo eodem modo potest similis effectus, vel conditio actus involuntarie non considerari, si nihil actu offeratur, quod sit sufficiens ad excitandam mentem, vel voluntatem, ut intellectum applicet ad hujusmodi considerationem (*DVI*, d.4, sec. iii.17: IV, 228).

[18] Again, cf. *DVI*, d.4, sec.iii.3.

When Suárez first undertakes to discuss how inconsideration can be voluntary, he problematizes the issue in a similar way. Although he gives three different accounts of the problem, they all seem to revolve around the same paradox: How can inconsideration ever be voluntary given that voluntariness requires that the agent possess knowledge, i.e. consideration? Is not the presence of *consideratio* logically incompatible with *inconsideratio*, in which case *inconsideratio* can never be voluntary?[19]

[19] There is no particular need to recount in the text his three diagnoses of the problem of voluntariness for *inconsideratio*. The basic idea is stated above. Nonetheless, I will recount one of them here in a footnote if the reader is interested. It has the following structure:

> (1) If failing to 'consider' something is a voluntary, culpable failure, the agent must in some way be able to consider that thing.
> (2) If the agent is not actually (*in actu*) considering that thing, it is not in the agent's power to consider it.
> (3) It is the same for something to be 'cognized' and to be 'considered' (at least in some sense).
> (4) An agent who is performing an action or omission and is doing so while accompanied by ignorance is thus failing to consider that of which she is ignorant. [3]
> (5) An ignorant agent, therefore, is not *in actu* considering that of which she is ignorant. [4]
> (6) It is therefore not in an ignorant agent's power to consider that of which she is ignorant. [2]
> (7) Therefore, an agent's ignorance cannot be a voluntary, culpable failure. [1]

The crucial step in this argument is (2). Why is an agent not able to consider something that she is not already considering? To answer this, let us think about how an agent could come about to consider something she is not considering. The answer seems to be that the contents of her intellect must change. How, though, could that happen? It could not come about by means of her own intellect; the intellect is not a free power such that it can determine itself. Furthermore, the will seems unable voluntarily to change the contents of the intellect, for such a (directly) voluntary action of the will would already presuppose some cognition of the considerandum. And if the change of intellectual contents were to come about by some other, external means, (e.g. if someone mentioned to the agent the considerandum, thus bringing it to her attention), such a change would not be in the agent's power in the first place. [Probatur minor, quia neque homo potest se applicare ad considerandum, quod non considerabat, per solam potentiam intellectivam, quia illa non est pontentia libera, unde non potest se determinare quoad exercitium, nisi vel ab objecto necessario excitetur, vel aliunde applicetur, sicut contingit in visu et aliis potentiis cognoscitivis: neque etiam est hoc in nostra potestate per voluntatem, quia voluntas non potest applicare intellectum ut consideret, nisi volendo ut consideret hanc vel illam rem: non potest autem voluntas hoc velle, nisi prius intellectus judicet bonum esse considerare de illa re, quia non potest ferri, nisi in cognitum et judicatum bonum: ergo talis voluntas supponit necessario aliquam considerationem illius rei, saltem quatenus potest esse objectum

There is one easy way to address this problem and resolve the initial paradox posed in (PA3). It could simply be suggested that a case of inconsideration is voluntary whenever there occurs (through whatever means) the lower-level consideration that one should think about something more (i.e. consider more) and yet the agent does not perform this further consideration. For example, someone might mention Goldbach's Theorem to me, causing me to realize that I really need to sit down and think about its truth. Realizing that I should consider this theorem in more detail, I could nevertheless choose not to consider it further. Such failure to consider further (i.e. such inconsideration) would then be voluntary.

There is no problem characterizing such failures to 'consider further' voluntary. Moreover, if it is such cases of inconsideration that (A3) is concerned with, the paradox easily disappears. The "act of consideration" can be taken to refer not to mere awareness, but rather to the more robust act of 'consider further' or 'consider in more detail.' Armed with the distinction between 'consider' as it refers to mere awareness, and 'consider' in the more robust sense of 'considering further,' (A3) is easily resolved, (PA3) answered, and the problems Suárez notices when he initially problematizes the issue vanish.

3. *The Inadequacy of the Just-Posited Solution*

While the explanation just offered may explain some instances of indirectly voluntary ignorance,[20] it is inadequate for solving our problem. In the Goldbach's Theorem example just discussed, the agent omits considering the theorem further *in light of the explicit knowledge* that she should consider it further. We have already explained, however, that ignorance arising in the face of such explicit knowledge would lead not to a *negligent* omission, but rather to a more or less *intentional* one.[21] Explaining the voluntariness of ignorance in this way is consequently not adequate.

---

considerationis intellectus: ergo si omnino nulla sit consideratio talis rei, non potest actio esse voluntaria (*DVI*, d.4, sec.iii.3: IV, 224)].

[20] Recall, *inconsideratio* is a form of ignorance. In the current case, inconsideration implies one is ignorant of the details one would have known if she had 'considered further.'

[21] Again, cf. 'Example 1' in the chapter on Aquinas.

Interestingly, Suárez himself clearly states that he does not intend by (A2) and (A3) to restrict indirectly voluntary ignorance to those cases in which there is explicit reflection upon one's obligation to consider further: "The other extreme [which we must avoid] will be if we were to say that only that inconsideration is voluntary when by a formal act the intellect is reflected on it [i.e. inconsideration]."[22] In other words, it is not even necessary for the indirect voluntariness of subsequent inconsideration that the agent reflectively begin to wonder whether she ought to inquire further.

Suárez takes this position no doubt because he believes there are many instances in which agents should be held as having erred or sinned by not considering something further (i.e. for having ignorance) even if they did not consider$_1$ (i.e. were not aware) that they should have considered$_2$ (i.e. consider further).[23] This claim, though, poses a difficult problem. If the agent has no explicit cognition regarding her ability to consider something further, it is unclear how the knowledge requirement can be fulfilled with regard to the subsequent inconsideration. And if, in turn, the knowledge requirement is thusly unfulfilled, it is further unclear how (A3), which requires for voluntariness that something be actually proposed to the intellect, could be fulfilled with regard to such inconsideration.

Suárez believes that both the knowledge requirement and (A3) can be fulfilled with regard to such further inconsideration. What is distinctive in his approach, however, is that (A3) is not satisfied in virtue of the knowledge requirement being fulfilled in such cases. Instead, it will turn out that the means by which (A3) is satisfied sets into motion a process that makes the fulfillment of the knowledge requirement possible. To show how this is possible will require some extensive inquiry in Suárez's corpus and some constructive analysis. This inquiry and analysis will be the focus of the next substantial section, after which we will be in a position to apply the findings specifically to the problem of NO's and the ignorance accompanying them.

---

[22] Alterum ergo extremum erit si dicamus, tunc solum inconsiderationem esse voluntariam, quando supra illam aliquo modo reflectitur intellectus actu formali, ut expresse advertendo se non satis considerasse hanc rem, et teneri ad exactius considerandum, vel saltem dubitet de sufficienti cogitatione, et de obligatione amplius cogitandi (*DVI*, d.4, sec.iii.21: IV, 229).

[23] Cf. *DVI*, d.4, sec.iii.22.

II. The Voluntariness of Further Inconsideration and Virtual Cognition

A. *Two types of voluntariness:* in se *and* in alio

At first glance, Suárez appears to claim that such further inconsideration (inconsideration in the absence of explicit knowledge that one could consider something further) can be voluntary in spite of failing to fulfill either (A3) or the knowledge requirement. He seems to do so by means of his distinction between types of voluntariness – that between voluntariness *in se* and voluntariness *in alio* – and his assertion that such further inconsideration may fulfill the conditions for the latter. Although Suárez does indeed believe voluntariness *in alio* permits the possibility of such further inconsideration being voluntary, it will turn out that this belief does not entail a disregard for either (A3) or the knowledge requirement. To see why it may initially appear otherwise, however, we need first discuss the distinction between these two types of voluntariness.

Voluntariness *in se* occurs when there is actual, explicit reflection in the intellect concerning that which is to be done. Suárez describes it as follows:

> for this that same reflection on the part of the intellect is necessary, because some thing is not able to be voluntary *in se*, unless it is proposed in its very self to the will, with the result that the will can freely do or suspend its act concerning that thing ... it being posited, moreover, that there is a reflection in the intellect concerning that very inconsideration, the will is able to have no act concerning it [i.e. the inconsideration] and concerning the application of the intellect to further consideration.[24]

Basically, voluntariness *in se* is the understanding of voluntariness we have had in mind all along, an understanding according to which the agent has some actual, present knowledge of that which she is, or is not, doing.

---

[24] ... et ad hoc necessaria est eadem reflexio ex parte intellectus, quia non potest aliqua res esse in se voluntaria, nisi in se ipsa sit proposita voluntati, ut ipsa possit libere operari, vel suspendere actum circa ipsam, nam in hoc distinguitur *voluntarium in se* a *voluntario in alio:* posita autem in illa reflexione intellectus circa inconsiderationem ipsam, potest voluntas nullum actum habere circa illam, nec circa intellectum applicandum ad ampliorem considerationem, sed solum circa hic et nunc faciendum (*DVI*, d.4, sec.iii.26: IV, 231).

Another type of voluntariness, the type that will characterize further inconsideration, is voluntariness *in alio*. Something is voluntary *in alio* when it is an effect following from an earlier voluntary *in se* act or omission. For example, to return to Thomas's illustration, if the captain of a ship omits to steer it and it subsequently sinks, the sinking of the ship is voluntary *in alio*.[25] The idea is that something is voluntary *in alio* if it is not willed *per se* itself, but occurs as a result of another voluntary act that one does intentionally do. Armed with this concept, Suárez is then able to say that an instance of inconsideration can be voluntary *in alio* if it follows from another voluntary *in se* act or omission.

This strategy for solving the problem of voluntary inconsideration, however, seems initially to be no more than a semantic ruse on Suárez's part. Unable (on account of the knowledge requirement) to find a way to characterize some instances of further inconsideration as voluntary, he appears to have simply said that there is a different kind of voluntariness defined in such a way that these cases of inconsideration can qualify. Clearly, such a solution would be unsatisfactory, for it is unclear what sort of moral import something merely voluntary *in alio* carries. If anything, it seems as if something voluntary *in alio* is voluntary only by denomination from an earlier voluntary act or omission. If so, voluntariness *in alio* perhaps would not carry its own moral import and thus not factor towards culpability. In that case it would not be relevant to our problem, nor would it serve the purposes for which Suárez initially wanted to make inconsideration voluntary – namely, so that certain cases of inconsideration could be considered blameworthy.

B. *Virtual Deliberation/Cognition*

1. *Preliminary Considerations*

Fortunately, Suárez does attempt to give voluntariness *in alio* a more robust sense when it comes to inconsideration. In fact, he even intimates that something voluntary *in alio* can fulfill the knowledge requirement. In such a voluntarium there is, according to him, "virtual" or "interpretative deliberation."[26] Since one cannot deliberate

---

[25] voluntarium autem in alio dicitur effectus subsecutus ex tali carentia actus imperati, vel elicit, ut est mors, verbi gratia, vel submersio navis, quae subsecuta est ex eo quod alius non subvenit, illa enim non est in se volita etiam indirecte, sed solum quatenus in alio priori volito virtute continetur (*DVI*, d.1, sec.v.6: IV, 178).

[26] These are the terms given to the concept by Cajetan and Durandus respectively: Atque eadem veritas colligitur ex aliis auctoribus, qui dicunt ad hoc voluntarium

without being aware of that over which one is deliberating, it seems to follow that 'virtual deliberation' would imply some level of 'virtual awareness' or 'virtual reflection.' But if one is 'virtually' aware of what it is one is virtually deliberating over, then when one acts or fails to act in response to the deliverances of that deliberation, one does it with what can be called 'virtual knowledge' or 'virtual cognition.' This virtual cognition, moreover, consequently, affords a way in which to understand voluntaria *in alia* as somewhat voluntary in their own right in that it fulfills the knowledge requirement with regard to them.

Before moving on, a terminological point must be made. When referring to virtual cognitive phenomena, Suárez seems to recognize no difference among different virtual cognitive states and appears to have the same phenomenon in mind in all cases. For example, there is no technical difference intended between 'virtual deliberation' and 'virtual reflection.' Instead, it appears that that for Suárez all cognitive descriptions (such as 'deliberation', 'reflection', and 'attention'), when modified by 'virtual,' should be simply understood as equivalent to what could be called 'virtual awareness' or 'virtual cognition' or 'virtual knowledge.' I will accordingly use all such phrases synonymously.

Suárez, therefore, posits the existence of some sort of virtual cognition that fulfills the knowledge requirement with regard to further consideration. The problem that remains, though, is to make sense of what a virtual cognition could be. Here is a first attempt to express what Suárez may have in mind. Consider a case of actual willing. It is not necessary that, in order to will q, the agent must will to will q. If it were, then it would likewise be necessary for the agent to will to will to will q, and so on, leading to an untenable infinite regress. Instead, it could be said that those higher-order willings are, in some manner, included in the initial act of willing. We could perhaps, for lack of a better term, say that those higher-order acts of will are included 'virtually.'[27]

Suárez seems to have something similar in mind when he discusses 'virtual' or 'interpretative' deliberation. To see this, let us turn to his example of two thieves and the stealing of money. He notes that there are two *consideranda* in such a theft. First, there is the *considerandum*

---

sufficere deliberationem virtualem, ut Cajetanus ait, vel interpretativam, ut Durandus in 2, d.24, q.6, n.5 (*DVI*, d.4, sec.iii.27: IV, 231).

[27] Cf., for example, Harry Frankfurt's idea that volitional commitments 'resound' through the higher orders of willing. See Harry Frankfurt, "Freedom of the Will and the Concept of a Person" *Journal of Philosophy* 68, no. 1 (1971): 5–20.

that what the agent is doing is stealing, and that it is evil. There is also the *considerandum* concerning the particular conditions of this act of stealing, e.g. how much money is being stolen.[28] It is very possible, claims Suárez, that two criminals could each intentionally steal money without either necessarily considering how much money he or she is stealing.[29] Now, suppose that each criminal realizes that he or she is committing the evil of stealing but does not consider any of the further circumstances of the act, and one criminal steals $100 while the other steals only $10. Suárez believes he is in unanimous agreement with all other theologians by saying that the one who steals $100 sins worse than the one who steals $10.[30] How, though, can this conclusion be correct, given that *ex hypothesi* they both equally considered the evil in the act of stealing (in general), and equally 'inconsidered,'[31] or did not think about, the particular circumstances concerning how much money they stole?[32] Suárez bases his answer on the claim that they must each be responsible for having voluntarily failed to consider the second *considerandum* and can thus be held responsible not only for the theft itself, but also for the particular details of their respective thefts.[33] To support the claim that they voluntarily failed to consider the second *considerandum*, he writes that "by that very fact" that the thieves' intellects apprehended, and thus considered, that stealing was an evil, they were

---

[28] This distinction, of course, is based upon Aristotle's distinction between the universal and the particular.

[29] Note that the actual amount stolen need not be the only 'inconsidered' detail that affects the gravity of some sins. It is possible that the person from whom one is stealing, or the place (e.g. church) in which one is stealing, could also affect the relative gravity of some sins even if those details were inconsidered. In Suárez's example, I take it that all factors are identical between the two thieves except for the amount stolen. The example could easily be altered without losing its point, however, by controlling for the amount stolen and varying the victims or location.

[30] If the difference between $100 and $10 is not enough to invoke this intuition, make the difference as large as one likes (e.g. $1,000,000 vs. $1).

[31] Due to linguistic requirements and ease of exposition, throughout this chapter I will refer to 'inconsideration' and other such non-actions as 'acts' or things to be 'performed,' although properly they are not. This phrasing should not affect any of the conclusions offered.

[32] cf. *DVI*, d.4, sec.iii.23–24 for this discussion.

[33] As Jorge Gracia has aptly pointed out to me, Suárez's contention that the two thieves sinned unequally even though they both equally 'inconsidered' the specific details of their thefts inevitably brings up questions of moral luck. Nonetheless, issues regarding moral luck need not be solved for us to gain from Suárez's discussion. The basic point for our purposes is that each of the thieves was in a position to consider his or her act in more detail, and this point holds regardless of one's position on moral luck.

also "able to will to consider [further], even if he or she should not have another act by which he or she considered that he or she was considering." And he explicitly ties this ability to will to consider further to the presence of a 'virtual reflection.' For such a willing to consider further, he writes, "virtual reflection suffices."[34]

The idea then is that simply by virtue of an act of considering, it is open to the will to cause that consideration to be pursued further and further. And the reason it is open to the will to push that consideration further is that there is always accompanying an act of consideration an implicit, 'virtual cognition' that one *could* consider the *consideratum* further. If this awareness were not implicitly there or were not sufficient, an agent could never voluntarily consider something more intensely without having a separate explicit act of the intellect by which she [considers that [she could consider further]]. But for this consideration to be voluntary under the assumption that some sort of virtual reflection does not suffice, she would have to have a further act of the intellect by which she [considers that [she could consider that [she could consider further]]] and so on. Since in such a case an agent could never freely begin to consider anything further, it must be that either voluntary acts of considering further never happen, or there is some sort of implicit, virtual reflection accompanying (at least some) acts of consideration, and these virtual reflections suffice for a voluntary act of the will. Since the former is obviously not the case, virtual reflections must exist and suffice.

Despite this explanation, it is admittedly difficult to get a precise understanding of what a virtual cognition is. To do so, we will need to turn to Suárez's larger corpus in order to discern how he came to this notion. Before we do that, however, let us briefly return to (A3) and our worries concerning it. Recall that (A3) requires that something be "actually proposed to the intellect" by which the "intellect is in such a disposition that the will could cause the intellect to" consider the

---

[34] Hoc ergo judicio, et apprehensione supposita in intellectu, antequam voluntas libere se determinet ad prosequendum objectum propositum, potest applicare intellectum ut perfectius conferat, vel dijudicet, vel ut conetur distincte concipere quod tantum confuse propositum est, vel alio modo simili: ad quod non semper requiritur novus actus intellectus, sed sufficit virtualis illa reflexio, quam rationalis consideratio virtualiter in se includit super se ipsam, ut Scotus supra notavit: qui enim considerat aliquam rem, hoc ipso potest velle considerare, etiam si non habeat alium actum quo consideret se considerare: et eadem ratione potest applicare intellectum ad considerandum in se et distincte, quod confuse ibi continetur (*DVI*, d.4, sec.iii.28: IV, 231–232).

second *considerandum.*[35] (A3) seems to pose a problem in cases of inconsideration in which there is no explicit cognition of the fact that one should perform some further consideration, for there seems to be nothing "actually proposed to the intellect" in those cases with regard to the possibility of further consideration. One might be tempted to think that the presence of the virtual cognition now under discussion satisfies (A3) in these cases. Such a resolution, however, would be fallacious. As we will soon discover, Suárez is adamant in drawing a distinction between a 'virtual' and an 'actual' cognition and denies that a virtual cognition could be considered actual. As such, the presence of a 'virtual' cognition could not fulfill (A3)'s call for something to be "*actually* proposed to the intellect."

Instead of being fulfilled by the virtual cognition that one could perform further consideration of some *consideratum x*, Suárez maintains that (A3) is fulfilled by the initial, actual consideration of *consideratum x* itself. Recall from the discussion above regarding the two thieves that they were able to perform further consideration "by that very fact" that they were actually considering stealing money and the evil inherent in it in the first place. It is the actual consideration of stealing that makes it possible that they consider their theft in more detail. An initial actual consideration, therefore, not only fulfills (A3) but (as just discussed above) also gives rise to a virtual cognition that can fulfill the knowledge requirement with regard to any subsequent inconsideration. That this is the correct way to interpret the relationship between (A3)'s fulfillment, virtual cognition, and inconsideration will become clear after a more extensive inquiry into the nature of Suárez's virtual cognition is undertaken. We now turn to that task.

2. *Suárez's References to Other Philosophers*

In his attempt to explain indirectly voluntary *in alio* inconsideration by means of virtual cognition, Suárez refers to the ideas of Cajetan (who mentioned a "virtual deliberation") and Durandus (who dubbed such deliberation "interpretative").[36] We can thus begin our exploration as to what is meant by virtual cognition by exploring these references.

---

[35] For the sake of reference, (A3) is here stated again: "A necessary condition for the voluntariness of inconsideration is that, in some way or other, something be actually proposed to the intellect with the result that the intellect is in such a disposition that the will could cause the intellect to perform an act of consideration."

[36] Atque eadem veritas colligitur ex aliis auctoribus, qui dicunt ad hoc voluntarium sufficere deliberationem virtualem, ut Cajetanus ait, vel interpretativam, ut Durandus in 2, d. 24. q. 6, n. 5 (*DVI*, disp. 4, sec. 3, n.27: IV, 231).

Unfortunately, the reference to Durandus's 'interpretative' deliberation is not very helpful. The passage referred to is concerned with whether the morose delight one may have while thinking about a sin is itself a mortal sin. Durandus simply answers that morose delight can be a mortal sin because it "supposes deliberation directly or interpretatively."[37] In other passages Durandus does mentions an 'interpretative' will. In those instances, however, he is concerned with the completely different issue of how a guardian's or parent's will can or cannot substitute, or be 'interpretative' of, someone else's such as a child's.[38]

By contrast, the reference to Cajetan is more fruitful. Suárez refers to Cajetan's discussion more than once and points out that Cajetan distinguishes between formal (actual) and virtual deliberation of the mind. In addition, Cajetan recognizes a further two-fold distinction in both types of deliberation. Formal (actual) deliberation is sub-divided into (a) perceptible and (b) imperceptible formal deliberation. The latter (b) occurs when there is actual deliberation in the mind that happens too quickly to be noticed by the agent.[39] Virtual deliberation, on the other hand, comes about "without this actual consideration [but] from habit, or custom, or from a prior deliberation already made."[40] Although Suárez is not as clear at this point as he could be, the two-fold distinction in Cajetan's text with regard to virtual deliberation is between (c) habit and custom on the one hand, and (d) that which comes about from a prior deliberation on the other.[41]

---

[37] Est etiam complacentia deliberative, cum sit morosa: voco enim nunc delectationem morosam, quae supponit deliberationem directe vel interpretative [D. Durandus, D. Dvrandi a Sancto Porciano, ord. praed. et meldensis episcopi, in Petri Lombardi Sententias Theologicas commentariorum libri IIII. Venetiis, Guerraea, 1571 (Ridgewood, NJ: Gregg Press, 1984), Bk 2, dist. 24, q. 6, n.5.]

[38] *Ibid*., Bk. 4, d. 4, q. 7. See also Bk 4, d.6, q.2, n.9, Bk. 2, d. 30, q.2, n.7.

[39] This passage will be referenced below in support of the contention that virtual deliberation cannot consist in actual yet frail and imperceptible deliberation. Deliberation that is imperceptible yet actual is actual (formal) and not virtual according to Cajetan and Suárez. Virtual deliberation is less robust that that which is actual.

[40] Eadem doctrina sumi potest ex Cajetano 2, 2, quaest. 88, art. 1, ubi distinguit duplicem deliberationem mentis, seu rationis, formaliem scilicet, et virtualem ... posteriorem vero significant fieri sine hac actuali consideratione ex habitu, vel consuetudine, vel ex priori deliberatione jam facta (*DVI* disp. 4, sec. 3, n.12: IV, 227).

[41] Primo, ille actus dicitur esse virtualiter ex collatione, de quo non in seipso, sed in sui principio collatio praecessit: et hoc modo artifices absque act'que actuali deliberatione, non tamen abseque virtuali operantur. Non nam cum quis pulsat, aut scribit, deliberat de singulis actibus: sed deliberauit de initio scribendi, au pulsandi, et universaliter de utendo tunc arte illa. Secundo actus ille voluntarius diciture esse ex collatione virtualiter, qui sic volenti consonat, ut nolit conferre de illo, ut contingit quando quis operatur ex habitu, seu consuetudine, aut negligentia. Qui nam consuetudinem suam

An example of a virtual deliberation resulting from (d) a prior deliberation is, for Cajetan, being in the process of writing. While in the process, nobody "deliberates about the individual acts" such as how to form each letter, spell each word, and put them together in proper grammatical form. One already in the process did, however, "deliberate about her starting to write" at the time at which she began to write. In other words, Cajetan is describing a scenario in which some virtual phenomenon is resulting from a preceding actual deliberation that is no longer taking place. The other type of virtual consideration (c) occurs when somebody just merely follows her custom without having actually deliberated or even having proposed to herself that she should act according to this custom. In these cases, there is not a prior deliberation from which the current action stems.

Cajetan's sub-division of virtual deliberation exemplifies, in Suárez's mind, an unjustified conflation between virtual and habitual phenomena made by many of his predecessors, such as Navarrus.[42] Navarrus had apparently tried to explain one's virtual intention as the purpose one would note if she were asked why she was doing something. For example, if one were asked why she had taken the breviary and she answered she did so for the purpose of reciting, then according to Navarrus she is virtually intending to perform a vocal prayer. In reality, however, Suárez claims that at most she had a habitual intention to pray, an intention that is not properly 'virtual.' The reason Suárez gives for it not being virtual is that there was *ex hypothesi* never any *actual* intention to do the moral act of praying or worshipping God per se. Any actual intention she may have had was only to do some act, such as reciting, which is itself "habitually associated with a moral act."

prosequitur in bono, vel in malo, non deliberat actualiter quoniam secundum illam operatur, nec umque forte proposuit uti illa consuetudine [Thomas de Vio Caietanus, *Summa totius theologiae S. Thomae de Aquino* (Hildesheim, Zurich, New York: Georg Olms Verlag, 2001), II-IIae, q. 88, art. 1]. It is interesting to note here that Cajetan includes, in the second type of virtual deliberation, negligence. Suárez mentions custom and habit, but leaves out negligence in his description of Cajetan's view. This difference may be no more than just accidental. As will become clear shortly, however, I believe Suárez would not classify this second type of Cajetanian virtual deliberation as properly 'virtual.' Instead, phenomena of this type will fall in the less robust category of phenomena resulting from habit. It is possible, therefore, that Suárez does not include negligence for he believes negligence is culpable and as such requires a more robust cognitive state than that associated with habit. If so, then this is in accordance with the general contention of this book.

[42] This is most likely Martín de Azpilcueta (1493–1586), also known as Dr. Navarrus. This biographical information can be found at: Jacob Schmutz,

The most that can be said therefore is that she had a habitual, not virtual, intention and such an intention "does not suffice for the moral property of the act."[43]

This reference to Navarrus points out that, of the two sub-types of virtual deliberation noted by Cajetan, only (d) that which follows from some actual deliberation made at the beginning of an activity properly counts as virtual for Suárez. Cajetan's other sub-type (c) is not a type of virtual phenomena at all, but is instead a description of "habitual" phenomena which carry no moral import in and of themselves.[44] In other words, Suárez wants to draw a sharp distinction between 'virtual' and 'habitual' phenomena and claim that virtual phenomena are (i) more robust than phenomena characterized by habit, (ii) less robust than those characterized by actuality, and yet (iii) robust enough such that they, unlike habitual phenomena, carry moral import.

3. *Suárez's Discussions of Virtual Phenomena*

Suárez elaborates upon his understanding of the distinction among actual, virtual, and habitual phenomena when he discusses which type of intention is sufficient for completing the sacraments.[45] Before diving into this discussion, it should be noted that the forming of an intention is an act of the will. Therefore, a virtual intention is a virtual will-act,

---

Scholasticon (3 June 2010), URL = http://www.scholasticon.fr/Database/Scholastiques_fr.php?ID=188.

[43] Navarrus autem supra explicat virtualem intentionem per illam conditionalem, quia si interrogaretur quare accipit Breviarium, responderet se id facere ad recitandum. Verumtamen hoc modo magis explicatur habitualis, quam virtualis intention. Et praeterea hujusmodi conditionalis proposition, nisi fundetur in aliquo actu absoluto, incerta est hominibus, nec sufficit ad proprietatem moralem actus. Igitur implicita intentio illa est, quae non terminatur expresse et formaliter ad actum moralem sub expressa ratione orationis, vel cultus divini, sed sub aliqua ratione magis generali, quae ex habitu vel consuetudine determinatur ad actum moralem. Talis est intentio in exemplo adducto a Navarro (*DOD* lib. 3, c. 3, n.6: XIV, 223–224).

[44] This is not to say that allowing oneself to do something habitually could not, for Suárez, be morally imputable. To follow the current example, if one were obligated to pray and at that point engaged in merely this habitual action, then one could be culpable for not having fulfilled one's obligation to pray. In other words, allowing oneself to perform something in only a 'habitual' mode when a more robust mode is called for could itself be blameworthy. The point being made here, however, is that the habitual intention for doing some act *x* (e.g. praying) is not sufficient for one to have actually performed act *x* in a morally relevant way. This does not preclude the possibility that somebody at the same time could do some act *y* (e.g. reciting words) in a way such that *y* could be a properly human act to which moral import could attach (if *y* were a morally-relevant act at all). Nonetheless, having a virtual or actual intention for *y* does not mean that there is also an actual or virtual intention for *x*. This is Suárez's main point in the example.

[45] *CDTP*, Disp. 13, sec. 3, n.3.

not a virtual cognition. It is not clear, however, that Suárez himself was always careful to separate discussion of acts of the will from acts of the intellect when referring to this distinction. At any rate, an exploration into his discussion of virtual intention should shed some light on Suárez's understanding of the actual/virtual/habitual distinction and will confirm some of our suspicions regarding virtual cognition arising from the Cajetan passage.[46]

According to Suárez, "pure habitual intention does not suffice for completing the sacrament, nor is actual intention required (although it is more perfect), but virtual attention can suffice."[47] Suárez states an actual intention comes about when the "will for performing the sacrament (*voluntas faciendi*) is elicited in act at the time at which the sacrament externally is taking place." In the cases of both virtual and habitual intention, by contrast, this "will for performing the sacrament" precedes the external action and is no longer actually being elicited.[48] The difference between these latter two is that in the case of habitual intention the *voluntas faciendi* "afterwards does not flow into (*influit*) the effect (the external action), and in no way is it afterwards in the memory or cogitation of the person, neither is it the cause of such action through itself nor through another effect." By contrast, virtual intention occurs when "something (*aliquid*) from [the *voluntas faciendi*] nevertheless remains left behind through which it is judged by its power to move [the agent] toward the action of the sacrament."[49] This only begs the question, though, as to what this *aliquid* is that somehow remains, and how that remainder can influence an act.[50]

---

[46] Suárez often cites this passage as his authoritative description of the difference between habitual, virtual, and actual phenomena. Looking at it, therefore, is essential for our investigation into virtual cognition.

[47] Intentio mere habitualis non sufficit ad sacramentum conficiendum, nec requiritur actualis, quamvis illa perfectissima sit, sed sufficere potest virtualis (*CDTP*, Disp. 13, sec. 3, n.3: XX, 250).

[48] There is the implication here that habitual intention can be preceded by an actual intention to do that act, and this seems a bit contrary to our initial understanding of habitual phenomena based upon the discussion of Navarrus's example. This problem will be addressed later in the chapter.

[49] Actualis satis est clara (consistit enim in hoc, quod actu eliciatur voluntas faciendi sacramentum, eo tempore, quo exterius fit); habitualis dicitur esse, quando praecessit voluntas faciendi sacramentum, et postea nullo modo influit in effectum, seu in actionem externam, quia neque ullo modo est postea in memoria, seu cogitatione hominis, nec per se aut per aliquem effectum, seu virtutem relictam, est causa talis actionis. Virtualis ergo dicitur, quando praecessit actualis intention, quae jam in se non existit, quando fit sacramentum, manet tamen aliquid ab illa relictum, per quod censetur virtute movere ad actionem sacramenti (ibid.).

[50] See also *DOD*, Lib. 3, c. 3, n.6 where the same point is made.

Suárez goes on to explain virtual intention in two different ways: morally and physically. The moral explanation, although a bit repetitive of the point that something of the original actual intention must remain, does add a condition: a virtual intention must begin with an actual intention which is not "revoked by a contrary intention" in the meantime.[51] As long as these conditions are fulfilled, the resulting external act is a properly human (i.e. morally-relevant) act.

This elaboration unfortunately does not clarify what exactly the *aliquid* is that is left over. The *aliquid* cannot merely be the absence of a subsequent revocation. Otherwise, his denials that habitual intention suffices would be based upon the claim that in a habitual intention the agent has revoked a former actual intention, and they are not. What, then, is the *aliquid* that is left behind and causes external actions even when the internal actual willing is no longer present?

Suárez surveys various possibilities for this left-over *aliquid* while offering the physical explanation. One suggestion is that the *aliquid* is some "actual attention" on the part of the intellect. This attention is "very frail and mild and does not include a reflection by which we advert to the fact that we are paying attention or willing." We consequently cannot even remember that we had such attention once the act is over. Nonetheless, this actual attention is there, and this actual attention clearly fulfills the knowledge requirement such that any action being taken at the time is voluntary.[52] The idea seems to be that if one is having frail actual attention upon an act that was the object of an earlier intention, that earlier intention is present virtually on account of the present actual attention to the act. Despite conceding that such frail attention probably happens, Suárez denies this is an adequate explanation of virtual intention. If it were, the distinction between virtual and actual phenomena would be largely extinguished. Moreover, this suggestion would contradict his discussion of Cajetan in *DVI* in which it is

[51] Necessarium tamen est, ut saltem in initio actionis, quando homo incipit se movere, et applicare ad sacramentum conficiendum, praecedat aliqua actualis voluntas, a qua inchoetur illa action, ut postea in progressu actionis virtualiter durare possit, … Unde tandem requiritur, quod illa intentio non sit per contrariam intentionem revocata, alioqui actio exterior jam non procederet ab illa, sed casu fieret praeter hominis intentionem (*CDTP*, Disp. 13, sec. 3, n.5: XX, 251).

[52] Respondetur, illam attentionem esse valde debilem et remissam, et non includere reflexionem, qua advertamus, nos attendere aut velle; et ideo, licet revera sit, ut exterior effectus probat, no stamen illam in se non experimur, quamdiu durat, nec, postquam transacta est, recordari aut dijudicare possumus, an illam habuerimus (ibid.: XX, 252).

stated that imperceptible yet actual consideration is one of the two subtypes of actual, not virtual, consideration.[53]

Another suggestion for understanding the left-over *aliquid* is based upon the understanding that the original actual intention impresses a "certain quality, or disposition or impetus ... on the motive powers' exterior organs."[54] This suggestion makes use of an analogy to a projectile which retains its motion even when the person who threw it is no longer touching it; the thrower endowed the projectile with certain dispositions that continue to carry it even after the thrower is no longer present. Suárez is similarly unconvinced by this approach because he "cannot understand how a physical impression of such a quality can come about in external members through an internal act of the will."[55] Nonetheless, since it is obvious to him that persons often walk "on account of a prior intention" while actually thinking of other things and not of their walking,[56] then it must be the case that a "virtual intention remains in that external motion itself."[57] He then speculates that "some actual motion of a *phantasia* and an appetite always concurs

---

[53] Eadem doctrina sumi potest ex Cajetano 2, 2, quaest. 88, art. 1, ubi distinguit duplicem deliberationem mentis, seu rationis, formalem scilicet, et virtualem, et priorem ait fieri cum actuali consideratione objecti, et militia ejus, seu prohibitionis, et aliarum circumstantiarum, quam considerationem interdum dicit esse perceptibilem, interdum vero imperceptibilem, quia nimirum velocissime fit, et absque magna reflexione; posteriorem vero significant fieri sine hac actual consideratione ex habitu, vel consuetudine, vel ex priori deliberatione jam facta (*DVI* disp. 4, sec. 3, n.12: IV, 227). The reader may be puzzled here in that the passage seems to imply virtual consideration can result from habit, whereas the denial of this claim is the topic of the present discussion in the body of the paper. In this quotation, Suárez is referring to Cajetan's and Biel's views. The *ex habitu* is not to be read as constituting his own view, but rather as the explanation that others have offered. As we have already discussed, Suarez criticizes others (such as Navarrus) for failing to adequately distinguish between habitual and virtual phenomena.

[54] Ad hanc difficultatem Richard., dist. 6, art. 1, quaest. 3, ad 2, censet, hanc virtutem esse quondam qualitatem seu dispositionem, ac veluti impetum, quae imprimitur ex vi talis intentionis exterioribus organis motivae potentiae, et durante cessante actuali intentione; nam sicut in projectis, cessante contactu projicientis, manet quidam impetus continuans motum, per quem dicitur projiciens virtualiter movere (*CDTP*, disp. 13, sec. 3, n.5: XX, 251).

[55] Nihilominus mihi etiam non placet ille dicendi modus, quia non intelligo, per actum interiorem voluntatis fieri in membris externis physicam impressionem alicujus qualitatis (ibid.).

[56] Quis enim dicat, quamdiu homo ambulat ex vi prioris intentionis seu applicationis, semper actu cogitare de ipsa ambulatione, praesertim cum inter ambulandum alias res attentissime meditatur, aut alia negotia tractat (ibid., n. 5).

[57] Quocirca dicendum censeo, cum Scoto et Gabr. supra, hanc intentionem virtualiem manere in ipsa motione externa (ibid., n.6: XX, 252).

with external action," leading us to believe that the motion of the *phantasia* and the appetite is the *aliquid*.[58]

From this discussion, we can draw a few insights into the description of virtual phenomena:

> (VT1): The virtual phenomenon must be preceded by an 'actual' phenomenon.
> (VT2): The virtual phenomenon must not have been revoked since the relevant original actual phenomenon.
> (VT3): The actual phenomenon has left behind an *aliquid* that somehow influences (*influit*) that which is virtual.
> (VT4): This *aliquid* probably consists of some sort of appetitive/phantasmatic movement.[59]

4. *The "Will Moving the Intellect" (WMI): The* Aliquid *Left Behind*

In order to try to discern what exactly this aliquid is that is largely constitutive of a virtual phenomenon, let us return to Suárez's discussion of the two thieves and its surrounding text. In the midst of that discussion, Suárez explains that when the common or universal ground of evil (*communis ratio mali*) inherent in theft itself is adverted to, that advertence is enough such that the "will can at the least move the intellect confusedly in order that it inquire what lies under that [more universal] common ground of evil."[60] This movement of the intellect by the will is done so that the agent can "more completely think about, or judge, or try to distinctly conceive what is merely confusedly proposed."[61] Often when the intellect is thinking about some act or object, there is much about that object which is not immediately clear. It is for

[58] Probabile autem est, cum actione externa semper concurrere actualem aliquam phantasiae et appetitus motionem (ibid.).

[59] I make use of a similar, but abbreviated, list in my "Voluntary Inconsideration, Virtual Cognition and Francesco Suárez," *Southwest Philosophical Studies* 31 (2010).

[60] … quia stante illa advertentia objecti communis, potest voluntas saltem confuse movere intellectum ut inquirat quid sub illo communi lateat: quae motio satis est ut intellectus possit pertingere ad considerandum id quod in re ipsa est (*DVI* disp. 4, sec. 3, n. 24: IV, 230, italics mine). Note that it is this actual advertence to the common *ratio* of the act that one is doing (in the current case, stealing) that fulfills (A3)'s requirement that something be *actually* proposed to the intellect such that further consideration or inconsideration can be voluntary. To explain how such advertence can fulfill (A3) is a burden that will be relieved shortly by means of the current discussion of WMI.

[61] Hoc ergo judicio, et apprehensione supposita in intellectu, antequam voluntas libere se determinet ad prosequendum objectum propositum, potest applicare intellectum ut perfectius conferat, vel dijudicet, vel ut conetur distincte concipere quod tantum confuse propositum est, vel alio modo simili (*DVI*, disp. 4, sec. 3, n.28: IV, 231).

this reason that the will can actually move the intellect so that it can think about that act or object in more detail. This phenomenon of the will moving the intellect I term 'WMI.'

There are two different ways in which WMI can be understood. On the one hand, WMI may refer simply to the phenomenon of the agent actively willing to try to understand something more that she already has a sense of but does not fully understand. This is the sense seemingly intended by the second quotation above: one understands something in a confused manner, and is now willing to try to clarify that confusion. If this were the only meaning of WMI, it would be uncontroversial but of no help to the current project. In fact, it seems to be nothing more than a different way in which to describe 'further consideration' itself, the lack of which we are trying to describe as a candidate for voluntariness by finding a related virtual cognition. As a result, such 'further consideration' simply understood could not be the *aliquid* left behind as a virtual cognition by an initial consideration of some general phenomenon.

Another understanding of WMI is suggested by the first quotation's statement that the "will can … move the intellect *confusedly*." As I suggest elsewhere,[62] this passage may be understood as positing that there is, within the intellect, a metaphorical searchlight that serves as the 'mind's eye' and which can be moved around 'confusedly.' As will be demonstrated, I believe this latter understanding of WMI, although not explicitly proposed by Suárez himself, is crucial for making sense not only of Suárez's discussion of virtual cognition and thus of voluntary inconsideration, but also of his distinction between virtual and habitual phenomena.

If there is indeed such a metaphorical searchlight within the agent's intellect, then the above quotation implies that whenever the agent considers some *consideratum x*, the agent's will causes her intellect's searchlight to cast its light *confusedly* throughout the *x*-related contents of the intellect; the searchlight is being 'jiggled around' by the will, so to speak. This 'jiggling' is performed so as to enable the agent to come into cognitive contact with any *x*-related information that may be stored within the agent's intellect and was not part of the content of the initial *consideratum x*. If the searchlight is working optimally, then it

[62] The following description of WMI as a 'searchlight' that is jiggled and that comprises virtual cognition is similarly proposed in my "Voluntary Inconsideration."

shines upon all such stored *x*-related contents, thereby giving the agent cognitive access to them. When some *x*-related content is illuminated by the searchlight, the agent could at that point decide whether to think about that *consideratum x*-related detail and thereby perform further consideration with regard to the initial *consideratum x*. The jiggling of the searchlight, therefore, is the means by which the agent can engage in further consideration.

Under this understanding of WMI, it is necessary to note that the jiggling of the intellectual searchlight does not in itself comprise further consideration. It is instead the means by which further consideration of some *consideratum x* can be performed; it is that by which the agent can gain some cognitive access to a *x*-related detail that may not have been initially obvious to her but was instead stored within the contents of her intellect. Once access has been made possible by the searchlight's shining upon some stored content, *then* further consideration of the initial *consideratum x* can, but need not, take place by means of the agent deciding to think about this additional content and how it may inform her understanding of the initial *consideratum x*.

An example related to our two thieves may be helpful. Suppose a consideration of stealing in general (call it 'consideration$_1$') with the content <I am committing the evil of theft>. Suppose also the related detail (call it 'detail$_1$') with the content <the amount of money being stolen determines how serious a theft it and one stealing should therefore pay attention to how much is being stolen>. Now, consider our thieves who *ex hypothesi* actually have consideration$_1$ but are not cognizing detail$_1$. According to my current proposal, their intellectual searchlights are being jiggled on account of them having consideration$_1$. This jiggling is enabling them the possibility of coming into cognitive contact with detail$_1$. Once their intellects' searchlights shine upon detail$_1$ as a result of WMI, they could then perform further consideration by considering detail$_1$ and its relation to consideration$_1$. If they were to perform such further consideration, they would then reach the conclusion that they need to think about how much money they are stealing. *Ex hypothesi*, however, our two thieves do not consider detail$_1$ after their searchlights have shined upon it. They thus fail to perform further consideration with regard to consideration$_1$ even though further consideration was possible by means of the cognitive access to detail$_1$ afforded them by WMI.

According to this proposal, therefore, there are potentially three discrete phenomena within the agent's intellect: the original cognition (consideration$_1$), WMI understood as the jiggling of the intellectual searchlight, and further consideration of consideration$_1$ via consideration (if performed) of illuminated stored contents such as detail$_1$. It is moreover my proposal is that WMI, understood as this jiggling, should be understood as the *aliquid* that is left behind by some actual consideration and which constitutes a virtual deliberation/cognition. As long as WMI originated from and is continuing after actual consideration of some *x*, the agent is engaged in a virtual cognition related to *x*: the *aliquid* is the act of WMI.

In support of this interpretation, let us observe how WMI thusly understood is in agreement with earlier insights regarding virtual phenomena. WMI is preceded by and results from some actual act of consideration that sets it into motion, matching observations made in (VT1) and (VT3). In addition, WMI is really a movement experienced by the intellect and may thus be regarded as an intellectual appetitive motion. This movement is moreover a movement in which the intellect may be shining upon *phantasm*-like contents since details stored in the intellect may be stored in some sort of phantasmic mode. Consequently, Suárez's speculating in (VT4) that the *aliquid* probably consists of some sort of appetitive/phantasmatic movement is compatible with the current understanding of WMI.[63] This leaves only (VT2) to be considered.

(VT2) states a necessary condition, but unfortunately one that is not very illuminative. Since it basically requires for the presence of a virtual phenomenon that it not be revoked, anything which can no longer persist after it has been revoked is consistent with this condition. Therefore, claiming that an act of WMI can no longer exist after it is revoked accords with (VT2). Such a claim in itself, though, does not help establish WMI as the *aliquid* constituting a virtual phenomenon; any quality or action that no longer exists after it is revoked would accord with (VT2). However, indirect support for the claim that WMI is that *aliquid* can be supplied if it can be shown that the distinction between virtual and habitual phenomena can be adequately explained in terms of a revocation of WMI.

Recall from our earlier discussion of voluntariness that Suárez denigrates the role of habit and habitual knowledge. A human act properly

[63] Cf. my "Voluntary Inconsideration, Virtual Cognition and Francesco Suarez" in which these points are similarly made.

speaking can "not *per se* stem from habit."[64] In addition, "habitually know[ing], or retain[ing] in memory" knowledge of some *x* is not sufficient for one to bring oneself to actual consideration of some *x* for Suárez.[65] Something over and above a mere habit must be present so that the agent can *here and now* consider *x*. The process of WMI fills this exact role. Let 'WMI$_{[x]}$' refer to the jiggling of the mind's eye around the *x*-related contents of the intellect as we have described it. If this jiggling is indeed that by which an agent has cognitive access to such content stored within her intellect, then it would make sense that without WMI$_{[x]}$ the agent would still possess *x*-related contents within her intellect but would have no immediate access to them in the here and now. In other words, it would make sense that without WMI$_{[x]}$ the agent's knowledge of *x*-related contents would fit Suárez's explanation of habitual knowledge, knowledge which is *here and now* outside the agent's actual cognitive grasp. On the other hand, the agent does indeed have cognitive access to those contents here and now if WMI$_{[x]}$ is present. Consequently, WMI appears well-suited to fill the role of the *aliquid* left behind relevant to virtual consideration and of the *aliquid* that is revoked when one moves from a virtual to a habitual state.

5. *A Case Study: Prayer, Virtual and Habitual Attention*

As support for my claim that WMI constitutes cognitive virtual phenomena, we now turn to a passage in which Suárez specifically discusses the cognitive state of 'virtual attention' and which *prima facie* appears to pose a problem to this claim. In doing so, we will also see how the current proposal not merely makes sense of Suárez's claim of a distinction between virtual and habitual phenomena but rather illuminates it. This demonstration will therefore, despite initial appearances to the contrary, provide support for the interpretation currently being offered.

In *DOD* Suárez examines the case of one praying the prayers at the canonical hours. For one to fulfill one's vow to pray the prayers, one need not have actual attention during the entire prayer, but must at least maintain 'virtual attention.' He notes that

> virtual attention only ceases to be when a person knowing and seeing that they are thinking of other things and not [actually][66] attending [to

[64] *DVI*, disp. 4, sec. 3, n.9.

[65] *DVI*, disp. 4, sec. 3, n.7.

[66] From the way in which *attendere* is contrasted with 'virtual attention,' it is clear that Suárez understands *attendere* in this passage as a case of actually attending to the prayer.

> the prayers], does not take care to start paying attention but neglects to do so, or else directly wills to speak only in that mode.[67]

The reason that virtual attention seems to cease at this point is the following: when one has realized she is not attending to the words and does not take steps so as to remedy that situation, one has thereby "revoked her earlier intention [of praying], because to will to be in this manner is not to will to pray, for with the will of speaking thusly optimally stands the will of not praying."

In order to glean as much as we can from this brief (and somewhat puzzling[68]) discussion, suppose two different priests, C & D. Let it be the case that both are reciting the canonical hours with the same virtual attention, and both are equally "thinking of other things and not [actually] attending to the prayers." Let it furthermore be the case that at one point, t_1, Priest C just happens to "know and see that he is thinking of other things" and subsequently fails to "take care to start paying attention." Instead, Priest C continues to think of other things at t_1 and afterwards. Nonetheless, he continues to say the words of the prayers "in that mode" in which he is not attending to the prayers but is thinking of other things. Let it also be the case that Priest D is in all ways similar to Priest C except for the following: neither at t_1 nor at any other point while saying the prayers does Priest D happen to "know and see that he is thinking of other things." Instead, he finishes his prayers while "thinking of other things and not [actually] attending to the prayers." According to the passage from *DOD*, Priest C would have had virtual attention before, but not after, t_1. Priest D, on the other hand, would apparently have maintained virtual attention for the entirety.

Let us set aside problems arising from this discussion that fall outside the scope of the present inquiry[69] and address a significant one that

---

[67] Quia tunc solum desinit esse virtualis attentio, quando homo sciens et videns se de aliis cogitare, et non attendere, non curat, sed negligit, vel directe vult illo tantum modo dicere; at hoc ipso jam non vult orare, sed revocat priorem intentionem; quia velle sic loqui, non est velle orare, nam cum voluntate sic loquendi stat optime voluntas non orandi; ergo (*DOD*, lib. 4, c. 26, n.13: XIV, 403).

[68] In addition to the points I am about to make, the passage is further puzzling in that virtual attention and virtual intention seem to become somewhat conflated by the end of it even though they are clearly differentiated earlier in the passage. The conflation need not be fatal since there are ways to explain it. These issues, however, are not directly pertinent to the current investigation and need not detain us.

[69] One potential problem would be that it seems as if it would have been better for Priest C not to have "known and seen that he was thinking of other things." If he had just not been so self-conscious and aware of himself (a laudable quality) so as to notice that his mind were wandering but were instead a bit less conscious and more

does. According to the understanding of virtual cognition currently being discussed, it seems there should no longer be any cognitive access to x-related content *here and now* once one revokes one's virtual attention understood as $WMI_{[x]}$ and reverts into a state of habit. According to my proposal, it appears that Priest C would have revoked $WMI_{[x]}$ at t_1 and should thereby have subsequently lost cognitive access in the *here and now* to all such prayer-related content. Suárez, however, seems to admit the possibility that Priest C could revoke the *aliquid* that is relevant to a virtual phenomenon related to x, revert to a habitual state with regard to x, and nonetheless apparently retain cognitive access to x-related content. Therefore, (so the objection goes), there must be a problem somewhere with the current proposal. Either WMI is not the *aliquid* constituting a virtual phenomenon, or, if it is, then it is not necessary that one's attention with regard to some x be as robust as 'virtual' so as to have cognitive access *here and now* to x-related contents; being in a habitual state (as Priest C was after t_1) would appear to suffice. This latter disjunct would, in turn, call into question Suárez's earlier claim that habitual phenomena are insufficient for either human acts or bringing oneself to full consideration.

My proposal that virtual cognitive phenomena be understood as WMI can not only respond to this formidable objection but can also help explain Suárez's comments regarding habitual cognitive states. To respond, consider Priest C and let y = 'praying the prayers at the canonical hours.' At the beginning, Priest C had an actual attention to y. After having begun y and yet before t_1, Priest C ceased paying actual attention to y. If my understanding of virtual cognition is correct, however, he maintained virtual attention to y by means of the continuance of $WMI_{[y]}$, an intellectual appetitive movement or jiggling of the mind's eye within the intellect set into motion by the initial actual attention. The persistence of $WMI_{[y]}$ within the agent does not mean that he was actually considering y-related contents. However, its persistence did give him some sort of immediate cognitive access to those contents; $WMI_{[y]}$ ensured that his mind's eye would move confusedly around y-related contents so that they could come to the forefront of his consideration.

---

neglectful of herself (a negative quality), then his virtual attention to the prayers would have presumably persisted and he would receive the additional moral merit for having performed them.

At t_1, Priest C apparently did 'see and know' that he was not paying actual attention to those contents and yet did not take remedial steps; instead, he continued to say the words "in that mode." Note that at this moment he has a *new actual* cognition – he actually sees and knows that he is saying the words of the prayer without really paying attention to them. By having this actual cognition and deciding in light of it to continue to say the words only 'in that mode,' he also forms a *new* actual intention (call it 'intention$_{[z]}$') - an intention to "say the words of the prayer only 'in that mode' of one who is not paying attention to the words." He also thereby has a new actual cognition$_{[z]}$ – a cognition of the fact that he is willing and intending to "say the words of the prayer only 'in that mode.'" Although forming this actual intention is a revocation of WMI$_{[y]}$, the accompanying new cognition$_{[z]}$ initiates WMI$_{[z]}$. He has actually considered doing *z* and has begun to carry it out in light of that actual consideration. At any point after t_1, he consequently either had an actual intention to 'say the words only in that mode (if he was continuing to actually cognize his act of just saying the words in that mode), or he had a virtual intention to 'say the words only in that mode' (if the actual cognition of that act was no longer present but WMI$_{[z]}$ persisted).

This description accords with the proposal that WMI is the *aliquid* constituting a virtual phenomenon. It moreover makes clear how Priest C still had cognitive access to the words of the prayer even after WMI$_{[y]}$ had ended. The words of the prayers are not merely *y*-related content; they are also *z*-related content. Given that at the very least WMI$_{[z]}$ occurred, Priest C had cognitive access to the words of the prayer. His saying them is therefore no mystery and would only be a challenge to the current proposal if the proposal required that intellectual contents be related to only one actual subject of consideration. No such requirement exists.

Note furthermore how well this response fits with Suárez's criticisms of Navarrus's conflation of habitual and virtual phenomenon. When Navarrus suggested that someone reciting a prayer is virtually praying, Suárez noted that the most that can be said is that she is 'habitually' praying since those words are 'habitually associated' with the moral act of praying. Since the actual saying of the words in that case did not result directly from a preceding actual intention, the one saying such a 'habitual prayer' cannot be considered to have done the moral act of praying. The same is the case here. After t_1, the saying of the words was not resulting from the earlier actual intention$_{[y]}$ ('to pray the prayers') but from another intervening intention$_{[z]}$ ('to say the words only in that mode'). At most, Priest C could be considered to have been habitually praying after t_1. Such praying, however, carries with it no moral merit so far as fulfilling the obligation to pray is concerned.

In summary, it can be said that Priest C was habitually praying the prayers after t_1. However, it was not by means of this 'habitual' aspect that he was able to move himself to say the words. He was able to move himself to say the words either through a separate actual or virtual aspect through which he intended to 'say the words only in that mode.' He was habitually praying only insofar as the words that he was saying are habitually associated with the prayer. Consequently, Suárez's claim that habit in and of itself is insufficient to allow someone to act *here and now* is consistent with the current proposal that a virtual cognitive state is constituted by WMI.

6. *Recap of Virtual Knowledge and Voluntary Inconsideration*

Recall the problem that we undertook this exploration in order to solve: how can the failure to perform further consideration about some *consideratum* fulfill the conditions for voluntariness in the absence of an explicit cognition along the lines of "I can consider this *consideratum* further"? In response to this question, Suárez claims that such inconsideration could be voluntary *in alio*. Furthermore, he claims that voluntary inconsideration *in alio* is a robust enough voluntariness such that it fulfills both (A3) and the knowledge requirement.

The knowledge requirement is fulfilled by the presence of a virtual cognition understood as WMI. WMI, understood as a jiggling among stored intellectual contents related to some *consideratum*, is itself a cognitive process and makes further consideration related to the *consideratum* possible. Consequently, it is uniquely qualified to play the role of a virtual cognition that is somehow equivalent to the explicit cognition with the content <I can consider this *consideratum* further>. If an agent fails to pursue such further consideration in light of this virtual cognition that one could consider the *consideratum* further, then such inconsideration fulfills the knowledge requirement and can be voluntary.[70] Given, moreover, that (i) it is the presence of WMI that

[70] Stated in an alternate manner, not pushing consideration further in light of this virtual cognition that one could is equivalent to not pursuing further consideration with the virtual cognition equivalent to the content <What I am doing is not considering this *consideratum* further>.

makes further consideration possible and (ii) it is the initial actual consideration of some *consideratum* that gives rise to WMI, then (iii) actual consideration of the initial *consideratum* in itself makes further consideration possible. This, in turn, confirms our earlier claim that actual consideration of the initial *consideratum* fulfills (A3)'s call that something be actually proposed to the intellect such that the will could cause the intellect to pursue the further consideration in question.

It can easily be seen how this interpretation helps make sense of the voluntary inconsideration of the two thieves. Each thief's inconsideration is to be understood as voluntary *in alio*, the *alium* being the voluntary *in se* act of stealing. During this voluntary act of stealing, the agent is actually considering the fact that he or she is stealing and adverts to the evil in it. This actual consideration subsequently initiates the virtual cognition, understood as WMI, that this act can be explicitly thought out in more detail. Given the presence of this 'virtual' cognition, the thief's omitting to explicitly further consider the theft in more detail is voluntary.

Consequently, virtual cognition makes it possible for Suárez to assert that the omission to perform further consideration can be voluntary even in the absence of an explicit cognition that one could perform such further consideration. This, in turn, provides a key for solving NO's in general. Before we apply the insights gained in this section to the problem of NO's, two final clarifications regarding virtual cognition ought to be made.

First, note that we have not explained *how* an actual consideration of some *consideratum* x will cause the intellect's searchlight to jiggle among x-related, as opposed to y-related, contents stored in the intellect, nor do we necessarily need to. Without making any assumptions as to the mechanics behind the intellect's functions, we can simply (and somewhat safely, I presume) assume that the contents of the intellect are structured and stored in such a way that there are logical connections between all x-related contents such that the consideration of one x-related *consideratum* leads, through the natural functions of the intellect, to other x-related *considerata*. We may leave it up to cognitive scientists to say more about this precise process.

This leads us to the second point. Nothing said here implies that, upon considering some *consideratum* x, *all* relevant x-related details come into cognitive grasp by means of WMI. It undoubtedly can happen that one considers some *consideratum* x, $WMI_{[x]}$ is subsequently initiated, and yet the intellect's searchlight just happens not to shine on some particular *x*-related detail through no fault of the agent. In such a case, inconsideration of that *x*-related detail would, for Suárez, not be voluntary or blameworthy; instead, the agent's temporary ignorance of that detail would be considered invincible and fall under the provisions of (A2). In addition, neither we nor Suárez have offered any algorithm by which to test whether any one particular case of inconsideration is blameworthy. Instead, we have shown how some case of inconsideration without explicit cognition regarding the possibility of such consideration can be voluntary *given the assumption* that such inconsideration is blameworthy.

III. Preliminary Conclusion to the Problem of NO's

A. *The Utility of 'Virtual Reflection' and WMI*

Given that actual consideration of some *consideratum* implies the presence of such virtual cognition that one could think about that *consideratum* further, Suárez has found a way to make inconsideration (not-thinking-about, temporary ignorance) voluntary. The agent's refusal to attempt further consideration in light of a virtual reflection that one could qualifies as a voluntary omission to cause further knowledge. The resulting ignorance or inconsideration, therefore, is voluntarily brought about.

It is interesting to note that Suárez regards the will's refusal to attempt further consideration as a case in which the will is "negligent." The will, he says, is negligent in "applying the intellect … to perfect and full consideration."[71] My overall solution to the problem of NO's will claim that the ultimate root negligence in NO's of all types consists in precisely this: the similar failure, or 'negligence' of the will to cause further consideration of some *consideratum*, leading to subsequent ignorance regarding one's obligation. And because this lack of performing further consideration can be regarded as voluntary, therein will lie the root of voluntariness in NO's.

Moreover, the claim that virtual, as opposed to explicit, cognition can fulfill the knowledge requirement for cases of inconsideration has

[71] et quidem si in hoc sit voluntas negligens, et statim sine ampliori consideratione se determinet, erit inconsideratio, et condition actus inconsiderata, voluntaria, vel indirecte, per carentiam actus, quem voluntas posset et deberet habere: vel aliquo modo per actum positivum, quo voluntas vult ad aliquid attendere, vel sequi passionem aliquam, quae talem considerationem impedit (*DVI*, d.4, sec.iii.28: IV, 232).

a further advantage. Recall that throughout the book the knowledge requirement has forced us into a sort of 'tight-rope' walk. On the one hand, we need knowledge so as to make the subsequent ignorance voluntary while, on the other hand, the presence of knowledge related to some action or omission that causes subsequent ignorance would seem to make that subsequent ignorance, and thus the NO, somewhat intentional and not negligent. For example, above in section I.C.3 ("The Inadequacy of the Just-Posited Solution") we discussed the case in which an agent reflects on the fact that she should consider Goldbach's Theorem in more depth. If she does not do so in spite of this knowledge that she should, any subsequent ignorance resulting from this refusal would seem more intentional than negligent.

The concept of virtual reflection, however, helps us walk this tightrope. If someone is only virtually cognizing the fact that they could or should consider some *considerandum x* in more detail and yet do not, it can still be said that the resulting inconsideration is done with knowledge; the knowledge requirement can thus be fulfilled. However, it is not so clear as it is in the Goldbach's Theorem case that we would call such a failure to consider 'intentional.'

To illustrate these points, recall the type of illustration used in chapter 4. Consider a person who is considering playing chess shortly before time to go to Mass. As a result of this consideration, it is open to her to consider further this act of playing chess. Let it be the case that she *explicitly* reflects on the fact that she should think further about playing chess right now and, in spite of that explicit reflection, decides not to and 'dives right in' to the game. In that case, we would be more inclined to call the resulting ignorance of the fact that playing chess may cause her to miss Mass intentional rather than negligent. She explicitly knew she should engage in further consideration and yet did not.

On the other hand, consider a case in which she is about to play chess and only virtually knows she could further consider the fact that she is about to play chess right now (i.e. virtually reflects on the fact that she could and/or should think further about playing chess right now by means of her intellectual searchlight jiggling among chess playing-related details) but does not *explicitly* reflect on the fact that she could think further about playing chess right now. It is not so obvious in this scenario that we would label the resulting ignorance of the consequences of her playing chess as 'intentional.' It seems we would be loath to so call it and would instead more likely refer to it as 'negligent.' The idea of virtual reflection, therefore, permits a way to understand ignorance as voluntary yet not necessarily, or overtly, intended.

B. *A Problem*

A difficulty remains. Suárez's appeal to virtual reflection and its relationship to performing further consideration of some *consideratum* is primarily made in the context of *commissions*. It is, for instance, when one is *committing* the act of stealing that one has the virtual reflection that one can consider that act further in its details. The topic of this book, however, is negligent *omissions*, not negligent *commissions*. Consequently, we face a particular obstacle in our appeal to virtual reflection to solve our problem.

Recall that for inconsideration/ignorance of some particular detail to be rendered voluntary, there must be some actual consideration of some *consideratum* that is somehow *related to* that *considerandum* which is ultimately not considered. For instance, the detail regarding how much money is being stolen is related to the actually-considered *considerandum* that one is committing a theft. In negligent omissions, however, there does not necessarily seem to be consideration of some *consideratum* that is in any way *related* to the omission for which one is presumably to be blamed.

For example, consider the general case of John. When he omits to pick up Des at 7:00, the relevant detail of which he is ignorant is that it is then time for him to pick up Des. According to the model above, ignorance/inconsideration of this particular detail could be voluntary if John is considering some *consideratum related to* this detail and could push this consideration further so as to arrive at this detail. It seems, though, that he does not. If he is considering anything, he is considering either the fact that he is watching TV or whatever it is on TV he is watching. But to push further his consideration either of the fact that he is watching TV or of what it is he is watching presumably would not lead John to consideration of the detail that he is supposed to pick up Des. What intrinsic connection, after all, does watching TV or the show on TV have with the detail that one must pick up Des?[72]

Consequently, it seems as if by watching TV John's intellect is *not* in such a disposition that his will could cause his intellect to consider further so as to reach awareness of the idea that he should pick up Des. The relevant sort of WMI seems not to be initiated.[73] At first glance, therefore, Suárez's concept of virtual cognition and its relationship to

[72] Similar points may be made regarding our chess player above.

[73] Alternatively, it could also be stated that (A3) seems not to be fulfilled in cases of NO.

certain types of inconsideration does not appear well-suited to make the specific instances of inconsideration relevant to NO's voluntary.

C. *The Solution: Combining Scotus and Suárez*

The resolution to this problem, and thus to the problem of NO's in general, will come primarily by combining certain elements from both Scotus's and Suárez's thought. In direct response to the problem just posed, let me first say that the point in time at which to focus upon the relevant ignorance in NO's being voluntarily caused is not necessarily TEF. The objection just raised above assumed that if an appeal to virtual cognition is to be helpful for explaining John's ignorance, there must have been open to John a way to have the relevant virtual cognition that he should perform some further consideration at 7:00, his TEF. This, as will be shown, is not necessarily the case. Often when a NO occurs, the ignorance is indirectly voluntarily caused (i.e. caused on account of a refusal to perform further consideration in the presence of the virtual cognition that one could) before TEF.

Second, I wish to recall the discussion above (section I.B) in which a Scotist explanation of indirectly voluntary ignorance was proposed. We discussed whether the presence of an indistinct intellection is adequate to impart the relevant knowledge needed such that either 'ignorance' or 'blameworthy ignorance' is voluntary. That is, we wondered whether the mere presence of some intellection *i* upon which an agent is failing to perform *complacere* entails knowledge of either: i' <what I am not doing is performing an act of *complacere* on intellection *i* and thus am causing subsequent ignorance of its object> (needed for the ignorance to be voluntary), or i'' <what I am not doing is performing an act of *complacere* on intellection *i* and thus am causing subsequent ignorance of its object *even though I should not be causing such ignorance*> (needed for the ignorance to be voluntary *and* blameworthy). We granted that Scotus must have thought the agent knows at least i', but were less optimistic about the agent's knowledge of i''.

The general outline of my solution to the problem of NO's will be this: in each type of NO, the agent at some point or other (not necessarily TEF) has a relevant intellection. This means that at some level the agent is aware of, or rather, somewhat 'considers,' this intellection's object. This consideration, in turn, implies that the agent has virtual cognition (contained within the awareness/consideration of that intellection) that she *should* consider that intellection's object further. That is, she has virtual cognition somewhat analogous to the content in i''

insofar as she knows that she *should* consider something further and thus should not allow herself to be ignorant of whatever further details she would have if she performed further consideration. In addition, it is the case that if she were to consider this intellection's object further, she would not have the subsequent ignorance that ultimately causes her NO. Her refusal, therefore, to further consider the object of that intellection, along with the fact that she virtually knows she *should* consider it further, means that her lack of further consideration, (i.e. the ignorance that causes the NO) is voluntary *in alio*.

Stated more precisely in terms of the discussion in this chapter, in all cases of NO, the agent has a Scotist intellection (whether distinct or indistinct) that is sufficient to fulfill (A3). The details will vary from type to type, but in all instances there will be an intellection such that (i) the agent, were she to consider its object further, would arrive at knowledge of her obligation, and (ii) on account of that intellection the agent's "intellect is in such a disposition that the will could cause the intellect" to consider that intellection's object further.[74]

In the concluding chapter, I will be able quickly to show how this combination of Scotist and Suárezian concepts is adequate to solve each of the types of NO we have been concerned with. I will then bring our exploration to a close by commenting on how the insights we discovered in the earlier chapters on Aristotle, Anselm and Aquinas contribute to and/or are consistent with this solution.

---

[74] This is of course the wording of (A3).

CHAPTER 9

AN ANSWER THAT CANNOT BE NEGLECTED

THE SOLUTION

At the end of the last chapter, I indicated the general strategy for my solution to the problem of culpability for NO's. The basic idea is that in every NO, the agent has some awareness or consideration of the object of an intellection. This consideration carries along with it the virtual reflection that one *should* further consider that intellection's object more. If the agent were to do this, she would arrive at knowledge of her obligation and be able to avoid the NO. *Ex hypothesi*, she does not perform further consideration even though she (virtually) knows she should and thus voluntarily causes ignorance.

What remains is to show how this general strategy can be applied to each of the different types of NO. After I do this, I will discuss how my ultimate solution relates both to the traditional understandings of the solution for NO's and to some of the insights gained from the other authors discussed in this book.

I. Explanation of the Different Types of NO

A. *Type-1 NO's*

1. *General Description of the Solution*

Recall the basic structure of Type-1 NO's. They are situations in which the time span between the last point at which one was specifically aware of one's obligation and the time of expected fulfillment (TEF) is short enough such that the agent is reasonably expected to keep her obligation in mind continuously until TEF so as to be sure not to forget it. In Chapter 5, we parsed this expectation in terms of the requirement that the agent continuously perform *complacere* on the obligation-related intellection such that it not cease. We then noted that in order to ascribe blameworthiness to an agent who does not keep that obligation continuously in mind, we must give some account of how the agent is to know that she *should* keep that obligation continuously in mind until TEF. We also noted that while doing so we must make sure that the account of that knowledge does not imply that her subsequent ignorance and omission are intentional.

We can now easily meet this two-fold task. To demonstrate how, let us return once again to Sample 1.[1] When John first undertakes the obligation at 6:55, he must at the very least be aware of the fact that he is undertaking that obligation; if he has no such awareness, it is difficult to understand how he could be obligated in the first place. Hence he has an intellection of the fact that he should pick up Des at 7:00 and must, at some level, be considering its object, his obligation. This act of consideration, in turn, means he has the virtual cognition that he can push this consideration further. If he were to push consideration further, he would come to realize explicitly (not virtually[2]) the following detail that is related to this initial *consideratum*: the TEF is near-enough such that he reasonably can and thus should keep the full obligation-related intellection in mind continuously.[3] In other words, he would realize that he is in a Type-1 scenario, a scenario in which he must keep the obligation continuously in mind. This further consideration would ideally then lead him to the yet further explicit consideration that, in order to do this, he must apply constant psychic attention to this obligation (i.e., perform *complacere*).[4] Consequently, it is within his power to know both how and that he should keep the full obligation-related intellection in mind continuously until TEF. Since he could have come to this knowledge by performing further consideration upon the initial

---

[1] Sample 1: At 6:55 p.m., John promises, and is thus morally obligated in some sense, to pick up his friend Des at the airport, for which he will need to leave at 7:00. At 6:56, a mere one minute after promising Des, John begins watching television and subsequently forgets to leave at 7:00 to pick Des up. It is not until 9:00, when Des calls John to ask him where he is, that John realizes he has omitted to fulfill his obligation.

[2] The only knowledge that is virtual is that concerning the possibility or requirement to perform further consideration of some *consideratum*. Knowledge arrived at on account of this further consideration is explicit, not virtual.

[3] If he pushed consideration further and did not reach this knowledge, his ignorance would be invincible and he would be blameless. Given that we are assuming a NO takes place, it must then be the case that the ignorance is not invincible and thus the agent can gain the relevant knowledge on account of further consideration.

[4] No problem arises from the fact that he may come to this further knowledge in step-wise fashion. It is possible that upon the first consideration of the obligation, he 'considered further' the obligation and arrived at knowledge that TEF is nearby. But now, the fact that TEF is nearby is itself being considered. It is thus open for him to consider this fact further, by which he would arrive at the knowledge of the fact that he must apply constant psychic attention. In other words, a detail arrived at on account of considering some prior *consideratum* further is itself something one is now considering, and it is open to the agent at this point to 'consider further' this fact.

consideratum, and virtually knew that he could perform such further consideration so as to consider the obligation contained in that initial *consideratum* more fully, his ignorance of these further details (i.e. the details that he should keep his obligation continuously in mind by focusing psychic attention on it) is voluntary. His ultimate ignorance of his obligation, consequently, can be traced back to the ignorance arising from his voluntary refusal to perform further consideration upon the initial *consideratum*.

It may be objected that by this demonstration I have not yet shown John to be blameworthy. All I have done is demonstrated that his subsequent ignorance of the fact that he needs to keep in mind the obligation (which leads to subsequent ignorance of his obligation) constitutes voluntary ignorance, but not *blameworthy* voluntary ignorance. In other words, I have only shown that the agent *could* have avoided ignorance, but have given no reason to assume that he could have been expected not to. Similar to a point made in the previous chapter, if John did not know that he *should* perform further consideration so as to consider the obligation further, any subsequent ignorance of details surrounding that obligation may be voluntary but is not necessarily blameworthy.

In response, I propose that John's virtual cognition upon first undertaking/considering his obligation should be understood as not merely equivalent to <I can consider this obligation further>, but rather to <I can and *should* consider this obligation further>. And the normative force within this virtual cognition arises from the fact that the object of the intellection is an *obligation*; it is an obligation, and not any generic object, that he is performing consideration upon. To consider an obligation is, at the very least, to consider that one must do something. It stands to reason that the WMI given rise to by such consideration would be a more demanding, exacting form of WMI – a jiggling so forceful such that it would (in a sense) demand and call out that the agent take it seriously. In other words, it seems reasonable to presume that the WMI initiated by a consideration of an obligation would create a significant-enough amount of cognitive dissonance such that there would arise, at some level, an imperative for the agent to take it seriously. If this is correct, then it seems fair to understand the virtual cognition accompanying an initial consideration of an obligation somehow equivalent to <I can and *should* consider this obligation further> instead of simply the more casual <I can consider this obligation further>.

2. Support for the Claim that Virtual Reflection has Normative Force

Support for my assertion that a virtual reflection accompanying consideration of an obligation includes the normative 'should' comes from several sources. On the one hand, there is intuitive support. It simply does not seem possible to consider the fact that one has/is undertaking an obligation without also knowing (at least virtually) that one should be sure that she can, and knows how to, fulfill it. That is part and parcel of undertaking an obligation in the first place.

Underlying this intuition is the notion that an obligation is inherently prescriptive. As such, it embodies a precept given to an agent. Precepts, moreover, have a certain affinity to the will. Suárez indicates that they sort of 'call out' to the will to pay attention to them.[5] It is, according to him, extremely difficult for a will to be unaffected by the intellect's presentation to it of an obligation/precept. If the will is to be so affected, however, surely the intellect's presentation to it is not merely equivalent to the generic 'this obligation *could* be considered further.' Such a presentation would hardly be distinctive in a way to explain the special affinity precepts supposedly have to the will. As a result, it is more reasonable to assume that if one is considering a precept, the intellect is also entertaining a virtual cognition that consideration of that precept *should* be furthered.[6]

---

[5] Suárez actually says that the affinity between a precept and the will is so great that "morally speaking" it is nearly impossible for the will to refrain from all action whatsoever with regard to it. This statement is important because in general the will can simply refuse to act (*non velle*) and does not have to will not-to-will in order for an omission to occur. In light of a precept, however, the possibility for a will simply to *non velle* is almost non-existent. Because of the precise way in which an obligation 'calls out' to the will, the will must either will for or will against that precept in some manner.

Of course, our position somewhat disagrees with Suárez's (but agrees with Scotus's) insofar as we are allowing the possibility that the will can simply *non velle* to perform further consideration in light of the virtual knowledge that one has an obligation/precept. Our position, however, is not so contrary to Suárez's as may first seem, for Suárez himself openly admits the theoretical possibility that such could be the case. Furthermore, it may be that Suárez is committed to his more stringent thesis that the will cannot refrain from acting in the face of precepts only when the precept is explicitly, as opposed to virtually, known. And while the precept itself may be explicitly known according to our position, the further precept that one should push one's consideration further is known only virtually. It thus may be that the will can refrain from acting (i.e. refrain from considering further) in response to that virtually-known precept.

At any rate, I am not sure it matters which position Suárez himself ultimately held in this regard. The important point is that there is nothing preventing the explanation I am offering in the text. (For Suárez's discussion, see *DVP*, d.3, sec.ii.4–7.)

[6] I realize I am using somewhat anthropomorphic language here. As stated at the beginning of Chapter 5, I do so only for the sake of clarity. Such usage is not to be

Secondly, Suárez seems to understand virtual reflection as in some sense inherently prescriptive. The point of virtual reflection and WMI for him is not simply to make ignorance voluntary, but to hold agents accountable for that ignorance. For example, the thieves' ignorance of how much they are stealing is blameworthy, for it is their ignorance that accounts for their ultimate difference in terms of culpability. When Suárez appeals to the thieves in the midst of explaining WMI and virtual reflection, he seems to assume that because the thieves could have considered further, they should have. His assumption is that the possibility of performing further consideration brings along with it the virtual recognition that one should when one can.

This last point may be objected to by saying that consideration *could* in many cases be pursued to an unreasonable extent. Certainly (so the objection goes) the fact that one *could* consider further does not necessarily entail that one should in all cases. Otherwise, consideration could at times be carried out *ad infinitum*. Consequently, the objection concludes that 'should' is not necessarily implied by 'could' when it comes to further consideration.

This objection can easily be answered by making a slight modification to our description of virtual reflection's prescriptive force. Instead of the unmodified 'should,' the injunction included in the virtual reflection is that 'one should push consideration further *to a degree that is adequate* given the particular circumstances of that which one is considering.' Of course, the objection is correct in that if consideration should always be pursued further whenever it could, performing any type of free action would be very difficult. The fact that it is impractical to expect consideration to be pushed to its upper limits in all cases, however, gives no reason to conclude that there are not some reasonable limits to which consideration should be pushed, limits that vary depending upon the particular act and circumstances inherent in the situation. We can thus insist that it is to these limits that the normative 'should' calls for consideration to be pushed.

That this is the position Suárez held is clear from his writings. In fact, not only did he assume a reasonable limit beyond which lack of further consideration is not blameworthy, but he even refused to call lack of further consideration beyond that point voluntary.[7] Apparently, he

---

interpreted as implying that intellects and wills are some sort of agents in their own right.

[7] Cf. *DVI*, d.4, sec.iii.28–29.

was hesitant to recognize a difference (as we have done) between voluntary and blameworthy ignorance, an assumption probably based on the idea that the only reason for inquiring into voluntariness is in service to moral evaluation.

We need not go (and have not gone) so far as to equate the voluntary with blameworthiness. Nonetheless, two important points emerge from noting that Suárez did. First, his doing so provides more support for my claim that he viewed virtual reflection regarding further consideration as prescriptive in the first place. His not distinguishing between voluntariness and blameworthiness with regard to the ignorance that arises from omitting to perform further consideration implies that virtual knowledge is not only of one's ability to perform such consideration, but also of the fact that one ought to exercise that ability. We have thus not violated the original spirit of Suárez's understanding of virtual reflection by positing that it is prescriptive.

Second, given that we (as opposed to Suárez) do recognize a difference between voluntary ignorance and blameworthy ignorance, we can grant the objection that one need not pursue consideration to its furthest extent just because one can. Nonetheless, we can still maintain that one *should* pursue it to an adequate extent given the nature of the object one is considering and the attendant circumstances. And since in the current case the object one is considering is one's obligation, an adequate extent to which to push consideration would be to the point of knowing what it is one must do so as to be sure to fulfill that obligation. We have hereby dealt with the objection and can maintain our claim that virtual reflection is prescriptive when it arises as a result of consideration of an obligation. Failure to perform further consideration as prescribed in that virtual reflection is thus blameworthy.

3. *Summary of the Conclusion to Type-1 and a Final Objection to it*

My claim is that the simple presence of an obligation-related intellection initiates within John's intellect a process of WMI. This process of WMI, furthermore, constitutes a virtual reflection equivalent to the cognition that he should consider his obligation further to an adequate extent. If he were to perform further consideration regarding his obligation, he would ideally come to the further knowledge that to fulfill his obligation in this particular scenario, he needs to keep the intellection continuously in mind. *Ex hypothesi*, John does not perform further consideration. Given that consideration of an obligation imparts the virtual knowledge that he should further his consideration to an adequate extent, his omitting to do so can be regarded as being done with the virtual knowledge that <what I am doing is failing to consider my obligation further even though I can and *should* do so>. His resulting ignorance of the fact that he should keep his obligation in mind continuously is hence voluntary *and* blameworthy.

There is one further wrinkle to worry about with respect to Type-1 NO's. What if John did push his consideration further initially at 6:55 and arrived at the knowledge that he should keep his obligation continuously in mind. When he started watching TV at 6:56, however, he seems simply to have forgotten about his obligation and the requirement to maintain it continuously. How can his failure in this case be explained given that my explanation above centers on whether one arrives at the knowledge that one must keep one's obligation in mind continuously until TEF, and John *ex hypothesi* did arrive at this knowledge at 6:55?

The response to this is actually simple. Consider the moment immediately before John completely forgot about his obligation. At that moment, he still had an intellection of his obligation (otherwise, the obligation would already be forgotten). According to the model I have offered, all the following must be the case: (i) Given the assumption he would forget his obligation at the next moment, he was not performing *complacere* on that intellection. (ii) Given that the intellection was nonetheless there, however indistinct, he had some awareness, and thus some consideration of the object of the intellection; namely, the obligation. (iii) Given this awareness/consideration, he had the virtual knowledge that he should pursue consideration of this obligation further. (iv) When, in the next moment he failed to perform *complacere* on that intellection or its object, he did so in the presence of virtual knowledge that he should pursue consideration of that obligation further. To do this, however, is exactly what we described in the last chapter as causing blameworthy ignorance.[8] He is thus culpable for his subsequent ignorance of the fact, after 6:56, that he must keep his obligation continuously in mind.

It may be objected that he need not perform further consideration at 6:56 so as to gain the knowledge that he must maintain his intellection continuously until TEF because he had already arrived at such knowledge at 6:55. According to this further objection, then, the response

[8] Recall our discussion of intellection *i''* in section II.C.3

I just gave does not hold; John is already actually aware of the fact that he must keep his obligation in mind. This objection, however, contradicts the *ex hypothesi* assumption that John's omission at 7:00 is a NO. If John is actually aware at 6:56 that he must keep his obligation continuously in mind until 7:00 and nonetheless fails to perform *complacere*, then his ignorance is more intentional and the resulting omission could not properly be considered negligent. Given that John's omission is negligent, it must then be the case that at the point at which he 'forgets' his obligation, he did not know that he must keep it in mind continuously. Type-1 NO's are hence solved.

B. *Type-2 NO's*

Recall that Type-2 NO's are those in which the time span between one's last awareness of one's full obligation and TEF is too long for the agent to be reasonably expected to keep in mind continuously the full obligation-related intellection. On the other hand, that time span is too short and the circumstances not serious enough such that she is reasonably expected to take extra precautions. Recall furthermore that Type-2 NO's come in two variations. In Variation A, the agent possesses the MOI/LII and experiences it as a warning at TEF. Despite experiencing this warning she ignores it and proceeds to do something else and hence omits to fulfill her obligation. In Variation B, the agent has no MOI/LII in the first place. I will discuss these in order.

1. *Variation A*

With regard to Variation A NO's, we noted that the only issue yet to be resolved is to determine how we can be sure that the agent experiences the MOI/LII as a warning and knows that she is failing to heed this warning. It is only if we can assume that the agent has this knowledge that her neglect of the warning will be voluntary. In Chapter 6, section III.E, we offered some general reasoning in support of the fact that such an agent would have such knowledge. Since it was not conclusive, I here want to buttress that reasoning.

Given our discussion of Type-1 NO's it should now be rather obvious how we can explain that the agent has such knowledge. Recall that the content of a MOI/LII is <I must do something>. "Must do something," however, is equivalent to "have an obligation." (In fact, there is nothing preventing us from initially wording the MOI in that way.) And given that the MOI is present, then the agent has some awareness/consideration of the object of that MOI, i.e. the fact that she must do something. Analogous to the reasoning presented in the section above, such consideration imparts the virtual knowledge not only that one can, but also that one should consider the object of that intellection further.

In fact, since the content of the MOI is merely the fact that one has an obligation without any specification as to what that obligation is, the normative force of that virtual knowledge would be even stronger. In other words, the fact that one knows she has an obligation without being aware of what that obligation is gives all the more reason to assume that the intellection 'calls out' to the will to pay attention to it and consider it further. As a result, it seems that an agent in such a position would experience the prescriptive force of this virtual knowledge to a high degree – an experience which could even perhaps be expressed in terms of being 'warned.'

If the agent were to heed the injunction presented by her virtual knowledge, she would perform further consideration in order to try to explicitly recall what the obligation is. Depending on the situation, she then may or may not perform even further consideration in order to come to explicit knowledge of what she needs to do to fulfill that obligation. If, on the other hand, the agent does not heed the injunction presented to her by her virtual knowledge, she omits to do so while having the virtual knowledge that she should not thus omit. That is to say, she would be omitting to perform further consideration while knowing <what I am doing is failing to perform further consideration (i.e. failing to heed the warning) even though I can and *should*>. The knowledge requirement is thus fulfilled, and the subsequent ignorance of what exactly she is obligated to do is voluntary and culpable.

2. *Variation B*

With regard to Variation B NO's, we noted that there were two possibilities for explaining how an agent lacks a warning: either (i) the agent began the process of creating and maintaining a MOI/LII but at some point before TEF did something else instead of continue to perform ContinualComp, leading to the cessation of the MOI/LII as an intellection, or (ii) the agent *neglected* to create the MOI and begin ContinualComp in the first place but did something else instead. The tasks that remained for us to demonstrate that the ignorance in Variation B NO's is voluntary were accordingly to show (i) how the MOI/LII can be understood to impart awareness that one must continue the MOI as a LII and not let it cease, and (ii) how the obligation-related intellection imparts awareness that one should create a MOI/LII in the first place. We can now easily make both demonstrations by appealing to argumentation given above.

In regard to explaining (i) [how a MOI/LII imparts awareness that one must continue the MOI as a LII], recall our response to the above-objection (section I.A.3) in which we discussed how my proposal can be adapted to cases of apparently forgetting one's obligation after initially continuing an intellection of it. In the present case, consider the moment immediately before the MOI ceases. At that moment, *ex hypothesi* the agent has forgotten that she must continue the MOI, but does have awareness/consideration of the fact that she must do something (otherwise, the MOI would not be present). This consideration, in turn, imparts the virtual knowledge that she should attempt to consider further specific details with regard to the object of that intellection, one of which is the fact that she should *continue* that intellection. At the next moment when she permits the MOI to cease as a result of not performing *complacere* on it, she consequently does so with the virtual knowledge that <what I am doing is letting an intellection cease without performing further consideration on it even though I know I *should* perform such further consideration>. Given that this omission is done with such virtual knowledge, the subsequent ignorance of the fact that she should continue the MOI (which entails further ignorance of her obligation) is blameworthy.

In regard to (ii) [how the obligation-related intellection imparts knowledge that one should create a MOI/LII], the explanation is nearly the same as that for Type-1 NO's. Upon undertaking an obligation, the agent has awareness/consideration of her obligation. This consideration imparts the virtual knowledge that she should think further about her obligation. If she were to think further, she would recognize that she is in a Type-2 scenario and that she should take some sort of psychic measure to insure that she not forget her obligation. That is to say, she would recognize that she must create a psychic warning mechanism, a MOI/LII. Since, *ex hypothesi*, she never creates the MOI/LII, it must be the case that she failed to perform such further consideration about her obligation when initially undertaking it. Since this omission to perform further consideration was done with the virtual knowledge that she should not omit to do such, the resulting ignorance of that fact that she should create a MOI, and the entailed ultimate ignorance of her obligation, is blameworthy.

C. *Type-3 NO's*

The explanation just given is equally applicable to Type-3 NO's. In a Type-3 NO, the agent was reasonably expected to take extra precautions. Either the seriousness of the obligation or the length of the time span from one's last awareness of the full obligation (which in most instances should be the point at which the obligation was initially undertaken)[9] to TEF was such that these extra precautions were reasonably called for. A NO occurs, therefore, when either precautions to remind oneself were not taken, or the precautions taken were not adequate.

An agent who commits a Type-3 NO could not have failed to take adequate precautions in light of the actual knowledge that she should; otherwise, the resulting omission would not be negligent. We must then find a way to blame her for her failure to have actual awareness that she should take such precautions. And that way is by appeal to a failure to do further consideration in light of a virtual reflection that one should.

Upon initially undertaking her obligation (or, upon last being explicitly aware of it while still in a Type-3 situation), her consideration of that obligation imparted the virtual reflection that she should consider it further. If she had, she would have recognized that the length of the time span and/or the particular circumstances were such that she should take extra precautions so as to remind herself of her obligation. Taking these precautions were thus in her power. Unfortunately, she did not consider her obligation further, a consideration that would have led to explicit knowledge of the need to take these extra precautions. This refusal to perform further consideration was furthermore done with the virtual knowledge that she should. Consequently, her subsequent ignorance of the need to take those precautions is voluntary and blameworthy. Culpability for Type-3 NO's, therefore, is hereby solved.

---

[9] For a Type-3 NO, it is possible that one's last awareness before TEF was not necessarily when the obligation was initially undertaken. If, however, that is the case, it must furthermore be the case that upon initially undertaking the obligation, one was at that time also in a Type-3 scenario. In such a case, given that a NO followed, the agent must have omitted, both at the initial undertaking of the obligation and at the later point, to take the proper steps so as to be sure to remind herself of her obligation (unless part of the special precaution was to remind oneself at a later point so that, at that point, even further precautions be taken).

D. *A Slightly Different 'Type'*

It might be thought that there is a slightly different kind of NO that I have not addressed. All my 'Types' of NO have assumed that there is a certain point at which an obligation must be fulfilled, a TEF. There are some instances, however, in which an obligation need not be fulfilled at any one particular time. Instead, the obligation can be fulfilled at any time over a particular time span up until a certain point, at which time it will be too late to fulfill it – a 'point of no return' ("PNR"), so to speak.[10] For example, one could be obligated to leave a key out for her roommate before she leaves the apartment. She can fulfill that obligation at any point between arriving home and her PNR, the time at which she leaves the apartment. Could the possible negligent omission of her not leaving the key out for her roommate (on account of ignorance of her obligation) be explained by my framework?

Before responding, I want to say that I think the reason this type of scenario may suggest a qualitatively different 'Type' of NO to some is that in it, the agent is not under obligation to recall her obligation at any one particular time. But this should cause no qualitative difference, for although she is not required to recall it at any one particular time, she *is* obligated to recall it at least by PNR. Consequently, PNR can be treated as TEF for all intents and purposes. Upon initially undertaking her obligation, therefore, she has open to her the possibility of performing WMI so as to determine what steps she needs to take (either keep the obligation continuously in mind, create a MOI/LII, or take additional special precautions) in order to be sure she fulfills her obligation by PNR. In other words, upon initially undertaking the obligation (or upon last recalling it), the agent can treat PNR as if it were TEF for the purposes of determining which type of scenario she is in.

If the agent takes the steps appropriate for the scenario she is in and just happens to recall her obligation before she has reached PNR (on account of, for example, her periodically heeding the LII as a warning as we discussed in Chapter 6, sec. III.C.3) and fulfills it, so much the better. But if she does not 'just happen' to recall it before PNR, then at least she should have already taken such steps that would cause her to

[10] An obligation that need not be fulfilled at any one particular time and yet must be fulfilled at some point has some affinity to the medieval understanding of precepts that bind *semper sed non ad semper*. Note also that for some obligations, it is possible that the PNR is death.

recall it at PNR. If she has not taken such steps, then her omission would be treated as a NO of the type corresponding to the type of scenario she was in. Consequently, the fact that some obligations can be fulfilled over a time span instead of having to be fulfilled at one particular point in time need cause no problem.[11]

E. *Summary of the Utility of my Proposal and Relation to Traditional Explanations*

Before moving on, I just want to reiterate some of the virtues of my framework. In all cases of NO, the agent is ultimately blameworthy for not performing some further consideration. Not doing so entails not coming to have explicit, actual knowledge of further details, i.e. being somewhat ignorant. Moreover, the agent virtually knows, on account of some act of actual consideration, that she *should* perform some further consideration, i.e that she should take steps so as not to be ignorant of further details. Consequently, the agent's subsequent ignorance is voluntary and blameworthy.

The appeal to virtual knowledge permits the knowledge requirement for the relevant ignorance to be voluntary while at the same time providing a way in which to understand the ignorance as not necessarily 'intentional.' If the agent explicitly knew she should pursue consideration further, refusal to do so would seem somewhat intentional as would the subsequent ignorance and resulting omission. The fact that the knowledge that one should think further is virtual, however, allows us to insist on the voluntariness of the ignorance while denying that it is of a type we would be less inclined to call negligent. We thereby maintain the distinction between negligent and non-negligent omissions.

The failure to perform further consideration also explains why we are tempted to attach the precise term 'negligence' to omissions of these types. In a NO, there was something the agent could have done, i.e. perform further consideration, which the agent just did not go so far as to do. She thus 'neglected' to do all she could to fulfill the obligation without necessarily trying not to fulfill it.

[11] In fact, in the example used throughout this book, that obligation could have been fulfilled at any point over a time-span. John could have left at any point before TEF to go to the airport so as to be there to pick up Des.

Finally, the proposal finds some kernel of truth in each of the generic explanations (discussed in the Introduction) given for culpability of NO's. The first explanation was that NO's are culpable because the agent could have 'thought harder' but neglected to do so. As it turns out, we agree, for our 'consider further' is a way of 'thinking harder.' What we have done in this book is to provide a way in which to understand how the agent can be expected to perform the relevant 'harder thinking.'

The second typical explanation was that a person is liable for failing to take special precautions. And in many of the types of NO, that is exactly what happens. The person either fails to take the special precaution to 'continue the obligation-related intellection continuously' or to 'create a MOI' or actually to take special precautions (as in Type-3 NO's.) Our proposal has the added benefits that it understands some precautions as intra-psychic and it offers reasons to believe that the agent should know to take those precautions.

II. How Our Results Accord with Aristotle's, Anselm's and Aquinas's Insights

A. *Aristotle*

Before ending, I briefly want to comment on how my proposal, drawn largely from Scotist and Suárezian concepts, accords with the insights of the other authors in this study. I will start by considering an objection to my proposal. My approach to locating culpability for NO's rests largely upon the concept of virtual deliberation/knowledge that one should consider something further. The virtual knowledge that one should consider something further suffices to fulfill the knowledge requirement such that refusals to consider something further (i.e. refusal to come to actually and explicitly know those details one would become aware of if consideration were pursued further) can be considered to create a voluntary *in alio* ignorance. It may be wondered, however, whether (contra Suárez's assertions) voluntariness *in alio* is a robust enough kind of voluntariness to count for moral culpability given that it depends upon this sort of 'virtual' and non-explicit knowledge. Stated differently, is virtual knowledge sufficient to satisfy the knowledge requirement such that acts or omissions carried out in its presence can have moral import?

Aside from Suárez's contention that virtual knowledge is sufficient, further support comes from my interpretation of Aristotle's akratic.

Recall that we ended Chapter 2 with a discussion of Aristotle's akratic in an attempt to discern how robust knowledge must be such that the knowledge requirement is fulfilled. My interpretation concluded that for Aristotle, some sort of 'half-used' knowledge was sufficient. It was at that time unclear in what 'half-used' knowledge could consist other than some sort of cloudiness of intellect. But whatever it is, we saw that (i) it is sufficient for the voluntariness of morally-relevant actions, (ii) it is not in the recesses of one's mind but (iii) somewhat occurrent (i.e the agent is somewhat aware of it), yet (iv) not fully used.

Suárez's description of 'virtual knowledge' seems to fit uniquely this description of half-used knowledge. Virtual knowledge is knowledge that is not merely in the recesses of one's mind but is somehow present to the agent. Nevertheless, it is not 'fully used' knowledge, for it is neither explicit nor actual. It seems to be somewhere in between full use and residing in the recesses. In other words, it seems 'half-used.' Virtual knowledge, then appears to be a type of knowledge perfectly situated to correspond to an Aristotelian notion of 'half-used' knowledge. One could even regard Suárez's discussion of virtual knowledge as an explanation of what Aristotle means by 'half-used' knowledge. And since (according to my interpretation), Aristotle holds that half-used knowledge is sufficient to fulfill the knowledge requirement, my proposal's reliance upon 'virtual knowledge' can be regarded as consistent with Aristotelian prescriptions for voluntariness.

Note also that in Aristotle's *di'agnoian*/*agnoōn* distinction, we have a reason to ascribe voluntariness to NO's. The NO's arise as a result of some ignorance for which the agent is responsible. In all cases of NO, the agent is responsible for her ignorance of the obligation because she voluntarily fails to perform some act of further consideration that would, if performed, lead in some way or other (depending on the specific scenario) to knowledge of her obligation. The agent is thus responsible for her ignorance, and subsequent acts or non-acts on account of that ignorance are performed, in Aristotle's terminology, *agnoōn* and are thereby culpable.

B. *Anselm*

With regard to our discussion of Anselm, we posited that if Anselm were to be consistent in his theory of the will, the devil's first sin must be the result of some sort of forgetting about his obligation. In Chapter 7, we discovered that one can adhere to the general doctrine of Anselmian affections without it necessarily implying that a first sin must result from a case of forgetfulness. If, however, one wanted to persist in the claim that a rational creature's first sin must be a form of negligence, we have discovered a way in which to make it voluntary and culpably ascribable to the agent.

Under Anselm's supposition that there is a devil, let us examine his first sin in light of our model if indeed that sin were a NO. When the devil sinned, he was willing a *commodum*. A *commodum* must thus have been in his mind. By having this *commodum* in mind, the devil must have been considering it. This consideration, in turn, would have imparted to him the virtual knowledge that he should consider that *commodum* and his willing of it further. This act of consideration would *ex hypothesi* have led to his realizing that he was willing the *commodum* inappropriately in that his willing was not moderated by concerns for justice. He did not, however, perform that further act of consideration, and thus the resulting ignorance of the demands for justice was voluntary. Given this voluntary ignorance of those demands, he was unable to will in accordance with justice. The root of the devil's omission to think about the demands of justice so that he could will accordingly would thus lie in an earlier voluntary refusal to consider further that which he was currently considering and willing. His ignorance of justice's requirements would thus be voluntary.

Finally, Anselm's claim that the devil sinned because he did not *pervelle* (a willing completely and continuously) can be seen as consistent with our explication of Type-1 (and, to an extent, Type-2) NO's. It can thus be said that Anselm put his finger on an essential component of the problem, even if he did not necessarily foresee that according to his theory the devil's sin must have been a NO.

C. *Aquinas*

We noted at the end of Chapter 4 that with Aquinas's insights, we had taken a significant step forward toward understanding culpability for NO's. Two major insights had been gained. First, we noted that for Aquinas the category of NO's does not collapse into that of non-negligent omissions. The unfolding of our solution has verified that position. The concept of virtual knowledge allows the omission to be understood as not so much intentional (i.e. non-negligent) while still as a *voluntarium* in which the knowledge requirement is fulfilled.

The other and more significant conclusion drawn in Chapter 4 was that for Aquinas, the root of every sin of negligent omission is a sin of non-negligent omission that causes the ignorance of one's obligation. It may seem that our ultimate solution partly contradicts this claim. In our ultimate solution, the ignorance of one's obligation is ultimately caused by the *negligent* omission to performing further consideration of some *consideratum*. That omission seems not able to be intentional (non-negligent) for if it were, the resulting ignorance would seem more affected and the omission, for that reason, more or less intentional.

Despite this potential conflict, I believe the Scotist-Suárezian solution accords rather well with Aquinas's views. In our explication of Aquinas, there were in general no appeals to any sort of 'half-used' or 'virtual' knowledge. Knowledge was regarded (with the exception of a brief discussion of habitual knowledge that is *in potentia accidentali* [more on this shortly]), in an all-or-none manner. Consequently, when we concluded that a NO must ultimately arise from a non-negligent omission, what was really meant was that a NO ultimately arises from an omission carried out in the presence of knowledge. In fact, it was even stated that a negligent omitter "knows that she should apply herself to avoid subsequent ignorance but does something else" instead. But this is exactly the position of my Scotist-Suárezian solution. According to the latter, every NO arises from some omission that is done in the presence of (virtual) knowledge that one should apply oneself to consider something further so as to avoid subsequent ignorance. Given this, it could be said that Aquinas's conclusion was 'correct in spirit' though perhaps 'not in the letter.' Our explorations of Aquinas, therefore, did indeed represent a significant step toward our solution.

Furthermore, our understanding of virtual cognition could be appealed to in order to explain the relevance of the concept of 'habitual knowledge,' or knowledge *in potentia accidentali*, to NO's. Those items of knowledge that would be arrived at *if* one heeded the virtual cognition that consideration should be further performed are those items that are somewhat 'within reach' of the agent without being actually occurrently present before the agent's mind. It is those items that the agent 'could' occurrently think about even though the agent is currently not doing so. My model thus offers a greater, more full understanding of what it can mean to say that one has knowledge *in potentia accidentali* that is not actually before one's mind but which one 'could' nonetheless think about.[12]

III. Conclusion

Despite the step forward taken in Chapter 4, we had to wait until we had discovered the sophisticated machinery present in the writings of Scotus and Suárez to construct a model fully capable of explaining culpability for NO's. The fact that the framework constructed out of this sophisticated machinery accords relatively well with the insights of earlier thinkers provides an added level of confidence in it. It is, however, the framework's utility in solving a significant and interesting problem that lends it the greatest credibility. And the fact that the problem of NO's, a problem confronting even contemporary philosophers and theologians, can be approached so effectively by a scholastic-based model provides great incentive for bringing the insights of medieval and post-medieval scholastic philosophy and theology into the current discussion.

[12] See especially Chapter 4, n.34, n.53, and section IX. I am making no claim that this is the understanding Aquinas himself had. Instead, I am here offering a way in which to understand these concepts and to suggest a way in which Aquinas might have, or at least could have, understood them.

APPENDIX A

TRANSLATION OF *NICOMACHEAN ETHICS* 1146B31–1147B19

1146b31 But since we call 'knowing' in two ways (for both the one having but not using knowledge and the one [having] and using are said to know) it will matter whether one has [knowledge] but is not contemplating it or [both] has and contemplates it [when one is doing] those things which one must not do. For this [i.e. doing that which one should not do when both having and contemplating knowledge] seems amazing [sc. impossible], but it is not amazing [for one to do what should not be done] if one is not contemplating [the knowledge]. Further, since there are two

1147a1 kinds of premises, nothing prevents one who has both premises from acting against knowledge while using only the universal [premise] but not the [premise] about the part [or, "not the particular premise"]. And [to help explain how this is possible and not amazing after all] there are different types of universals [in both the universal and particular premises];

1147a5 for on the one hand there is (a) that which refers to the agent and on the other hand there is (b) that which refers to the object. An example [of this] is that ('A1' - the universal premise with a focus on universal term 'a') dry things are profitable to *every human being*, and that ('A2' - particular premise with focus on universal term 'a') he himself is a human being, or that ('B1' - a somewhat universal but less universal premise than the universal premise proper, with focus on universal term 'b') this such-a-thing is dry; but whether ('B2' - particular premise with focus on universal term 'b') this thing is this such-a-thing, either [the one who acts against knowledge] does not have this knowledge or does not use it. Now according to these [different premises which we have just delineated] it matters to a great extent which ways [i.e. premises] that [one knows], so that it does not seem out of place [to have acted against knowledge] when one knows in one way [i.e. when lacking 'B2'], but [to act against knowledge] when knowing in another way [i.e. 'B2'] is amazing [or impossible].

1147a11 Further, it is possible for human beings to have knowledge in a different way from those ways we have now described; for we see a split in the way of having knowledge but not using it [i.e. there are different ways of having but not using knowledge], so that in a way one can both have and not have [this type of knowledge, i.e. knowledge which is not being fully used]. Examples of these are the sleeper and the mad person and the drunk person. But, truly they who are affected by feelings (or, passions) are disposed in this way;

1147a16 For emotions and sexual desires and others such as these clearly even change the body, and even produce madness in some people. Therefore it is clear that it must be said that the akratics have [knowledge] in the same way. And saying the words which come from knowledge is no sign; for those who are in these states will recite geometrical demonstrations and say verses of Empedocles,

1147a21 And people learning for the first time on the one hand will speak words, but they do not yet know them; for it is necessary that the knowledge the words express grow into them, and this takes time. This leads us to a result (*hōste*) that one must suppose that it is in the same way as actors repeating lines that akratics say the words. Further, we can also investigate the cause [of acting against knowledge] in reference to human nature. For on the one hand there is a universal belief,

1147a26 and on the other hand there is the different particular belief, sense perception already being the master [of the latter]; and whenever one [belief] arises out of these, it is necessary there for the soul to affirm the conclusion which has been drawn, and [further] when it is in regard to practical things to act immediately [on the conclusion]. For example, if everything sweet must be tasted, and this one particular this is sweet, it is necessary for the one who is able and not hindered to do this [i.e. taste it] at the same time.

1147a32 Therefore suppose that on the one hand there is the universal belief hindering one from tasting, and on the other hand the belief that everything sweet is pleasant, and that this is sweet (and this latter belief is active), and appetite is present in the situation. Therefore, on the one hand the belief says to flee this, but on the other hand appetite leads one on (for it is capable of moving each of the parts). Hence it comes to pass that one acts akratically in a certain way because of reason and belief. The [second] belief is not contrary to correct reason in itself, but coincidentally [or, according to coincidence] (for the appetite is opposite to correct reason, but not the [second] belief). For this reason wild animals are not akratic,

1147b5 because they do not have universal judgments, but they only have particular images and memory. But how is the ignorance removed and the akratic to regain his or her knowledge? The same account that concerns both the drunk and the sleeper [also applies here] and this account is not particular to this way of being affected. It is necessary to learn this from the physicists.

1147b10 And since the last proposition is a belief and of sensible things and is a lord of actions, either he does not have this when he is being affected or he has it in a way which is not knowledge but in the way of saying [words] just as the drunk person says the words of Empedocles. And since the last term seems to be neither universal nor expressive of knowledge in the same way as the universal,

1147b15 even [the situation] has become like that which Socrates was seeking to bring about. For it does not seem fully to be knowledge present to the one who is affected or who is drug around because of being affected, but it is a knowledge of sensible things. Therefore, concerning knowing and not knowing and how, while knowing, it happens to someone that he or she is incontinent, enough has been said.

BIBLIOGRAPHY

Primary Sources

Aquinas, Thomas. *On Evil.* Translated by Jean Oesterle. Notre Dame, Indiana: University of Notre Dame Press, 1995.

——. *Opera Omnia.* Recognovit ac instruxit Enrique Alarcón automato electronico Pampilonae ad Universitatis Studiorum Navarrensis aedes a MM A.D. (Leonine edition). http://www.corpusthomisticum.org/iopera.html.

——. *Summa Theologicae.* Edited by. Blackfriars. London: Eyre & Spottiswoode, and New York: McGraw-Hill, 1970.

Aristotle. *Introductory Readings.* Translated by Terence Irwin and Gail Fine. Indianapolis, Cambridge: Hackett, 1996.

——. *The Basic Works of Aristotle.* Edited by Richard McKeon. New York: Random House, 1941.

Anselm. *Anselm of Canterbury: Collected Works.* 2nd American Edition. Translated and edited by Jasper Hopkins and Herbert Richardson. Toronto, New York: Edwin Mellen, 1975.

——. *S. Anselmi Cantuariensis Archiepiscopi Opera Omnia.* Ad fidem codicum recensuit Franciscus Selesius Schmitt. Stuttgart - Bad Cannstatt: Friedrich Frommann Verlag, 1968.

Caietanus, Thomas de Vio. *Summa totius theologiae S. Thomae de Aquino.* Hildesheim, Zurich, New York: Georg Olms Verlag, 2001.

Durandus. *D. Dvrandi a Sancto Porciano, ord. praed. et meldensis episcopi, in Petri Lombardi Sententias Theologicas commentariorum libri IIII. Venetiis, Guerraea, 1571.* Ridgewood, NJ: Gregg Press, 1984

Plato. *Protagoras.*

Scotus, John Duns. *Opera Omnia.* 21 vols. to date. Città del Vaticano: Typis Polyglottis Vaticanis, 1950.

——. *Opera Omnia.* Editio nova / juxta editionem Waddingi XII tomos continentem a patribus franciscanis de observantia accurate recognita. 26 v. Westmead, Farnborough, Hants : Gregg International, 1969.

——. *Quaestiones super libros Metaphysicorum Aristotelis: Libri VI-IX*, vol. 4 of *Opera Philosophica.* Edited by G. Etzkorn, R. Andrews, G. Gál, R. Green, F. Kelly, G. Marcil, T. Noone, and R. Wood. St. Bonaventure, NY: The Franciscan Institute, 1997.

——. *Reportatio.* 2A.6 Oxford, Merton College, MS 61.

Suárez, Francisco. *R.P. Francisci Suarez … Opera Omnia.* 28 vols. in 30, editio nova, a D.M. André …, juxta editionem venetianam XXIII tomos in-f° continentem, accurate recognita, reverendissimo ill. domino Sergent … ab editore dicata: Parisiis, apud Ludovicum Vivès, 1856–78.

Secondary Sources

Adams, Marilyn McCord. "Ockham on Identity and Distinction." *Franciscan Studies* 14 (1976): 5–74.

——. *William Ockham.* Notre Dame, IN: University of Notre Dame Press, 1987.

——. "St. Anselm on Evil: De casu diaboli." *Documenti e studi sulla tradizione filosofica medievale 3* (1992): 423–451.
——. "Duns Scotus on the Will as Rational Power." In *Via Scoti: Methodologica ad mentem Joannis Duns Scoti*. Edited by Leonardo Sileo, 839–854. Roma: PAA-Edizioni Antonianum, 1995.
Adams, Robert M. "Involuntary Sins." *Philosophical Review*, January 94 (1985):3–31.
Ando, Takatura. *Aristotle's Theory of Practical Cognition*. 3rd ed. Hague: Martinus Nijhoff, 1971.
Barnwell, Michael. "Voluntary Inconsideration, Virtual Cognition and Francesco Suarez." *Southwest Philosophical Studies* 31 (2008).
Boler, John. "An Image for the Unity of the Will in Duns Scotus." *Journal of the History of Philosophy 32* (1994): 23–43.
——. "Transcending the Natural: Duns Scotus on the Two Affections of the Will." *American Catholic Philosophical Quarterly* 67 (1993): 109–26.
Bonansea, Bernadine M. "Duns Scotus' Voluntarism." In *Studies in Philosophy and in the History of Philosophy*, vol. 3: John Duns Scotus, 1265–1965. Edited by John K. Ryan and Bernardine M. Bonansea, 83–121. Washington DC: Catholic UP, 1965.
Bostock, David. *Aristotle's Ethics*. New York: Oxford University Press, 2000.
Brown, Robert. "Some Problems with Anselm's View of Human Will." *Anselm Studies* 2 (1988): 333–342.
Charles, David. *Aristotle's Philosophy of Action*. Ithaca, NY: Cornell University Press, 1984.
Charlton, William. *Weakness of Will*. Oxford: Basil Blackwell, 1988.
Cross, Richard. *Duns Scotus*. Oxford: Oxford University Press, 1999.
Curren, Randall. "The Contribution of *EN III.5* to Aristotle's Theory of Responsibility." *History of Philosophy Quarterly* 6: 261–277.
Dahl, N.O. *Practical Reason, Aristotle, and Weakness of Will*. Minneapolis: University of Minnesota Press, 1984.
Deme, Daniel. "The 'Origin' of Evil According to Anselm of Canterbury." *Heythrop Journal* 43 (2002): 170–184.
Dewan, Lawrence. "St. Thomas and the First Cause of Moral Evil." In *Les philosophies morales et politiques au Moyen Âge*. Edited by C.B. Bazán, E. Andújar, and L.G. Sbrocchi, 1223–1230. New York, Ottawa, Toronto: Legas, 1995.
Dumont, Stephen D. "Did Duns Scotus Change His Mind on the Will?" In *Nach der Verurteilung von 1277. Philosophie und Theologie an der Universität von Paris im letzten Viertel des 13. Jahrhunderts. Studien und Text*. Edited by Jan. A. Aertsen, Kent Emery Jr., and Andres Speer, 719–794. Berlin and New York: Walter de Gruyter, 2001.
——. "Duns Scotus's Parisian Question on the Formal Distinction." *Vivarium* 43, no. 1 (2005): 7–62.
Ekenberg, Tomas. "Free Will and Free Action in Anselm of Canterbury." *History of Philosophy Quarterly* 22, no. 4 (1980): 301–318.
Engberg-Pedersen, Troels. *Aristotle's Theory of Moral Insight*. Oxford: Clarendon, 1983.
Frankfurt, Harry. "Freedom of the Will and the Concept of a Person." *Journal of Philosophy* 68, no. 1 (1971): 5–20.
Gallagher, David M. "Free Choice and Free Judgment in Thomas Aquinas." *Archiv für Geschichte der Philosophie* 76 (1994): 247–277.
Gosling, Justin. "Mad, Drunk or Asleep? - Aristotle's Akratic." *Phronesis* 38, no. 1 (1993): 98–104.
——. *Weakness of the Will*. London, New York: Routledge, 1990.
Hause, Jeffrey. "Thomas Aquinas and the Voluntarists." *Medieval Philosophy and Theology* 6 (1997): 167–182.
——. "Voluntariness and Causality: Some Problems for Aquinas' Theory of Responsibility." *Vivarium* 36, no. 1 (March 1998): 55–66.

Hardie, W.F.R. *Aristotle's Ethical Theory*. 2nd ed. Oxford: Clarendon, 1980.
Hedwig, Klaus. "Actus indifferens: Über die Theorie des indifferenten Handelns bei Thomas von Aquin und Duns Scotus." *Philosophisches Jahrbuch* 95 (1988): 120–131.
Hoffmann, Tobias. "Aquinas and Intellectual Determinism: The Test Case of Angelic Sin." *Archiv für Geschichte der Philosophie* 89 (2007): 122–156.
Hopkins, Jasper. "Anselm on Freedom and the Will: A Discussion of G. Stanley Kane's Interpretation of Anselm." *Philosophy Research Archives* 9 (1983): 471–494.
Irwin, Terry, ed. and trans. *Aristotle; Nicomachean Ethics*. 2nd ed. Indianapolis, Cambridge: Hackett, 1999.
Kane, G. Stanley. *Anselm's Doctrine of Freedom and the Will*. Lewiston, NY: The Edwin Mellen Press, 1981.
Kenny, Anthony. *Aristotle's Theory of the Will*. New Haven, CT: Yale University Press, 1979.
——. *Aquinas on Mind*. New York: Routledge, 1993.
King, Peter. "Scotus on Metaphysics." In *The Cambridge Companion to Duns Scotus*. Edited by Thomas Williams. Cambridge, UK: Cambridge University Press, 2003.
Lee, Patrick. "The Relation between Intellect and Will in Free Choice According to Aquinas and Scotus." *The Thomist* 49 (1985): 321–342.
Lee, Sukjae. "Scotus on the Will: The Rational Power and the Dual Affections." *Vivarium*36, no. 1 (March 1998): 40–54.
Loughran, Thomas J. "Aquinas, Compatibilist." In Human and Divine Agency. Edited by F. Michael McLain and W. Mark Richardson, 1–39. Lanham, New York, Oxford: University Press of America, 1999.
MacDonald, Scott. "Aquinas's Libertarian Account of Free Choice." *Revue Internationale de Philosophie*, 52 (1998): 309–328.
——. "Practical Reasoning and Reasons-Explanations: Aquinas's Account of Reason's Role in Action." In *Aquinas's Moral Theory*. Edited by Scott MacDonald, 133–160. Ithaca, NY: Cornell University Press, 1998.
——. "Primal Sin." In *The Augustinian Tradition*. Edited by Gareth B. Matthews London. Berkeley: University of California Press, 1999.
Maritain, Jacques. *St. Thomas and the Problem of Evil*. Milwaukee: Marquette University Press, 1942.
——. *Existence and the Existent*. Garden City, NJ: Doubleday, 1948.
——. *God and the Permission of Evil*. Milwaukee: The Bruce Publishing Co., 1966.
McCluskey, Colleen. "Happiness and Freedom in Aquinas's Theory of Action." *Medieval Philosophy and Theology* 9 (2000): 69–90.
——. "Intellective Appetite and the Freedom of Human Action." *The Thomist* 66 (2002): 421–456.
Mele, Alfred R. "Aristotle on *Akrasia* and Knowledge." *Modern Schoolman* 58 (1981):137–59.
Pasnau, Robert. *Thomas Aquinas on Human Nature*. Cambridge, UK: Cambridge University Press, 2002.
Pickavé, Martin and Jennifer Whiting. "Nicomachean Ethics 7.3 on Akratic Ignorance." *Oxford Studies in Ancient Philosophy* 34 (2008): 323–371.
Rogers, Katherin. *Anselm on Freedom*. Oxford, New York: Oxford University Press, 2008.
Ross, David. *Aristotle*. 5th ed. London: Methuen, 1949.
Schedler, George. "Anselm and Aquinas on the Fall of Satan: A Case of Retributive Punishment." *Proceedings of the American Catholic Philosophical Association* 56 (1982): 61–69.
Schmutz, Jacob. "Azpilcueta, Martín de." Scholasticon. http://www.scholasticon.fr/Database/Scholastiques_fr.php?ID=188 (accessed June 3, 2010).
Sheets, John R. "Justice in the Moral Thought of St. Anselm." *Modern Schoolman* 25 (January 1948): 132–139.

Smith, Patricia G. "Contemplating Failure: The Importance of Unconscious Omissions." *Philosophical Studies* 59 (June 1990): 159–176.

Staley, Kevin M. "Aquinas: Compatibilist or Libertarian?" *The Saint Anselm Journal* 2, no. 2 (2005): 73–79

Stump, Eleonore. "Intellect, Will, and the Principle of Alternate Possibilities." In *Christian Theism and the Problems of Philosophy*. Edited by Michael D. Beaty, 254–285. Notre Dame: University of Notre Dame Press, 1990.

——. "Aquinas's Account of Freedom: Intellect and Will." *The Monist* 80 (1997): 576–597.

——. Aquinas. London, New York: Routledge, 2005.

Tyvoll, Stan R. "Anselm's Definition of Free Will: A Hierarchical Interpretation." *American Catholic Philosophical Quarterly* 80, no. 2 (2006): 155–171.

Visser, Sandra and Thomas Williams. Anselm's Account of Freedom." *Canadian Journal of Philosophy* 31 (June 2001): 221–244.

——. "Anselm's Account of Freedom." In *The Cambridge Companion to Anselm*. Edited by Brian Davies and Brian Leftow. Cambridge, UK: Cambridge University Press, 2004.

——. *Anselm*. Oxford, New York: Oxford University Press, 2009.

Van Inwagen, Peter. *Metaphysics*. Boulder: Westview, 1993.

Walsh, James Jerome. *Aristotle's Conception of Moral Weakness*. New York: Columbia University Press, 1963.

Williams, Thomas. "Introduction." In *The Cambridge Companion to Duns Scotus*. Edited by Thomas Williams, 1–14. Cambridge, UK: Cambridge University Press, 2003.

Wolter, Allan B. "The Formal Distinction." In *John Duns Scotus 1265–1965*. Edited by J. K. Ryan and B. M. Bonansea. Washington DC: Catholic University of America Press, 1965.

——. *Duns Scotus on the Will and Morality*. Washington, DC: Catholic University Press, 1986.

——. The *Philosophical Theology of John Duns Scotus*. Edited by Marilyn McCord Adams. Ithaca, NY: Cornell University Press, 1990.

Wright, John H. "Human Freedom and Divine Action." In *Human and Divine Agency*. Edited by F. Michael McLain and W. Mark Richardson, 41–47. Lanham, New York and Oxford: University Press of America, 1999.

INDEX

www.ingramcontent.com/pod-product-compliance
Lightning Source LLC
LaVergne TN
LVHW010632300926
849162LV00001B/131
* 9 7 8 9 0 0 4 1 8 1 3 5 9 *